'Convincing brand management has become a central challenge for all HEIs. The book presented by Nguyen, Melewar, and Hemsley-Brown offers an excellent opportunity to mentally penetrate and analyse the specific problem situation of HEIs and develop appropriate brand strategies and action programs. I am convinced that not only students but also practitioners in particular will benefit from reading the book'.

Professor Dr Klaus-Peter Wiedmann, *Full Chaired Professor of Marketing and Management and the Director of the Institute of Marketing and Management at the Leibniz University Hannover, Germany*

'Strategic Brand Management in Higher Education offers a unique, robust and useful perspective to all university stakeholders. The book is well organised around a strategic planning structure, updated by contemporary branding developments like co-creation. Building blocks are strategy, planning, co-creation and metrics. Well-timed to effectively meet the sector's challenges'.

Professor Bill Merrilees, *Professor of Marketing, Griffith Business School, Australia*

'The book *Strategic Brand Management in Higher Education* is a very timely topic since higher education institutions undoubtedly face severe competition, not only concerning student attraction, but also financing and funding challenges, and in attracting companies for co-operation within teaching and research. This places more pressure on institutions to move from mere communication approaches towards developing the university brand in a strategic way. The book also has an important angle since most universities' communication is handled by administrative staff with very limited understanding on strategic marketing and branding'.

Anne Rindell, *Associate Professor in Marketing, Hanken School of Economics, Finland*

'This book provides a comprehensive text on all aspects of corporate brand management in the higher education sector. The editors are leading academics in the fields of corporate branding and higher education and they have assembled an excellent cast of experts to produce the most comprehensive book in this specialised field. The topics covered will be valuable to students as well as practitioners in this highly competitive sector'.

Professor Russell Abratt, *Professor of Marketing, Huizenga College of Business and Entrepreneurship, Nova Southeastern University, Florida, USA*

Strategic Brand Management in Higher Education

University branding has increased substantially, due to demands on universities to enrol greater numbers of students, rising tuition fees, the proliferation of courses, the growing 'internationalization' of universities, financial pressures, and reliance on income from foreign students. As higher education continues to grow, increased competition places more pressure on institutions to market their programs. Technological, social, and economic changes have necessitated a customer-oriented marketing system and a focus on developing the university brand.

This book is unique in providing a composite overview of strategy, planning, and measurement informed by ground-breaking research and the experiences of academics. It combines theoretical and methodological aspects of branding with the views of leading exponents of branding in different contexts and across a range of higher education institutions. Expert contributors from research and practice provide relevant and varying perspectives allowing readers to access information on international trends, theory, and practices about branding in higher education.

Readers are exposed to the critical elements of strategic brand management, gain insights into the planning process of higher education branding, and gain a solid understanding of the emerging research area of branding concepts in higher education. Advanced students, and researchers will find this book a unique resource and it will also be of interest to brand practitioners in both education and public sector markets.

Bang Nguyen is Professor at the University of Southern Denmark, Kolding, Denmark.

T C Melewar is Professor of Marketing and Strategy at Middlesex University Business School, London, UK.

Jane Hemsley-Brown is Professor of Marketing at Surrey Business School, Surrey, UK.

Routledge Studies in Marketing

This series welcomes proposals for original research projects that are either single or multi-authored or an edited collection from both established and emerging scholars working on any aspect of marketing theory and practice and provides an outlet for studies dealing with elements of marketing theory, thought, pedagogy and practice.

It aims to reflect the evolving role of marketing and bring together the most innovative work across all aspects of the marketing 'mix' – from product development, consumer behaviour, marketing analysis, branding, and customer relationships, to sustainability, ethics, and the new opportunities and challenges presented by digital and online marketing.

1 **Addiction as Consumer Choice**
 Exploring the Cognitive Dimension
 Gordon R. Foxall

2 **The Psychology of Consumer Profiling in a Digital Age**
 Barrie Gunter

3 **Contemporary Consumer Culture Theory**
 Edited by John F. Sherry, Jr and Eileen Fischer

4 **Marketing and Mobile Financial Services**
 A Global Perspective on Digital Banking Consumer Behaviour
 Edited by Aijaz A. Shaikh and Heikki Karjaluoto

5 **Ethnic Marketing**
 Theory, Practice and Entrepreneurship
 Guilherme D. Pires and John Stanton

6 **Relationship Marketing in the Digital Age**
 Robert W. Palmatier and Lena Steinhoff

7 **Strategic Brand Management in Higher Education**
 Edited by Bang Nguyen, T C Melewar, and Jane Hemsley-Brown

Strategic Brand Management in Higher Education

Edited by Bang Nguyen, T C Melewar, and Jane Hemsley-Brown

LONDON AND NEW YORK

First published 2019
by Routledge
2 Park Square, Milton Park, Abingdon, Oxon OX14 4RN

and by Routledge
52 Vanderbilt Avenue, New York, NY 10017

Routledge is an imprint of the Taylor & Francis Group, an informa business

© 2019 selection and editorial matter, Bang Nguyen, T C Melewar, and Jane Hemsley-Brown; individual chapters, the contributors

The right of Bang Nguyen, T C Melewar, and Jane Hemsley-Brown to be identified as the authors of the editorial matter, and of the authors for their individual chapters, has been asserted in accordance with sections 77 and 78 of the Copyright, Designs and Patents Act 1988.

All rights reserved. No part of this book may be reprinted or reproduced or utilized in any form or by any electronic, mechanical, or other means, now known or hereafter invented, including photocopying and recording, or in any information storage or retrieval system, without permission in writing from the publishers.

Trademark notice: Product or corporate names may be trademarks or registered trademarks, and are used only for identification and explanation without intent to infringe.

British Library Cataloguing-in-Publication Data
A catalogue record for this book is available from the British Library

Library of Congress Cataloging-in-Publication Data
A catalog record has been requested for this book

ISBN: 978-0-367-13942-1 (hbk)
ISBN: 978-0-429-02930-1 (ebk)

Typeset in Sabon
by Wearset Ltd, Boldon, Tyne and Wear

Contents

Notes on contributors ix

1 Introduction to *Strategic Brand Management in Higher Education* 1
BANG NGUYEN, T C MELEWAR, AND JANE HEMSLEY-BROWN

PART I
Strategy 23

2 Co-creating brand identity: the case of UK higher education 25
JULIE ROBSON, SANJIT KUMAR ROY, CHRIS CHAPLEO, AND HSIAO-PEI (SOPHIE) YANG

3 Organizational culture in higher education branding: branding the core values and beliefs 41
CLÁUDIA SIMÕES

4 Brand leadership and brand support: influencing employees via internal branding 58
NARISSARA SUJCHAPHONG AND PAKORN SUJCHAPHONG

5 Competition in higher education 74
FRANCESCA PUCCIARELLI AND ANDREAS KAPLAN

PART II
Planning 89

6 Corporate brand communication in higher education 91
ELIF KARAOSMANOGLU AND GULBERK GULTEKIN SALMAN

7 Corporate design: what makes a favourable university logo? 118
PANTEA FOROUDI AND BANG NGUYEN

8 Brand image and reputation development in higher education institutions 143
ADELE BERNDT AND LINDA D. HOLLEBEEK

9 Co-creation of value: a customer-integration approach 159
TIM HUGHES AND IAN BROOKS

PART III
Measurement   177

10 Measuring higher education brand performance and brand impact 179
CHRIS CHAPLEO AND LOUISE SIMPSON

11 Building a trustworthy university brand: an inside-out approach 196
SANJIT KUMAR ROY, SAALEM SADEQUE, AND SATHYAPRAKASH BALAJI MAKAM

12 Scale development in higher education: university corporate brand image, student satisfaction, and student behavioural intention 217
SHARIFAH FARIDAH SYED ALWI AND NORBANI CHE-HA

13 Evaluating branding scales in higher education 233
LESLEY LEDDEN, STAVROS P. KALAFATIS, AND ILIA PROTOPAPA

14 Conclusion to *Strategic Brand Management in Higher Education* 255
BANG NGUYEN, T C MELEWAR, AND JANE HEMSLEY-BROWN

Index 269

Contributors

Editors

Bang Nguyen, PhD, is Professor of Marketing at the Institute of Entrepreneurship and Relationship Management, University of Southern Denmark, Kolding, and Adjunct Professor at the Department of Management at Shanghai University, China. He is Editor-in-Chief of *The Bottom Line*, a journal on the economics of information, and on the Editorial Board of the *Journal of Marketing Management*. Previously, he held positions at East China University of Science and Technology, Oxford Brookes University, and RMIT University Vietnam, and was a Visiting Scholar at China Europe International Business School (CEIBS). His research interests include branding, customer relationship management (CRM), entrepreneurship, BtB marketing, and innovation management. Bang has extensive knowledge in technology and service organizations and has published widely in journals such as *Business Ethics Quarterly, Industrial Marketing Management, Journal of Business Research, European Journal of Marketing, Journal of Marketing Management, Information, Technology & People*, and so on. He has published in more than 150 peer reviewed scientific articles, books, conference papers, and book chapters. In addition, he has published six books: *Ethical and Social Marketing in Asia* (Elsevier), *The Dark Side of CRM* (Routledge), *Services Marketing Cases in Asia* (Springer), *Asia Branding* (Palgrave Macmillan), *Internet Retailing* (Routledge), and *Strategic Brand Management in Higher Education* (Routledge). Bang is an experienced consultant and advises on marketing and brand development for SMEs and start-ups. He has lived and worked professionally in Denmark, the USA, the United Kingdom, Vietnam, China, and Taiwan.

T C Melewar (BSc, MBA, PhD, HFAM), is Professor of Marketing and Strategy and the Head of Department (Marketing, Branding and Tourism) at the Business School, Middlesex University London, UK. Prior to joining Middlesex in August 2013, he was Professor at Brunel University and Zurich University of Applied Sciences (ZHAW) in Switzerland. He has also held academic positions at the University of Warwick

(Warwick Business School) and De Montfort University in the UK and MARA Institute of Technology, Malaysia. T C's research interests include corporate identity/branding and international marketing strategy. He has published over 140 journal articles in academic journals such as *Journal of International Business Studies, International Marketing Review, European Journal of Marketing, Journal of World Business, Industrial Marketing Management, International Journal of Management Review, Business Ethics Quarterly, Journal of Business Research* among others. He has written seven books in the area of corporate branding/identity and international marketing with publishers such as Routledge, Emerald, and Palgrave. He was the former Editor-in-Chief of the *Journal of Brand Management*. Now he is the Editor Emeritus of this journal. He is currently on the Senior Advisory Board of the *Journal of Product and Brand Management*, and on the Editorial Board of several academic journals. T C is the Founder and Chair of the following colloquia: Corporate Branding, Identity, Image and Reputation (COBIIR); Place Branding; Design, Branding and Marketing (ICDBM). T C was awarded the Honorary Fellow and Life Member of the Academy of Marketing (HFAM) (2016) and the Honorary Fellowship from the Faculty of Marketing, Bucharest University of Economic Studies, Romania (2016).

Jane Hemsley-Brown (PhD Soton, MA Soton, DipHE, BEd IoE London), is Professorial Fellow in Marketing at the University of Surrey. She has held a number of Principal and Senior Research Fellow posts prior to her appointment at Surrey Business School: Post Doctoral Fellow at the University of Greenwich, London (1995–1996), Senior Researcher at the University of Southampton (1996–2001); and a Principal Researcher with NFER (National Foundation for Educational Research) (2001–2002). Jane joined the University of Surrey (School of Management) in 2002. Her research interests are in the fields of Education Marketing (Higher Education Marketing), Branding, and Research Utilization (RU) (the effective dissemination of research outcomes, for utilization by managers and practitioners). Prior to her role as Professorial Fellow, Jane was a Reader in Marketing (2007–2014), Head of Division of Business (2007–2011), Deputy Head of Surrey Business School (2013–2014), and Associate Dean (International) for the Faculty of Business, Economics and Law (2011–2014 and 2015–2016). Jane is the author of over 100 publications on consumer behaviour, choice in education markets and management decision-making, including 3 books: *Higher Education Consumer Choice* (2015 with Oplatka), *The Management and Leadership of Education Marketing: Research, Practice and Applications* (2013 with Oplatka), and *Choosing Futures: Young People's Decision-making in Education, Training and Careers Markets* (2001, with Foskett). Funded research projects are related to attitudes to technical and digital innovation and impact on the delivery of health care, innovation in online shopping environments, and customer relationship management in higher education. Jane is also Editor-in-Chief of the *Journal of Marketing for Higher Education*.

Contributors

Julie Robson is Associate Professor at Bournemouth University and she specializes in financial services marketing. She helped to develop several professional groups including the General Insurance Market Research Association (MRS) and the Financial Services Marketing Group (CIM). More recently Julie's research has been extended to include marketing within the banking, insurance, broker and Islamic finance sectors; and she has secured grants from the ESRC and HEIF to support this work. Julie is on the editorial board of the International Journal of Bank Marketing and is currently chair of the Qualifications Examination and Assessments Committee of the Chartered Insurance Institute (CII).

Sanjit Kumar Roy is Senior Lecturer in Marketing at University of Western Australia, Australia. His research interests include services marketing, technology and marketing and transformative service research. He has published in journals including *European Journal of Marketing*, *Journal of Business Research*, *Journal of Marketing Management*, *Internet Research*, *Studies in Higher Education*, *Journal of Services Marketing*, *Journal of Service Theory & Practice*, *Journal of Brand Management*, and *Computers in Human Behaviour*, among others. He co-edited *Marketing Cases for Emerging Markets*; *Services Marketing Cases in Emerging Markets – An Asian Perspective*; and *Strategic Marketing Cases in Emerging Markets*.

Chris Chapleo is the Head of The Department of Marketing at Bournemouth University. Dr Chapleo has published widely in international journals on marketing and branding, specializing in non-profit organizations and the education sector. He has also presented key notes and papers at many conferences across the world and has combined this with consultancy and enterprise work for leading organizations. Prior to academia he held senior marketing roles in publishing and leisure and is also Director of Brand Education, specializing in HE brand consulting.

Hsiao-Pei (Sophie) Yang is a Senior Lecturer in Marketing at Coventry University, Faculty of Business and Law. Sophie held several marketing posts in industry prior to joining academia. She has a PhD in Marketing and an MA in International Marketing and her research interests are in the marketing of higher education and the consumption of services. Since acquiring her doctorate, Sophie has published in a number of journals such as the *Journal of General Management*. In addition, she has written book chapters and case studies in mainly the services marketing area.

Cláudia Simões (PhD from University of Warwick, UK) is an Associate Professor in Marketing at University of Minho in Portugal. Her research interests are in strategic marketing, co-creation and corporate identity, brand and reputation. Her work has been published in the *Journal of the Academy of Marketing Science*, *Business Ethics Quarterly*, *Journal of Business Research*, *European Journal of Marketing*, and *Industrial Marketing Management*, among others. She was, in the past, a visiting scholar at Warwick Business School/UK (visiting fellow), Open University Business School/UK (senior visiting research fellow) and Scheller College of Management, Georgia Institute of Technology/USA (visiting scholar).

Narissara Sujchaphong is a Lecturer at Mahasarakham Business School, Mahasarakham University, Thailand. She obtained a PhD in Management from Brunel University and an MA in Marketing from London Metropolitan University. She has published in internationally refereed journals and contributed to several books. Her research interests span areas of internal branding, university branding and brand-related leadership.

Pakorn Sujchaphong is a Lecturer at Mahasarakham Business School, Mahasarakham University, Thailand, where he developed the undergraduate program in International Business and then served as its coordinator. He earned his BEng degree from Chulalongkorn University, his MIB degree from Monash University, and his PhD degree in Management from the University of Texas at Arlington. His research interests are in the area of human capital, strategic human resource management, and organizational behaviour.

Francesca Pucciarelli has worked as management consultant both with international companies and with small and medium enterprises, mostly in projects concerning business development through customer focus, value added services and digitalization. After three years managerial experience as Digital and Social Media Marketing Manager of ESCP Europe Turin campus, currently Professor Pucciarelli is Academic Director of the MBA in International Management. Her research interests concern higher education evolution, challenges and competitiveness, with a special focus on business schools. She is also working in the field of experiential learning and impact of digital advancement on learning experience.

Andreas Kaplan has over a decade of senior level experience in higher education. Currently Rector of ESCP Europe Berlin, Professor Kaplan previously served as Dean for Academic Affairs, Director of Brand and Communications, as well as elected Head of the Marketing faculty. With almost 20,000 citations on Google Scholar, Kaplan counts among the top 50 Business and Management authors in the world according to John Wiley & Sons. His publications treat the digital revolution in higher education through the arrival of MOOCs, SPOCs, and artificial intelligence (AI), as well as general strategic and competitive issues in today's higher education sector.

Elif Karaosmanoglu is an Associate Professor Doctor of Marketing at Istanbul Technical University, who holds her PhD from Warwick Business School, UK and is a Fulbright Alumna. Her research streams mainly focus on corporate marketing and branding, and consumer-technology interactions. Her papers have appeared in leading journals such as *Journal of Business Research*, *Journal of Product and Brand Management*, *European Management Review*, *European Journal of Marketing*, *Journal of Brand Management*. She serves as an editorial board member for the *Journal of Product and Brand Management*. She was the Turkey Representative of EMAC (2010–2016) and chaired the EMAC 2013 in Istanbul. She is currently the co-coordinator of ITU-SUNY Business Administration dual degree program.

Gulberk Gultekin Salman is an Assistant Professor Doctor of Marketing at Bahçeşehir University. She is a PhD graduate of Marmara University. Her research areas mainly concentrate on sport marketing, consumer and fan behaviour, and services marketing. Her papers have appeared in *Journal of Brand Management* and *International Business and Economics Research Journal* as well as at several leading international conferences. She formerly held the administrative role of Vice-Director of the Graduate School of Social Sciences at Bahçeşehir University and she is currently the coordinator of the Sport Management Graduate degree program. She is also a member of the Women's Committee of the International Tennis Federation and a member of the Education Board of the Turkish Tennis Federation.

Pantea Foroudi (PhD, FHEA, MSc (Honours), MA, BA (Honours)) is Senior Lecturer in Marketing, Branding, and Tourism, Middlesex University, London, UK as well as Advisor at Foroudi Consultancy London. She earned her PhD from Brunel University, London and completed her MA in Marketing and Communication Management at the University of The Arts London (LCC), UK and has an MSc in Graphic Design from Azad University, Tehran, Iran. Pantea began in her corporate position in 1996. She has over 25 years of experience as a creative innovator and practical problem-solver in visual identity, graphic design, and branding in different sectors such as airlines and travel; arts and entertainment; banking; fashion and retail; healthcare and hospitality; institutions and non-profit organizations.

Adele Berndt, PhD is Associate Professor of Business Administration at Jönköping International Business School (JIBS), Sweden, member of the Media, Management and Transformation Centre at JIBS and an affiliated researcher at Gordon Institute of Business Science at the University of Pretoria. She studied and worked in South Africa prior to moving to Sweden in 2012. Her research interests include services marketing and consumer behaviour, having presented conference papers and edited books on these topics. She has authored articles appearing in various marketing journals. She is a member of the Academy of Marketing Science and the European Media Management Association.

Linda D. Hollebeek, PhD is Senior Associate Professor at Montpellier Business School, Full Professor (Adj.) at Tallinn University of Technology, and Associate Professor (Adj.) at the Norwegian School of Economics. Her research centres on customer engagement, brand relationships, and value, and to date has appeared in the *Journal of the Academy of Marketing Science*, *Journal of Service Research*, *Industrial Marketing Management*, *Journal of Business Research*, and *Journal of Interactive Marketing*, among others. She is Associate Editor of *European Journal of Marketing* and is currently guest editor for the *Journal of Service Research* and *International Journal of Research in Marketing*, while also co-editing *The Handbook of Research on Customer Engagement* (Edward Elgar).

Tim Hughes worked in senior marketing management roles at Heinz and Nestle before moving into financial services marketing at Skipton and Bristol & West Building Societies. He then ran his own marketing consultancy for seven years, working in the UK and internationally. Since joining the University of the West of England (UWE) in 2002, Professor Hughes has focused on doing research that, while rigorous, is also relevant to practice. He formed the Applied Marketing Research Group to support this type of work. He has published extensively in high quality academic journals. The current focus of his work is on co-creation and collaboration.

Ian Brooks is a Senior Lecturer in Sustainable IT at UWE Bristol, UK and a Senior Teaching Fellow at the University of Bristol. He teaches and supervises student research at the intersections of sustainability, technology, and entrepreneurship. He is a faculty member for the research and enquiry capstone module on the BA Business (Team Entrepreneurship) programme at UWE Bristol. He is undertaking his PhD research into the use of the UN Sustainable Development Goals as requirements in Systems Engineering. He has over 20 years management consultancy and shareholder value management experience for multi-national companies with Price Waterhouse, PwC and IBM.

Louise Simpson is Founding Director of The Knowledge Partnership UK. She is an expert in higher education reputation and brand strategy, leading research for universities and government bodies in the UK and globally. Before setting up a higher education agency, she was Director of

Communications at the University of Cambridge and a commissioning editor for Reed Elsevier. In 2007 she set up The World 100 Reputation Network, which now has 50 leading member universities across the globe. She established an annual reputation academy for university directors of communications and marketing, and her latest project is an online reputation tracker for benchmarking universities with multiple audiences. Based in the UK, Louise is a graduate of Cambridge University and Manchester University Business School.

Saalem Sadeque is Lecturer in Marketing at the Perth campus of the University of Western Australia. He previously worked in the Marketing discipline at the University's School of Business from 2012 to 2016. He has over 14 years of teaching experience spread across Australia and overseas. His research interests include consumer marketing, retailing and branding. He has published in *Journal of Business Research*, *Technological Forecasting and Social Change*, *Journal of Gambling Business and Economics*, and *Education Research and Perspectives*.

Sathyaprakash Balaji Makam (M. S. Balaji) is an Associate Professor in Marketing at Nottingham University Business School China (NUBS). He was a visiting research scholar at Whitman School of Management, Syracuse University, USA between August 2007 and July 2008. Dr Balaji has published his research in leading marketing and business management journals including *Journal of Business Research*, *European Journal of Marketing*, *Information and Management*, *International Journal of Hospitality Management*, *Journal of Services Marketing*, *Service Industries Journal* and others. He serves as a reviewer for many leading marketing and business management journals.

Sharifah Faridah Syed Alwi is a Senior Lecturer in Corporate Brand Management and Director for MSc Corporate Brand Management at Brunel Business School, Brunel University London, UK. She received her PhD from Manchester Business School, The University of Manchester, UK. Her research interests are in B-to-C branding and cover several levels such as firm, corporation, product and services across different sectors such as higher education and services. Her work has appeared in several journals such as *Business Ethics Quarterly*, *Journal of Business Research* and *European Journal of Marketing*. To date, she has published several chapters and co-authored two edited books, namely *Corporate Branding* and *Islamic Branding and Marketing*, both for Routledge.

Norbani Che-Ha is an Associate Professor and Head of Department of Marketing, Faculty of Business and Accountancy, University of Malaya, Kuala Lumpur. She received her PhD from Monash University, Australia, and MBA and BsBA from University of Denver, Colorado USA. Her research interests are in marketing capabilities, branding, halal marketing, consumer behaviour and small and medium enterprises. She publishes widely in several journals such as *Journal of Business Research*, *Journal of Strategic Marketing*, *Marketing Intelligence and Planning* and many others. She has co-authored several book chapters and has many books on her own. She is also actively involved in consultancy work for private and public institutions in Malaysia.

Lesley Ledden is a Senior Lecturer in Marketing at Kingston Business School, Kingston University London. Her research focuses on the consumer value construct in experiential service contexts in general and higher education in particular, the latter being the subject of her PhD gained at Kingston University. Her work has been published in, among others, the *Journal of Marketing Management*, *Journal of Business Research*, and *Studies in Higher Education*. She is an active member of the Academy of Marketing Special Interest Group in Marketing of Higher Education, hosting the annual colloquium at Kingston Business School in 2017.

Stavros P. Kalafatis is Professor of Business Marketing at Kingston Business School, Kingston University, London and a Visiting Professor at the University of Suffolk, Ipswich. His research focuses on business segmentation, relationship marketing, value creation and brand alliances. He is a member of the editorial board of Industrial Marketing Management and his research has been published in, among others, *European Journal of Marketing*, *Industrial Marketing Management*, *Journal of Business Research*, and *Journal of Marketing Management*.

Ilia Protopapa is a PhD Researcher and a Graduate Teaching Assistant at Kingston Business School, Kingston University, London. Her research focuses on consumer behaviour, consumption value, regulatory focus theory and brand alliances. Prior to her doctoral studies she was awarded a Master's degree in Marketing and Brand Management and a Master of Research in Business and Management. Her research has been presented in a number of international conferences and doctoral colloquia.

1 Introduction to *Strategic Brand Management in Higher Education*

Bang Nguyen, T C Melewar, and
Jane Hemsley-Brown

1 Introduction

As higher education continues to grow, increased competition has placed more pressure on higher education institutions (HEIs) to market their programs (Kaplan, 2018; Sujchaphong, Nguyen, and Melewar, 2017). Technological, social, and economic changes have necessitated a customer-oriented marketing system (Adams and Eveland, 2007) and a focus on developing the university brand (Judson, Gorchels, and Aurand, 2006; Lowrie, 2017). Researchers suggest that, in recent years, university branding has increased substantially (Binsardi and Ekwulugo, 2003; Chapleo, 2017; Melewar and Akel, 2005; Naudé and Ivy, 1999). These researchers propose a number of reasons, namely, a consequence to governmental demands on universities to attract and enrol greater numbers of students, rising tuition fees, the proliferation of courses on offer, the growing 'internationalization' of universities, escalating advertising costs, financial pressures, and, in many universities, heavy reliance on income from foreign students (Bennett and Ali-Choudhury, 2009; Binsardi and Ekwulugo, 2003; Ivy, 2001; Lowrie, 2017).

A university's brand is defined as a manifestation of the institution's features that distinguishes it from others, reflects its capacity to satisfy students' needs, engenders trust in its ability to deliver a certain type and level of higher education, and helps potential recruits to make wise enrolment decisions (Bennett and Ali-Choudhury, 2009; Bick, Jacobson, and Abratt, 2003; Sujchaphong, Nguyen, and Melewar, 2017). These are only some of the issues marketers should address.

Due to these complexities, the study of branding in higher education is a timely topic for further investigation. This book, **'Strategic Brand Management in Higher Education'**, will include academic and practitioner perspectives and be of interest to a wider audience than students studying marketing and branding. It aims to address the following:

Strategy: Readers are exposed to the critical elements of strategic brand management in higher education, such as the development of a mission, vision, values, organizational design, leadership, and so on, examining the effects of these on stakeholder behaviour and brand performance by drawing from extant strategy and organizational theories and research. This enables the readers to understand different characteristics of brand strategy and subsequent applications towards managing these in higher education.

Planning: Readers will gain insights into the planning process of a higher education branding from different perspectives. The planning aspects of higher education branding include elements such as architecture, visual identity, image, reputation, communication, and so on. This enables readers to compare, contrast and comprehend how a brand is implemented and sustained at different levels in a higher education institution and how plans for brand management are created and managed.

Measurement: An exciting aspect of this book is the presentation of the measurement of branding concepts in higher education, which is an emerging research area. This section highlights the operationalization of the branding concepts in practice and covers the measuring of brand performance, brand equity, and scales for measurement. Readers are exposed to differing measurement approaches, which, once applied to a university, would increase chances of success in improving branding efforts and successful implementation and management of branding across the sector.

The editors of this book also edit the *Journal of Marketing for Higher Education* which involves working closely with academics and academic authors regarding research and practice in education marketing and, in particular, brand management in higher education. The editors also guest edit special issues on branding for well-known journals. Last summer (2017), for example, saw the publication of a special issue of the *Journal of Business Research*, looking at the impact of branding on higher education, across the areas of 'BIMIR' – brand identity, meaning, image, and reputation.

2 Introducing key concepts of branding in higher education

In the present chapter, we review the role of branding in the higher education sector, focusing on contemporary issues such as brand equity in higher education, the positioning of the university brand, the branding of business schools and their MBA programs, the emergence of online programs, brand personality and communication, and student perceptions of the university brand. Finally, we present the book's coverage and content is briefly summarized chapter by chapter to provide an overview of the most current issues of branding in the higher education sector. A topic that permeates the book is that of brand identity. Researchers have long acknowledged that a university brand influences students' beliefs about individual attributes (Melewar and Nguyen, 2015). It is said that brand identity for a university is 'the essence of how you would like alumni, prospective students, legislators, and the public to perceive your institution' (Lawlor, 1998, p. 19). Universities thus increasingly recognize that knowledgeable, prospective students are more likely to process their college choices based on the institution's brand identity. Consequently, many universities are taking the necessary steps to alter the market position of their institution in order to attract targeted groups of prospective students (Judson et al., 2006; Sujchaphong, Nguyen, and Melewar, 2015).

Brand definitions

Previously, Ambler and Styles (1996) defined a brand as the promise of attributes that someone buys, and said that these attributes may be real or illusory, rational or emotional, tangible or invisible. Balmer and Gray (2003), reflecting on the idea that a brand involves a collection of promises concerning the brand's physical and emotional benefits to buyers, used the term 'brand covenant'. Scholars posit that the brands' characteristics, as a covenant, are particularly appropriate for services because of their intangibility and heterogeneity. Intangibility stresses the associations with the brand's values (de Chernatony and Segal-Horn, 2003). Fan (2005) suggests that these brand core values include trustworthiness, honesty, and integrity. Thus, researchers note that the promises embodied in a brand should be in line with the organization's values and behaviour (e.g. Hatch and Schultz, 2003). However, Gutman and Miaoulis (2003) demonstrated how marketing communications in the university sector frequently made promises of benefits that the universities could not deliver. They proposed that universities must link all the benefits promised in communications to the real attributes and capabilities of an institution, coherently and consistently (Bennett and Ali-Choudhury, 2009).

Keller (2002) notes that branding involves the development of expectations about desired outcomes in the mind of the buyer that differentiates the brand from its competitors. These outcome expectations, consequently, provide meaning for the brand among consumers and indicate differences in the products' benefits (Keller, 2002). Thus, a successful brand is expected to deliver the most desired benefits (Heslop and Nadeau, 2010). In addition, researchers suggest that brand definitions are based on 'emotional' and 'rational' factors (Caldwell and Freire, 2004; de Chernatony and McWilliam, 1990). Pringle and Thompson (1999) note that these two main constituents explain a brand's authority, namely, its rational or performance benefits and its emotional or image ones. Louro and Cunha (2001), highlighting brands' multidimensionality, add 'strategic' and 'relational' dimensions in their conceptualization. In a symbolic sense, a brand consists of the name, which should be relevant and distinct (Berry, Lefkowith, and Clark, 1988), logos, typefaces, colour schemes, stationery, forms, receptionists' uniforms, vehicles, and premises (LeBlanc and Nguyen, 1996). These *aesthetic designations* are customers' observed touch points and influence their opinions about the organization (Pratt and Rafaeli, 1997). Visual aesthetic designations, or visual identity, are employed to symbolize numerous aspects of an organization's aims and values (Melewar and Karaosmanoglu, 2006). The aim is to create and sustain organizational meaning (Simoes, Dibb, and Fisk, 2005). Stern, Zinkhan, and Jaju (2001) note how symbolism is important for service organizations due to the intangibility aspects (Bennett and Ali-Choudhhury, 2009). Symbolic branding is thus particularly important for universities if they are to brand themselves successfully. This is typically seen in university logos and merchandising, which students use as a way to develop an affiliation with their university brand.

Brand equity in higher education

Research into brands in higher education has been extensive, and studies are attempting to describe the university brands' substantive components. Scholars emphasize three basic ingredients that are present within a university brand, namely (a) a collection of promises concerning the brand's benefits (e.g. 'covenant'); (b) a set of distinctive features that define the brand's inherent nature and reality (the quiddity); and (c) an assortment of aesthetic designations and external communications that describe the brand (symbolic and external representation (Bennett and Ali-Choudhury, 2009)).

Universities establish strong brands in order to (a) enhance market awareness among potential recruits, their parents, and careers advisors; (b) improve their ability to recruit high-calibre faculty and administrators; (c) differentiate themselves from rival new universities; and (d) gain market share. For example, in the UK, the new university sector's increased branding activities has encouraged 'older' and more traditional institutions to market themselves more aggressively in order both to retain market share and to maintain their student intakes' quality (Bennett and Ali-Choudhury, 2009; Melewar and Akel, 2005; Naudé and Ivy, 1999). Scholars suggest that to achieve the above, a university brand should communicate both the 'cognitive' and 'affective' dimensions. Specifically, those responsible for conveying the university image should communicate attributes that address these distinct components (Palacio, Meneses, and Pérez, 2002), which, it is suggested, are manifest through 'functional values' (cognitive) and 'emotional values' (affective).

The next section presents an in-depth look at branding at several levels, including overall university brand image, business school MBA brands, and online programs.

University brand image and positioning of university brands

Despite increasing research into branding as an instrument for improving university competitiveness and reputation (Melewar and Akel, 2005), scholars argue that a university may be too complex to be encapsulated by one brand or identity definition (Wæraas and Solbakk, 2008). This complexity is driven by the mis-match between brand perceptions and delivery in terms of tuition fees, competitive differentiation, league tables, and university statuses (Stamp, 2004). The increased need for international recruitment is also forcing universities to consider international brand image, and in doing so, confront dilemmas of standardized or adapted brand strategies (Chapleo, Durán, and Diaz, 2011; Gray, Fam, and Llanes, 2003). However, with rising national and international competition, universities all over the world are continuing to brand themselves in order to create a unique brand identity. Many universities are under pressure to act as businesses (Chapleo *et al.*, 2011) forcing them to adopt the concepts and practices of corporate branding.

Corporate branding and, in particular, corporate image, are described as the associations created from personal experience, word-of-mouth, advertising, and promotion (Lemmink, Schuijf, and Streukens, 2003). A corporate image is a multi-dimensional construct (Boiger, 1959; Spector, 1961) and suggested to be the sum of impressions (Bromley, 1993; Davies and Chun, 2012) or set of perceptions (Holzhauer, 1999) held by stakeholders. For universities to overcome previous mis-matches and successfully create a corporate image, we posit that universities must use both marketing resources and internal operations to construct a desired image in the minds of various stakeholders. Dowling (1993) demonstrates that corporate image is the result of organizations aligning themselves with their stakeholders' perceptions through communication efforts. We suggest that the mis-matches may not be as problematic, as individuals will not have the same perception of a university brand (Nguyen and LeBlanc, 2001), suggesting that a university does not have a single image, but rather multiple images. The key is to manage a university image with an understanding of how a corporate image is formed and how it is measured. Furthermore, it is crucial to attain knowledge and understanding of current images and what they are based on (Dowling, 1986). Brown and Dacin (1997) refer to 'corporate association', as the umbrella of information a person holds about a company, including their cognition, judgment, and association. For universities, a clear market positioning and a unique corporate image is thus the key to overcome existing issues. For example, to successfully promote degree programs, universities must include marketing to industry, selling convenience, and emphasizing interactive technologies (Carnevale and Olsen, 2003). Promoting academic reputation includes the emphasis on several factors including successful graduates, facilities, rigour, and distinguished faculties (Adams and Eveland, 2007; Conard and Conard, 2001).

Bennett (2007) reveals that recruitment messages should heavily feature (pictorially and textually) imagery associated with social and learning environments. Specifically, a university's learning environment attracts students with the quality and extent of student support services, high-calibre teachers, and a student-friendly administration (Gatfield, Barker, and Graham, 1999; Gutman and Miaoulis, 2003). Other desirable elements of the social environment include numerous societies, clubs, and sports facilities, and opportunities to socialize on campus (Bennett, 2007; Gatfield, Barker, and Graham, 1999). Many universities also brand their promises about a person's job and career prospects on graduation (Moogan, Baron, and Bainbridge, 2001), focusing on two aspects, namely (1) whether the degree will be useful in general terms (i.e. relevant to other job types) (Ivy, 2001) and/or (2) whether a degree confers high status on the graduate (Gray, Fam, and Llanes, 2003). Scholars note the importance of an organization's publicly stated mission and vision, as it implies certain promises (de Chernatony, 1999; Melewar and Jenkins, 2002). Claims can be made in formal mission and vision statements or perhaps more implicitly in joining particular groupings of universities (e.g. the Russell Group), which are known for distinct orientations (research led, or teaching led). A university's position in published university league tables also indicates its mission (Bennett and Ali-Choudhury, 2009).

In building strong brands, research identifies several challenges. Chapleo (2007) identifies that universities face barriers such as organizational resistance towards change, difficulty in capturing the university's complex nature, lack of a clear branding direction, and the competing interests of schools' images with that of their faculties within the university (Wæraas and Solbakk, 2009). To overcome the complexity of a university as a barrier to implementing branding, studies suggest that universities must account for the contributions of schools and faculties in the overall brand image of the university (Hemsley-Brown and Goonawardana, 2007; Heslop and Nadeau, 2010). In that way, universities will be more aware of the link between what they 'stand for' in terms of values and characteristics and how they are perceived (Melewar and Akel, 2005). With a clear differentiation strategy, students and academic staff will perceive the university as a more attractive place (Chapleo, 2004; Chapleo et al., 2011; Hemsley-Brown and Goonawardana, 2007).

Brand personality and brand communication

Brand models have evolved to focus more on additions of the 'promise' (Villafañe, 2004). When conceptualizing a brand, the concept of 'brand personality' is an important expression of the brand. Chapleo et al. (2011) suggest that before communicating, universities must elaborate on their 'brand promise' using their brand personality. Balmer and Liao (2007) suggest that the strength of student identification with a brand is established based on awareness, knowledge and experience of a brand and its interactive personality.

Brand personality is a set of human characteristics associated with a brand and carries the symbolic meanings, which the brand represents (Aaker 1997). Brand personality allows consumers to identify their selves through the connection to a brand (Belk, 1988; Kleine, Kleine, and Allen, 1995; Malhotra, 1988). Brand personality is developed through the personality traits linked to the brand (Aaker, 1997) and can ensure differentiation in product categories where intrinsic cues are very similar (Freling and Forbes, 2005). When consumers strongly identify with a brand, more time and money will be spent upon it, leading to consumers' brand preferences and subsequent purchase intentions. With regular interaction, long lasting consumer-brand relationships and increased purchases are evident (Carlson, Donavan, and Cumiskey, 2009).

To ensure differentiation and induce customer brand preferences, Veloutsou, Lewis, and Patton (2004) identify the following 'information requirements' for a university: (1) reputation of university and program ('functional and emotional values'), (2) location of university ('functional and emotional values'), (3) institutional infrastructure ('functional values'), (4) costs of study at institution ('functional values'), (5) career prospects ('emotional and functional values') and (6) quality of life during study ('emotional values') (Chapleo et al., 2011). These models and requirements relate to functional and emotional values (Keller, 2002; Veloutsou, Lewis, and Patton, 2004; Villafañe, 2004) and have some commonality with a university's brand personality. The application of these values to the university context can best be explained through these points: 'Functional': the basic running of universities in order to manage quality and innovation. 'Emotional': empathy characteristics that brands offer to their publics (Chapleo et al., 2011). In combination, these form the university's brand personality traits.

Stern (2006) observes how an organization's central, enduring, distinctive identity constitutes one of the key elements of a corporate brand (personality). These organizational features are sometimes defined as the organizational identity (Hatch and Schultz, 1997), which includes both the organization's core values and its underlying and actual behavioural characteristics (Balmer, 1998). Balmer (2001) suggests that a corporate brand is a derivative of an organization's identity. Thus, in the higher education context, a university's brand personality is determined by its organizational identity or 'educational identity' (Bennett and Ali-Choudhury, 2009). Such identity is established by (a) the composition of its student body (e.g. the proportions of ethnic minority and non-traditional students that it enrols (Bennett and Kottasz, 2006)); (b) internal values (Chapleo, 2007), that is whether the university is elite and exclusive or inclusive and comprehensive; (c) whether it has traditional as opposed to contemporary (mass-market) educational values (Alreck and Settle 1999); and (d) whether it values research above teaching (Gatfield et al., 1999; Ivy, 2001). Bennett and Ali-Choudhury (2009) suggest that further relevant considerations may include the nature (theoretical versus practical) and level of difficulty of the institution's courses (Binsardi and Ekwulugo, 2003; Moogan, Baron, and Bainbridge, 2001; Palacio, Meneses, and Pérez, 2002), student dropout rates (Bennett, 2007), and faculty qualifications and publication records (Gatfield et al., 1999; Gray et al., 2003). These elements make up the identity and brand personality of the university and are factors that make a university unique.

A university is also represented by its formal marketing communications (advertising, prospectuses, public relations, etc.) and by its more general corporate communications with government agencies, funding bodies, etc. (Bennett and Ali-Choudhury, 2009). Other determinants of an organization's public image can include its behaviour, history, strategies and organization structure. Image is 'what the audience sees' (Hatch and Schultz, 1997, p. 336), and may or may not reflect reality (Simoes, Dibb, and Fisk, 2005). Researchers have found that a university's image affects student recruitment (Palacio et al., 2002), the attitudes of governmental funding authorities (Landrum, Turrisi, and Harless, 1998), public perceptions of an institution's prestige and quality (McPherson and Schapiro, 1998), and a university's overall competitiveness (Parameswaran and Glowacka, 1995). Naudé and Ivy (1999) note that communicating a favourable university image is essential, due to two reasons: First, the goal of student recruitment is continually to seek *new* entrants rather than to retain 'existing customers'. Second, very few potential students have deep factual knowledge of the institutions they are considering entering. Thus, a university's image is likely to represent a primary influence on enrolment decisions (Bennett and Ali-Choudhury, 2009).

Over time, a more consistent reputation may be formed from the university brand image. Reputation is a consequence rather than a cause of how a university brand is perceived (Bennett and Ali-Choudhury, 2009). Specifically, the university brand's objective is to create a favourable reputation. Herbig and Milewicz (1997, p. 25) defines reputation as the 'estimation of the consistency over time of an attribute of an entity ... based on its willingness and ability to perform an activity repeatedly in a similar fashion'. Thus, reputation is established when an organization fulfils its promises over a prolonged period via its marketing and other activities. Balmer (2001) notes how a corporate brand invariably contained a covenant, but that a reputation need not do so. Moreover, a brand can be established quite quickly, whereas a reputation must be nurtured through time (Marwick and Fill, 1997). Fombrun and Rindova (1998) demonstrate that, over the years, leading organizations that had projected their core values and identities systemically and consistently had achieved higher reputational rankings than others (Bennett and Ali-Choudhury, 2009).

Student perceptions and choice of university brands

When deciding on a university, student choices are affected by a variety of elements (e.g. Nguyen *et al.*, 2016). The institution's practicability relating to its physical location and convenience represents a critical factor. From the student's point of view, practicability arises when a university has entry requirements that allow the person to matriculate, and offers a desired degree program (Binsardi and Ekwulugo, 2003). In addition, it is important that the university exists in a suitable physical location, e.g. within traveling distance of the student's home (Alreck and Settle, 1999), and has affordable fees and costs of accommodation (Bennett and Ali-Choudhury, 2009; Binsardi and Ekwulugo, 2003). Apart from the practicability of the institution, other important dimensions of a university brand include the institution's physical actuality e.g. architecture and campus layout, safety and security, the facilities of the city in which the university is located (Gray *et al.*, 2003; Moogan *et al.*, 2001). Another crucial element is the composition of a university's student body, particularly the proportion of the institution's attendees that come from 'non-traditional' backgrounds (Bennett and Ali-Choudhury, 2009).

Prospective students with positive attitudes towards a strong university brand may respond in the following ways: (a) they intend to apply for enrolment at the institution and (b) they engage in favourable word-of-mouth about the university. Other responses could incorporate the beliefs that the university is 'good' (Palacio *et al.*, 2002), that it should be admired and respected (Fombrun, Gardberg, and Sever, 2000), and that attendance would be 'good value for money' (Davis, 2002). Finally, responses that incorporate affect might involve feelings among prospective students that they would be pleased to enrol at the university and thereafter be seen attending the institution and that the university is pleasant and appealing.

Webb and Allen (1995) found that graduate business students were looking to get five benefits from their program choice: analytical skills, competitive advantage, monetary reward, career advancement, and job enrichment. In another study, Chen (2008) found that graduate students in research-focused programs were interested in financial aid, faculty reputation, and the quality or reputation of the university or program as important selection criteria. In addition, those in graduate professional programs had different criteria, emphasizing program rankings and tuition costs as salient criteria (Chen, 2008). In a survey of alumni, Business Week (2008) gathered information about graduates evaluating MBA programs to include education, career change, salary increase, job promotion, international appeal and networking opportunities (Heslop and Nadeau, 2010).

Carrel and Schoenbachler (2001) found MBA students' major decision criteria, which influenced their program choice, were both process-related (length of program, timing of classes, curriculum relevance) and outcome-related (increased knowledge, improved employability and promotability, and investment 'payoff'). They noted some differences related to institution tier level (Heslop and Nadeau, 2010). Stiber (2001) also found that the most important factors among MBA students included the chosen MBA characteristics, namely, input factors (accreditation of the institution, quality and responsiveness of faculty, and quality students) and process factors (relevant and interesting curriculum, convenient class schedule, and challenging courses) (Heslop and Nadeau, 2010).

Graduating MBA students were asked about important criteria in choosing potential employers (Phillips and Phillips, 1998). Although not a direct question about MBA programs, the students' responses provide further insight into the underlying motivations for pursuing an MBA and desired outcomes from that educational experience (Judson et al., 2006). Interestingly, salary was not mentioned as a top factor; rather, students responded that opportunity for advancement, challenging or interesting work, positive organizational climate, job security, good training program, and good health insurance were important considerations in selecting an employer (Phillips and Phillips, 1998).

Developing the university brand requires continually probing into students' perceptions and choices. This is particularly important for universities operating within the services sector as they face challenges of developing brands for an intangible and complex offering (Judson et al., 2006). In order to evaluate an intangible offering, students look to people within the organization for clues. Berger and Wallingford (1996) apply the hierarchy of communication goals, widely used in consumer advertising, to higher education in an effort to connect with the prospective students' state of mind when selecting a college to attend. Research suggests that 'academics' and 'reputation' (less concrete factors) are the two most important factors in selecting a college to attend, with 'cost' and 'location' (more concrete factors) following closely behind (Judson et al., 2006). Sevier (1994, 2001) suggests that college students generally offer four reasons for their college choice: (1) image or reputation, (2) location, (3) cost, and (4) the availability of a particular major. When asked to choose among the four factors, students invariably choose image (Judson et al., 2006). This signifies the important role of branding in higher education.

3 Coverage and content of the book

This book will be unique in its layout and focus in that it reveals the composite overview of strategy, planning and measurement through groundbreaking research and experiences of academics. It combines theoretical and methodological aspects of branding in different contexts and across multiple higher education institutions in a comprehensive text with the views of leading exponents of branding. Top researchers and users of brand management have converged to make submissions that are grouped accordingly, drawing attention to the relevant context and from varying perspectives. Students and academics can therefore, access information on trends, theory and practices about branding in higher education, across the areas of strategy, planning and measurement.

With limited space and resources, it would have been difficult to cover all aspects of branding activities in higher education. Hence, there is a carefully selected a range of topics that encompass emerging and contemporary issues, covering backgrounds built on the three theme-based perspectives of strategy, planning, and measurement of branding. In the following sections, a description of each of the chapters is presented briefly.

The first part of the book revolves around the strategic aspect of brand management in higher education. In Chapter 2, authors consider the co-creation of a brand identity in the case of UK higher education. It is recognized that the business ecosystem, a community that co-evolves with an organization, can be used to determine stakeholders, highlight interactions and foster a wider system perspective on brand identity co-creation. Such an ecosystem provides the basis for a potential framework for HEIs to develop their brand identity. This chapter draws on the theories of brand identity, service dominant logic, value co-creation, stakeholder management and business ecosystems to provide a framework in which HEIs can co-create brand identity. In so doing, this chapter advances theory in brand identity co-creation and service ecosystems and has implications for managers in providing guidance on how HEIs can co-create their brands within their own ecosystems.

Chapter 3 focuses on the connection between organizational culture and the corporate brand (CB) in HEIs. Organizational culture is based on common values and beliefs that form understandings about the functioning of an organization. The CB is an expression of organization's essence and uniqueness to be communicated among stakeholders. This chapter discusses how, in the higher education context, the brand ought to reflect the organizational culture through the vision/mission and values. Chapter 4 demonstrates how a leader can influence academic staff to support the brand of the institution via internal branding. Based on existing literature in several fields (including higher education management, brand management, corporate communication, human resource management, marketing management and leadership), this chapter suggests that a transformational leader of an institution not only is a role model for his or her followers to act in alignment with the brand, but also either initiates or influences internal branding activities in the institution, thereby creating brand support among followers. Therefore, institutions that want to build brand support from the academic staff should ensure that the leaders of their academic staff exhibit transformational leadership characteristics. This chapter is expected to be valuable in advancing current knowledge about internal branding in universities and will be useful for higher education management that wants to encourage academic staff to support their university's brand.

Chapter 5 explores the competition aspect of higher education in which branding is a necessary competitive tool for universities to stand out from the crowd and attract the attention and retention of key stakeholders. This chapter introduces higher education sector contemporary challenges and the impact of the increasing competition on both stakeholders' perceptions and universities' strategies. In re-affirming the growing need for differentiation and branding as a crucial part of corporate strategy to remain competitive, recommendations coming from extant literature and real-life examples are presented. In particular, with the aim of illustrating how higher education institutions organize and manage their competitive strategy, the chapter uses international business schools branding, with a special focus on ESCP Europe, as these institutions experience higher market pressure and as, by teaching a lot of strategy and branding, they should be better equipped to walk the talk and brand themselves successfully.

In the second part of the book, the planning aspects of branding in higher education are presented. Chapter 6 explores the domain of corporate brand communications and its relevance for the sector of higher education. The primary argument is that brand positioning for higher education institutions (HEI) requires the management of controlled (managerial/organizational communication and marketing communications) and uncontrolled communications. This chapter discusses how HEIs should internally and externally communicate their corporate and individual brand values as a means of improving their image with stakeholders. By drawing on the literature on corporate branding and higher education marketing, this chapter discusses how HEIs can communicate their corporate identities via conventional and digital means of communication. The chapter concludes with suggestions regarding the managerial steps that can be taken for planning and executing HEI brand communication programs, while also offering options for future research in brand communications in the context of HEIs.

In Chapter 7, the book examines the university logo as an effective means of corporate design by developing knowledge from a multidisciplinary approach to explore its relationships with its antecedents and its consequences. A qualitative exploratory approach is taken, comprising 12 in-depth interviews with key informants involved in the implementation of corporate visual identity and 7 focus groups (22 women and 17 men) with internal-stakeholders of three London-based-universities in the UK to encourage a sufficient level of group interaction and discussion on university logos. Findings reveal convergence in views concerning the main components of the university logo (name, colour, design/graphic, and typeface). Also, the classification offers the key antecedents (university's identity and strategy) and its consequences (integrated marketing communication, image, reputation/trust creation, engagement, commitment, and loyalty). The results will be valuable for marketing decision-makers, branding and communication professionals who are engaged in improving visual identity considering perceptions of managers, employees, and students about their image and loyalty.

Chapter 8 focuses on the development of brand image and reputation in higher education institutions. Building a brand image is critical for any organization, as an institution's brand image will directly impact the quality of faculty and students, which will in turn contribute to further develop its brand image in the broader community. The development of a clear, value-laden brand identity serves as an important foundation for institution-based brand communication with its stakeholders, including the message and symbols used to create and communicate this identity. Appropriate management of the institution's brand identity is required, particularly in today's rapidly-changing environment.

Chapter 9 examines the co-creation of value from a customer-integration approach. The increasing influence of market competition on higher education has been criticized for a focus on short-term gains rather than scholarly development. An alternative view of the market that may be more appropriate is provided by Service-Dominant logic (S-D Logic). Value co-creation takes place through resource integration and service exchange, enabled and constrained by institutions and institutional arrangements. Lecturers combine their knowledge with that of the students to develop the students' resources. A co-creative approach based on S-D Logic challenges universities to take on board how they create value for their students and other stakeholders. Implications are discussed for the student experience and student engagement. In addition, the role of the university in developing collaborative ecosystems in the wider community is discussed. A case study is provided to stimulate discussion on how far students can and should co-create their own curriculum.

The third part of the book covers the measurement perspective of higher education branding. In Chapter 10, brand performance and brand equity in academic and practice contexts are examined, and the link to the role of reputation and rankings is explored through the academic lens. This section ends by summarizing contributions in the literature. The perspective of the practitioner is then explored, with personal insights from a UK agency on terminology, approaches and challenges. This moves into a specific case study from a UK university. It is concluded that brand and reputation in HE are of great significance and, although clarity is increasing, there are still conceptual and practical challenges in assessing brands in the sector. This chapter is clear in its aim to blend academic and practice views to offer a thought provoking and challenging assessment of branding in modern HE.

In Chapter 11, the authors conduct a study, the purpose of which is to propose an 'inside-out' approach for HEI branding. This inside-out approach requires excellent brand communication to connect students to the HEI brand values and perceptions. It is proposed that branding efforts should engage students in the form of student citizenship behaviours, which can contribute to building a strong and trustworthy higher education brand. The study conducted in this chapter examines how university brand communication affects students' university identification, university brand commitment, and citizenship behaviours, which in turn build a trustworthy university. Results show that university brand communication promotes university brand through student citizenship behaviours such as word-of-mouth, suggestions for improvement, affiliation, and participation in future activities. It is also found that student citizenship behaviours positively influence students' trust in the university. These findings have important managerial implications for HEIs.

Chapter 12 presents the topic of scale development in higher education, focusing on university corporate image, student satisfaction and student behavioural intention. Corporate brand image has been argued as the way forward for business schools' brand differentiation and reputation building, though empirical work in this area remains to be done. In theoretical terms, the study presented in this chapter contributes by exploring and developing the dimensions of corporate brand image in business schools and empirically tests it on student's satisfaction and their behavioural intention (recommendation). The study's findings are based on responses from 558 respondents. Also, the potential ways in which educators can design their university corporate brand are discussed.

Chapter 13 evaluates branding scales in higher education and reviews multi-item scales employed in the study of branding in higher education, based on 42 papers that contain operationalizations of a variety of branding constructs. The authors find that, with few exceptions, the employed scales are borrowed from other fields and disciplines. The analysis of the borrowed scales leads the authors to identify the following issues, (a) omission to specify the source of the scale; (b) incomplete evidence of scale modifications; (c) non-credible sources; (d) unclear mapping to the source scale; and (e) limited transferability of scales developed in other fields/disciplines to the HE context. The authors of this chapter provide examples that illustrate the above and make suggestions to help managers when using published scales. The authors encourage researchers in the field to carry out a rigorous examination of the stability of functional relationships of constructs operationalized using scales borrowed from other fields and/or disciplines and provide a case study example of how such an investigation can be carried out.

4 Conclusion

University brands represent a topic that has garnered great interest in recent years. Branding in higher education is of great value when attracting program applicants. Recent publications have focused on university branding activities (Chapleo, 2017; Kaplan, 2018; Lowrie, 2017), exploring a diversity of topics such as examining image differences between students and senior administrators (Belanger, Mount, and Wilson, 2002), the popular image of the graduates of the institution (Parameswaran and Glowacka, 1995), and the opinions alumni held about their former universities (McAlexander, Koenig, and Schouten, 2006), the role of internal branding activities (Judson et al., 2006), and the identity formulation perspectives of how the university builds a brand image (Heslop and Nadeau, 2010; Melewar and Akel, 2005). In this book, we cover these diversities of branding and offer suggestions on how to build a brand in the higher education sector. We highlight the important role of the Internet and digitalization, including social media. Higher education institutions should consider using their web presence to maintain (or gain) market share, establish a clear advantage in brand identity, and take advantage of their inherent resources. At the same time, there are public concerns over accreditation, fraud and abuse that are sensitive issues for accredited online institutions to consider (Adams and Eveland, 2007). Therefore, continued research into these pitfalls and dark sides of branding in higher education should be researched.

In this book, 14 chapters, all with case studies, are written by internationally recognized expert contributors, covering specific issues related to strategy, planning, and measurement in higher education branding. We hope that these interesting chapters will encourage further discourse in this ever-interesting research field of brand management in higher education. Above all, we are most grateful for our contributors' insights and for their time and effort in developing these highly directional and informative chapters. We hope you will enjoy the book and become inspired to contribute to branding in higher education.

References

Aaker, J. (1997) "Dimensions of brand personality." *Journal of Marketing Research* 34(3), pp. 347–356.

Adams, J. and Eveland, V. (2007) "Marketing online degree programs: How do traditional-residential programs compete?" *Journal of Marketing for Higher Education* 17(1), pp. 67–90.

Alreck, P. and Settle, R. (1999) "Strategies for building consumer brand preference." *Journal of Product and Brand Management* 8(2), pp. 130–144.

Ambler, T. and Styles, C. (1996) "Brand development versus new product development: Towards a process model of extension decisions." *Marketing Intelligence and Planning* 14(7), pp. 10–19.

Balmer, J. (1998) "Corporate identify and the advent of corporate marketing." *Journal of Marketing Management* 14(5), pp. 963–996.

Balmer, J. (2001) "Corporate identity, corporate branding and corporate marketing: Seeing through the fog." *European Journal of Marketing* 35(3/4), pp. 248–291.

Balmer, J. and Gray, E. (2003) "Corporate brands: What are they? What of them?" *European Journal of Marketing* 37(7/8), pp. 972–997.

Balmer, J. and Liao, M. (2007) "Student corporate brand identification: An exploratory case study." *Corporate Communications: An International Journal* 12(4), pp. 356–375.

Belanger, C., Mount, J., and Wilson, M. (2002) "Institutional image and retention." *Tertiary Education and Management* 8, pp. 217–230.

Belk, R. W. (1988) "Possessions and the extended self." *Journal of Consumer Research* 15, pp. 139–168.

Bennett, R. (2007) "Advertising message strategies for encouraging young White working class males to consider entering British universities." *Journal of Business Research* 60(9), pp. 932–941.

Bennett, R. and Ali-Choudhury, R. (2009) "Prospective students' perceptions of university brands: An empirical study." *Journal of Marketing for Higher Education* 19(1), pp. 85–107.

Bennett, R. and Kottasz, R. (2006) "Widening participation and student expectations of higher education." *International Journal of Management Education* 5(2), pp. 47–65.

Berger, K. A. and Wallingford, H. P. (1996) "Developing advertising and promotion strategies for higher education." *Journal of Marketing for Higher Education* 7(4), pp. 61–72.

Berry, L., Lefkowith, E., and Clark, T. (1988) "In services, what's in a name?" *Harvard Business Review* 66(1), pp. 28–30.

Bick, G., Jacobson, M., and Abratt, R. (2003) "The corporate identity management process revisited." *Journal of Marketing Management* 19(5), pp. 835–855.

Binsardi, A. and Ekwulugo, F. (2003) "International marketing of British education: Research on the students' perception and the UK market penetration." *Marketing Intelligence and Planning* 21(5), pp. 318–327.

Boiger, J. F. (1959) "How to evaluate your company image." *Journal of Marketing* 24, pp. 7–10.

Bromley, D. B. (1993) *Reputation, Image and Impression Management*. Chichester: John Wiley & Sons.

Brown, T. J. and Dacin, P. A. (1997) "The company and the product: Corporate associations and consumer product responses." *Journal of Marketing* 61, pp. 68–84.

Business Week. (2008) "The best schools: Full-time MBA rankings." Cited from Heslop, L. A. and Nadeau, J. (2010) "Branding MBA programs: The use of target market desired outcomes for effective brand positioning." *Journal of Marketing for Higher Education* 20(1), pp. 85–117.

Caldwell, N. and Freire, J. R. (2004) "The differences between branding a country, a region and a city: Applying the Brand Box Model." *Journal of Brand Management* 12(1), pp. 50–61.

Carlson, B. D., Donavan, D. T., and Cumiskey, K. J. (2009) "Consumer-brand relationships in sport: Brand personality and identification." *International Journal of Retail & Distribution Management* 37(4), pp. 370–85.

Carnevale, D. and Olsen, F. (2003) "How to succeed in distance education." *The Chronicle of Higher Education* 49(40), A31. From http://chronicle.com/weekly/v49/i44/44a02501.htm.

Carrel, A. E. and Schoenbachler, D. D. (2001) "Marketing executive MBA programs: A comparison of student and sponsoring organization decision considerations." *Journal of Marketing for Higher Education* 11(1), pp. 21–29.

Chapleo, C. (2004) "Interpretation and implementation of reputation/brand management by UK university leaders." *International Journal of Educational Advancement* 5(1), pp. 7–23.
Chapleo, C. (2007) "Barriers to brand building the UK universities?" *International Journal of Nonprofit and Voluntary Sector Marketing* 12(1), pp. 23–32.
Chapleo, C. (2017) "Exploring the secret of successful university brands," in *Advertising and Branding: Concepts, Methodologies, Tools, and Applications*. Hershey, PA: IGI-Global, pp. 288–303.
Chapleo, C., Durán, M. V. C., and Díaz, A. C. (2011) "Do UK universities communicate their brands effectively through their websites?" *Journal of Marketing for Higher Education* 21(1), pp. 25–46.
Chen, L. H. (2008) "Internationalization of international marketing? Two frameworks for understanding international students' choice of Canadian universities." *Journal of Marketing for Higher Education* 18(1), pp. 1–33.
Conard, M. J. and Conard, M. A. (2001) "Factors that predict academic reputation don't always predict desire to attend." *Journal of Marketing for Higher Education* 11(4), pp. 2–18.
Davies, G. and Chun, R. (2012) "Employee as symbol: Stereotypical age effects on corporate brand associations." *European Journal of Marketing* 46(5), pp. 663–683.
Davis, S. (2002) "Implementing your BAM strategy: Eleven steps to making your brand a more valuable business asset." *Journal of Consumer Marketing* 19(6), pp. 503–513.
de Chernatony, L. (1999) "Brand management through narrowing the gap between brand identify and brand reputation." *Journal of Marketing Management* 15(2), pp. 157–179.
de Chernatony, L. and McWilliam, G. (1990) "Appreciating brands as assets through using a two dimensional model." *International Journal of Advertising* 9(2), pp. 111–119.
de Chernatony, L. and Segal-Horn, S. (2003) "The criteria for successful service brands." *European Journal of Marketing* 37(7/8), pp. 1095–1118.
Dowling, G. R. (1986) "Managing your corporate images." *Industrial Marketing Management* 15(2), pp. 109–115.
Dowling, G. R. (1993) "Developing your company image into a corporate asset." *Long Range Planning* 26(2), pp. 101–109.
Fan, Y. (2005) "Ethical branding and corporate reputation." *Corporate Communications: An International Journal* 10(4), pp. 341–350.
Fombrun, C., Gardberg, N., and Sever, J. (2000) "The reputation quotient: A multi-stakeholder measure of corporate reputation." *Journal of Brand Management* 7(4), pp. 241–255.
Fombrun, C. and Rindova, V. (1998) "Reputation management in global 1000 firms: A benchmarking study." *Corporate Reputation Review* 1(3), pp. 205–214.
Freling, H. and Forbes, L. (2005) "An empirical analysis of the brand personality effect." *Journal of Product and Brand Management* 14(7), pp. 404–413.
Gatfield, T., Barker, M., and Graham, P. (1999) "Measuring communication impact of university advertising materials." *Corporate Communications: An International Journal* 4(2), pp. 73–79.
Gray, B., Fam, K., and Llanes, V. (2003) "Branding universities in Asian markets." *Journal of Product and Brand Management* 12(2), pp. 108–120.

Gutman, J. and Miaoulis, G. (2003) "Communicating a quality position in service delivery: An application in higher education." *Managing Service Quality* 13(2), pp. 105–111.

Hatch, M. and Schultz, M. (1997) "Relations between organizational culture, identity and image." *European Journal of Marketing* 31(5/6), pp. 356–365.

Hatch, M. and Schultz, M. (2003) "Bringing the corporation into corporate branding." *European Journal of Marketing* 37(7/8), pp. 1041–1064.

Hemsley-Brown, J. and Goonawardana, S. (2007) "Brand harmonization on the international higher education market." *Journal of Business Research* 60(9), pp. 942–948.

Herbig, P. and Milewicz, J. (1997) "The relationship of reputation and credibility to brand success." *Pricing Strategy and Practice* 5(1), pp. 25–29.

Heslop, L. A. and Nadeau, J. (2010) "Branding MBA programs: The use of target market desired outcomes for effective brand positioning." *Journal of Marketing for Higher Education* 20(1), pp. 85–117.

Holzhauer, F. F. O. (1999) "Corporate image en brand image – Wat merkartikelreclame doet voor het corporate image," in C. B. M. Van Riel (ed.), *Handboek corporate communication, studenteneditie* (2nd edition). Samson, Alphen aan den Rijn, the Netherlands, pp. 177–220.

Ivy, J. (2001) "Higher education institution image: A correspondence analysis approach." *International Journal of Educational Management* 15(6), pp. 276–282.

Judson, K. M., Gorchels, L., and Aurand, T. W. (2006) "Building a university brand from within: A comparison of coaches' perspectives of internal branding." *Journal of Marketing for Higher Education* 16(1), pp. 97–114.

Kaplan, A. (2018) "Academia goes social media, MOOC, SPOC, SMOC, and SSOC: The digital transformation of Higher Education institutions and universities," in B. Rishi and S. Bandyopadhyay, *Contemporary Issues in Social Media Marketing*. Abingdon, Oxon: Routledge.

Keller, D. L. (2002) *Building, Measuring, and Managing Brand Equity*. Upper Saddle River, NJ: Pearson Education.

Kleine, S. S., Kleine III, R. E., and Allen, C. T. (1995) "How is a possession me or not me? Characterizing types and an antecedent of material possession attachment." *Journal of Consumer Research* 22(3), pp. 327–343.

Landrum, R., Turrisi, R., and Harless, C. (1998) "University image: The benefits of assessment and modelling." *Journal of Marketing for Higher Education* 9(1), pp. 53–68.

Lawlor, J. (1998) "Brand identity." *Case Currents* 24(9), pp. 16–23.

LeBlanc, G. and Nguyen, N. (1996) "Cues used by customers evaluating corporate image in service firms: An empirical study in financial institutions." *International Journal of Service Industry Management* 7(2), pp. 44–56.

Lemmink, J., Schuijf, A., and Streukens, S. (2003) "The role of corporate image and company employment image in explaining application intentions." *Journal of Economic Psychology* 24(1), pp. 1–15.

Louro, M. J. and Cunha, P. V. (2001) "Brand management paradigms." *Journal of Marketing Management* 17(7/8), pp. 849–875.

Lowrie, A. (2017) *Understanding Branding in Higher Education: Marketing Identities*. Boston, MA: Springer.

Malhotra, N. K. (1988) "Self-concept and product choice: An integrated perspective." *Journal of Economic Psychology* 9(1), pp. 1–28.

Marwick, N. and Fill, C. (1997) "Towards a framework for managing corporate identity." *European Journal of Marketing* 31(5/6), pp. 396–409.

McAlexander, J. H., Koenig, H. F., and Schouten, J. W. (2005) "Building a university brand community: The long-term impact of shared experiences." *Journal of Marketing for Higher Education* 14(2), pp. 61–79.

McPherson, M. and Schapiro, M. (1998) *The Student Aid Game*. Princeton, NJ: Princeton University Press.

Melewar, T. and Akel, S. (2005) "The role of corporate identity in the higher education sector: A case study." *Corporate Communications: An International Journal* 10(1), pp. 41–57.

Melewar, T. and Jenkins, E. (2002) "Defining the corporate identity construct." *Corporate Reputation Review* 5(1), pp. 76–90.

Melewar, T. and Karaosmanoglu, E. (2006) "Seven dimensions of corporate identity: A categorisation form the practitioners' perspectives." *European Journal of Marketing* 40(7/8), pp. 846–869.

Melewar, T C and Nguyen, B. (2015) "Five areas to advance branding theory and practice." *Journal of Brand Management* 21(9), pp. 758–769.

Moogan, Y., Baron, S., and Bainbridge, S. (2001) "Timings and trade-offs in the marketing of higher education courses: A conjoint approach." *Marketing Intelligence and Planning* 19(3), pp. 179–187.

Naudé, P. and Ivy, J. (1999) "The marketing strategies of universities in the United Kingdom." *International Journal of Educational Management* 13(3), pp. 126–134.

Nguyen, N. and LeBlanc, G. (2001) "Image and reputation of higher education institutions in students' retention decisions." *International Journal of Educational Management* 15(6), pp. 303–311.

Nguyen, B., Yu, X., Melewar, T C, and Hemsley-Brown, J. (2016) "Brand ambidexterity and commitment in higher education." *Journal of Business Research* 69(8), pp. 3105–3112.

Palacio, A., Meneses, G., and Pérez, P. (2002) "The configuration of the university image and its relationship with the satisfaction of students." *Journal of Educational Administration* 40(5), pp. 486–505.

Parameswaran, R. and Glowacka, A. (1995) "University image: An information processing perspective." *Journal of Marketing for Higher Education* 6(2), pp. 41–56.

Phillips, C. R. and Phillips, A. S. (1998) "The tables turned: Factors MBA students use in deciding among prospective employers." *Journal of Employment Counseling* 35(4), pp. 162–168.

Pratt, M. and Rafaeli, A. (1997) "Organizational dress as a symbol of multilayered social identities." *Academy of Management Journal* 40(4), pp. 862–898.

Pringle, H. and Thompson, M. (1999) *Brand Spirit: How Cause Related Marketing Builds Brands*. Chichester: John Wiley & Sons.

Sevier, R. A. (1994) "Image is everything: Strategies for measuring, changing, and maintaining your institution's image." *College and University* 69(2), pp. 60–75.

Sevier, R. A. (2001) "Brand as relevance." *Journal of Marketing for Higher Education* 10(3), pp. 77–97.

Simoes, C., Dibb, S., and Fisk, R. (2005) "Managing corporate identity: An internal perspective." *Journal of the Academy of Marketing Science* 33(2), pp. 153–168.

Spector, A. J. (1961) "Basic dimensions of the corporate image." *Journal of Marketing* 25(6), pp. 47–51.

Stamp, R. (2004) "The new challenge of branding buy-in." *Education News* Winter, p. 7.

Stern, B. (2006) "What does brand mean? Historical analysis method and construct definition." *Journal of the Academy of Marketing Science* 34(2), pp. 216–223.

Stern, B., Zinkhan, G., and Jaju, A. (2001) "Marketing images: Construct definition, measurement issues, and theory development." *Marketing Theory* 1(2), pp. 201–224.

Stiber, G. (2001) "Characterizing the decision process leading to enrollment in master's programs: Further application of the enrollment process model." *Journal of Marketing for Higher Education* 11(2), pp. 91–107.

Sujchaphong, N., Nguyen, B., and Melewar, T C (2015) "Internal branding in universities and the lessons learnt from the past: The significance of employee brand support and transformational leadership." *Journal of Marketing for Higher Education*, 25(2), pp. 204–237.

Sujchaphong, N., Nguyen, B., and Melewar, T C (2017) "Towards a branding oriented higher education sector: An overview of the four perspectives on university marketing studies." *The Marketing Review* 16(2), pp. 87–116.

Veloutsou, C., Lewis, J. W., and Patton, R. A. (2004) "University selection: Information requirements and importance." *The International Journal of Educational Management* 18(3), pp. 160–171.

Villafañe, J. (2004) *La buena reputación, Claves del valor intangible de las empresas"* [The good reputation: Intangible key business value]. Madrid: Pirámide.

Webb, M. S. and Allen, L. C. (1995) "Benefits of a graduate business degree: Students' perspectives and universities' challenges." *Journal of Marketing for Higher Education* 6(2), pp. 57–71.

Wæraas, A. and Solbakk, M. N. (2009) "Defining the essence of a university: Lessons from higher education branding." *Higher Education* 57(4), pp. 449–462.

Further readings

Clayton, M. J., Cavanagh, K. V., and Hettche, M. (2012) "Institutional branding: A content analysis of public service announcements from American universities." *Journal of Marketing for Higher Education* 22(2), pp. 182–205.

Haytko, D. L., Burris, G., and Smith, S. M. (2008) "Changing the name of a major university: A case study and how-to guide." *Journal of Marketing for Higher Education* 18(2), pp. 171–185.

Lawton, L. and Lundsten, L. (1998) "Contracts between benefits expected and delivered among MBA inquires, students, and graduates." *Journal of Marketing for Higher Education* 8(3), pp. 15–29.

McAlexander, J. H. and Koenig, H. F. (2010) "Contextual influences: Building brand community in large and small colleges." *Journal of Marketing for Higher Education* 20(1), pp. 69–84.

Opoku, R. A., Hultman, M., and Saheli-Sangari, E. (2008) "Positioning in market space: The evaluation of Swedish universities' online brand personalities." *Journal of Marketing for Higher Education* 18(1), pp. 124–144.

Osei, R. W. C. Jr, and Omar, M. (2012) "Higher education institution branding as a component of country branding in Ghana: Renaming Kwame Nkrumah University of Science and Technology." *Journal of Marketing for Higher Education* 22(1), pp. 71–81.

Rosen, D. E., Curran, J. M., and Greenlee, T. B. (1998) "College choice in a brand elimination framework: The high school student's perspective." *Journal of Marketing for Higher Education* 8(3), pp. 73–92.

Rosen, D. E., Curran, J. M., and Greenlee, T. B. (1998) "College choice in a brand elimination framework: The administrator's perspective." *Journal of Marketing for Higher Education* 8(4), pp. 61–81.

Sharma, A. A., Rao, V. R., and Popli, S. (2013) "Measuring consumer-based brand equity for Indian business schools." *Journal of Marketing for Higher Education* 23(2), pp. 175–203.

Syed Alwi, S. F. and Kitchen, P. (2014) "Business schools brand image: A design perspective." *Journal of Business Research* 67(11), pp. 2324–2336.

Watkins, B. A. and Gonzenbach, W. J. (2013) "Assessing university brand personality through logos: an analysis of the use of academics and athletics in university branding." *Journal of Marketing for Higher Education* 23(1), pp. 15–33.

Part I
Strategy

2 Co-creating brand identity
The case of UK higher education

Julie Robson, Sanjit Kumar Roy, Chris Chapleo, and Hsiao-Pei (Sophie) Yang

1 Introduction

Operating in a turbulent environment and with a diverse range of stakeholders (Knox and Gruar, 2007), higher education institutions increasingly recognize the value of marketing (Foroudi et al., 2017) and the need for a strong brand identity (Tapp, 1996). However, branding of HEIs has received less attention from scholars than the branding of commercial companies (Ewing and Napoli, 2005; Balaji et al., 2016) and as a result both academics and practitioners often lack the knowledge and tools to enable them to effectively co-create a strong brand identity.

The traditional marketing perspective suggests that an organization centrally develops a brand identity which it then communicates to its customers. However, as our understanding of branding has evolved it has been recognized that brand identity is not owned or created by an organization, but it is the customer who co-creates a brand with an organization and that customer is just one of many stakeholders that work together with an organization to co-create brand identity (Iglesias et al., 2013; Ramaswamy and Ozcan, 2015). As the marketing discipline is called upon to move away from its rather restrictive focus on customers toward acknowledging the interrelatedness of stakeholders and their impact on marketing practice (Hillebrand et al., 2015), a focus on the co-creation of brand identity within a wider ecosystem context comprising many different members is timely.

The context for this chapter is the HEI sector and specifically UK Higher Education (HE). Higher education institutions joined the marketing discussion late (Salamon and Anheier, 1992). As a result, many gaps remain in our understanding of HEI marketing in general and branding specifically. We do acknowledge that universities have more recently become more marketing-orientated in order to attract prospective students, particularly in response to increased global competition; however, branding remains embryonic in this sector (Lomer, Papatsiba, and Naidoo, 2018).

Underpinned by the business ecosystem concept, a dynamic community where members interact and create value, the purpose of this chapter is to develop a conceptual framework that provides insight and aids understanding of how HEIs can work with their ecosystem to co-create brand identity. The structure of this chapter is as follows: first, we draw on service dominant logic to understand how value is co-created generally and in a brand identity construct. Stakeholder theory is then examined to provide insight into the importance of stakeholder identification, management and their role in brand identity co-creation. Next, the business ecosystem is reviewed and its appropriateness in a brand identity construct established. We conclude with theoretical and managerial implications and suggested directions for further research. Finally, focusing on the UK HE sector, a framework is applied in a case study to identify co-creation opportunities within the HE service ecosystem.

After reading this chapter, you should be able to understand:

- The role of brand identity for higher education institutions (HEIs).
- The role of business ecosystem for HEIs.
- The role of value co-creation for HEIs.
- The relationship between co-creation processes, stakeholder theory and brand identities.

2 Review of the literature on brand identity and co-creation

Brand identity co-creation

There is a consensus among academics and practitioners that brands are the most valuable assets for organizations (Madden, Fehle, and Fournier, 2006) and hence there is burgeoning research on building brands (Schouten, McAlexander, and Koenig, 2007). Aaker (1991) defines brand identity as the sum of brand meanings expressed as a product, organization, symbol and person. Marketers of an organization position the brand in stakeholders' minds to create a brand identity (Brown *et al.*, 2006; Anisimova, 2014). Therefore, what an organization does and how it does it are all a part of its brand identity (Balmer, 2008, 2010; Anisimova, 2014). However, brand managers of organizations are not the sole creators of brand identity (Csaba and Bengtsson, 2006; Von Wallpach *et al.*, 2017). Stakeholders also contribute to the branding of organizations by co-creating brand identity with an organization (Schau, Muñiz, and Arnould, 2009). Two types of co-creation are relevant to this, first value co-creation and, leading on from this, brand identity co-creation.

The concept of co-creation was examined by Vargo and Lusch (2004) who contended that the dominant logic of marketing has shifted towards a new logic, which they refer to as service-dominant (S-D) logic. S-D logic considers service as the common denominator of the marketing exchange whereby a process orientation is the key and the customer is endogenous to value creation. One of the foundational propositions (FP 6) of S-D logic

(Vargo and Lusch, 2008) posits that the customer is always a co-creator of value. S-D logic therefore illustrates that customers co-create value as they are inherently involved in the value co-creation process (Vargo and Lusch, 2008). Customers engage with the value co-creation process through a range of actions and interactions (Arnould *et al.*, 2006), however they also interact with other collaborators in the customer's service network (McColl-Kennedy *et al.*, 2012). These activities represent the customer's cognitive and behavioural performance and the interactions represent customers' engagement with others, for example stakeholders or actors, in a service ecosystem.

In S-D logic, Vargo and Lusch (2004) focus on co-creating value but pay little attention to the concept of branding and how brand identity might be co-created. Consequently, Brodie, Glynn and Little (2006) have called for research to examine brand building for an organization, involving its customers and other stakeholders. Merz, He and Vargo (2009, p. 328) argue that there is a need 'to rethink the logic of brand and branding' to take into account the S-D Logic. They term this the new brand logic which underscores that brand value is co-created between the organization and its different stakeholders (Merz *et al.*, 2009).

Brand value co-creation has a process orientation and views different stakeholders as endogenous to this process. Brand value is co-created dynamically through social interactions in the stakeholder-based ecosystems (Merz *et al.*, 2009). This view is consistent with the propositions of Muñiz *et al.* (2001) that a brand is a continuous social process and brand value is co-created via stakeholder-based negotiations. The multiplicity of stakeholders in construing the meaning of brands and brand value co-creation is also mentioned in the works of Berthon, Pitt, and Campbell (2009). The full stakeholder-based brand co-creation process is based on stakeholder knowledge, stakeholder engagement and action and the alignment between the internal and external stakeholders (Gregory, 2007; Hatch and Schultz, 2010). Indeed, co-creation entails an active role by participants (e.g. customers, employees, partners and other stakeholders) (Ramaswamy and Ozcan, 2015, Ballantyne *et al.*, 2011; Frow and Payne, 2011). These actors interact with each other to create value via a process which does not distinguish between respective roles and actions (Grönroos and Ravald, 2011; Grönroos, 2011). As a result, brand identities are consistently shaped by the interactions between the brand and its stakeholder networks (Merz *et al.*, 2009). As stakeholder identities and brand identities emerge from the social processes between the brand and its multiple stakeholders (Csaba and Bengtsson, 2006), organizations need to identify who their stakeholders are in order to involve them in the brand management and co-creation process.

This section has demonstrated how brand identity can be co-created and the role of stakeholders in this process. In the next section, we will explore what is meant by stakeholders and the need to identify and classify stakeholders to manage the brand identity co-creation process.

Stakeholder management

The issue of stakeholder management is relatively well understood in private sector organizations (Carroll and Buchholtz, 2002; Christopher *et al.*, 2002; Rutterford *et al.*, 2006). However, whilst stakeholder theory has been advanced in commercial arenas (Donaldson and Preston, 1995), within the area of public and not-for-profit organizations literature there is less research (Bryson, 2005), particularly in a HE context.

Freeman (1984) defines stakeholders in the commercial arena as any group or individual that can affect or is affected by the achievement of the organization's objectives, showing some congruence with Bryson (2005), who talks of persons, groups or organizations that must be taken into account. It is clear that the term stakeholder is relevant to a broad number of groups and stakeholder management can therefore be complex.

Identifying stakeholders and understanding their impact on the organization is a key marketing task (Mitchell, Agle, and Wood, 1997) and underpins the essence of stakeholder management. Indeed, research suggests that attention to multiple stakeholders leads to organizational wealth and stakeholder value (Hillebrand *et al.*, 2015). There is however a key question of how should stakeholders be identified and grouped? Mitchell *et al.* (1997) discuss the need for a theory of stakeholder identification that can reliably separate stakeholders from non-stakeholders, as each group will exist within a complex network of intertwining relationships and needs to be represented systematically. The variety of approaches taken to classify stakeholder has arguably given rise to confusion over what factors to consider when grouping stakeholders. Mitchell *et al.* (1997) identify three key factors: power, legitimacy, and urgency. Johnson and Scholes (2002) suggest classification of stakeholders in terms of how *interested* each stakeholder is to impress its expectations on the organization and whether they have the *power* to do so. Reed (2008) discussed the nature of participation of stakeholders as a classification basis.

Despite the importance of identifying and managing stakeholders, few studies have examined the impact of the multiple stakeholders of organizations on branding (Miles, 2017; Roper and Davies, 2007) and most research has focused on co-creating value with direct customers alone, rather than considering multiple stakeholders in the network (Healy and McDonagh, 2013). As a result, much less is known concerning multiple stakeholders' roles on brand identity co-creation. Thus, we argue the importance of multiple stakeholder identification and adopt an ecosystem approach since HEI stakeholders often have complex inter-organizational relationships that are intimately involved in the achievement of the organizational goals and marketing strategy development (Knox and Gruar, 2007). However, value creation for stakeholders is challenging for organizations, as multiple stakeholders often hold diverse interests that bring both opportunities and tensions for organizations. For example, in the HE sector, Bolton and Nie (2010) reveal how a collaborative partnership, between two universities from two countries, struggled to balance stakeholders' different needs, when the diverse stakeholder groups ranged across governments, industries, professional associations, students, parents and broader communities. An ecosystem approach can provide insight into such challenges and will be discussed next.

Business ecosystems

Drawing from the strategic management literature, the business ecosystem was first conceptualized by Moore (1993). Ecosystems contain a large number of interconnected actors, members or stakeholders that depend on each other for their effectiveness and survival (Iansiti and Levien, 2004). This is a dynamic community where members actively interact and create value (Moore, 1993; Iansiti and Levien, 2004). The emphasis within an ecosystem is not therefore on the individual organization, but on the ecosystem as a whole (Power and Jerjian, 2001, p. 3). As such the ecosystem concept aligns well and provides a useful context to consider the brand identity co-creation as it recognizes the importance of the community and the value contributed by different members within the ecosystem.

Ecosystem members include organizations and individuals with direct and indirect links to a central organization (Baghbadorani and Harandi, 2012). Moore (1998) defined an ecosystem as an 'extended system of mutually supportive organizations; communities of customers, suppliers, lead producers, and other stakeholders, financing, trade associations, standard bodies, labour unions, governmental and quasigovernmental institutions, and other interested parties' (Moore, 1998, p. 168). Members of one ecosystem may also be members of other competing ecosystems.

Business ecosystem participants are typically classified into groups or layers (see for example, Rong and Shi, 2015, p. 46). At the centre, the focal organization and the nature of that organization, i.e. the different business sectors in which the organization operates, are commonly stated. At level one is the core business (e.g. internal departments of an organization, direct suppliers, distribution channels); level two is the extended enterprise (e.g. direct customers, standards bodies); and level three, other ecosystem partners who can have an impact on the core business (e.g. government, trade organizations, unions, investors). Unlike marketing frameworks (see for example, Akaka *et al.*, 2013), in the business ecosystem, the customer is not located at the core, but in the extended layer as the business ecosystem was originally developed to create innovation to develop new products and satisfy customers (Moore, 1996, p. 76). This aligns well with the call by Hillebrand *et al.* (2015) to move the focus of marketing from the customer to include other stakeholders as the ecosystem extends this view to consider all stakeholders within the system.

The ecosystem is not confined to one single industry, but extends to a variety of industries where the direct or indirect members may be located (Moore, 1993). An ecosystem can therefore include hundreds, if not thousands, of members. Ecosystems can be complex and difficult to map due to the sheer number of members that need to be included in an ecosystem. Indeed, some users (see for example, Townsend, 2014) have coined the phrase 'ecosystem blindness' to describe the inability to both understand and describe an organization's ecosystem and the complex web of relationships in which their organization operates.

The concept of ecosystems has been used in a wide range of business sectors (Adner and Kapoor, 2010) and more recently have been adopted by marketing scholars (Vargo and Akaka, 2012; Akaka *et al.*, 2013). Ecosystems can aid understanding of a complex context by mapping out the key stakeholders, identifying inter-relationships and providing a stakeholder hierarchy within the ecosystem (Akaka *et al.*, 2013; Baghbadorani and Harandi, 2012). Business ecosystems are therefore a way of making interdependencies more explicit (Adner and Kapoor, 2010). However, despite the concept of ecosystems having existed for more than 20 years, understanding of ecosystems is still evolving (Iansiti and Levien, 2004; Anggraeni, Hartigh, and Zegveld, 2007). Indeed, scholars point to the need to comprehensively explore and structure the concepts, boundaries and theoretical systems of ecosystems (Rong and Shi, 2015). Application of the ecosystem concept in new and different contexts, such as marketing and brand co-creation, can help advance understanding.

Brand ecosystems

Winkler (1999) was the first to use the term 'brand ecosystem' to describe the different stakeholders in a brand. However, Winkler's approach adopted a company centric view rather than considering the wider interactions that take place on different levels within an ecosystem (Bergvall, 2006). Others have used different terms interchangeably, for example, lifecycle and brand bio-ecology (Zi-Xian and Qing-Hua 2013). In addition, other writers have adopted the ecosystem but retained a consumer focus, placing the customer or the customer-firm dyad at the centre (see for example, Vargo and Lusch, 2004, 2008 who link S-D Logic with the ecosystem; and Pinar and Trapp, 2008 who apply the ecosystem in a HE context).

Few, if any, have used Moore's original framework (Moore, 1993) as the basis of their work, taking into account the idea of a brand community with direct and indirect brands. Mackalski and Belisle (2011, p. 401) come closest, defining a brand ecosystem as representing 'an environment consisting of all brands that could potentially impact and interact with each other in a competitive space'. They included the brands of related product categories, competing brands and private label brands in their study on the impact of product recall on brands. In this chapter, we adopt the original definition of a business ecosystem and consider the potential role of all members in brand identity co-creation.

A framework of higher education ecosystems

The business ecosystem presented in Figure 2.1 provides a framework in which HEIs can better understand and manage their brand identity. It identifies the wide range of the different stakeholders a HEI has and at the same time emphasizes the importance of the ecosystem as an entity in itself. It is well recognized within the ecosystem literature that an organization is likely to have hundreds, if not thousands, of stakeholders. It is impossible for any organization to identify all of them. Use of the framework will help organizations, such as HEIs, reduce what practitioners term ecosystem blindness (Townsend, 2014) by identifying many more of their stakeholders and help them to explore and understand which ones contribute currently to their brand identity and which ones may present an opportunity for future collaborative work.

The business ecosystem framework is not however simply about identifying and locating stakeholders in a framework. Its application extends beyond this to understanding what it means to be a part of a brand ecosystem. It has already been established that brand identity is co-created,

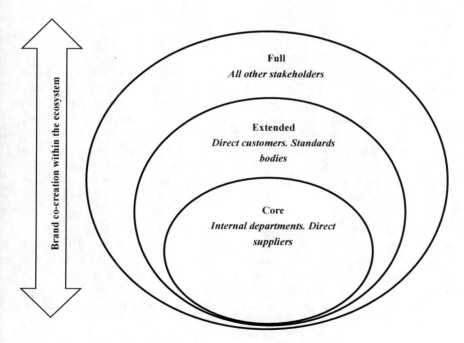

Figure 2.1 Higher education ecosystem.

however the ecosystem approach highlights the need for organizations to consider the brand identities of others within their ecosystem. Iansiti and Levien (2004) identify the need for ecosystems to be healthy to ensure survival and growth (Iansiti and Levien, 2002). Value creation and therefore brand identity co-creation can be considered to be a key part of this. Ecosystem health can be achieved through interdependency, integration and impact (Iansiti and Levien, 2004, p. 10)

In a brand identity co-creation context, interdependency recognizes that an organization needs to influence others within the ecosystem if it is to manage its own brand identity, others which are outside of its direct control. HEIs needs to identify which stakeholders within the ecosystem are most important to them in co-creating their own brand identity and how they can influence those organizations and individuals. As Iansiti and Levien (2004) explain, this has implication for strategy, operations and policy. For example, which stakeholder(s) does the university want to co-create their brand with and form closer alliances, relationships and links? Consideration of those organizations, possibly with indirect relationships, in the outer 'full' level may give rise to more innovative brand identity co-creation opportunities. In addition, which stakeholders have identified the university as an important stakeholder, how is this in turn impacting the university brand and how can this be managed going forward?

Integration is about identifying what resources exist within the ecosystem that can be used to enhance an organization's brand. Within the HEI ecosystem, universities have access not only to their own resources but potentially those of all other stakeholders. For example, working with local colleges as 'customers' for their student 'product' can result in brand identity co-creation depending on the activities undertaken and the nature and strength of the college brand. The HEI can benefit from college resources where these are used to position and promote the college and HEI as partners. In addition, many HEI brands are closely linked to the brand identity of their geographic locations in terms of the region, or city, or town. This can give rise to a geographically bound ecosystem where the fate of the location adds or detracts value from the HEI's brand. HEIs can draw on the resources of local government and organizations to co-create their brand value.

Finally, HEIs need to be aware of the impact of their own actions on the ecosystem to which they belong. It is therefore important to consider not only how a university's action may influence its own brand identity, but also how it can affect other members of the ecosystem and the ecosystem itself. The lesson here is that HEIs do not compete with other universities, but the HEI ecosystem competes with other HEI ecosystems to which the competitors belong.

3 Managerial implications

From a managerial perspective, this chapter proposed a framework that aims to encourage HEI brand managers to focus on three key questions: what is their core business mix; who are their stakeholders; and how can they draw on their ecosystem to co-create their brand identity? The key managerial implication for many HEIs therefore is that education is one business focus and students are one, albeit important, stakeholder within their ecosystem. HEIs therefore need to move their focus from the students at the centre of the ecosystem to consider other stakeholders and the ecosystem as a whole when considering brand identity. This wider perspective highlights that brand identity is not linear; brands are intricately intertwined (Bergvall, 2006, p. 174) and co-creation takes place on a number of different levels with a wide range of direct and indirect actors. HEIs need to take a wider, holistic approach to brand identity.

4 Conclusion

This chapter has addressed the call to help academics and practitioners alike better understand and manage stakeholder co-creation of brand identity for HEIs. It has achieved this by proposing an ecosystem framework for HEIs. In so doing this chapter makes several contributions to the theoretical literature.

First, the ecosystem framework helps identify and simplify the complex array of stakeholders that HEIs have. The framework categorizes stakeholders into core, extended and full. By focusing on understanding the ecosystem as a whole, rather than the contextual challenges, researchers and practitioners can better understand and deal with the complexities (Akaka, Vargo, and Lusch, 2013, p. 2; Ramaswamy and Ozcan, 2015). The ecosystem has provided a framework to guide and inform the identification of co-creation opportunities.

Second, the ecosystem provides a framework in which existing theory on co-creation, brand identity, and stakeholder identity can be applied in a holistic manner. HEI branding efforts have often focused on external elements of branding (e.g. promotion and identity) without seeming to understand the full nature of an HEI brand. The ecosystem framework identifies core, extended and full stakeholders whose inter-relationships work together to contribute to the overall brand of a HEI organization and the community in which it operates.

Third, by applying the ecosystem to brand identity co-creation we have responded to the call by Hillebrand *et al.* (2015) to move away from a customer–focused view of marketing. The ecosystem has however broadened this perspective considerably by providing community perspective and emphasizing the ecosystem entity as a brand identity in which individual organizations are located. This in turn has highlighted additional considerations in brand identity co-creation, namely interdependency, integration and impact.

Finally, development of the business ecosystem in a brand identity context has added to the need to comprehensively explore and structure the concepts, boundaries and theoretical systems of ecosystems (Rong and Shi, 2015). It has demonstrated the appropriateness of the business ecosystem in a marketing and brand context. The framework proposed builds on the earlier application by Pinar *et al.* (2011) and Khanifar *et al.* (2013) and suggests that the business ecosystems could well provide insights into further areas of marketing that are characterized by complexity.

5 Case study: applying the HE ecosystem in the UK HE sector

Recent reports suggest that the HE sector in the UK generates approximately £11 billion per year in export earnings. At the same time, the UK HE sector contributed £21.5 billion to GDP, which is approximately 1.2 per cent of the UK's GDP (Universities UK 2015). Increasing competition in the global higher education sector underscores the importance of branding in the UK HE sector (Lomer *et al.*, 2018). The UK HE sector is poised to face certain challenges in the present times which are (a) global competitive pressures; (b) increased student expectations; (c) increasing cost structures; (d) recruiting global talent; and (e) creating an environment of research and innovation. In the wake of such challenges, branding of the UK HE sector and looking at it from an ecosystem perspective might provide avenues for managing the HE brands.

An HE ecosystem framework, based on Moore's original business ecosystem (Moore, 1993) and adapted to take into account brand identity co-creation, is presented in Figure 2.1. At the centre of the framework, the business of HEIs is stated. Although others have focused solely on education and the student (Pinar *et al.*, 2011; Khanifar *et al.*, 2013), education is just one of several activities that universities engage in. HEIs also produce research and provide professional practice services (e.g. consultancy to businesses). Education may well be the largest contributor in terms of income for most HEIs, but education does not exist in isolation and the overall university brand will be determined by the interplay between these different areas. In addition, although stakeholders for each activity may overlap, others may be unique to one strand, for example, research or consultancy, and will need to be identified and managed separately.

Stakeholders present in the core of the framework include the internal departments and staff of the HEI – both academic (e.g. University Vice Chancellor, Professors and Lecturers) and support staff (e.g. Administrators) and those located in central business function departments (i.e. Personnel and Estates). In addition, direct suppliers such as local schools, colleges, agents, publishers and consultants are also located here.

In level two, the extended enterprise, the direct customers and standards bodies for each of the core business areas are located. These include students, parents, influencers, student funders, partner institutions, academic and research bodies/funding councils, national charities, local employers/businesses, national employers/businesses, governors, course accreditors and professional bodies, taxpayers, the National Union of Students (NUS), other student organizations, and trustees.

At level three, all other ecosystem stakeholders who can have an impact on the core business are included. For example, Government and the EU, learned societies, networking societies/lobbying groups, trade unions, other NGOs, local government/city/authorities, local community, media and the press, qualifications authorities (e.g. A level boards), UK HE marketing organizations, local police, local charities, competitors and other stakeholders.

The ecosystem aids the understanding of brand identity co-creation as it highlights that co-creation can take place between the HEI and any of the organizations/individuals in each of the layers. In addition, co-creation can also take place between organizations and individuals external to the HEI. The ecosystem concept thus contributes to the notion of brand identity co-creation by recognizing that the HEI's ecosystem as a whole also has a brand identity which all ecosystem members contribute to. This ecosystem brand identity will differ from the brand identity of other ecosystems to which competing HEIs belong. Consequently, neither the branding theory nor the practice of the ecosystem brand identity have been previously embraced by HEIs for developing and maintaining successful HEI brands and they therefore warrant further investigation.

Discussion points:

1 What are the characteristics of HEI brands?
2 Why do HEIs need to embrace branding?
3 What is the usefulness of understanding and applying the ecosystem brand identity framework?
4 Critically examine the stakeholder and process oriented view of branding for HEIs.
5 Critically examine the different components of HEI brand identity.

6 Further investigation

In offering a new direction for the co-creation of brand identity, this chapter suggests a number of avenues for further research. First the non-linear and intertwined nature of brand identity co-creation needs to be explored further. How can organizations prioritize and manage these different relationships while at the same time taking into account the needs of the wider ecosystem. In addition, what guidance can we provide to managers in this context?

Our conceptual framework presents one static ecosystem. We have not considered the dynamic nature of an ecosystem (Rong and Shi, 2015); and the impact of this on brand identity co-creation as new members join or existing members leave, or where a HEI may be a member of more than one ecosystem. Future research could explore the impact these changes have on the HE brand identity co-creation.

Given the different nature of HEIs, it would also be useful to explore the use of this framework within a range of HEIs with different business mixes (e.g. from a teaching only HEI to a research based HEI) to assess both the accuracy of the framework, in terms of the range and location of different stakeholders, and their different contributions to the co-creation of brand identity. The results will also further our understanding of ecosystems and enrich knowledge in this important area.

Finally, this is a conceptual chapter and therefore this work requires empirical testing. In particular, given that many HEIs have come late to marketing, are brand managers willing to take the leap forward from a student-customer focus to a wider ecosystem-community perspective when developing their brand identity?

References

Aaker, D. A. (1991) *Managing Brand Equity: Capitalizing on the Value of a Brand Name*. London: The Free Press.

Adner, R. and Kapoor, R. (2010) "Value creation in innovation ecosystems: How the structure of technological interdependence affects firm performance in new technology generations." *Strategic Management Journal* 31(3), pp. 306–333.

Akaka, M. A., Vargo, S. L., and Lusch, R. F. (2013) "The complexity of context: A service ecosystems approach for international marketing." *Journal of Marketing Research* 21(4), pp. 1–20.

Anggraeni, E., Den Hartigh, E., and Zegveld, M. (2007, October) "Business ecosystem as a perspective for studying the relations between firms and their business networks," in *ECCON 2007 Annual meeting*. Bergen aan Zee, The Netherlands.

Anisimova, T. (2014) "Benchmarking desired corporate brand image in relation to stakeholders: a managerial perspective." *Qualitative Market Research: An International Journal* 17(4), pp. 441–463.

Arnould, E. J., Price, L. L., and Malshe, A. (2006) "Toward a cultural resource-based theory of the customer," in R. F. Lusch and S. L. Vargo (eds), *The Service-dominant Logic of Marketing: Dialog, Debate and Directions*. New York: Routledge, pp. 320–333.

Baghbadorani, M. F. and Harandi, A. (2012) "A conceptual model for business ecosystem and implications for future research." *International Proceedings of Economics Development and Research* 52(17), pp. 82–86.

Balaji, M. S., Roy, S. K., and Sadeque, S. (2016) "The antecedents and consequences of university brand identification." *Journal of Business Research* 69 (8), pp. 3023–3032.

Ballantyne, D., Frow, P., Varey, R. J., and Payne, A. (2011) "Value propositions as communication practice: Taking a wider view." *Industrial Marketing Management* 40(2), pp. 202–210.

Balmer, J. M. (2008) "Identity based views of the corporation: Insights from corporate identity, organisational identity, social identity, visual identity, corporate brand identity and corporate image." *European Journal of Marketing* 42(9/10), pp. 879–906.

Balmer, J. M. (2010) "Explicating corporate brands and their management: Reflections and directions from 1995." *Journal of Brand Management* 18(3), pp. 180–196.

Bergvall, S. (2006) "Brand ecosystems," in J. E., Schroeder, M. Salzer-Mörling, and S. Askegaard (eds), *Brand Culture*. Abingdon, Oxon: Taylor & Francis.

Berthon, P., Pitt, L. F., and Campbell, C. (2009) "Does brand meaning exist in similarity or singularity?" *Journal of Business Research* 62(3), pp. 356–361.

Bolton, D. and Nie, R. (2010) "Creating value in transnational higher education: The role of stakeholder management." *Academy of Management Learning & Education* 9(4), pp. 701–714.

Brodie, R. J., Glynn, M. S., and Little, V. (2006) "The service brand and the service-dominant logic: Missing fundamental premise or the need for stronger theory?" *Marketing Theory* 6(3), pp. 363–379.

Brown, T. J., Dacin, P. A., Pratt, M. G., and Whetten, D. A. (2006) "Identity, intended image, construed image, and reputation: An interdisciplinary framework and suggested terminology." *Journal of the Academy of Marketing Science* 34(2), pp. 99–106.

Bryson, J. (2005) "What to do when stakeholders matter." *Public Management Review* 6(1), pp. 21–53.

Carroll, A. B. and Buchholtz, A. K. (2002) *Business and Society: Ethics and Stakeholder Management* (5th edition). South Western College Publishing.

Christopher, M., Payne, A., and Ballantyne, B. (2002) *Relationship Marketing: Creating Stakeholder Value* (2nd revised edition). Mason, USA: Butterworth-Heinemann.

Csaba, F. F. and Bengtsson, A. (2006) "Rethinking identity in brand management," in J. E. Schroeder and M. Salzer-Mörling, *Brand Culture*. London: Routledge, pp. 118–135.

Donaldson, T. and Preston, L. (1995) "The stakeholder theory of the corporation: Concepts, evidence, and implications." *Academy of Management Review* 20(1), pp. 65–91.

Ewing, M. T. and Napoli, J. (2005) "Developing and validating a multidimensional nonprofit brand orientation scale." *Journal of Business Research* 58(6), pp. 841–853.

Foroudi, P., Dinnie, K., Kitchen, P. J., Melewar, T C, and Foroudi, M. M. (2017) "IMC antecedents and the consequences of planned brand identity in higher education." *European Journal of Marketing* 51(3), pp. 528–550.

Freeman, R. E. (1984) *Strategic Management: A Stakeholder Approach*. Chicago: Chicago Press.

Frow, P. and Payne, A. (2011) "A stakeholder perspective of the value proposition concept." *European Journal of Marketing* 45(1/2), pp. 223–240.

Gregory, A. (2007) "Involving stakeholders in developing corporate brands: The communication dimension." *Journal of Marketing Management* 23(1–2), pp. 59–73.

Grönroos, C. (2011) "Value co-creation in service logic: A critical analysis." *Marketing Theory* 11(3), pp. 279–301.

Grönroos, C. and Ravald, A. (2011) "Service as business logic: Implications for value creation and marketing." *Journal of Service Management* 22(1), pp. 5–22.

Hatch, M. J. and Schultz, M. (2010) "Toward a theory of brand co-creation with implications for brand governance." *Journal of Brand Management* 17(8), pp. 590–604.

Healy, J. C. and McDonagh, P. (2013) "Consumer roles in brand culture and value co-creation in virtual communities." *Journal of Business Research* 66(9), pp. 1528–1540.

Hillebrand, B., Driessen, P. H., and Koll, O. (2015) "Stakeholder marketing: Theoretical foundations and required capabilities." *Journal of the Academy of Marketing Science* 43, pp. 411–428.

Iansiti, M. and Levien, R. (2002) *The New Operational Dynamics of Business Ecosystems: Implications for Policy, Operations and Technology Strategy.* Harvard Business School Working Paper, No. 03-030, September 2002.

Iansiti, M. and Levien, R. (2004) "Strategy as ecology." *Harvard Business Review* 82(3), pp. 68–81.

Iglesias, O., Ind, N., and Alfaro, M. (2013) "The organic view of the brand: A brand value co-creation model." *Journal of Brand Management* 20(8), pp. 670–688.

Johnson, G. and Scholes, K. (2002) *Exploring Corporate Strategy.* Harlow, England: Prentice Hall.

Khanifar, H., Esfidani, M. R., Nazari, H., and Naderi, J. (2013) "Evaluation of Tarbiat Modares University brand based on University Brand Ecosystem Model." *International Journal of Academic Research in Business and Social Sciences* 3(7), pp. 628–642.

Knox, S. and Gruar, C. (2007) "The application of stakeholder theory to relationship marketing strategy development in a non-profit organization." *Journal of Business Ethics* 75(2), pp. 115–135.

Lomer, S., Papatsiba, V., and Naidoo, R. (2018) "Constructing a national higher education brand for the UK: Positional competition and promised capitals." *Studies in Higher Education* 43(1), pp. 134–153.

Mackalski, R. and Belisle, J. F. (2011) "Measuring the short-term spillover impact of a product recall on a brand ecosystem," in *AMA Educators' Proceedings Marketing* 2011. San Francisco, USA.

Madden, T. J., Fehle, F., and Fournier, S. (2006) "Brands matter: An empirical demonstration of the creation of shareholder value through branding." *Journal of the Academy of Marketing Science* 34(2), pp. 224–235.

McColl-Kennedy, J. R., Vargo, S. L., Dagger, T. S., Sweeney, J. C., and van Kasteren, Y (2012) "Health care customer value cocreation practice styles." *Journal of Service Research* 15(4), pp. 370–389.

Merz, M. A., He, Y., and Vargo, S. L. (2009) "The evolving brand logic: A service-dominant logic perspective." *Journal of the Academy of Marketing Science* 37(3), pp. 328–344.

Miles, S. (2017) "Stakeholder theory classification: A theoretical and empirical evaluation of definitions." *Journal of Business Ethics* 142(3), pp. 437–459.

Mitchell, R. K., Agle, B. R., and Wood, D. J. (1997) "Toward a theory of stakeholder identification and salience: Defining the principle of who and what really counts." *Academy of Management Review* 22(4), pp. 853–886.

Moore, J. F. (1993) "Predators and prey: A new ecology of competition." *Harvard Business Review* 71, pp. 75–86.
Moore J. F. (1996) *The Death of Competition: Leadership and Strategy in the Age of Business Ecosystems.* New York: Harper Business.
Moore, J. F. (1998) "The rise of a new corporate form." *Washington Quarterly* 21(1), pp. 167–181.
Muñiz, Jr, A. M., Albert, M., and O'Guinn, T. C. (2001) "Brand community." *Journal of Consumer Research* 27(4), pp. 412–432.
Pinar, M. and Trapp, P. S. (2008) "Creating competitive advantage through ingredient branding and brand ecosystem: The case of Turkish cotton and textiles." *Journal of International Food and Agribusiness Marketing* 20(1), pp. 29–56.
Pinar, M., Trapp, P., Girard, T., and Boyt, T. E. (2011) "Utilizing the brand ecosystem framework in designing branding strategies for higher education." *International Journal of Educational Management* 25(7), pp. 724–739.
Power, T. and Jerjian, G. (2001) *Ecosystem: Living the 12 Principles of Networked Business.* FT. com.
Ramaswamy, V. and Ozcan, K. (2015) "Brand value co-creation in a digitalised world: An integrative framework and research implications." *International Journal of Research in Marketing* 33(1), pp. 1–14.
Reed, M. (2008) "Stakeholder participation and environmental management: A literature review." *Biological Conservation* 141, pp. 2417–2431.
Rong, J. and Shi, Y. (2015) *Business Ecosystems: Constructs, Configurations, and the Nurturing Process Hardcover.* London and New York: Palgrave Macmillan.
Roper, S. and Davies, G. (2007) "The corporate brand: Dealing with multiple stakeholders." *Journal of Marketing Management* 23(1–2), pp. 75–90.
Rutterford, J., Upton, M., and Kodwani, D. (2006) *Financial Strategy: Adding Stakeholder Value* (2nd edition). New York: John Wiley and Sons.
Salamon, L. M. and Anheier, H. K. (1992) "In search of the non-profit sector. I: The question of definitions." *International Journal of Voluntary and Nonprofit Organizations* 3(2), pp. 125–151.
Schau, H. J., Muñiz Jr, A. M., and Arnould, E. J. (2009) "How brand community practices create value." *Journal of Marketing* 73(5), pp. 30–51.
Schouten, J. W., McAlexander, J. H., and Koenig, H. F. (2007) "Transcendent customer experience and brand community." *Journal of the Academy of Marketing Science* 35(3), pp. 357–368.
Tapp, A. (1996) "Charity brands: A qualitative study of current practice." *International Journal of Nonprofit and Voluntary Sector Marketing* 1(4), pp. 327–336.
Townsend, M. (2014) *Curing Ecosystem Blindness: Your Company's Place in the Business Ecosystem.* Available from www.corpedgroup.com.
Universities UK. (2015) *Patterns and Trends in UK Higher Education 2015.* London: Universities UK.
Vargo, S. L. and Akaka, M. A. (2012) "Value cocreation and service systems (re)formation: A service ecosystems view." *Service Science* 4(3), pp. 207–217.
Vargo, S. L. and Lusch, R. F. (2004) "Evolving to a new dominant logic for marketing." *Journal of Marketing* 68(1), pp. 1–17.
Vargo, S. L. and Lusch, R. F. (2008) "Service-dominant logic: Continuing the evolution." *Journal of the Academy of Marketing Science* 36(1), pp. 1–10.

Von Wallpach, S., Voyer, B., Kastanakis, M., and Mühlbacher, H. (2017) "Co-creating stakeholder and brand identities: Introduction to the special section." *Journal of Business Research* 70 (January), pp. 395–398.

Winkler, A. (1999) *Warp-speed Branding: The Impact of Technology on Marketing* (Vol. 6). New York: Wiley.

Zi-Xian, W. and Qing-Hua, L. V. (2013) "A new study on cultural branding from the perspective of brand ecosystem." *Journal of Chemical and Pharmaceutical Research* 5(11), pp. 106–111.

3 Organizational culture in higher education branding
Branding the core values and beliefs

Cláudia Simões

1 Introduction

Higher education institutions (HEIs) increasingly operate in transforming and complex environments. For example, the international scope of universities has been widened to a global reach by the proliferation of student and/or research exchange programs (e.g. Erasmus Mundus), universities compete for funding and deal and communicate with multiple stakeholders (e.g. students, staff, researchers, community, accrediting agencies) with very diverse interests (Hénard, Diamond, and Roseveare, 2012; Ng and Forbes, 2008). Such dynamics call for the development of a consistent corporate behaviour and marketing instruments that allow the institution to act and present itself in a coherent and competitive way.

However, extant research is not clear on how to transpose marketing principles and notions to higher education in general and universities in particular (Dholakia and Acciardo, 2014). This fact is reflected in the evolving nature of marketing practice into capturing a multifaceted and wide scope of activities both at the strategic and tactical levels (Dibb, Simões, and Wensley, 2013), denoting an increasing complexity due to challenging environments (Ng and Forbes, 2008) (e.g. increasing competition and technology). The fact that HEIs operate in competitive contexts (Khanna, Jacob, and Yadav, 2014) when compared to other social/nonprofit institutions makes more difficult the application of instruments, such as branding (Dholakia and Acciardo, 2014). The variety of stakeholders and their distinct motivations exacerbate the complexity of branding in higher education (Jevons, 2006).

This chapter focuses on the connection between organizational culture and the corporate brand (CB) in HEIs. The organizational culture reflects the shared values and beliefs of an organization that support behaviours (Deshpande and Webster, 1989). Values ought to be crystalized in a cohesive CB as a means of expressing the organization's posture and way of 'doing things' (Knox and Bickerton, 2003). Hence, the organizational culture should be reflected and articulated in the CB, so that stakeholders are presented with a clear sense of the organization. The application of brand principles to HEIs is relevant to establish differentiation in the market, enhance student preference, loyalty and identification (Balaji, Roy, and Sadeque, 2016) and, ultimately, foster stakeholder commitment. The study discusses how the CB may be instrumental in sustaining and embedding the organizational culture in higher education. In addition, the CB ought to be developed and based on strong identity features such as the institution's mission/vision and values.

After reading this chapter, you should be able to:

- Understand how higher education institutions may express their organizational culture in the corporate brand.
- Understand the multitude and divergence of stakeholders in higher education.
- Critically assess the central role of mission/vision and core values in defining the higher education brand.
- Reflect on the challenges higher education institutions face when developing their corporate brand.

2 Review of the literature on organizational culture and branding the core values and beliefs in HEIs

The link between organizational culture and branding is not fully understood in the brand literature, and in the higher education context. In fact, applying the notions of marketing to education institutions and, in particular, to universities is somewhat challenging and controversial. The idea of the marketization of the university is often considered as an unsuitable approach. For example, using the word 'consumer' to refer to the student has, in the past, raised a debate on its adequacy. As Gibbs (2007, p. 1001) states:

> The adoption of marketing techniques, originally developed for more immediate consumption and used within education, encourages a foreshortening and a representation of temporal futures dependent on short-term operational goals, evident in semester courses, modular degrees, etc. The real danger is that this closure begins to determine the form of higher education. However, if higher education is not a product or service for consumption in this manner but is also a way of encouraging transcendental self-development, then educators need to do something to prevent the values of marketing becoming the values of education.

Hence, considering the nature of higher education, the definition of the essence and core existence of the institution has a peculiar background. The connection between organizational culture and CB are now discussed.

Shaping the organizational culture and identity

Organizational culture is based on common understandings about the functioning of an organization. It may be defined 'as the pattern of shared values and beliefs that help individuals understand organizational functioning and thus provide them norms for behaviour in the organization' (Deshpande and Webster, 1989, p. 4). Organizational culture captures

> the internal values, beliefs and basic assumptions that embody the heritage of the company and communicate its meanings to its members; culture manifests itself in the ways employees all through the ranks feel about the company they are working for.
> (Hatch and Schultz, 2003, pp. 1047–1048)

It is expected that organizations with a strong organizational culture have cohesive managerial values that express the way the organization works. Such values are consubstantiated in the organization behaviour towards different stakeholders (Barney, 1986). Ultimately the organizational culture endures the organization's personality, character and history (CMI, 2015). As Schein (2004, p. 8) explains,

> [p]erhaps the most intriguing aspect of culture as a concept is that it points us to phenomena that are below the surface, that are powerful in their impact but invisible and to a considerable degree unconscious. In that sense, culture is to a group what personality or character is to an individual. We can see the behavior that results, but often we cannot see the forces underneath that cause certain kinds of behavior. Yet, just as our personality and character guide and constrain our behavior, so does culture guide and constrain the behavior of members of a group through the shared norms that are held in that group.

When addressing the culture in organizations, various aspects should be taken into account so that the organizational life is understood. In fact, pertaining to culture are physical and managerial dimensions. Schein (2004) refers to three levels of culture: artifacts, espoused beliefs and values, underlying assumptions. The artifacts level captures the objective dimensions of the organization, such as visible or physical aspects (e.g. observed rituals, architecture, etc.). Espoused beliefs and values involve the 'strategies, goals, philosophies (espoused justifications)' (p. 26). The underlying assumptions level apprehends the 'Unconscious, taken-for-granted beliefs, perceptions, thoughts, and feelings (ultimate source of values and action)' (p. 26).

Referring specifically to higher education institutions, Tierney (1988, 2008) presents a culture framework constituted by the following dimensions: mission (the primary ideology of the institution); environment (ways actors describe their environment); leadership (forms and leadership styles – e.g. formal/informal); strategy and information (the ways strategy and information are depicted, depending on the cultural interpretations of actors); socialization (the ways employees learn about the institution). Although this framework assists addressing the organizational culture of a university, there is not a unique model that would be adequate to all universities. Tierney (2008, p. 28) further explains:

> a cultural framework assumes that organizational life is interpretive, no one key model fits all organizations. Thus, an effective mission in one institution will not be effective in another; the successful socialization of individuals in one university may be an abysmal failure in another, and so on. Nevertheless, the worth of such a framework is that it enables an analysis of the interconnections that exist in organizational life and encourages participants and scholars alike to investigate ways to strengthen culture and highlights how the ignorance of culture can stymie innovation.

The organizational culture helps sustain the expression of what the organization is. Nuances in the organizational culture suggest forms of differentiation and uniqueness. Such rationale leads to the idea that, similarly to any other institution, each university is a unique organization with its own ways of doing things and behaving. Organizations ought to internalize a cognitive structure of what the organization stands for and where the organization intends to go – that is, create the essence of the organization's identity. The idea of a unique organizational identity relies on meaning, emotion and human aspects (Albert *et al.*, 2000). *Organizational identity* is what is central (i.e. the character), enduring and distinctive about an organization (Albert and Whetten, 1985). Identity may be mirrored in aspects such as shared values and beliefs, mission and the organizational climate. This identity needs to be shared among an organization's members. The higher the consistency and coherence of the organization's character (solid culture), the greater the internalization (Ashforth and Mael, 1989, pp. 21–22).

Expressing organizational culture in the corporate brand

The connection between culture and identity has been widened in the marketing literature by taking into consideration internal and external stakeholders. The notions of corporate identity and CB (Hatch and Schultz, 2003) have particular relevance in such context. Corporate identity represents the uniqueness and being of the organization (Simões, Dibb, and Fisk, 2005). The notion of corporate identity expands the organizational identity views by focusing on internal as well as on external stakeholders. Pertaining to the management of corporate identity are features such as the diffusion of mission and values, consistent image implementation and visual identity implementation. In particular, considering the behavioural component of identity, the mission and values dissemination at the internal level, allows for triggering employees' sense of belonging and consistency in behaviours (Simões et al., 2005).

Uniqueness and identity lead to the idea of corporate brand. The concept of CB expands the notion of product brand to be applied at the organizational level (Aaker, 2004). As Abratt and Kleyn (2011, p. 1053) explain, the CB concerns 'expressions and images of an organization's identity', and hence is pivotal in conveying the organization's identity. The CB 'involves the conscious decision by senior management to distil and make known the attributes of the organization's identity in the form of a clearly defined branding proposition' (Balmer, 2001, p. 281). In this line of thought, brand identity is 'a unique set of brand associations that the brand strategist aspires to create or maintain. These associations represent what the brand stands for and imply a promise to customers from the organization members' (Aaker, 1996, p. 68).

The identity structure is formed by core and extended identities. The former embodies the timeless *essence* of the brand – the soul, brand values and beliefs, organizational competencies and organizational mission. The extended identity represents a more detailed layer and encompasses dimensions that complete and give texture to the brand (e.g. visible associations with the brand). Yet, the brand identity is dynamic and evolves over time. Brand identity 'originates among insiders, and develops through mutually influencing inputs from insiders and outsiders, entailing distinguishing, central, and enduring attributes, where enduring takes a dynamic meaning' (da Silveira et al., 2013, p. 31).

In this sense, the CB defines what the brand does and who the brand is (Keller and Richey, 2006), including the core defining values (Ind 1997). In the higher education context, the brand ought to be regarded as

> a manifestation of the institution's features that distinguish it from others, reflect its capacity to satisfy students' needs, engender trust in its ability to deliver a certain type and level of higher education, and help potential recruits to make wise enrolment decisions.
> (Bennett and Ali-Choudhury, 2009, pp. 85–86)

Ultimately the HEI brand outlines the distinctive essence of the university, leading to a cohesive message among internal and external stakeholders (Chapleo, 2011) and expressing a unique identity.

In the higher education context one of the core features of the brand is reflected in aspects such as vision, values and culture (Sataøen, 2015). The organizational culture becomes a dimension of brand identity involving aspects such as, 'outstanding mission and vision' and 'professional management style' (Goi, Goi, and Wong, 2014, p. 67). The mission statement and core values set the strategic direction for the university. The CB emerges from the organizational culture (Chapleo, 2005) and captures the unified brand among the various schools/faculties or departments consistent with the core brand identity and brand values (Hemsley-Brown and Goonawardana, 2007). The management of a university needs to be involved in a comprehensive view of the brand and value (Rauschnabel et al., 2016). Because CB has a multiple stakeholder perspective (Gylling and Lindberg-Repo, 2006), it needs to be developed, presented and managed in a coherent way through the various channels and platforms of communication (Balmer, 2012). Strategic aspects, such as, the definition of the institution's vision, mission and values become fundamental for the development of a sound organizational culture and relevant in the development of the CB.

Yet, differentiation in higher education remains a challenge. There is a tension in expressing the uniqueness of a HEI when in many ways the reason for its existence ought to be analogous to other similar institutions (e.g. educational role) (Sataøen, 2015). A way of presenting the CB is to attribute a personality to its existence (Simões, Singh, and Perin, 2015). Rauschnabel et al. (2016) developed a university brand personality scale entailing six dimensions: prestige, sincerity, appeal, liveliness, conscientiousness, and cosmopolitan. Such an idea of personality is used in university leaders' communications as a way to attribute human features to the brand. For example, the Harvard University (USA) President refers to the institution in her final speech with human characteristics: '[m]ay Harvard be as wise as it is smart, as restless as it is proud, as bold as it is thoughtful, as new as it is old, as good as it is great' (Faust, 2017).

The broader role that the University has as 'a way of encouraging transcendental self-development' (Gibbs, 2007, p. 1001) ought to be reflected in the content of the values and mission of the institution. In addition, the specificity and variety of constituents (in particular students, researchers, faculty, staff, alumni, parents, employers) with multiple interests in the institution call for a comprehensive idea of what the university stands for and its brand. Table 3.1 presents ways that different universities around the world use to capture their uniqueness in their corporate mission/vision and values. These suggest the tone for behaviour as present in the CB. The elements of the university's corporate foundation become the pillars sustaining the CB. The examples show a variety of expressions with the common denominator of innovation, formation of responsible citizens, inclusiveness/education for all and vision for the future.

3 Managerial implications

University branding involves the definition of the essence of the university's existence and its core features. Expressing the CB in a single succinct brand proposition is a challenge (Chapleo, 2011). The development of a strong

Table 3.1 University mission/vision and values

University/Country of origin	Setting the tone for behaviour through the CB – University Mission/Vision and Values	Source
University of Warwick/UK	Our vision is to be a world-class university – one with a dynamic, enterprising approach to solving global challenges; one that enables students to create their place in the world; one that defines the university of tomorrow. So, what does our future hold? Our current strategy lays out the following goals: • Enable our students to succeed • Deliver world-class research • Secure our global position • Engage our communities • Champion social, cultural and economic growth • Secure our future sustainability. Values: Pursuit of excellence; Ambition and drive; Enterprising; Making a difference; Community; Accessible; Global perspective; Independence.	University of Warwick, 2018
Maastricht University/ Holland	Maastricht University (UM) is a young university (…), with a distinct global perspective and a strong focus on innovative education and research strategies. We see ourselves first and foremost as an open and inclusive academic community (…). UM's mission and strategy for the future are built on four core values: • To be an innovator in education and research by introducing the CORE philosophy at our university; • To adopt an inclusive approach and to open our doors to all students and staff who fit with our profile and subscribe to our values; • To take our social responsibility seriously by linking the university to society, from the local to the global level; • To be a sustainable institution in the broadest sense. CORE stands for: Collaborative Open Research Education. • Collaborative: education and research are best organized in teams rather than individually • Open: being open minded and inclusive • Research Education is about the integration of research and education.	Maastricht University, 2018

continued

Table 3.1 Continued

University/Country of origin	Setting the tone for behaviour through the CB – University Mission/Vision and Values	Source
Sorbonne University/France	*A world-class research university inventing the knowledge of tomorrow* Sorbonne University will mobilize all fields of knowledge – science, medicine, engineering, humanities, social sciences, the arts, business and management – to offer the highest quality of university education and multidisciplinary research, to create informed and engaged citizens, and to benefit society at large. To achieve this, Sorbonne University is: • Developing the pedagogical and scientific transdisciplinary approaches needed to understand complex and wide-ranging problems (…). • Fostering the success of each and every student (…). • Increasing international cooperation to consolidate the excellence of its training and research activities and strengthening its hosting services for international students and researchers in order to better support them and help them integrate. • Encouraging and enhancing university and campus life thanks to ambitious social, cultural and sporting programs.	Sorbonne University, 2018
University of Minho/Portugal	*Mission* 'The University's mission is to create, spread and put knowledge into application, with free thinking and pluralism as its core values. Our goals are to promote higher education and to contribute to shape a model of society based on humanistic principles, in which knowledge, creativity and innovation contribute towards growth, sustainable development, well-being and solidarity'. *Goals* '[S]cientific research plays a leading role in close articulation with teaching, by pursuing the following goals: a achieve the highest level of education, in our ethical, cultural, artistic, scientific, technical and professional dimensions by providing a diversified range of educational options in a proper educational environment (…)	University of Minho, 2018

Organizational culture in HE branding   49

University/Country of origin	Setting the tone for behaviour through the CB – University Mission/Vision and Values	Source
University of Minho/Portugal	b to do research and to participate in scientific institutions, and events, for the sake of the permanent quest for excellence as well as creativity as a source of innovative and unique solutions and also to seek responses to the major challenges faced by society; c to transfer, exchange and enhance scientific and technological knowledge through the development of suitable solutions, community service projects and continuous training and development support on the basis of reciprocal enhancement and the promotion of entrepreneurship; d to promote the development of activities in order to provide access to and enjoyment of culture by all people and groups, whether internal or external to the University; e to promote the cultural, scientific and technical exchange of students, teaching staff, researchers, non-teaching and non-research staff as well as national and international institutions and organizations; (…) f to interact with society by fostering people's understanding of culture along with the analysis of solutions to address the main problems of everyday life (…) g to contribute to the social and economic development of Minho which includes the development of knowledge, and the protection and spread of its natural and cultural heritage; h to promote the University's institutional sustainability and competitiveness in a global context'.	University of Minho, 2018
Cornell University/ USA	*University Mission* Learning. Discovery. Engagement. Cornell is a private, Ivy League university (…). Cornell's mission is to discover, preserve and disseminate knowledge, to educate the next generation of global citizens, and to promote a culture of broad inquiry throughout and beyond the Cornell community. Cornell also aims, through public service, to enhance the lives and livelihoods of students (…)	Cornell University, 2018

continued

Table 3.1 Continued

University/Country of origin	Setting the tone for behaviour through the CB – University Mission/Vision and Values	Source
Cornell University/ USA	*University Vision* Cornell aspires to be the exemplary comprehensive research university for the 21st century. Faculty, staff and students thrive at Cornell because of its unparalleled combination of quality and breadth; its open, collaborative and innovative culture; its founding commitment to diversity and inclusion; its vibrant rural and urban campuses; and its land-grant legacy of public engagement.	Cornell University, 2018
Zhejiang University/China	*The University Motto:* Zhejiang University encourages all its faculty members and students to follow the spirit of 'pursuing the truth, being rigorous and earnest, exerting oneself for never-ending progress, and pioneering new trails'. In short, the university motto is 'Seeking Truth and Pursuing Innovation'.	Zhejiang University, 2018

CB and its implementation call for higher education leaders to address and integrate innovative features into their brand definition and management. Of particular interest are leadership, CB consistency and co-creation, and internal brand living.

The leadership vision for the HEI constitutes a core aspect in brand building. Brand leaders are strategists that set the tone for behaviour and strategic direction of the organization. The connection between the higher education institution culture and the CB is articulated in the connection of the institution's mission/vision and values as initially defined by the institution's leadership (also reflected in the organizational culture) (Hatch and Schultz, 2003). Branding becomes linked to the business philosophy which concerns the entire organization (Simões and Dibb, 2001) and stakeholders. Nonetheless, HEI leaders should be aware that the development of the CB is dynamic. For example, the current organizational context points to a process of interconnectedness and co-creation emerging from the links between the higher education brand and the consumer (student) (Khanna et al., 2014). This process involves internal and external stakeholders (in particular consumers – the student) in defining core aspects of the brand (da Silveira, Lages and Simões, 2013). Such dynamics ought to be incorporated in the management and preservation of the brand. This vibrant context has implications in the way leaders in universities define the institution's scope and philosophy and become open to the incorporation of stakeholder engagement.

Organizational culture in HE branding 51

The underlying principles of corporate branding ensure that there is cohesion in the organization's internal and external posture. Hence the CB ought to be considered a strategic instrument (Webster and Keller, 2004) that organizations apply when approaching stakeholders. The presentation of an institution's mission and values becomes a feature of expression of the CB (Simões et al., 2015). The perception of brand meaning that stakeholders hold tends to be aligned with the mission of the university (Wilson and Eliot, 2016). There is a dilution in the organization's borders where consumers and other stakeholders become co-creators of value (da Silveira et al., 2013). Such intertwinedness of roles between consumers (and other stakeholders) and the higher education brand lead to the strengthening of the relevance of a strong connection between organizational culture and branding. The organizational culture ought to set the tone and platforms for brand co-creation. As Dholakia and Acciardo (2014, p. 144) explain:

> people are a critical element of the brand and the service marketing paradigm. For a successful implementation of the branding approach, it is expected that people – faculty, staff and students – will live the brand and the co-creation process will generate the value.

The way the brand is communicated and explained inside the corporation is of the utmost importance. Of particular relevance becomes the internal brand management, addressing the 'processes by which employees understand the brand concept, commit to the brand and thus live the brand' (Merriliees and Frazer, 2013, p. 159). Internally, the brand ought to be pervasive throughout the organization (Simões and Dibb, 2001). Employees' stance towards the corporation and brand (e.g. in terms of pride or passion) is crucial in the organization of branding (Chernatony and Harris, 2000). Employees have a relevant role in making the brand distinctive and unique by underlining the values and organizational culture. When building the brand internally, 'the core values link mission, vision and organizational values' (Gylling and Lindberg-Repo, 2006, p. 262). Hence, brand management and performance should be embedded throughout the company with all departments involved. The essence of a brand – the major features that shape the brand and form its distinctiveness – must always be present and embedded in activities (Rubinstein, 1996) of the organizations. Corporate branding becomes the strategic direction for an organization's activities, providing consistency through the connection between positioning, communication and staff working style or behaviour (Chernatony, 1999). Employees co-create brand meaning over time through interactions with the brand and social interactions (Dean et al., 2016).

4 Conclusion

Throughout this chapter it became visible that branding in higher education is a challenging and often diffuse endeavour. This study addressed the connectedness between organizational culture and the CB. Ultimately, mission statement and core values become vital for market positioning and tying up the institution into a coherent and cohesive self. This is particularly relevant in HEIs with different faculties/schools showing often distinctive brands. The pervasiveness of the institutional culture articulated in the mission and values creates a relevant tone to deal with inconsistencies.

Future research ought to gain deeper insights into the connectedness between the organizational culture and the CB in higher education. HEIs present higher levels of complexity in what concerns brand management and stakeholder engagement. Further research may include the development of insights and metrics that would allow for a better understanding of the role and impact that different stakeholders may have in the higher education brand. In particular, it is important to further understand the motivation and relevance for the higher education brand. In addition, as university stakeholders (e.g. employees) may show little loyalty towards the organization and, ultimately, negatively affect the brand, it would be relevant to further develop measurements that would capture their impact on brand assessment (Chapleo, 2011). Moreover, it is not yet known how the co-creation process occurs in higher education institutions with internal and external stakeholders. Future research ought to capture the impact such context may have for brand building and management. The controversy around the marketization of higher institution as well as the impact that student co-creation may have in the higher education offer (see, Nixon, Scullion, and Hearn, 2018) calls for deeper insights and analysis.

5 Case study: University of Coimbra – uniqueness with tradition and history

The University of Coimbra is the oldest university in Portugal. The University was created in Lisbon in 1290 by King Dinis and in 1537 King João III relocated the institution to the city of Coimbra. The University expanded its scope and influence throughout the centuries and is currently formed of eight Faculties: Arts and Humanities, Law, Medicine, Sciences and Technology, Pharmacy, Economics, Psychology and Education Sciences, Sports Sciences and Physical Education. The University of Coimbra has over 22,000 students (UC, 2018).

The CB at the University of Coimbra is based on the general aspects referred to earlier as relevant for universities, for example, values such as education, innovation, citizenship, inclusion, etc. The essence of the University's CB is also reflected in the University's vision and mission.

The mission reflects aspects such as, the 'dissemination and transfer of knowledge' and the contribution of the institution to society and the world (Table 3.2).

As a form of differentiation, the CB of the University of Coimbra relies on pillars such as its historical heritage (over 725 years of existence), classification as UNESCO World Heritage since 2013, rituals associated with local student tradition (rites and ceremonies that are unique), and the University's elite alumni, including high profile people (e.g. politicians). The

Table 3.2 Support of the University of Coimbra's brand

	Corporate brand support
Vision and Mission	*Vision* 'The affirmation of the University of Coimbra as the best Portuguese-speaking university and as a major player in the forefront of the advancement of knowledge, capable of attracting the best students and teachers and of decisively contributing to the progress and well-being of society'. *Mission* The University of Coimbra is an institution in which creation and critical analysis coexist with the transmission and dissemination of culture, science and technology. The university contributes research, education and services to the economic and social development of the community, the protection of the environment, social justice and responsible citizenship, and the consolidation of knowledge-based sovereignty. It is the University's duty to contribute to: • The public understanding of the humanities, the arts, science, and technology by promoting and staging initiatives aimed at the dissemination of humanistic, artistic, scientific and technological culture, and making the required resources available; • The development of society-oriented activities, notably for the dissemination and transfer of knowledge and the economic enhancement of scientific knowledge; • The fostering of effective mobility of the teaching staff, researchers, students and graduates, both at national and international level, in particular in the European space of higher education and among the community of the Portuguese-speaking countries' (Statutes of the University of Coimbra, Article 2).
Values	Openness to the world; Co-operation; Cultural interaction; Independence; Tolerance; Dialogue; Tradition; Contemporariness; Innovation; Enhancement of people; Intellectual accuracy; Freedom of opinion; Ethics; Scientific humility; Stimulating creativity; Recognizing and fostering merit

Sources: UC 2011, 2018.

following quotes from former students capture the brand uniqueness and this stakeholder's connection to the brand: 'Humanism, rigor and weight of a live and contagious history make the University of Coimbra a unique institution. You should not miss the opportunity to study in Coimbra (...)'; 'University with centuries of existence yet always young in the search for knowledge, informal yet rigorous, partner and friend of current and former students. An alumnus of this university will always feel as an ambassador' (www.uc.pt/alumni). The brand is further cultivated and expressed to current and new students in social media with the following descriptors: notable, world heritage, inspiring, cosmopolitan, current, unique.

6 Further investigation

- What are the challenges of developing a corporate brand in a higher education institution context?
- How can HEIs incorporate their organizational culture in the CB?
- What type of content is relevant to include in the shared values and mission of a HEI that fosters the wider role of a university in its environment?
- How should a University's CB be managed over time?

References

Aaker, A. D. (2004) "Leveraging the corporate brand." *California Management Review* 46(3), pp. 6–18.
Aaker, D. (1996) *Building Strong Brands*. New York: The Free Press.
Abratt, R. and Kleyn, N. (2011) "Corporate identity, corporate branding and corporate reputations, reconciliation and integration." *European Journal of Marketing* 46(7/8), pp. 1048–1063.
Albert, S., Ashforth, B., and Dutton, J. (2000) "Organisational identity and identification: Charting new waters and building new bridges." *Academy of Management Review* 25(1), pp. 13–17.
Albert, S. and Whetten, D. (1985) "Organisational identity." *Research in Organisational Behaviour* 7, pp. 263–295.
Ashforth, B. and Mael, F. (1989) "Social identity theory and the organisation." *Academy of Management Review* 14(1), pp. 20–39.
Balaji, M., Roy, S., and Sadeque, S. (2016) "The antecedents and consequences of university brand identification." *Journal of Business Research* 69, pp. 3023–3032.
Balmer, J. M. T. (2001) "Corporate identity, corporate branding and corporate marketing: seeing through the fog." *European Journal of Marketing* 35(3–4), pp. 248–291.
Balmer, M. T. (2012) "Strategic corporate brand alignment. Perspectives from identity based views of corporate brands." *European Journal of Marketing* 46(7/8), pp. 1064–1092.
Barney, J. (1986) "Organizational culture: Can it be a source of sustained competitive advantage?" *The Academy of Management Review* 11(3), pp. 656–665.

Bennett, R. and Ali-Choudhury, R. (2009) "Prospective students' perceptions of university brands: An empirical study." *Journal of Marketing for Higher Education* 19, pp. 85–107.

Chapleo, C. (2005) "Do universities have 'successful' brands?" *The International Journal of Educational Advancement* 6(1), pp. 54–64.

Chapleo, C. (2011) "Exploring rationales for branding a university: should we be seeking to measure branding in UK universities?" *The Journal of Brand Management* 18, pp. 411–422.

Chernatony, L. and Harris, F. (2000) "Developing corporate brands through considering internal and external stakeholders." *Corporate Reputation Review* 3(3), pp. 268–274.

CMI (2015) *Understanding Organizational Culture*. Chartered Management Institute: Northants.

Cornell University (2018) *University Mission and Vision*. www.cornell.edu/about/mission.cfm (accessed April 2018).

da Silveira, C., Lages, C., and Simões, C. (2013) "Reconceptualizing brand identity in a dynamic environment." *Journal of Business Research* 66(1), pp. 28–36.

de Chernatony, L. (1999) "Brand management through narrowing the gap between brand identity and brand reputation." *Journal of Marketing Management* 15(1–3), pp. 157–179.

Dean, D. Arroyo-Gamez, R., Punjaisri, K., and Pich, C. (2016) "Internal brand co-creation: The experiential brand meaning cycle in higher education." *Journal of Business Research* 69(8), pp. 3041–3048.

Deshpande, R. and Webster, F. E. (1989) "Organizational culture and marketing: Defining the research agenda." *Journal of Marketing* 53, pp. 3–15.

Dholakia, R. and Acciardo, L. (2014) "Branding a state university: Doing it right." *Journal of Marketing for Higher Education* 24(1), pp. 144–163.

Dibb, S., Simões, C., and Wensley, R. (2014) "Establishing the scope of marketing practice: insights from practitioners." *European Journal of Marketing* 48(1/2), pp. 380–404.

Faust, D. (2017) *Future Plans*. www.harvard.edu/president/news/2017/future-plans (accessed April 2018).

Gibbs, P. (2007) "Marketing and education – A clash or a synergy in time?" *Journal of Business Research* 60(9), pp. 1000–1002.

Goi, M., Goi, G., and Wong, D. (2014) "Constructing a brand identity scale for higher education institutions." *Journal of Marketing for Higher Education* 24(1), pp. 59–74.

Gylling, C. and Lindberg-Repo, K. J. (2006) "Investigating the links between a corporate brand and a customer brand," *Journal of Brand Management* 13(4/5), pp. 257–267.

Hatch, M. and Schultz, M. (2003) "Bringing the corporation into corporate branding," *European Journal of Marketing* 37(7/8), pp. 1041–1064.

Hemsley-Brown J. V. and Goonawardana, S. (2007) "Brand harmonisation in the international higher education market," *Journal of Business Research* 60, pp. 942–948.

Hénard, F., Diamond, L., and Roseveare, D. (2012) *Approaches to Internationalization and their Implications for Strategic Management and Institutional Practice, A guide for Higher Education Institutions*, OECD – IMHE.

Ind, N. (1997) *The Corporate Brand*. London: Macmillan Press.

Jevons, C. (2006) "Universities: A prime example of branding going wrong." *Journal of Product & Brand Management* 15(7), pp. 466–467.

Keller, K. L. and Richey, K. (2006) "The importance of corporate brand personality traits to a successful 21st century business." *Brand Management* 14(1/2), pp. 74–81.

Khanna, M., Jacob, I., and Yadav, N. (2014) "Identifying and analyzing touchpoints for building a higher education brand." *Journal of Marketing for Higher Education* 24(1), pp. 122–143.

Knox, S. and Bickerton, D. (2003) "The six conventions of corporate branding." *European Journal of Marketing* 37(7/8), pp. 998–1016.

Maastricht University (2018) *Mission & Strategy*. www.maastrichtuniversity.nl/about-um/organisation/mission-strategy (accessed April 2018).

Merrilees, B. and Frazer, L. (2013) "Internal branding: Franchisor leadership as a critical determinant." *Journal of Business Research* 66(2), pp. 158–164.

Ng, I. and Forbes, J. (2008) "Education as service. The understanding of university experience through the service logic." *Journal of Marketing for Higher Education* 19(1), pp. 38–64.

Nixon, E., Scullion, R., and Hearn, R. (2018) "Her majesty the student: Marketised higher education and the narcissistic (dis)satisfactions of the student-consumer." *Studies in Higher Education* 43(6), pp. 927–943.

Rauschnabel, P., Krey, N., Babin, B., and Ivens, B. (2016) "Brand management in higher education: The University Brand Personality Scale." *Journal of Business Research* 69(8), pp. 3077–3086.

Rubinstein, H. (1996) "Brand first' management," *Journal of Marketing Management* 12(4), pp. 269–280.

Sataøen H. (2015) "Higher education as object for corporate and nation branding: Between equality and flagships." *Journal of Higher Education Policy and Management* 37(6), pp. 702–717.

Schein, E. (2004) *Organizational Culture and Leadership*. San Francisco: Jossey-Bass.

Simões, C. and Dibb, S. (2001) "Rethinking the brand concept: New brand orientation," *Corporate Communications: An International Journal* 6(4), pp. 217–224.

Simões, C., Dibb, S., and Fisk, R. (2005) "Managing corporate identity: An internal perspective," *Journal of the Academy of Marketing Science* 33(2), pp. 153–168.

Simões, C., Singh, J., and Perin, M. (2015) "Corporate brand expressions in business-to-business companies' websites: Evidence from Brazil and India." *Industrial Marketing Management* 51, pp. 59–68.

Sorbonne (2018) *About us – Our vision*. www.sorbonne-university.com/about-us/our-vision/ (accessed April 2018).

Tierney, W. (1988) "Organizational culture in higher education: Defining the essentials," *The Journal of Higher Education* 59(1), pp. 2–21.

Tierney W. G. (2008) "Trust and organizational culture in higher education," in J. Välimaa and O. H. Ylijoki (eds), *Cultural Perspectives on Higher Education*. Dordrecht: Springer.

UC. (2011) *University of Coimbra, "University of Coimbra 2011–2015 Strategic Plan."* www.uc.pt/en/planning/ficheiros/UC_Strategic_Planning_2011_2015_out 2012.pdf (accessed April 2018).

UC. (2018) University of Coimbra. www.uc.pt (accessed April 2018).
University of Minho. (2018) *Institutional Information.* www.uminho.pt/EN/uminho/institutional-information/Pages/Mission.aspx (accessed April 2018).
University of Warwick. (2018) *Essential Warwick – University Profile.* https://warwick.ac.uk/about/profile/ (accessed April 2018).
Webster, F. and Keller, K. (2004) "A roadmap for branding in industrial markets." *Journal of Brand Management* 11(5), pp. 388–402.
Zhejiang University (2018) *About Zhejiang University.* www.zju.edu.cn/english/wbout/list.htm#right_box_02 (accessed April 2018).

Further reading

Asaad, Y., Melewar, T C, and Balmer, J. (2013) "Universities and export market orientation: An exploratory study of UK post-92 universities." *Marketing Intelligence & Planning* 31(7), pp. 838–856.
Rutter, R., Lettice, F., and Nadeau, J. (2016) "Brand personality in higher education: Anthropomorphized university marketing communications." *Journal of Marketing for Higher Education* 27(1), pp. 19–39.
Schlesinger, W., Cervera, A., and Pérez-Cabañero, C. (2016) "Sticking with your university: The importance of satisfaction, trust, image, and shared values." *Studies in Higher Education* 42(12), pp. 2178–2194.
Winter, E. and Thompson-Whiteside, H. (2017) "Location, location, location: Does place provide the opportunity for differentiation for universities?" *Journal of Marketing for Higher Education* 27(2), pp. 233–250.

4 Brand leadership and brand support

Influencing employees via internal branding

*Narissara Sujchaphong and
Pakorn Sujchaphong*

1 Introduction

Leaders are vital in an organization. Leaders are able to influence a group of individuals towards the achievement of a particular goal (Drouillard and Kleiner, 1996). They are the group of stakeholders who provide the organization with time, skills and human capital commitment (Hill and Jones, 1992). Leaders tend to play a critical role in shaping an organization's value and orientation (Hambrick and Mason, 1984).

In a higher education institution context, educational institutions are concerned with the need to develop organizational leadership and the quality of that leadership (Dearlove, 1995; Askling, Bauer, and Marton, 1999). Research has concluded that leadership is needed for higher education institutions if they are to perform effectively (e.g. Jarrett Report, 1985 cited in Barry, Chandler, and Clark, 2001, p. 89; Cohen and March, 1986). According to Dearlove (1995, p. 167), academics tend to prefer being left alone to do their own work, typically teaching and research. For this reason, 'they may be prepared to trust empathetic leaders to do their organizational thinking for them' (Dearlove, 1995, p. 167). Due to continuing changes in government policies (Askling *et al.*, 1999) and the increase of competition in the higher education sector, universities are encouraged to act in a more business-like manner (Davies, Hides, and Casey, 2001). Moreover, higher education institutions are striving to pay more attention to the quality of leadership as the quality of their leadership indicates something about their capacity to change and influence society for the better (Dearlove, 1995).

Chapter 4 considers how the development of brand leadership and brand support influence employees via internal branding in higher education. Diversities and issues are explored. The aim is to enable readers to comprehend how universities organize and manage their internal branding in different parts of the organization. Furthermore, this chapter presents important aspects of decision making processes that influence stakeholders' perceptions towards higher education branding. Theories on internal branding in higher education are reviewed and extant research presented.

Learning objectives

After reading this chapter, you should be able to:

- Understand a brand leadership concept and its roles in encouraging brand support.
- Understand the ways in which institutions organize and manage their internal branding.
- Understand the relationships among brand leadership, internal branding, and brand support.

2 Review of the literature in brand leadership and brand support

Brand leadership in a university: influencing employees via internal branding

Ramsden (1998) agrees that the purpose of leadership in higher education institutions is to produce change and also to align and motivate followers. In the higher education context, Ramsden (1998, p. 8) argues that 'leadership is about tensions and balances'. The focus of leadership studies is to find how leaders attempt to persuade group members to achieve the group's goals (Bargh, Bocock, Scott, and Smith, 2000). House (1971), for example, considers the motivational functions of the leader – for instance, making personal rewards both intrinsic (e.g. work satisfaction) and extrinsic (e.g. promotions and salary increases), as well as ensuring that each person's work has the necessary direction and support to attain its goals. However, in order to be successful, a leader may need a particular style of leadership, depending on the situation and which style will enable them to exert influence over the group members (Fiedler, 1967).

Brand leadership is a style of leadership where a leader has characteristics that are likely to encourage employees to behave in alignment with the brand. Brand leadership characteristics are likely to be related to transformational leadership characteristics. It has been noted by several authors (e.g. Burmann and Zeplin, 2005; Morhart, Herzog, and Tomczak, 2009) that a leader with transformational leadership characteristics tends to be the most effective in influencing employees' brand support behaviour. In addition, transformational leadership has primarily been identified by those leadership characteristics which produce greater changes in educational institutions (e.g. Leithwood, 1992; Fink, 2005). According to Burns (1978), transformational leadership tends to be concerned with the process of encouraging one's followers to accomplish great work. Transformational leadership results in employees' performance which goes well beyond what is expected (den Hartog, van Muijen, and Koopman, 1997; Northouse, 2004). This type of leadership is concerned with the performance of followers and with developing followers to their fullest potential (Bass and Avolio, 1990; Avolio, 1999).

The characteristics of leaders within an organization are likely to encourage employees' brand commitment by, for example, influencing the culture of the organization (Schein, 1983; Kotter and Heskett, 1992). According to the types of control defined by Jaworski (1988), this situation may occur because of the informal control mechanisms, which are unwritten mechanisms that influence the behaviour of individuals or groups. Specifically, informal controls are characterized by personal interaction between leaders and employees, which can be seen as 'social control' and/or 'culture control' (Jaworski, 1988; Henkel, Tomczak, Heitmann, and Herrmann, 2007).

Northouse (2004, p. 171) provides a good extension to Burns' transformational leadership theory (1978): that '[transformational leadership] refers to the process whereby an individual engages with others and creates a connection that raises the level of motivation and morality in both the leader and the follower'. Northouse (2004, p. 175) describes leaders 'who exhibit transformational leadership [and who] often have a strong set of internal values and ideals ... [being] effective at motivating followers to act in ways that support the greater good rather than their own self-interests'. Furthermore, transformational leaders facilitate collective actions based on the institution's values, i.e. the institution's mission and vision (Leithwood, 1992; Roberts, 1985). According to Urde (2003), an organization's values are an important part of brand value which enables employees to understand 'what we are', 'what our organization stands for' and 'what it is that makes us who we are'. These could therefore enable employees to act in a way which supports the brand (Urde, 2003).

Furthermore, the characteristics of transformational leadership could be identified as follows (Bass and Avolio, 1990; Northouse, 2004): (1) **idealization influence or charisma** are attributes of leaders who act as strong role models for their followers and provide them with a clear vision and sense of mission. The followers identify with these leaders and want to imitate them; (2) **inspirational motivation** is attributed to leaders who communicate high expectations to their followers, inspiring them through motivation to become committed to and a part of the shared vision within the organization; (3) **intellectual stimulation** comes from leaders who stimulate their followers to be creative and innovative and to challenge their own beliefs and values and those of the leaders and the organization; and (4) **individual consideration** is given by leaders who provide a supportive climate in which they listen carefully to the individual needs of followers and act as advisers trying to assist specific ways of working.

The definitions of transformational leadership as discussed above suggest that a transformational leader is likely to motivate employees' brand support by providing a supportive climate, i.e. being a role model, acting as an adviser and giving positive and constructive feedback. Along with the studies on internal branding (e.g. Burmann and Zeplin, 2005; Morhart *et al.*, 2009), transformational leadership characteristics tend to be the most effective ones in influencing employees' brand support behaviour.

Creating brand support in a university

The delivery of the brand promise to the employees of an educational institution has been recognized as having the same importance as delivering it to people outside the institution (Sujchaphong, Nguyen, and Melewar, 2017; Whisman, 2009). As presented in Table 4.1, university employees are heavily influential in representing higher education institutions' brands to the public (for example, in terms of staff reputation, research output and top-quality teaching).

Baker and Balmer (1997, p. 367) refer to the fact that 'individual members of a university are, by definition, experts in their own right and so consider that they are the best judge of how to fulfil this role'. Thus, if staff members do not clearly understand the institution's brand values, their acts may reflect their own values more than the university's brand values (Jevons, 2006). Besides, if they do not present an institution's brand characteristics, the brand of the institution becomes unreliable (Stensaker, 2005). Stensaker (2005) supports the view that universities need to align employee behaviour with brand values. It is noted that employees' beliefs and actions may not match the externally generated brand image (Melewar and Karaosmanoglu, 2006; Ind, 2007); hence, universities need to ensure that employees understand the corporate brand values and are able to incorporate the brand values into their work activities, so-called 'brand support'.

Internal branding

The alignment of employees' attitudes and behaviour with the values of the corporate brand is viewed by Judson, Gorchels and Aurand (2006) as the main task of internal branding in universities. Internal branding is about aligning employees' behaviour with brand values by promoting and educating them about the brand values (Aurand, Gorchels, and Bishop, 2005). Internal branding, from the marketing and communications based perspective (Karmark, 2005), consists of two important aspects (i.e. the brand-centred training and development activities factor and the internal brand communications factor).

Brand-centred training and development activities include, for example, training activities, performance evaluation, setting standard procedures and providing the skill set necessary to deliver an institution's values. On

Table 4.1 Research on university branding in relation to internal brand support

Author(s)	Authors' comments
Baker and Balmer (1997)	A strong visual identity has a positive impact on leading the university's internal stakeholders to be loyal to the institution. A weak visual identity may occur due to weaknesses in corporate strategy, corporate culture and/or formal corporate communications policies.
Maringe (2005)	From internal people's point of view, marketing activities are implemented in Higher Education Institutions (HEIs). However, from the customers' (students') point of view, HEIs still communicate inadequate information about product, price, place, promotion, physical evidence and people. In addition, the elements of product, price and people are seen by the students as the most important elements to influence their decision where to study.
Judson, Gorchels, and Aurand (2006)	Internal brand communication activities have a positive impact on employees' understanding and incorporating the brand into their work activities.
Whisman (2009)	Internal branding helps an institution overcome internal resistance to branding efforts. It helps the institution take an identity-development strategy beyond traditional approaches (e.g. new logos and advertising campaigns) in order to take an embedded cultural approach which guides the ways in which the institution should run its activities (e.g. communications, fund-raising, marketing, enrolment management and programme development).
Judson, Aurand, Gorchels, and Gordon (2009)	A university's brand image has a strong impact on guiding university administrators to do their job, but less of an impact upon how they manage their staff and how their staff reflect the brand in their everyday work. Moreover, private university administrators are likely to have a greater brand clarity than public university administrators.
Chapleo (2010)	For the success of branding, a university should pay more attention to internal brand engagement.
Sujchaphong, Nguyen, and Melewar (2015)	The knowledge of internal branding and employee brand support in higher education institutions is based on knowledge imported from the business sector, and more practices should be adapted and implemented. Transformational leadership tends to be the essential element to the successful implementation of internal branding. However, it has been little researched in the internal branding context.
Bagautdinova, Gorelova, and Polyakova (2015)	There is the need to link external brand promises with internal branding efforts to avoid loss of its credibility. The study emphasizes the link between the choice of potential consumers evaluating a complex intangible offering of the university and the degree to which people within an organization use the university brand value in their everyday work.
Sujchaphong *et al.* (2017)	Although internal branding has become important for universities in increasingly competitive markets, it is still recognised as a new phenomenon and therefore more research is needed in this area.
Yu, Asaad, Yen, and Gupta (2018)	The effect of internal market orientation on employees' university brand commitment varies among employees of different demographic groups.

Source: adapted from Sujchaphong *et al.* (2017).

the basis of the theory of marketing control (Jaworski, 1988), as a result of controls, employees are more likely to behave in ways consistent with 'organizational goals', the 'true aims of the organization' and the 'best interest of the organization'. An empirical study conducted by Punjaisri and Wilson (2007) shows that training activities are the processes which help an organization to develop and reinforce employees' behaviour in alignment with the organizational brand. In addition, several researchers (e.g. Gotsi and Wilson, 2001; Aurand *et al.*, 2005; Ind, 2007) insist that communicating brand values through human resource activities can encourage the staff to support the organizational brand. Along with the types of control distinguished by Jaworski (1988), it is likely that brand-centred training and development activities can be categorized as formal control activities, which focus on behaviour, actions and/or activities as well as end results. The sub-types of formal control are input control, process control and output control (Jaworski, 1988).

First, with input control (Jaworski, 1988), an organization provides its employees with working guidelines (which do not need to be in the form of a specific working process) which are related to the institution's values, including the institution's goals, mission and vision, in order to ensure that employees are producing the desired results for attaining the organization's goals. Providing brand related training or seminars, is likely to help academic staff to have a clearer understanding of the brand. Being well informed about the brand values and the appropriate way of working could help an employee to clearly understand the brand and be able to apply this knowledge in their work activities. The brand support behaviour which could be produced by these types of control includes the ability of an employee to clearly explain the institution's brand values' and to use his/her knowledge of the institution's brand values to prioritize her/his tasks.

Second, setting standard procedures for delivering an institution's values (e.g. providing employees with training to help them use brand values), could be seen as process control activities. Universities may encourage the brand support behaviour of an employee by *informing him/her of a specific way of working*, through the use of training and development activities. When these process control activities are provided, the focus is on the behaviour and/or activities of the employees (Jaworski, 1988), which consequently direct employees *how to* behave in alignment with their institution's brand values.

Third, Jaworski (1988) suggested that employees' behaviours are likely to be controlled by a system of performance reviews, which can be seen as an output control. Brand-centred training and development activities may not only provide directions for employees, but may also, to some extent, control the brand supportive behaviours of employees. Through the use of annual performance reviews and key performance indicators (KPIs) which are related to the brand, employees' behaviours are directed by an output control tool. The examples of employees' behaviours which tend to be directed by the output control tool are, (1) considering reviews of their work performance when making decisions on the work activities and (2) following the institutional rules.

The discussion above points to the important role of brand-centred training and development activities, as control activities that generate brand support. In other words, these activities are also seen by academic employees as presenting the rules and guidelines to help them to *clearly understand the brand* and be *able to apply this knowledge in their work activities*. According to Sujchaphong (2013), employees with better knowledge will deliver better performance. In the next paragraph, the role of internal brand communications in building brand support is discussed.

Internal brand communication activities have been found to have a positive impact on brand support. Judson et al. (2006) make the point that when internal brand communication tools (i.e. university brochures, campus meetings, e-mail messages and university memos) have been implemented, university staff tend to have a 'clearer understanding of their respective universities' brand values and are subsequently better able to use these brand values in their everyday work' (Judson et al., 2006, p. 105). With reference to the types of formal control (Jaworski, 1988), internal brand communication activities in universities tend to illustrate 'input control'. As stated earlier, with this type of control, the organizations may not formally communicate specific ways of working to their employees or even list them. Rather, in order to ensure that the employees produce the desired results for achieving organization goals, the organization communicates the organization's goals, for example, its mission and vision (Jaworski, 1988). According to Urde (2003), the brand values are typically attached to some forms of organizational values such as the organization's mission and vision. Thus, the institution's values (including mission, vision and goals) could enlighten an employee on how the institution wants to be seen from outside, by communicating brand values to them through internal mass communications, for example, newsletters, memos and brochures.

As input control tools which inform the employee about the organization's brand values, these activities could help her/him to *understand the value* and to be able to clearly explain the institution's brand values. Furthermore, internal communication media are generally available for organizations to keep repeating the importance of the brand (Ind, 2007). Communicating brand messages through communication media, for example the institution's song, newsletter and promotional items can provide an opportunity for the institution to keep repeating its brand massages, thus enhancing the possibility that employees will recognize the brand messages.

However, in line with Karmark (2005), brand values which are communicated through communication media (e.g. websites, brand book, billboard) can be irrelevant to the day-to-day operations and the actual working situation of employees. Therefore, it can be hard to attract an employee's attention using these types of communication activity. As a result, it can be a challenge for employees to memorize these brand values and apply them to their work activities. According to Baker and Balmer (1997), the values of an institution which are communicated through the institution's goal, mission and vision are unlikely to be memorized by employees.

This means that an employee may not be able to remember the institution's values (including the institution's policy, goal, mission and vision). According to Baker and Balmer (1997), those messages may perhaps be too detailed for easy memorization. Furthermore, as stated above, internal brand communications in universities (i.e. university brochures, campus meetings, e-mail messages and university memos) are input control activities which communicate the institution's goals without specifying any procedures (Jaworski, 1988). Thus, these activities may not be able to ensure that employees understand 'the whys and the hows of the brand delivery' (Kunde, 2000, p. 171). Therefore, the brand-centred training and development activities should be used as control tools which tend to provide specific rules and guidelines for employees to follow. On the other hand, internal communication activities are control tools which communicate the institution's goals without specifying any procedures. Therefore, in order to create brand support, institutions should use both the internal communication media and the brand-centred training and development activities.

To sum up, brand support formation is a complex process that is influenced by multiple marketing activity factors including the factors of formal control activities and informal control activities. Thus, this chapter provides an inclusive model of the way in which brand support could be created within an organization through the use of marketing control tools, both formal (i.e. training and development activities and internal brand communications activities) and informal (i.e. transformational leaders).

3 Managerial implications

This chapter offers practical guidelines for the university' management team to manage the university's brand from the inside out. Basically, this chapter recommends that a university could enhance brand support behaviour from the academic staff by communicating institutional brand values to them via transformational leaders and internal branding activities. In practice, it could be a useful guideline for the management team of educational institutions, as well as those in other industries, above all service industries, to encourage brand support effectively.

This chapter suggests to management that transformational leaders are likely to have power over the formation of brand support and the operation of internal branding. Thus, the academic staff's leaders with transformational leadership characteristics should be seen as an important factor which can greatly affect the building of brand support behaviour among academic staff. In an organization, what is needed to influence brand support is transformational leaders who tend to facilitate collective actions and systems based on the institution's values, i.e. the institution's mission and vision (Leithwood, 1992; Roberts, 1985). They can encourage or initiate internal branding activities (i.e. brand-centred training and development activities and internal brand communication activities), thereby indirectly creating brand support. Since a head of department with transformational leadership tends to identify and prioritize the training activities related to the institution's values, such activities could be supported efficiently by his/her provision of financial support for the training activities, for example, or for an academic staff member to attend the activities.

Moreover, this chapter suggests that the brand support behaviour of employees can be directly affected by transformational leaders, immediate leaders in particular. Thus, apart from operating internal branding activities, ensuring the existence of transformational leaders within the organization is another way for management to encourage the building of brand support. For example, the organizations can provide their leaders with leadership training courses related to the brand, concentrating on the immediate leaders of academic staff. A study by Morhart et al. (2009) insists that brand-specific transformational leadership can be learned through management training. Therefore, by providing brand leadership training, leaders can specifically learn how to build brand support behaviour among their followers through the characteristics of transformational leadership. Regarding the characteristics of transformational leadership, this study suggests that the organization should ensure that its leaders are capable of being role models, providing followers with more freedom, advice, counselling and other psychological support and communicating high expectations to the followers, in order to inspire and demonstrate to followers an appealing image of what they might accomplish as brand supporters.

The four-dimensions of transformational leadership characteristics provided in this chapter could be used by the management as a guideline for creating a leadership training programme and also for monitoring the behaviour of leaders. Organizations may also provide this guideline for leaders to evaluate themselves. In addition, the organizations could adapt the activities of internal brand communications and brand-centred training and development activities suggested in this chapter as a basic checklist to monitor the degree of internal branding activities within organizations. Thus, the operations and the consistency of internal branding activities and the transformational characteristics of leaders could be audited and monitored in order to ensure the effectiveness of the internal branding process in building brand support.

4 Conclusion

This chapter has sought to comprehensively discuss how brand leadership encourages employees' brand support via internal branding. For academic staff to behave in alignment with the institutional brand value, having an immediate leader with transformational leadership characteristics is one of the key factors that directly influence an increase of desirable behaviour on the employees' part. Moreover, the level of internal brand communication activities and brand-centred training and development activities may be dependent on immediate leaders' characteristics. Therefore, apart from internal branding activities, leaders with transformational leadership characteristics are needed in institutions in order to build the institution brand from the inside out.

It is crucial for the university to ensure that the immediate leaders of academic staff do exhibit transformational leadership characteristics because such leadership characteristics not only encourage employees to give brand support, but also either initiate or influence internal branding activities, thereby creating further brand support.

For the possible areas for future research, the relationships between brand support, internal branding and transformational leaders should be investigated from many perspectives (e.g. those of leaders and of management). The reader could examine the gaps between the employees' and the managers' perceptions of the internal branding activities. At the same time, the factors which create such gaps could also be investigated. In addition, a study of Morhart *et al.* (2009) revealed a set of items for measuring brand related-transformational leadership characteristics. Employing this set of items for future research could help researchers to better capture the relationships between transformational leadership characteristics and brand support.

5 Case study

In emerging markets, universities are increasingly recognizing the importance of corporate branding which emphasizes the roles of employees in the brand building process (Istileulova, 2010). Moreover, in Thailand, the new public management approach resulted in reduced financial support from the Thai government for higher education. One business school located in northeast region of Thailand, like other Thai public institutions, received financial support from the government, such as human resource development loan funds and student loan funds. The reduced funding from the government was one of the main reasons why the school began to apply a marketing strategy, because it needed to be marketing oriented and to find alternative revenue streams.

Being located very close to a top class university, recruiting new students could be challenging for this school. In 2011, the school name did not appear even in the national top 100 undergraduate course choice rankings. However, five years later, there was a significant change. In 2016, the school name appeared in the top five undergraduate course rankings. In 2017, the school name appeared as the top undergraduate course choice. In addition, the number of academic positions as well as journal publications increased significantly. This significant change makes this school a very interesting case study for investigating how it encouraged its staff to support the school brand value.

As the government allowed universities more control over their staff, budget and internal organization, this encouraged the school to develop efficient systems for supporting the self-development of academics. In turn, this increased service quality and efficiency. This business school offers more than 20 degrees (undergraduate and postgraduate) with over 100 lecturers. Therefore, it was a challenging task to encourage academics to support the school brand value. Since 2006, the school has created various strategies for allocating and managing their academic staff. The goals of the school were relayed to their academic staff to help them understand the school's goals and represent the school well. This process helped the school to raise its ranking in certain indicators (e.g. staff qualifications, research quality). The institution tried to improve its brand and image, for example by encouraging staff to publish research papers, or by providing scholarships in foreign countries such as the UK, the USA and Japan to raise academics' levels of education. It communicated its brand value to employees in several ways, including through communication media, training and leadership.

Brand leadership

In this school, lecturers tended to put extra effort into relating the organization's brand to their work activities when their leader exhibited the characteristics of transformational leadership. In the following paragraphs, four ways in which the leader of this school influenced brand support are discussed.

First, the leader of the school was seen to be an intelligent person (**the characteristic of 'idealization influence'**). Lecturers seemed to be quite proud to work with their leader as the leader was an intelligent person and he was also a person of good morals. Moreover, the leader was the role model for them. It was said that if the leader followed what the university wanted, the lecturers would definitely do it too. In addition, the behaviour of the leader (i.e. coming to work early and working hard) could be imitated by lecturers. Specifically, the lecturers knew the right behaviour by observing their leader's behaviour.

Second, the leader inspired and motivated his followers to apply institutional brand values in their work activities by providing appealing images about what his followers could do (**the characteristic of 'inspiration motivation'**). In order to efficiently communicate high expectations to lecturers, the leader recognized the general capabilities of each lecturer and was able to identify exactly how each lecturer could perform. The leader clearly understood each lecturer's abilities and knew what each lecturer should do to achieve the university's goals.

Third, the leader was a great supporter (**the characteristic of 'intellectual stimulation'**). The leaders let his followers think for themselves and then judged appropriateness. If a proposal was not appropriate, he did not reject the project, but instead suggested ways of improving it. This really motivated them to work for the school because he allowed them to think independently.

Fourth, the leader usually gave positive feedback which made employees enthusiastic to continue working and made them feel worthy to work for the organization (**the characteristic of 'individual consideration'**). The leader tended to talk to lecturers face to face as that can create positive feeling for the lecturers. It was good for academic staff because they wanted to develop themselves and their leader was able to help them. This approach was vital for motivating behaviour change.

Internal communication and training

The missions of the school are to provide an educational service, to preserve Thai culture, to provide a business education with high moral standards and to be a research institution. The school communicated policies and what it wanted to be by using meetings, internal letters, memos, emails and social media such as Facebook. In addition, there was a strategy map which extracted the school's values that was communicated through the school's activities. Also, new lecturers received guidelines or a booklet. These activities built the understanding of brand, reinforced values, and enhanced understanding of the brand for academic staff who had already done things in alignment with the brand without realizing it.

In general, brand values of this school were communicated to lecturers: (1) individually; (2) specifically to each grouping and (3) to all of them together through mass communications. Sometimes, there were group meetings, for example new lecturers' meetings and department meetings. In the new lecturers' meeting, the dean of the school talked about what the institution expected new lecturers to do. New lecturers were likely to be impressed by this meeting because knowing specifically what the institution expected from the school gave them a good sense of direction so that they could work in alignment with the institution's goals. Moreover, in meetings, there were discussions about what the institution wanted the lecturers to do in relation to its mission, vision, and policy, such as activities for the local community which is the focus of the institution. In the meeting, they could all discuss the projects of the school in more detail, so lecturers understood the objectives and the details of the plan. The meetings helped them to understand each other and remember things better because they allowed two-way communication. Also, these were chances for lecturers to interact with the source of information.

Moreover, the school provided lecturers with training and financial support for conducting research. As a result, many lecturers had started conducting research. There was a training activity, called 'quality assurance training'. From this training, employees learnt about the school's goals and what they needed to do to support the goals. Lecturers were notified about the assessment of their work quality (performance indicators), so that they knew the ways of working in alignment with the school's goals, for example how to integrate knowledge about local culture in course activities and assignments. In addition, the school communicated brand values (i.e. policy, mission and vision) through the KPIs (key performance indicators). Training programmes related to the KPIs were provided, so that the employees could work in alignment with the institution's brand. In addition, the annual performance reviews of the institution were likely to reflect the institution's mission, vision, and policy.

The school encouraged academic staff to conduct research by setting research training modules. The school also encouraged academics who had only a Master's degree to get a PhD degree abroad, providing lecturers with courses in English and scholarships for a PhD course in the USA and the UK. These kinds of support activities helped academics to know specifically what they needed to do. It was a work directive. Furthermore, the school encouraged lecturers to learn more technological knowledge. After lecturers had an IT training course, they knew how to develop websites that benefited their students.

In conclusion, this school created brand support by using both brand leadership and internal branding. The leader of the school initiated internal branding activities. Apart from initiating internal branding activities, the leader tended to influence employees' perception of institutional values, such as by emphasizing what lecturers needed to do in staff meetings. As a result, lecturers gained more brand support by perceiving the brand values in the leader and through the internal branding activities

6 Further investigation

1 What are the ideal characteristics of brand leadership?
2 What are the important tools that can be used in internal branding activities?
3 What are the ideal characteristics of the brand support behaviours of employees?
4 What are the best methods for brand-centred training and development activities?
5 Apart from leadership influences and internal branding activities, what are the other approaches that can influence brand support behaviours of employees?

References

Askling, B, Bauer, M., and Marton, S. (1999) "Swedish universities towards self-regulation: A new look at institutional autonomy." *Tertiary Education and Management* 5(2), pp. 175–195.
Aurand, T. W., Gorchels, L., and Bishop, T. R. (2005) "Human resource management's role in internal branding: An opportunity for cross-functional brand message synergy." *Journal of Product and Brand Management* 14(3), pp. 163–169.
Avolio, B. J. (1999) *Full Leadership Development: Building the Vital Forces in Organizations*. Thousand Oaks, CA: Sage Publications.
Bagautdinova, N. G., Gorelova, Y. N., and Polyakova, O. V. (2015) "University management: From successful corporate culture to effective university branding." *Procedia Economics and Finance* 26, pp. 764–768.
Baker, M. J. and Balmer, J. M. T. (1997) "Visual identity: Trappings or substance?" *European Journal of Marketing* 31(5/6), pp. 366–382.
Bargh, C., Bocock, J., Scott, P., and Smith, D. (2000) *University Leadership: The Role of the Chief Executive*. London: Open University Press.
Barry, J., Chandler, J., and Clark, H. (2001) "Between the ivory tower and the academic assembly line." *Journal of Management Study* 38(1), pp. 87–101.
Bass, B. M. and Avolio, B. J. (1990) "The implications of transactional and transformational leadership for individual, team, and organizational development." *Research in Organizational Change and Development* 4, pp. 231–272.
Burmann, C. and Zeplin, S. (2005) "Building brand commitment: A behavioural approach to internal brand building." *Journal of Brand Management* 12(4), pp. 279–300.
Burns, J. M. (1978) *Leadership*. New York: Harper & Row.
Chapleo, C. (2010) "What defines 'successful' university brands?" *International Journal of Public Sector Management* 23(2), pp. 169–183.
Cohen, M. D. and March, J. G. (1986) *Leadership and Ambiguity: The American College President* (2nd edition). Boston, Massachusetts: Harvard Business School Press.
Davies, J., Hides, M. T., and Casey, S. (2001) "Leadership in higher education." *Total Quality Management* 12(7/8), pp. 1025–1030.
Dearlove, J. (1995) "Collegiality, managerialism and leadership in English universities." *Tertiary Education and Management* 1(2), pp. 161–169.
den Hartog, D. N., van Muijen, J. J., and Koopman, P. L. (1997) "Transactional versus transformational leadership: An analysis of the MLQ." *Journal of Occupational and Organizational Psychology* 70(1), pp. 19–34.
Drouillard, S. E. and Kleiner, B. H. (1996) "Good leadership." *Management Development Review* 9(5), pp. 30–33.
Fiedler, F. E. (1967) *A Theory of Leadership Effectiveness*. New York: McGraw-Hill.
Fink, D. (2005) "Developing leaders for their future and our past," in M. J. Coles and G. Southworth (eds), *Developing Leadership: Creating the Schools of Tomorrow*. Berkshire: Open University Press, pp. 1–20.
Gotsi, M. and Wilson, A. (2001) "Corporate reputation management: Living the brand." *Management Decision* 39(2), pp. 99–104.
Hambrick, D. and Mason, P. (1984) "Upper echelons: The organisation as a reflection of its top managers." *Academy of Management Review*, 9(2), pp. 193–206.

Henkel, S., Tomczak, T., Heitmann, M., and Herrmann, A. (2007) "Managing brand consistent employee behaviour: Relevance and managerial control of behavioural branding." *Journal of Product and Brand Management* 16(5), pp. 310–320.

Hill, C. W. L. and Jones, T. M. (1992) "Stakeholder-agency theory." *Journal of Management Studies* 29(2), pp. 131–154.

House, R. J. (1971) "A path-goal theory of leader effectiveness." *Administrative Science Quarterly* 16(3), pp. 321–339.

Ind, N. (2007) *Living the Brand* (3rd edition). London: Kogan Page.

Istileulova, Y. (2010) Higher education of central Asia and Russia: Building corporate brand. *Paper presented at the Nation Branding in a Globalized World: An International Conference on the Economic, Political, and Cultural Dimensions of Nation Branding*, 2010.

Jaworski, B. J. (1988) "Toward a theory of marketing control: Environmental context, control types, and consequences." *Journal of Marketing* 52(3), pp. 23–39.

Jevons, C. (2006) "Universities: A prime example of branding going wrong." *Journal of Product & Brand Management* 15(7), pp. 466–467.

Judson, K. M., Aurand, T. W., Gorchels, L., and Gordon, G. L. (2009) "Building a university brand from within: University administrators' perspectives of internal branding." *Services Marketing Quarterly* 30(1), pp. 54–68.

Judson, K. M., Gorchels, L., and Aurand, T. W. (2006) "Building a university brand from within: A comparison of coaches' perspectives of internal branding." *Journal of Marketing for Higher Education* 16(1), pp. 97–114.

Karmark, E. (2005) "Living the brand," in M. Schultz, Y. M. Antorini, and F. F. Csaba (eds), *Corporate Branding: Purpose/People/Process*. Copenhagen: CBS press, pp. 103–124.

Kotter, J. P. and Heskett, J. L. (1992) *Corporate Culture and Performance*. New York: The Free Press.

Kunde, J. (2000) *Corporate Religion*. London: Prentice Hall.

Leithwood, K. A. (1992) "The move toward transformational leadership." *Educational Leadership* 49(5), pp. 8–12.

Maringe, F. (2005) "University marketing: Perceptions, practices and prospects in the less developed world." *Journal of Marketing for Higher Education* 15(2), pp. 129–153.

Melewar, T C and Karaosmanoglu, E. (2006) "Seven dimensions of corporate identity: A categorisation from the practitioners' perspectives." *European Journal of Marketing* 40(7/8), pp. 846–869.

Morhart, F. M., Herzog, W., and Tomczak, T. (2009) "Brand-specific leadership: Turning employees into brand champions." *Journal of Marketing* 73(5), pp. 122–142.

Northouse, P. G. (2004) *Leadership: Theory and Practice*. London: Sage Publications.

Punjaisri, K. and Wilson, A. (2007) "The role of internal branding in the delivery of employee brand promise." *Journals of Brand Management* 15(1), pp. 57–70.

Ramsden, P. (1998) *Learning to Lead in Higher Education*. New York: Routledge.

Roberts, N. (1985) "Transformational leadership: A process of collective action." *Human Relationships* 38(11), pp. 1023–1046.

Schein, E. H. (1983) "The role of the founder in creating organizational culture." *Organizational Dynamics* 12(1), pp. 13–28.

Stensaker, B. (2005) Strategy, identity and branding – re-inventing higher education institutions. *Paper presented to the city higher education seminar series (CHESS)*, 7 December. London: City University.

Sujchaphong, N., Nguyen, B., and Melewar, T C (2015) "Internal branding in universities and the lessons learnt from the past: The significance of employee brand support and transformational leadership." *Journal of Marketing for Higher Education* 25(2), pp. 204–237.

Sujchaphong, N., Nguyen, B., and Melewar, T C (2017) "Towards a branding oriented higher education sector: An overview of the four perspectives on university marketing studies." *The Marketing Review* 17(1), pp. 87–116.

Sujchaphong, P. (2013) *Individual Human Capital and Performance: An Empirical Study in Thailand* (Doctoral dissertation), The University of Texas at Arlington, Texas, USA.

Urde, M. (2003) "Core value-based corporate brand building." *European Journal of Marketing* 37(7/8), pp. 1017–1040.

Whisman, R. (2009) "Internal branding: A university's most valuable intangible asset." *Journal of Product & Brand Management* 18(5), pp. 367–370.

Yu, Q., Asaad, Y., Yen, D. A., and Gupta, S. (2018) "IMO and internal branding outcomes: An employee perspective in UK HE." *Studies in Higher Education* 43(1), pp. 37–56.

Further reading

Sujchaphong, N., Nguyen, B., and Melewar, T C (2017) "Employee brand support, transformational leadership and brand-centred training of academic staff in business schools," in B. Nguyen, T C Melewar, and D. E. Schultz (eds), *Asia Branding: Connecting Brands, Consumers and Companies*. London: Palgrave Macmillan, pp. 199–214.

5 Competition in higher education

Francesca Pucciarelli and Andreas Kaplan

1 Introduction

The age in which higher education (HE) was considered as a public good with a clear societal mission has evolved into an increasingly global, diverse, complex and crowded education market (Schofield *et al.*, 2013). This marks a major shift in discussion of the adequacy of the traditional way in which universities are managed, marketed and communicated (Nicolescu, 2009). Academic institutions are nowadays asked to act as both: a public good addressing societal aspiration and the pursuit of academic excellence, and also as competitive business entities competing for status, rankings, talent and funding, etc., to further operate, create value and ultimately generate growth (Pucciarelli and Kaplan, 2016). Universities, for their part, are not new to competition and managerial practices typical of for-profit business sectors, such as market orientation, relationship marketing and branding, which have become commonplace for HE institutions over the last few years (Temple and Shattock, 2007; Gibbs and Murphy, 2009; Waereaas and Solbakk, 2009).

This book chapter takes a close look at the competitive dynamics influencing the rules of the game in higher education and emphasizes the need for differentiation strategy and branding (Chapleo *et al.*, 2011). Then it introduces different competitive tools available to analyse the market and the competitive landscape. In addition, applied examples of competitive differentiation initiatives are used to increase readers' understanding of how universities manage their brands so that they stand out from the crowd in the large and growing education market.

A specific sub-category of higher education institutions is used to put theory into practice: business schools. Business schools have been chosen by the authors because of the greater market pressure they are subject to, owing, for example, to the introduction of international rankings by media in the late 1980s. Intense competitive pressure suggesting that business schools, even more urgently than other universities – with which they share trends and destinies in general – must practice what they teach: and they are teaching marketing strategy and branding.

After reading this chapter, readers should have a clearer understanding of:

- WHY universities do need a clear competitive strategy to establish their market space.
- WHAT challenges universities' decision makers encompass in building a strong brand.
- HOW universities can organize and manage their branding effort to truly differentiate themselves from competition and leverage those elements valued by key stakeholders.

2 Review of the literature in HE competition

The new rules of the game: the 3Es framework for competitiveness in higher education

The higher education sector has been subject to a series of fundamental challenges in past decades. Education today is a global market populated by an increasing number of quasi-commercial service providers (Brookes, 2003), in which institutional, national and global competition are different but feed into each other (Marginson, 2006) and technological, social and economic changes have necessitated a customer-oriented approach (Nguyen, Hemsley-Brown and Melewar, 2016), giving universities no choice but to market themselves with holistic competitive strategy.

Pucciarelli and Kaplan (2016) synthesize the new rules of the game underpinning higher education institutions' competitiveness in the long run in the so-called 3Es for higher education framework. The first E stands for Enhance and relates to a given higher education institution's prestige and market share in the consolidating global educational market. The second E is Embrace and relates to developing a deeper entrepreneurial mind-set, with corresponding modus operandi and decision-making approaches coming from increased final autonomy (because of the decrease of public funding) and thus accountability and responsibility in funding and investing decisions. Last, the third E represents the need to Expand links, interactions, and value co-creation with key stakeholders leveraging new forms of collaboration with old and new partners, exploring opportunities in the digital world. The 3Es are further explored in the next sections.

E – Enhance prestige and market share

As higher education continues to grow, increased competition places more pressure on institutions to market themselves and their programmes (Melewar and Nguyen, 2015). Pressure is intensified by the need for universities to complement (or even substitute) decreasing public funding through support with private sources (Nicolescu, 2009).

Many higher education institutions are recognizing the need to implement marketing concepts, which other industries have recognized as necessary for success, and have increased their marketing effort and spending (Guilbault, 2017). Furthermore, several universities, making a virtue of necessity, have come up with brand-building approaches (Chapleo, 2017) to reach potential key targets, to communicate to them their value proposition, with the aim of becoming the favoured educational reference in their minds and thus attracting vital resources, such as donors, students and company sponsorship for executive development and research.

Potential students, for their part, are digital natives, who act as rational, informed and autonomous – i.e. thanks to the web 2.0 – in forming their opinions about one university or another and choosing what and where to study (Temple and Shattock, 2007). Thus it is a matter of fact that market evaluation is and will be increasingly crucial, with the consequence that universities should carefully manage and nurture their brand reputation. It is not a secret that, for example, university rankings have gained popularity around the world and are now a significant factor shaping university reputation and influencing prospective students and their parents in selecting a university (Hazelkorn, 2015). It can also be safely argued, taking an employer perspective, that it will not only be valuable for a candidate to have a certain level academic degree, such as for example an MBA, but that the academic institution where the MBA was earned will also always be important, and will become even more important in a future.

Extant research suggests that higher education institutions are encouraged on all sides to become more market oriented (Sujchaphong, Nguyen, and Melewar, 2017), embracing branding effort as a way to assist students in choosing education institutions that better address their needs (Chapleo, 2017). In the same direction, Bunzel (2007) suggests that universities could substitute ranking positioning for market share, to get closer to a definition of a successful brand; arguing that there is little evidence that higher education branding effort really drives a change in perception or ranking of a university.

Arguably, brand success comprises both consumer based criteria and business based ones. Thus, if it is true, a sharp look at how markets assess and evaluate academic institutions is a fundamental preliminary exercise in determining the key brand attributes sought by students, as a basis for defining which university capabilities should be included as unique selling points in the value proposition. On the other hand, to articulate in a few sentences (i.e. university's mission, vision, brand statement, motto, etc.) how the education mission is brought to life by an individual university to provide a unique experience is anything but simple (Chapleo, 2015). This is why the rest of this chapter will focus on this challenging task.

E – Embrace a deeper entrepreneurial mind-set

Education is nowadays a quasi-commercial service market, in which universities are required to behave as corporations in many respects and to engage in increasingly complex marketing activities to gain their market space, encompassing multiple targets, multiple media, and multiple geographies.

Notably, the HE sector's attempts to catch up with other, more commercial, sectors in the adoption of a marketing ethos in education is widespread nowadays – as branding has been in recent years, – and as such is no longer a matter for debate (Wæraas and Solbakk, 2009; Chapleo, 2017). The potential benefits of applying marketing theories and concepts that have been effective in the business world are gradually being recognized by researchers in the field of higher education marketing (Hemsley-Brown and Oplatka, 2006). Several studies have sought to observe how broad marketing concepts can be applied in the context of HE, investigating scope, adaptations and limits (Gibbs and Murphy, 2009; Kaplan and Haenlein, 2009) and even warning about the risk of diluting teaching, research, with selection quality standards neglected in the pursuit of recruitment and market share (Nicolescu, 2009).

Extant literature agrees on the suggestion that further enhancement of marketization of academia is needed, which can be deduced from the simple fact that the appointment of a marketing director and/or a formal brand manager is still quite new to higher education (Chapleo, 2017). Pioneering institutions that could be mentioned as examples are Leeds University, which introduced its first brand's guardian only in 2004 (Times Higher Education Supplement, 23 July 2004); and *École Supérieure de Commerce de Paris* (ESCP Europe) appointing, in the same position, an experienced professional coming from another industry – instead of a faculty member – in 2014.

Whilst some academic institutions are encouraging academic personnel to participate actively, asking for specific contributions to universities' decision making and management, others are channelling faculty contributions toward marketing and PR activities, such as fund-raising and promotion (Kaplan, 2017), for example by supporting applied research commercialization to sustain universities' financing, but also as a means to preserve the strategic value of knowledge creation whilst benefitting the larger research diffusion beyond pure academic pursuits.

Some other universities have instead interpreted the need for more entrepreneurial solutions as a quest for becoming more responsive to students' demands in terms of curricula and media used in delivering teaching, experimenting, for example, with certificates in Coursera or creating their own online education propositions, as in the case of Harvard University's HBX initiative.

The adoption of new media could also be used for communication with the incoming flux of digital natives in promoting a given academic institution, as in the case of Cambridge University, by fostering faculties' active participation in social media with their personal accounts, communicating their affiliation to Cambridge and acting as online advocates of university-generated content. Notably these types of tactics, working in the direction of internal branding, encourage faculty and administrative staff to align their behaviour in support of corporate brands and are more in use in private universities, probably because of their major dependency upon tuition fees (Sujchaphong et al., 2017).

E – Expand links and value co-creation with key stakeholders

The third and last 'E' requires defining who key stakeholders are, starting by solving the never-ending debate about who the customers are and then striving to expand links, interactions and value co-creation by rethinking the relationships, touch-points, and joined activities – and a university's place within them.

Research has shown that market orientation can enable the organization to compete by creating and maintaining superior value through the appreciation of the importance of customers. It appears logical then that higher education institutions can benefit from market orientation in developing successful customer relationship management strategies, as education is a service industry and, like any service, it requires active engagement of both provider and customer – which translated into education settings will mean learning requires active engagement of both teachers and students.

The customer can be viewed as the students – potential, current, and former – the employers, and other stakeholders (Guilbault, 2017). Thinking of students as consumers is a natural consequence of talking of marketing in higher education (Cuthbert, 2010) and even if this concept attracts antipathy – or even denial – by some faculty, accepting the students as customers does not mean giving away education nor that students must be given 'As' to be satisfied; instead it means providing an excellent customer experience across the student experience lifecycle (Kaplan, 2017). Also, students for their part already consider themselves customers and expect to be satisfied. Thus higher education institutions will be challenged to truly be what they generally claim to be: lively learning and experiential communities, based upon personal interactions and collaboration to discover, understand, and apply new knowledge.

This collaboration could, for example, take the form of engaging former students and corporates in revising curricula to better define the relevant, up-to-date, enlarged set of competences needed to meet job market requirements. This would positively impact the employability of university graduates, the university value of positional goods, and thus, ultimately, the university's brand reputation (Marginson, 2006), not to mention the advantages of simply bringing back school alumni, a crucial group of stakeholders who could support the university in a number of ways – from scholarships and other resources that support university fundraising to stronger linkage with the corporate world, or simply via positive word-of-mouth promotion in their offline and online networks (Kaplan and Haenlein, 2016).

How to successfully compete in today's higher education: differentiate or die

To successfully compete in the marketplace, higher education institutions are required to re-think their strategy for the future to better address today's increased complexity and new challenges coming from the globalization and marketization of the education sector.

An interpretation of strategy that concentrates on the idea of 'more' is what universities around the world have used for the past half-a-century, with academic institutions occupied in offering more programmes, serving more students – including adding more seats per class whenever possible– and being in more places. This has resulted in a lack of real differentiation in the sector in general (Chapleo, 2004; Kaplan, 2014), making it difficult to differentiate between universities – including those in the top league – that address the same educational mission by using the same strategies and the same key ingredients (Temple and Shattock, 2007) to describe themselves (see Figure 5.1 below).

For example, values such as exceptionally strong alumni network, a highly ranked MBA programme, international experience, excellent career service, world class teaching faculty, excellent research reputation, are common descriptors of many top business schools around the globe. As a consequence, it is easy to replace one university name with another and find that the mission and vision statements are still equally applicable (see Figure 5.2 below).

Going back to definitions, the creation of successful brands requires three elements: an effective product, a distinctive identity and added value (Doyle, 2001). This is why, to succeed in attracting students and academic staff, universities should thus fight higher education sector uniformity by establishing a unique value proposition (Kaplan, 2014) and institutional positioning (Maringe, 2006) to differentiate themselves from competitors.

The idea of differentiation being critical to successful university brands is supported by a number of authors (Chapleo, 2017). Differentiation strategy consists in capitalizing on the inherent capabilities that define the university in terms of its basic identity, in the attempt to be distinguished – and distinguishable – from competitors in such a way that the target audience will value it, and thus the university will establish its competitive advantage. Nowadays, more than in a recent past, to stay ahead of competition, a further interpretation of the concept of distinctive values that meets consumers' perceived needs is required from universities, which

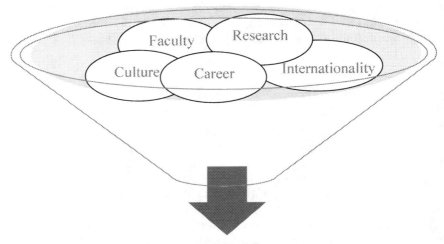

Figure 5.1 Higher education mission key common components.

should focus more on the idea of 'being different' rather than just offering more of the same.

This means that universities should be much more aware of the niche they fill – or want to fill – in the educational marketplace, starting from a clear sense of who the potential customer is: 'is that the potential student population or potential donors? And if the target is potential students, which type of student to attract? With which programs?'

Knowing the customer is the first step in differentiation, and it enable universities to start drawing value propositions which are more compelling, because they adopt the customer point of view in answering strategic questions such as: 'what is the role of research? which other core attribute is heavily considered by potential candidates: scholarship, international experience, career progression of what else?' with the result that these universities' value propositions differentiate in ways that their audiences care about.

Wharton - University of Pennsylvania	Motto: 'Knowledge for action'	Motto: *'Apprendre à oser'* (The more you know, the more you dare)	HEC Paris
INSEAD	Tagline: 'The Business School for the World'	Taglines: 'European Identity Global Perspective' 'The World's First Business School (est. 1819)'	ESCP Europe Business School
ESSEC Business School	'Our ultimate goal: to create a global world that has meaning for us all'	'To have a profound impact on the way the world does business'	London Business School
Harvard Business School	'We educate leaders who make a difference in the world'	'We develop brave leaders who inspire growth in people, organizations and markets'	Kellogg School of Management

Figure 5.2 Guess who? Top business schools' mottos and taglines.

Last but not least, real differentiation cannot be achieved without a close look at the competitive landscape. In as differentiating your own university from competitor universities, you should know who those universities are, as well as what their strengths and weaknesses are. The identification of the right key competitors (i.e. the schools that share candidatures and/or admitted students), is thus as fundamental as the right definition of the key targets to refine brand message (improving the ability to convey the right message, including comparing against competitors). So that even if many business schools' core offerings could appear similar to a prospective student, awareness and acknowledgement of differences in cost, location, outcomes, rankings and other factors, could drive brand building by weaving these items into a convincing narrative.

3 Managerial implications

Universities have long competed for status and ranking, talent, and funding, though the most important consequence of the heightened competition is the need for differentiation and it is likely that colleges and universities will become more differentiated and have more distinct strategic missions in terms of the type of students and stakeholders to attract, programs to offer, and the role of research and scholarship in their academic life. The existing literature mainly draws on the strategic management perspective that argues that HE Institutions are pressured to develop brands which differentiate them from their competitors and enable key stakeholders to differentiate between the various propositions on the market (Hazelkorn, 2015).

Branding is a crucial part of corporate strategies for remaining relevant in an increasingly competitive landscape. This is also true in higher education where it is arguably more difficult to implement branding successfully because of the complexity of the institutions involved and the difficulty of encapsulating the whole university spirit in the brand statement. Moreover, even if higher education institutions are in fact obligated to include research, world class teaching, a second-to-none experience and a student focus as elements of their identity – because of the common education mission –by consciously leveraging curriculum, experience and tradition, academic institutions can stand out as destinations for prospective students in what is an incredibly competitive marketplace.

It is important to highlight that enhancing a higher education institution's prestige and market share will necessitate passing through the stages of adoption of a market orientation, putting customers first, being responsive to potential students' needs and considering who the competitors are from their perspective, plus a bit of competitive intelligence to get to know the 'enemy' value proposition better (see Figure 5.3).

Then as branding entails defining the essence of what a university 'is', what it 'stands for', and what it 'is going to be known for', successful university brands should keep telling us as loudly as possible why their academic institution is different (instead of just offering more) to ensure a

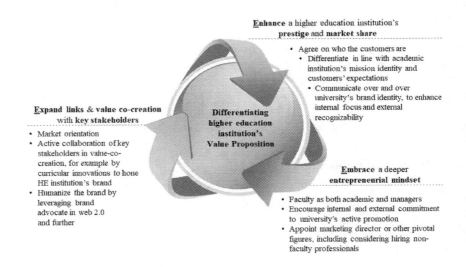

Figure 5.3 3Es for higher education framework in action.

shared brand meaning and foster internal commitment to the brand, facilitating internal culture change on top of enhancing institutional reputation externally. Communication should exit traditional circuits, leveraging entrepreneurial solutions in broadening the audience and making university projects more visible and impactful, including using other's voices (not just the institutional one) such as those of engaged students, alumni, and faculty in humanizing the brand.

Making that connection between university and students is vital for the success of the brands, because the truth is that the brand is about the people – who ultimately give life and own the brand – and the experience. A great brand can make all the difference when a student is deciding what and where to study, but it cannot replace a poor experience. Highly ranked MBAs have to thank their faculties and their graduates, who have gone on to do great things, for their positioning and prestige.

4 Conclusions

Today, academic institutions do not really have a choice but to develop adequate strategies in response to the outlined challenges, resulting from several evolutions and developments within the higher education sector which is becoming ever more dynamic, competitive, and complex. Based on critical analyses of the extant literature and on field examples, this chapter explores branding as a tool of strategic differentiation in higher education by using the case of Business Schools. These institutions were chosen based on the fact that they teach a lot of branding and thus, even more than other universities, they should themselves apply branding ideas and techniques.

In accordance with the 3Es of higher education competitiveness framework, three main ways exist for universities to stand out from competition in the crowded education market and attract the attention of potential students (or other key stakeholders groups) through: institutional prestige thanks to a strong and recognized brand built on the basis of differentiation of curriculum, experience and culture; an entrepreneurial mindset at all levels of the organization to commit all levels of the university in promoting the brand and ensuring consistent brand experience; and garnering long-term commitment and support from key stakeholders, *in primis* from students as they will become alumni and potential success-stories, employers, and even supporters (in financing their former university).

Further research

This chapter answers the call for a better understanding of marketing concepts application to the higher education sector (Chapleo, 2017; Guilbault, 2017), and in particular it re-affirms the centrality of branding as a competitive differentiation tool, in line with extant literature. This acknowledgment though represents a starting point for further researches and much remains to be done in analysing how branding adds value to universities, raising several questions that may be in need of further exploration. First, work on the definition of what 'successful higher education brands' are appears to be desirable, as it seems that some university branding may have an unclear purpose. Thus, filling this gap in literature is necessary and it will serve also to drive future effort to suggesting appropriate models for brand management in the specific context of higher education. Second to identify the areas where the engagement of students is weak to assess whether universities' functional areas have truly embraced a customer orientation. Another area of interest would be internal brand engagement as it seems to be increasingly important in ensuring brand consistency and organization 'buy-in' of brand identity. This has recently received the attention of university leaders, although little has been done so far in researching internal branding applied to a university. A last emerging issue, and suggested direction worthy of considerable investigation, regards the experiential branding area applied to education.

Last but not least, as strategy is built on twin pillars, namely knowledge of the current situation and uncertainty about what the future will look like, authors strongly believe that continuous effort is needed to observe and anticipate incoming issues and opportunities in the education market.

5 Case study: ESCP Europe Business School, the world's first business school (est. 1819)

ESCP Europe, established in 1819, is the world's first business school and as such invented the concept of the management school nearly 200 years ago. With its six campuses in Berlin, London, Madrid, Paris, Torino, and Warsaw, ESCP Europe's strong European identity establishes a unique style of cross-cultural business education with a global perspective on international management issues. ESCP Europe's network of more than 100 partner universities extends the school's reach worldwide.

ESCP Europe Business School is one institution interconnected across its six European campuses. During the scope of their studies, students have the option as well as obligation to move from one campus to another depending on their programmes. Within, e.g. the three-year Bachelor programme, students annually move from one campus to another studying in three different countries, becoming at least trilingual by the end of their studies. The Masters in Management programme goes even further and allows students to study at up to four different campuses with the possibility of spending one or two semesters with an international partner during the two-year programme (minimum of one semester per location). All ESCP Europe students study in at least two of the School's campuses.

Enhance a higher education institution's prestige and market share: Triple-crown accredited (EQUIS, AACSB, AMBA), the ESCP Europe brand's key element and unique selling proposition is without a doubt its European positioning. With six campuses and a vastly diverse student body, being European for ESCP Europe implies embracing cultural diversity at minimal geographical distances. This makes ESCP Europe a natural expert in cross-cultural management and entrepreneurship, not only in Europe but all around the world. Not limiting oneself to Europe but enlarging the School's scope to a worldwide one, has prominently been promoted in ESCP Europe's slogan 'European Identity, Global Perspective'. This motto, connected to the School's baseline 'The World's First Business School (est. 1819)', has created a strong and highly differentiated brand identity in comparison to its competitors worldwide.

ESCP Europe's target group thus consists of adventurous, open-minded students who are interested in experiencing cross-cultural management in theory and practice, moving around different countries in a relatively short period of time, learning and improving their foreign language skills, as well as planning on pursuing an international career. This is also expressed in the School's mission statement:

> ESCP Europe connects and shapes the business world by advancing cross-cultural management knowledge and practice. Teaching management from an interdisciplinary perspective at the highest level of academic excellence, we develop culturally intelligent, multilingual leaders, who are open-minded, adaptable and responsible. As managers and entrepreneurs, ESCP Europe's graduates are equipped to lead and inspire in a globalised world.
> (www.escpeurope.eu/mission-and-values)

Embrace a deeper entrepreneurial mind-set: Consisting of six different campuses in six European countries, ESCP Europe is quite a complex organization. Therefore, managerial processes need to be clear, allowing for certain (entrepreneurial) liberties in order to quickly react to local realities and cultural differences. Each of the School's campuses is managed by a local dean in charge of all local academic and operational matters, the development of its respected campus faculty, its undergraduate and graduate programmes, its executive education and corporate relations, its student and alumni relations, its social diversity and inclusion policy, its fundraising activities, and the evolution of its national as well as international profile. Federal directors, such as the dean of faculty, the dean of academic affairs, the director of brand and communications, are in charge of keeping the campus deans' positions consistent across all six campuses. Both the campus and federal deans and directors work together in a matrix organization managed by an overall dean/executive president of ESCP Europe.

With respect to branding, social media plays an important role at ESCP Europe. Also, here one needs to be more open to an entrepreneurial mind-set due to the character and spirit of these communication tools. To be the first business school in the world also means to be the oldest. This carries the risk of being considered old-fashioned. Social media helps ESCP Europe to show that the school is innovative, dynamic, and modern. ESCP Europe has a Digital Manager Europe, reporting to the Director of Brand and Communications. The Digital Manager Europe is in charge of the web and social media strategy across the various campuses. On each of its campuses there is one person dedicated to web and social media activities who reports to the local Head of Communications and Marketing, yet is functionally dependent on the Digital Manager Europe. In addition, several other employees work with social media, including the marketing managers for the different programmes, all coordinated by the Digital Manager Europe.

Expand links and value co-creation with key stakeholders: ESCP Europe Business School hosts approximately 5,000 students and 5,000 executives from 90 different nations every year. The alumni network accounts for 50,000 members in 150 countries and 200 different nationalities. To involve students as well as alumni in an institution's branding and communications activities is of increasing importance in today's competitive business school landscape. Looking at YouTube, several student- and alumni-made videos about ESCP Europe can be found. Some of them were produced in the course of viral video competitions organized by the school; others were created as course assignments; and others are students' own initiatives in promoting ESCP Europe's student life. Overall, the number of videos produced and implemented by students and alumni has dramatically increased over the years.

Also, faculty participates in these branding activities: as an example one can cite the course titled 'Social Media and Viral Marketing' within the School's Masters in Management programme elective portfolio. As part of this course, groups of about six students were involved in the production of a viral marketing video about some of the School's specific aspects. Subjects included: 'ESCP Europe – the expert in cross-cultural management'; 'ESCP Europe – the World's First Business School (est. 1819)'; 'ESCP Europe – a cross-border multi-campus European business school'. Some of these productions were even posted on the School's official social media channels or integrated into the School's website. This obviously led to high motivation amongst students. One notable video was 'ESCP Europe – A Love story' which was posted on the School's alumni section of its website.

6 Further investigation

1 What are the dangers but also the opportunities in the higher education market becoming more and more competitive?

2 Are there areas/higher education disciplines that are more exposed to competition than others? If yes, why is that the case?
3 Who are your institution's main competitors and why? How do they differ from each other?
4 How could students and alumni be integrated in your institution's branding and communication activities in order to strengthen it in its competitive landscape?
5 Do you think your institution embraces an entrepreneurial mind-set? Could it go further, and if yes, how?

References

Brookes, M. (2003) "Higher education: Marketing in a quasi-commercial service industry." *International Journal of Nonprofit and Voluntary Sector Marketing* 8(2), pp. 134–142.
Bunzel, D. (2007) "Universities sell their brands." *Journal of Product & Brand Management* 16(2), pp. 152–153.
Chapleo, C. (2004) "Interpretation and implementation of reputation/brand management by UK university leaders." *International Journal of Educational Advancement* 5(1), pp. 7–23.
Chapleo, C. (2017) "Exploring the secret of successful university brands," in *Advertising and Branding: Concepts, Methodologies, Tools, and Applications: Concepts, Methodologies, Tools, and Applications*. Hershey PA, IGI-Global, pp. 288–303. DOI: 10.4018/978-1-4666-4860-9.ch007.
Chapleo, C., Carrillo Duran, M. V., and Castillo Diaz, A. (2011) "Do UK universities communicate their brands effectively through their websites?" *Journal of Marketing for Higher Education* 21(1), pp. 25–46.
Cuthbert, R. (2010) "Students as customers." *Higher Education Review* 42(3), pp. 3–25.
Doyle, P. (2001) *Marketing Management and Strategy*. Hemel Hempstead: Prentice Hall
Gibbs, P. and Murphy, P. (2009) "Implementation of ethical higher education marketing." *Tertiary Education and Management* 15(4), pp. 341–354.
Guilbault, M. (2017) "Students as customers in higher education: The (controversial) debate needs to end." *Journal of Retailing and Consumer Services* 40: pp. 295–298.
Hazelkorn, E. (2015) *Rankings and the Reshaping of Higher Education: The Battle for World-class Excellence*. London, UK: Springer.
Hemsley-Brown, J. and Oplatka, I. (2006) "Universities in a competitive global marketplace: A systematic review of the literature on higher education marketing." *International Journal of public sector management* 19(4), pp. 316–338.
Kaplan, A. (2014) "European management and European business schools: Insights from the history of business schools." *European Management Journal* 32(4), pp. 529–534.
Kaplan, A. (2017) "Academia goes social media, MOOC, SPOC, SMOC, and SSOC: The digital transformation of higher education institutions and universities," in B. Rishi and S. Bandyopadhyay, *Contemporary Issues in Social Media Marketing*. Abingdon; New York: Routledge, pp. 20–30.

Kaplan, A. M. and Haenlein, M. (2009) "The increasing importance of public marketing: Explanations, applications and limits of marketing within public administration." *European Management Journal* 27(1), pp. 197–212.

Kaplan, A. M. and Haenlein, M. (2016) "Higher education and the digital revolution: About MOOCs, SPOCs, social media, and the Cookie Monster." *Business Horizons* 59(4), pp. 441–450.

Marginson, S. (2006) "Dynamics of national and global competition in higher education." *Higher Education* 52(1), pp. 1–39.

Maringe, F. (2006) "University and course choice." *International Journal of Educational Management* 20(6), pp. 466–479.

Melewar, T C and Nguyen, B. (2015) "Five areas to advance branding theory and practices." *Journal of Brand Management* 21(9), pp. 758–769.

Nguyen, B., Hemsley-Brown, J., and Melewar, T C (2016) "Branding higher education," in F. Dall'Olmo Riley, J. Singh, and C. Blankson (eds), *The Routledge Companion to Contemporary Brand Management*. London; New York: Routledge, p. 407.

Nicolescu, L. (2009) "Applying marketing to higher education: scope and limits." *Management & Marketing* 4(2), pp. 35–44.

Pucciarelli, F. and Kaplan, A. (2016) "Competition and strategy in higher education: Managing complexity and uncertainty." *Business Horizons* 59(3), pp. 311–320.

Schofield, C., Cotton, D., Gresty, K., Kneale, P., and Winter, J. (2013) "Higher education provision in a crowded marketplace." *Journal of Higher Education Policy and Management* 35(2), pp. 193–205.

Sujchaphong, N., Nguyen, B., and Melewar, T C (2017) "Towards a branding oriented higher education sector: An overview of the four perspectives on university marketing studies." *The Marketing Review* 17(1), pp. 87–116.

Temple, P. and Shattock, M. (2007) "What does branding mean in higher education?" in B. Stensaker and V. D'Andrea, *Branding in Higher Education Exploring an Emerging Phenomenon, EAIR Series Research, Policy and Practice in Higher Education*. Amsterdam, the Netherlands: EAIR, pp. 73–82.

Times Higher Education Supplement, (2004) www.timeshighereducation.com/academic/digital-editions, 23 July 2004

Wæraas, A. and Solbakk, M. N. (2009) "Defining the essence of a university: Lessons from higher education branding." *Higher Education* 57(4), p. 449.

Further readings

Kotler, P., Kartajaya, H., and Setiawan, I. (2016) *Marketing 4.0: Moving from Traditional to Digital*. Hoboken, NJ: John Wiley & Sons.

Lowrie, A. (2017) *Understanding Branding in Higher Education: Marketing Identities*. Boston, MA: Springer.

McHaney, R. (2011) *The New Digital Shoreline: How Web 2.0 and Millennials Are Revolutionizing Higher Education*. Sterling: Stylus Publishing, LLC.

Niessing, J. and Chandon, P. (2017) Who's #1: INSEAD, Harvard, Wharton, LBS? (A) and (B) Designing research to measure the strength of business schools brands. Case A reference no. 517–0184–1 and Case B reference no. 517–0184–8. INSEAD.

Sola, D. and Couturier J. (2014) *How to Think Strategically. Your Roadmap to Innovation and Results*. Harlow: Pearson Education Limited.

Part II
Planning

6 Corporate brand communication in higher education

Elif Karaosmanoglu and Gulberk Gultekin Salman

1 Introduction

Diminishing university funds and government pressure on universities to respond to trends in global student mobility while serving local needs are indicative of the growing importance of branding and brand communication in higher education (Hemsley-Brown and Goonawardana, 2007; Chapleo, 2010). While universities are in a battle for international student attraction, they are also seen as the pillars of domestic social and economic development. In particular, emerging countries are trying to compete with developed countries to prevent brain drain, while at the same time seeking to attract better international students in order to increase the quality of their universities. These countries are also trying to increase the number of local universities and guide them towards areas of specialization that are vital for the specific needs of certain districts or regions. For example, the Council of Higher Education in Turkey (YOK) recently announced a programme that includes five pilot universities that are going to position themselves locally on areas of study dealing with agriculture, geothermal technologies, and the fields of textiles, leatherwork and ceramics, as well as husbandry, health and the environment (www.yok.gov.tr/web/guest/yok-ten-universitelere-kalkinma-cagrisi). At the same time, YOK supports the older and more established top tier Turkish universities to attract international students via exchange programmes such as Erasmus, Erasmus+ and TURQUAS, and Erasmus Mundus, in addition to government scholarships (www.yok.gov.tr).

International, governmental and societal pressure forces institutions of higher education to juggle multiple identities. These external changes have been identified as leading to a shift from private to public financing of higher education (Caruana, Rameseshan, and Ewing, 1998; Pusser, 2002; Kinser, 2006), consumerist approaches to students, and managerial approaches to faculty retention and recruitment (Maringe, 2006; Eggins, 2007). While this shift has been criticized for leading to the commodification of education (Barrett, 1996; Hemsley-Brown and Goonawardana, 2007), brand orientation has become crucial for universities so they can respond to this new environment (Cassidy, 2013; Gromark and Melin, 2013; Williams and Omar, 2014) as it makes it possible for institutions of higher education to establish and maintain a distinct image and hence a competitive advantage in an increasingly competitive market (Hemsley-Brown and Goonawardana, 2007).

This chapter focuses on the brand communication of universities in two controllable areas: management/organizational communication and marketing communication. The chapter also explores the uncontrolled communications of higher education institutions.

After reading this chapter, you should be able to understand:

- How internal and external communication is harmonized in order to create a favourable basis for relationship-building among all relevant groups of a higher education institution.
- How the vision and mission are disseminated internally and externally as a way to create a strong reputation.
- How promotional mix elements can be geared towards supporting preferences regarding the services and goods offered by higher education institutions.
- How unconscious and unplanned communication can be integrated with the brand communication of universities.

2 Review of the literature on corporate brand communications

Controlled corporate communication and corporate branding in higher education

Higher education is characterized by its intangible and inseparable nature (Lowrie, 2007) which is manifested in continuous and formal relationships with students and graduates, commitment cultivation and retention mechanisms for outstanding faculty and support staff, a high level of customization in knowledge development, and delivery and multiple service delivery touch-points (e.g. in-class or online courses, continuous learning centres, laboratories, technology development centres, career support offices, schools and faculties, sports and art centres, libraries and so on) (Hemsley-Brown and Oplatka, 2006; Hemsley-Brown and Goonawardana, 2007; Khanna, Jacob, and Yadav, 2014; Williams and Omar, 2014). The success of a higher education institution is largely dependent on its ability to communicate well on all these fronts, thereby developing a strong reputation and prestige among its audiences (Balmer and Liao, 2007; Williams and Omar, 2014). 'Targeted at multiple stakeholders, any higher education institution brand is externally focused on positioning and marketing and internally focused on the organization and promotion of values/culture/vision' (Williams and Omar, 2014, p. 223). Therefore, the scope of brand communication in higher education can be seen within the border framework of corporate communication.

Corporate communication provides an interface for communicating organizational values between the corporation and its multiple stakeholders (de Chernatony, Cottam, and Segal-Horn, 2006; Schultz and Kitchen, 2004) and it covers all of the ways that an organization communicates with its all stakeholders (Balmer and Greyser, 2006). Thus, all of the messages that an organization disseminates and all the activities it carries out create a certain image in the minds of its stakeholders (Balmer, 1998, 2001). Corporate communication can be intentionally designed and managed by organizations to leverage fruitful and prolonged relationships with their audiences (controlled communication). However, that can also unintentionally occur among third parties, especially with the use of digital technology capabilities (uncontrolled communication) (Melewar and Karaosmanoglu, 2006).

Every organization is faced with a major communication challenge: it should have a corporate communication system that integrates internal and external communications because what an organization stands for is predicated upon how its internal and external audiences perceive it and what they seek for from it (Hatch and Schultz, 2003; Cornelissen, 2017). Internal communication processes should be geared towards developing organizational goals, creating a sense of belonging to the corporate identity, and the dissemination of common organization values among its internal members. At the same time, external communication processes should be directed towards gathering and interpreting external data about external audiences' expectations and preferences so that the right brand messages can be designed along with activities held at the corporate or individual product/brand level (Varey and White, 2000).

Two major components of controlled corporate communication are management/organizational and marketing communications (Grunig, 1993). Management communication, as coined by Olins (1989), concerns the establishment of a favourable image and hence a long-term reputation among internal and external audiences by communicating the vision and mission of the organization. Organizational communication refers to relationship-building activities among the audiences with which an organization has interdependent links, such as investors, intermediaries, and employees (van Riel, 1995). While the former mostly deals with how corporate identity is reflected in the mission and how the vision is perceived, the latter focuses on how corporate identity is collaboratively developed by the central and peripheral members of a relationship network (Hatch and Schultz, 1997). Marketing communication is related to supporting the sales of an organization's products via positioning and product/service brands. Although it is difficult to clearly distinguish between external and internal audiences and hence communication practices for contemporary organizations that are defined via networks, delayering (Hatch and Schultz, 1997), co-production, and co-creation practices (Vargo and Lusch, 2004), this distinction can be drawn based on whose main responsibility lies in areas of related communications.

Management/organizational communication and branding in higher education

Organizational/management communication has mainly focused on the cultivation of an organizational culture among internal members with the aim of increasing organizational commitment and identification (Ashfort and Mael, 1989; Hatch and Schultz, 1997; Gioia, Schultz, and Corley, 2000; Gioia and Patvardhan, 2012). It helps promote 'a collective and commonly shared understanding of the organization's distinctive values and characteristics' (i.e. organizational identity) (Hatch and Schultz, 1997, p. 357) with the aim of ensuring that all the organization's members have a consistent voice during their interactions with outside audiences (de Chernatony, 2001).

The role of managerial leadership in this field of communication is twofold: expressing organizational goals directly to internal audiences (Kiriakidou and Millward, 2000) and removing barriers so that a cooperative and interactive communication environment that encourages opportunities of value sharing can blossom (Varey and White, 2000; de Chernatony *et al.*, 2006). As organizational studies have argued (e.g. Ashfort and Mael, 1989; Hatch and Schultz, 1997, 2000; Gioia *et al.*, 2000; Gioia and Patvardhan, 2012), while managers communicate a strategically designed corporate identity to internal members via visual means (e.g. corporate name, logos, nomenclature, etc.) and vision and mission statements, it is interpreted by organizational members via daily work practices, social interactions that are both internal and external, and cultural patterns (Hatch and Schultz, 1997).

These ongoing interactions highlight the importance of branding the organization (i.e. corporate brand) internally and externally since internal members' sense-making is also influenced by what image their organizations have in outsiders' minds (Dowling, 1993; Hatch and Schultz, 1997, 2003; Karaosmanoglu and Melewar, 2006). While internal members' interactions with each other help delineate what impression other members have, internal-external member interactions (e.g. a salesperson helping a customer) help internal members learn about how outsiders view their organizations. Fabricated corporate brand messages communicated by top managers or spokespersons are as much an attempt to influence outsiders' views as an effort to have an impact on external constituencies (Hatch and Schultz, 2002, 2003). Accordingly, management/organizational communication involves all managerial work that is geared to articulating the organization's essence to internal and external audiences through clear and coherent corporate brand messages (Harris and de Chernatony, 2001; van

Riel and Fombrun, 2007; Wæraas and Solbakk, 2009) and establishing a distinctive positioning for the organization that is superior to that of its competitors (Harris and de Chernatony, 2001; Hatch and Schultz, 2003).

In order to achieve a distinctive place in the minds of its stakeholders, an organization should start with cultivating an internal culture that aligns with the mission and vision of it (Downey, 1986; Hatch and Schultz, 1997; Melewar and Karaosmanoglu, 2006, Whisman, 2009; Cornelissen, 2017). The study by Saurombe, Barkhuizen and Schutte (2017) argues that the generation of an appealing internal environment by the management of HEIs is vital for employee retention and attraction. The internal newsletters and announcements on websites or on official social media accounts are major means of conveying the cultural values of an organization to its employees (Cornelissen, 2017). Especially, empowering employees by sharing their success stories and their contribution to the organizations' overall success reinforces the employees' identification with their organizations (Dutton, Dukerich, and Harquail, 1994). The higher organizational identification makes employees take up a brand ambassador role while communicating with outsiders (Thomson and Hecker, 2001; Gelb and Rangarajan, 2014). In the HEI context, acknowledging the scientific excellence of academics and the support of administrative members in these projects can provide a great opportunity to increase the belongingness of internal members to their universities. Such initiatives also may serve as a proof for the funding bodies who seek legitimate grounds to collaborate with HEIs for business and public service purposes.

Corporate design is also an important instrument for gathering an organization's employees around common qualities of the firm, since the slogan, logo, architecture and office layout are the main artefacts that express a corporation's common values (De Chernatony, Cottam, and Segal-Horn, 2006). These also indicate the leadership and professionalism quality of the organization which are its most appealing aspects for prospective students, investors, suppliers, and governmental organizations (Melewar and Karaosmanoglu, 2006; Cornelissen, 2017). HEIs should be very selective in the choice of design elements in order to distinguish themselves from their equivalents. They should consistently emphasize their visual identity elements in all the communication materials they use while interacting with their relevant audiences. A very effective approach could be increasing possession of merchandise with their universities' visual identifiers by their staff and students, and admirers who would like to be a part of this educational culture.

The other valuable assets of the organizational/management communication of an organization are its founder and top managers (Melewar and Karaosmanoglu, 2006). The vision they exert publicly shows the leadership and structural strength of the organization so that business partners start considering it a very reputable organization to work with (Cornelissen, 2017). It also gives pride to current employees so that they identify with the corporate identity of the organization they work for (Saurombe, Barkhuizen, and Schutte, 2017). The public appearances and speeches given by the rector, vice-rectors and heads of the major research centres may inspire business collaborators, funders, academicians, administrative staff and current and prospective students who are or want to be part of such vision and culture.

Lastly, how an organization behaves in the public sphere and supports social causes influences its image in the eyes of its current and prospective employees and society at large (Turban and Greening, 1997). Corporate social responsibility (CSR) literature provides evidence that corporations' collaborations with non-profit organizations for social and environmental issues that require immediate action to reduce their threat to society's well-being are highly regarded by current and prospective employees (Lii and Lee, 2012). Such behaviours of organizations are important for keeping and attracting better talents. HEIs are expected to contribute to society not only by producing research that serves social and economic welfare, but also by partnering with non-profit organizations. Especially they should encourage their students to be aware of social issues and take active role in the causes that the HEI supports.

Marketing communications and branding in higher education

Brand messages are communicated mainly through corporate communications and marketing communications. In corporate communications, a company sends messages on its overall business practices and philosophies, whereas in marketing communications, product/service brand messages are administered, seeking consistency and coherence in order to build enduring relationships between the brands of an organization and their targeted audiences (Duncan and Moriarty, 1998).

All messages in communications need to be translated into symbols that are embodied in visual identity, products/services, societal behaviours of organizations, promotional activities, and materials (Hatch and Schultz, 1997) and should convey the intended meaning of an organization's and its brands' identities (Blythe, 2006). Since these outward expressions are translated by various audiences (e.g. customers, suppliers, regulators, investors and so on), these different audiences hold different external images about the organization (i.e. corporate image) and its brands (i.e. brand images). Marketing communications address this challenge of differing images and, hence, deal with activities that need to be coherent and consistent over time to achieve the highest communication impact about corporate identity at product and services level (Keller, 2009).

Marketing communications help external audiences learn about a product's maker, what it stands for (i.e. corporate identity) (Van Riel and Balmer, 1997; Balmer, 2001, 2011), and what its brands promise so that marketing communications can generate brand and product preferences and form the desire to make a purchase (Busch, Seidenspinner, and Unger, 2007). In other words, marketing communication is the united term for all communication elements used for promoting products/services with the purpose of adding convincing value to them for customers (Kitchen and De Pelsmacker, 2004).

According to Batra and Keller (2017), marketing communications result in higher brand awareness, association, and salience by conveying detailed information about the brand, its benefits, and performance, and also by establishing imagery and personality for the brand so that consumers can relate and develop relationships with it. Along with these outcomes, marketing communications help in building trust, eliciting emotions, inspiring action, instilling loyalty, and connecting with people (Batra and Keller, 2016).

Sevier (1999) has indicated that integrated marketing is a relatively new concept in higher education and it should be treated as a strategic asset so that not only the integration of the '4Ps' of the marketing mix (product, place, price and promotion) but also the integration of marketing communications as a function of the last P (promotion) should be strategically planned and executed. This is in line with Schultz and Schultz (2004) who suggest that integrated marketing communications (IMC) drive brand communication programs, not just promotion programs, as a strategic business process.

Porcu, del Barrio-Garcia, and Kitchen (2012) assert that IMC is the achievement and maintenance of a unique image and positioning with clear delivery of coherent messages through online and offline marketing communication tools that are geared towards interactivity to achieve long-term relationships. To be effective, IMC should be implemented both at tactical and strategic levels to support an organization's brand. Departments of marketing and communication in higher education institutions should take on formal and informal contact efforts in order for integrated marketing communications to be useful (Edmiston-Strasser, 2009).

Marketers are confronted with how to use communication tools in order to deliver their messages effectively and efficiently. Belch and Belch (2009) assert that finding the right combination of IMC tools and techniques, delineating their roles and use, and coordinating them will increase the success of institutions. Similarly, Ivy (2008) states that universities should use all communication tools to provide their markets with information on their offerings.

The traditional non-personal communication tools are used for managing image and building brands where the message is transmitted indirectly using TV advertising, event sponsorship, sales promotion, etc. (Kitchen and De Pelsmacker, 2004). On the other hand, personal communication is used for creating a rapid response and/or transaction and, also, for managing sales, service and customers by delivering the message directly (Dahlen, Lange, and Smith, 2010). Direct marketing helps to create and maintain a relation and ongoing dialogue with precisely targeted audiences (Dahlen *et al.*, 2010) and involves many activities such as database management, direct selling, telemarketing, and direct response ads through direct mail (Belch and Belch, 2018). The higher education institutions apply these traditional communication activities in order to attract best talents and minds. They open stands in major education fairs, send brochures to prospects' addresses, organize 'open days' on their main campuses and make their academic staff from different disciplines available for the prospective students' queries about the degrees offered. Higher education institutes also keep an alumni database in order to have life-long bonds with them so that the alumni act as brand ambassadors. Alumni are useful sources of promotion whereby publication of past students' careers and progression since leaving university can be advertised (Moogan, 2011). Although advertising is a principle element for image creation (Meenaghan, 1995) and can be utilized to create brand images and symbolic appeals for institutions (Belch and Belch, 2018), Schüller and Rasticová (2011) have reported that traditional forms of advertising are the least attractive sources of information for university prospects due to their overly commercial content (Lauer, 2007). On the other hand, the university's website, open days, fliers and fairs are more influential in the decision-making process of prospective students. Visits from admissions and faculty for campus open houses or high school assemblies provide a personal touch for prospective students (Berger and Wallingford, 1997).

Although these conventional methods are still viable communications means, interactive marketing elements have achieved a striking importance in promotional mix activities (Cowles and Kiecker, 1998; Belch and Belch, 2018). In recent years, due to intensive technological advancements and disintegration of traditional advertising media, different options for marketing communications in the form social media, websites, display ads, search ads, email, etc. are becoming overly important (Keller, 2001; Batra and Keller, 2016; Belch and Belch, 2018). There is a need to combine traditional and interactive activities in marketing communications, since they bring higher ease-of-reach and one-to-one communication opportunities with individuals in real-time that is cultivated by consumers' online search activities and social network interactions (Schultz, Macdonald, and Baines, 2012).

Batra and Keller (2016) suggest that a wide range of alternatives in online communication options help companies to offer targeted information and engage customers with their special interests and behaviours. Since university students use various digital screens, such as smart phones, desktop devices, tablets, laptops and other mobile devices (Harris and Rea, 2009), they have a higher tendency to search the Internet to be informed about specific topics, including university rankings, reputations, etc. (Royo-Vela and Hünermund, 2016). Sponsored search advertising can more easily target prospects who spend more effort with less popular keywords in their search (Batra and Keller, 2016) and, hence, can bring higher visibility to higher education institutions (Ramos and Cota, 2008; Shih, Chen, and Chen, 2013). Click-through rates and conversation rates are increased by achieving higher places on paid ad lists as well as by good use of display ads. The application of these new advertising methods by higher education institutions may yield almost 10 per cent more website visits (Batra and Keller, 2017).

Websites are used as the primary means for searching for information on what higher education institutions to attend (Moogan, 2011; Saichaie and Morphew, 2014). Websites deliver the message of a higher education institution's purpose, and enable prospective students to look at what one higher education institute offers that is better than the rest (Saichaie and Morphew, 2014). Gomes and Murphy (2003) indicate that students look into more customized content on university websites. Prospective students are more likely to be attentive to personalized emails (Batra and Keller, 2016) so that, for higher education institutions, use of targeted emails become vital.

Social media presence aids universities' contacts and relationships with various stakeholders by providing an interactive communication environment that reduces information asymmetry and increases engagement and sharing (Kietzmann *et al.*, 2011; Nevzat *et al.*, 2016) which results in greater brand trust (Laroche, Habibi, and Richard, 2013; Nevzat *et al.*, 2016). Peruta and Shields (2018) cite Barnes and Mattson's works indicating that 90 per cent of higher education admissions offices rely on social media for their recruiting programs. Peruta and Shields' (2017) findings highlight that a presence in Facebook helps higher education institutions to maintain strong identification with their alumni and the community and to engage current students. Rutter, Roper, and Lettice (2016) posit that Twitter provides a good opportunity for higher education institutions to signal student recruitment success in the number of followers. However, it should be noted by universities that when institutions have more than one social media venue, it is important to evaluate the differences across platforms in order to create a consistent and coherent institutional image (Batra and Keller, 2016).

Uncontrolled communication and branding in higher education

Corporate brand communication aims to create a holistic impression of an organization's corporate brand in the minds of its stakeholders (Balmer, 2001) so that it can achieve a distinctive positioning in the market (Harris and de Chernatony, 2001). The value propositions of corporate brands are based on the sense-making of organizational members about what they represent, i.e. corporate identity, which is nurtured by the organizational culture (Hatch and Schultz, 2003). Organizations communicate those values by fabricated and deliberately designed and orchestrated communication activities (controlled corporate communication). However, especially as the notion of Service-Dominant-Logic reveals (Vargo and Lusch, 2004; Merz, He, and Vargo, 2009), all of the stakeholders of an organization co-create brand value since value emerges as long as the beholder perceives it, and that perception is influenced by all stakeholders. All members in the relationship network of a corporate brand interact with each other, resulting in a situation in which not only internal-internal and internal-external interactions but also external-external interactions influence one another's sense-making of corporate brand promises (Dean et al., 2016; Hatch and Schultz, 2010; Merz et al., 2009).

Research on brand communities has demonstrated that brand meanings and hence brand values are co-created by dynamic social processes that occur during negotiations, symbolic meaning interpretations, and personal experience exchanges within brand communities (Muñiz and O'Guinn, 2001; Muñiz and Schau, 2005). Moreover, brand community researchers (e.g. Godwin-Jones, 2005; Gregory, 2007; Ind and Bjerke, 2007) have argued that such social processes not only occur among members but also among non-members or non-customers, so corporate brand co-creation should take a 'bazaar approach ... where every member is a natural partner in a collective process of product and brand development' (Ind and Bjerke, 2007, p. 140). These intra-brand community-member and inter-non-member relationships bring about notions of negotiated brands (Gregory, 2007) and the corporate community (Halal, 2000), so organizations need to develop processes of dialogue and negotiation that are responsive to stakeholders' input (Merz et al., 2009). Even though such interactions cannot be fully controlled as management and organizational and marketing communication activities designed by the organizations, through the management of response mechanisms, their feedback can be integrated into the re-design of former activities. Since services are consumed through communications, experiences, and activities in a holistic manner (Finne and Strandvik, 2012), interactions among the players involved in a holistic service experience co-create the value of the brand in the minds of the service receiver (Merz et al., 2009). Consequently, actors working in services are more likely to share feelings and opinions which cannot be fully controlled by the organizations.

Melewar (2003) defines uncontrolled communication as the sending of signals which are not created intentionally or knowingly by a company. Any element of a communication created by sources such as other customers, competitors, or the press which is rooted in a market setting represents an uncontrollable form of communication and the organization has no or little influence over their outcomes (Finne and Strandvik, 2012). In the context of higher education, Melewar et al. (2017) assert that uncontrolled communications are 'signals that are not created deliberately or consciously by the university, and could be created by other external parties to build rewarding relationships with the various stakeholders'

(p. 16). Swanson and Kelley (2001) argue that uncontrolled communications such as non-paid publicity and word-of-mouth have a stronger effect on brand attitudes. Customers base their image of an organization on word-of-mouth, interaction among brand communities, and their own experiences over time (Finne and Strandvik, 2012).

Word-of-mouth (WOM) is an unplanned message which is correspondingly embraced as a part of the overall brand communication of a company (Lindberg-Repo and Gronroos, 1999). WOM is a personal communication of 'unexpected contact' made by friends, associates, neighbours, or family members (Belch and Belch, 2018, p. 28). In a services context, WOM is 'the message about an organization, its credibility and trustworthiness, its way of operating and its services, communicated from one person to another' (Gronroos, 1990, p. 158). University education is an investment product bought only once or twice in a lifetime, and word of mouth is a more powerful tool than mass communication efforts (De Pelsmacker, Geuens, and Van den Bergh, 2013).

For this reason, universities should give audiences 'something to talk about', in other words 'an organized WOM' that is disseminated through the personal networks of universities' stakeholders (De Pelsmacker *et al.*, p. 24). By doing so, a certain buzz can be spread by the power of social media (e.g. Facebook, Twitter, YouTube, or Instagram) which turns traditional WOM into viral 'word-of-mouse' with the speed of a click (Belch and Belch, 2017). Melewar *et al.* (2017) show that social and digital media are a significant communication stage in obtaining an immediate response from communication between students, and that can help the university boost traffic to its website and search rankings.

The other uncontrolled communication tool is non-paid publicity. It involves unexpected messages made by other sources such as print or broadcast stories about the organization or its brands in the media or experts who write about products and services (Belch and Belch, 2017). Negative publicity tends to have a greater influence on consumers than positive publicity (Grace and O'Cass, 2005). Earned media (or free media) are generated by outside bodies such as the media or the public which the organization or the brand did not have to pay for in order to achieve greater exposure; however, it is generated by public relations or publicity efforts or through positive word-of-mouth. With the growth of social media, earned media may become stronger than other owned and paid alternatives so that organizations should focus on getting consumers and the media to share information through tweets and re-tweets on Twitter, posts on Facebook or Instagram, product reviews, blogs, vlogs, video sharing and discussion in online communities (Belch and Belch, 2017).

However, DiFonzo and Bordia (2007) draw attention to the fact that commercial or non-commercial rumours (non-verified information) can be the most difficult problem for organizations. They spread rapidly through social media and blogs and state or imply undesirable or repellent information about the target (Shimp and Andrews, 2013). Higher education institutions should find a social media voice that is tuned for its target audiences so that they can increase the chance of enjoying positive social chatting or conversation among its stakeholders. If they can activate social media influencers who have the potential to add a subtle irony on planned messages of higher education institutions, even though their views stand in opposition to what is actually being expressed in the story (Shimp and Andrews, 2013), they may attract attention and recognition for the organizational and individual brands of a university.

Not only the online influencers, but also the opinion leaders, opinion formers, and followers are major sources for the uncontrolled communication process. Getting them to advocate for the corporate brand may offer some control over the communication process and targeting the right people who will pass along the right message is critical (Copley, 2007). In particular, opinion formers, who are professionals with power and authority (Copley, 2007), such as education councils, high school teachers and counsels, represent good sources for the right messages to be passed along to prospective students. One critical aspect here could be the effect of the integrity and honesty of motivated internal customers (academics, administrative personnel, students, etc.) communicating with external stakeholders (Melewar and Karaosmanoglu, 2006).

3 Managerial implications

The sections above highlight the role of corporate communications in HEIs' brand communication to their stakeholders. In summary, the following could be suggested for HEIs to follow:

First, HEIs should have a managerial approach that provides an environment that is open to interaction and value exchange that nurtures the organizational culture among their members. Commonly shared values help academic and administrative staff to identify with their university and hence help motivate them to produce better research to contribute to society at large. The motivated internal members advocate and promote their institutions favourably to external audiences. Such leadership also signals professionalism to funding bodies, business collaborators and governmental organizations so that HEIs can have external financial support. This could give them a better leverage against their competitors in the higher education industry. The same professional look also attracts better minds to universities and gives the existing ones a reason to stay. The main communication tools for disseminating common organizational values are newsletters, announcement of achievements on websites and official social media accounts, top management speeches and public appearances and visual identifiers. The HEIs' behaviours on social issues are also an influential means of establishing a favourable image and better reputation over time.

Second, marketing communications should be geared so that they can create awareness, association, and salience in higher education as a means of building trust, eliciting emotions, inspiring action, instilling loyalty, and connecting with prospective students, alumni, and other stakeholders through personal and non-personal connections. Since prospective and enrolled students use the websites of HEIs to obtain information, they should be fresh, up-to-date and user friendly. Attracting new students will be easier if links offer new information, including pages about departments, academicians, and student life, along with current news about the HEI, how to apply and so forth. For enrolled students, such websites create a platform that promotes engagement with the university, by means of which news and information can be shared with students and alumni. By taking advantage of the popularity and ease of access to social media, HEIs should also pursue different venues that can render them more visible and easier to access. Since young people often use mobile devices, the utilization of social media applications would create a strong platform for HEIs to connect with prospective and current students. Organizing open days, arranging visits at high schools, attending education fairs, and sending brochures can also be beneficial. While television advertising is generally not seen as an effective means of communication, other forms of paid advertisement, such as billboards or magazines, can be effective. Given the fact that prospective students use search engines to obtain information about HEIs, sponsored search and display advertising could also be a vital means of connecting with them and their families.

Third, and especially, the most suitable and relevant content generation for various social media platforms such as Facebook, Instagram, YouTube, and LinkedIn plays a pivotal role in dealing with the potential harm of uncontrolled communication on the brand positioning of HEIs. A well-managed approach to the use of owned media can help reduce the risk of the creation of negative images and reputations by engaging a broader array of audiences and in that way they can disseminate favourable information about them. The power of digital consumers is influential in terms of how universities can develop brand communities around their corporate image, making it possible for them to identify digital influences that can help in acquiring and stimulating earned brand advocates.

In order to benefit from the capacity of controlled and uncontrolled corporate communications, HEIs should make a paradigm shift that targets corporate marketing, which in turn would make it possible to incorporate a philosophy and communication management roadmap aiming for a sound and successful higher education brand. The corporate marketing view suggests that marketing should take on a strategic and organization-wide role. In light of that, universities should maintain a stakeholder-based view and see every relevant audience as being a strategic partner. In addition, a corporate-wide philosophy should be manifest in all communications. Such efforts should have the ultimate aim of establishing and maintaining positive relationships with prospective and current customers, as well as stakeholders and society at large (Balmer, 2001, 2011; Balmer and Greyser, 2006).

In particular, a corporate communication strategy for HEIs within the realm of corporate marketing should involve a process that positions the various views of the stakeholders of an HEI in line with the University's mission and vision. Accordingly, the corporate communication practitioners involved with HEIs should design, plan, and implement communication programmes that include staff-stakeholder interactions, outreach activities, and community initiatives. Such programmes should start off by stating the strategic intent of the HEI's brand positioning and then the HEI should define specific communication objectives that target particular stakeholder groups (e.g. employees, currently enrolled students, alumni, funding bodies, and prospective students). In line with the strategic intent that has been specified, messages should be created that appeal to stakeholders as a means of generating a supportive view or behaviour regarding the HEI's corporate and individual brands after identifying and prioritizing target audiences. The following step should involve the participation of media activities that are relevant to those targeted groups so that alternative offline or online tools can deliver the intended meaning of the HEI's brands. Lastly, a budget should be drawn up and the effectiveness of programmes should be assessed on the basis of the prospective return on investments (Cornelissen, 2017).

4 Conclusion

This chapter has discussed corporate communications and two major sub-areas of controlled and uncontrolled communications via reflections on higher education brands. In particular, it addressed the role of managerial/organizational communications, marketing communications, and the role of interactions among different stakeholders, offline and online, in HEI brand positioning. It stressed that the mission and vision of HEIs are the central pillars to building a favourable corporate identity. This chapter makes the claim that HEI managers should create an environment that supports academic and administrative staff in their internalization of the core corporate brand values that are manifest in mission and vision statements, which would also be effective in delivering and representing those values to external stakeholders such as students, alumni, government representatives, businesses, investors, the public and non-profit organizations. This chapter also emphasizes the notion that the tools of conventional and digital marketing communications should be integrated so that they can result in the efficient and effective reflection of core corporate brand values on the individual services and degrees that an HEI offers. In addition, this chapter draws attention to the potentially harmful impacts of earned media on HEI brand positioning brought about by improper management of owned media, concluding with the recommendation that HEIs should shift to an understanding of corporate marketing that offers a managerial philosophy for corporate brand management and suggesting that a process of planning communication programmes and campaigns be implemented for HEIs.

Further studies in this field could address some of the following issues in order to improve our understanding of brand communications in the sector of higher education. The majority of earlier studies on brand communications about HEIs focus on how to attract prospective students or alumni relationships. For that reason, we need to better understand how various audiences aside from prospective students and graduates construct the brand meanings of HEIs at the corporate and individual levels. In addition, other research could focus on the medium and content of brand messages, as well as their interactions in terms of persuasion. Yet other research could focus on the antecedents of brand value co-creation and co-destruction within the context of HEIs; even though those concepts have been recently examined (primarily in service failure studies), to date little work has been done regarding the higher education sector. Furthermore, an engaging line of approach could take up the issue ethnographically and try to examine how interactions among individual-initiated brand communities are beneficial in developing the meanings of HEI brands and how social media leverages or hinders their position in the market.

5 Case study – Bahçeşehir University

Best education brand in Turkey and best in 500 big service exporters in education

The Bahçeşehir-Ugur Education Foundation was first established as a university exam preparation centre in Istanbul in 1968. Today, it runs over 35 primary schools, 18 high schools, 47 kindergartens, 177 special education centres and 16 preparation high schools in Turkey, employing over 5,000 teachers (and it also includes 100 Bahçeşehir high schools and 126 Ugur schools as franchises).

Bahçeşehir University (now called BAU Global Network) was established as part of the Bahçeşehir-Ugur Education Foundation in Bahçeşehir, Istanbul in 1998 with four departments. Although it first started as a local higher education institution, after signing an academic collaboration agreement with San Diego State University in 1998, it started to become a global player. Today, it operates a global network of five universities, four language schools and three BAU Global Centers on three continents (North America, Europe, and Asia). With programs of study in major fields such as architecture, art, business, design, education, engineering, information technologies, law, health sciences, and medicine, it offers many degrees at the undergraduate, graduate and PhD levels.

Table 6.1 The main global establishments of Bahcesehir University

University campuses	Language schools	Global centers

1 BAU Cyprus
2 BAU Istanbul
   a North Campus
   b South Campus
   c Galata Campus
   d Goztepe Campus
3 BAU International University Batumi
4 BAU International University Washington D. C.
5 BAU International Berlin – University of Applied Sciences
	• Fulford Academy – Ontario
	• CES Toronto and CES Junior Summer Schools
	• Mentora Sprachschule
	• Mentora College
	• BAU Global Cologne
		• BAU Global Silicon Valley Incubation Center
		• International Academy of Rome
		• BAU Global Hong Kong

Looking at BAU's vision and mission

VISION: As a higher education institution dedicated to teaching, research, and service to our society, the mission of Bahçeşehir University is to educate the leading work force of future who will have an inquiring mind and a critical thinking ability; who will be sensitive to local and global issues; achieve international standards; contribute to scientific, technological, and cultural knowledge; and be strong supporters of universal ideas and values.

MISSION: BAU Global expects to be the leading force regionally and nationally in the enhancement of knowledge. BAU Global aims to educate students who are committed to promoting respect for the rights of others, who are considerate and appreciative of human differences, and of the constructive expression of ideas. https://bauglobal.com/vision-mission/

The founder of this network, Mr. Enver Yucel states:

> Having recognized the importance of being a global citizen, we have institutionalized our international programs and partnerships and today we encourage our students to study at least one of their semesters abroad. BAU students are also able to explore their areas of study in any of our eight global centres and campuses – Berlin, Hong Kong, Toronto, Washington DC, Boston, Silicon Valley, Rome, and Baku. Through our academic partnerships with universities and foundations worldwide, BAU students are exposed to and equipped with the skills and knowledge needed for today's increasingly multinational and multicultural business world fulfilling the needs of both the global and domestic workplace. With the support of our talented and devoted faculty members, who have dedicated themselves to their students' educational success, and our world-class curriculum that combines classroom education with relevant extracurricular activities and internship opportunities, students at BAU are uniquely prepared for their future careers.

Table 6.2

BAU Istanbul in numbers and honours
- 9 faculties, 1 language school and 2 vocational schools
- 4 graduate schools
- 27,210 students
    - 17,487 undergraduate students
    - 8,405 graduate students
    - 1,318 vocational school students
- 1,047 faculty members
- 506 administrative personnel
- Collaboration with 193 different universities in 36 countries
- In 2017, granted the awards of 'Best Education Brand in Turkey' and 'Best in 500 Big Service Exporters in Education'
- Only higher education brand that has received the TURQUALITY Export Support of the Turkish State

Corporate communications management

Bahçeşehir University has a corporate communications department that handles all communications with various public entities. A number of coordinators are responsible for disseminating news to a broad array of recipients, ranging from students to the media:

- Corporate Communications Director
- Media Relations Director
- Student Resources and Publicity Director
- Publicity Coordinator – Istanbul
- Publicity Coordinator – Anatolia
- Apply BAU Representative
- Organizations Coordinator
- Sound and Vision Systems Coordinator
- Digital Media and Web Coordinator
- Graduate Program Coordinator
- Agency Tasks Coordinator

The corporate communication department informs academic and administrative personnel about upcoming events, as well as the university's achievements, via email.

Corporate behaviour

BAU is also very active in terms of student activities. The BAU Dean of Students' Office oversees a wide range of student clubs, including the Social Responsibility Club and the BiSoluk Café. The latter, which was founded by a BAU student with the sole aim of funding social causes, provides a venue for students to sell baked foods, stationery, and school apparel. Some of the other clubs are dedicated to matters such as economics, finance and sports, and BAU supports campaigns by collecting books, clothes, stationery and the like for schools in disadvantaged areas of Anatolia.

Controlled communication tools

CEO AS A SPOKESPERSON

Enver Yucel is a leading figure in Bahçeşehir University's communication efforts. News about his accomplishments and the awards he receives is communicated via his private account and the university's accounts on social media, as well as the university's website, billboards, magazines, newspapers and within the institute by e-mail.

STAKEHOLDER ENGAGEMENT

BAU created awareness by organizing 'Society Academy' to inform parents of prospective students about the professions during its first years. These meetings are held throughout the country and inform millions of prospective students not only about the structure of the university, but also about how different occupations bring value to a prospective student's life.

Co-op is a cooperative education program that draws together business and university worlds, where students benefit either by enrolling in a branded course as an elective course or through internship. BAU has more than 30 branded courses in different departments where a business gives its name to the course, i.e. IBM 'Big Data and Analytics', Samsung 'Advanced Developing Application for Android Devices', 'Financial Analysis with Bloomberg'. Co-op also provides internship opportunities for students in line with the needs of its partner corporations. While the students get an opportunity for practical feedback and on-the-job experience via the help of internships offered by Co-op Office partner organizations, with the help of *Reverse mentoring*, Co-op Office partners also get insights into the world of Y generation students. Both the university and the businesses benefit from this reciprocal mentoring opportunity in their understanding of their internal and external customers.

VISUAL IDENTITY

The University's visual identity is portrayed consistently throughout all its printed and broadcast materials. Its logo uses an academic navy colour and rays which represent the broad scope of disciplines, the enlightening power of education, and its vision of global expansion. The university's name appears under the logo with a softer typography.

ADVERTISING

Bahçeşehir University periodically uses advertising to promote its programs, especially before university entrance exams and student registration. Newspapers, billboards, and magazines are the traditional means of advertising that Bahçeşehir prefers to use. Brochures, leaflets and catalogues are also used not only in printed format but also digitally on the university's main website.

WEBSITE

The website of Bahçeşehir University not only focuses on enrolled students but also provides links for prospective students. Every department, both academic and non-academic, has its own page and content and the design is similar for each. The departments are responsible for maintaining and updating the content on their pages. The university also offers intranet services by means of which students and academic faculty members can interact. Through the intranet, students can also see their transcripts, class schedules, and course materials, and faculty members can share course materials and use the platform for communicating with students. Faculty members can also use this platform to see and check on the enrolment status of students and schedule the courses offered by the university.

ApplyBAU is a platform on the BAU official website by means of which prospective students can apply for scholarships by writing about their backgrounds and accomplishments; each department evaluates the applications and grants scholarships accordingly. Outstanding applicants are called in for interviews.

PUBLICITY VIA OPEN DAYS AND FAIRS

BAU also attends leading education fairs, not only in Turkey, but in other countries as well. It welcomes high schools for visits and provides information on campus life and university overall not only in open days but also by appointment. Another form of publicity used by BAU is to visit high schools either by appointment or upon request. Either way, BAU attempts to understand the needs of the students and bring them into interaction with academics or alumni according to their field of interest.

SOCIAL MEDIA ACCOUNTS FOR DIFFERENT DEPARTMENTS

The university uses social media effectively. In particular, Twitter is utilized as a medium for immediate news dissemination and students and Bahçeşehir affiliates are kept up to date with postings. Notably, Enver Yucel has more followers than the university's official account and he often provides information before the university makes announcements. He also corresponds with enrolled and prospective students, faculty members and anyone else who contacts him via Twitter. In addition, deans, department heads and departments also have official Twitter accounts, by means of which they post news about the university and current issues. Announcements are made via Twitter before they are published on the website. Instagram is also utilized by the university and its departments as well as by the founder, but it is not used very actively and there are far fewer followers than on Twitter. There are also pages on Facebook for the various departments, but again they are not used as much as Twitter. The BAU Alumni Department is responsible for relations with alumni and it is active on Twitter, Facebook and Instagram.

Overall view of corporate communication in BAU

As illustrated above, BAU has an understanding of corporate marketing, which embraces the notion of blending institutional strategy with its corporate and individual brand communication. Accordingly, it assigns responsibility to a specific corporate communications department which has experts as managers of controlled and uncontrolled communication areas. It integrates its main stance (i.e. corporate identity) in the higher education business sphere into its corporate and individual brands. It also recognizes the fact that multiple audiences are stakeholders of BAU so that constant, consistent, responsive, mutually beneficial, and timely communication via conventional and digital communication media is the key for a successful global higher education brand.

6 Further investigation

It would be beneficial for students to explore further the following issues in order to internalize how corporate and uncontrolled communication should be managed by higher institution organizations:

1. Discuss how stakeholder theory could provide a framework for higher education institutions for detecting opportunities and challenges regarding the communication of their corporate brands to different stakeholders.
2. Identify further what skills the corporate communication managers in higher education institutions should have. How could they blend the role of communication practitioner and communication strategy developer and executer?
3. Discuss how the model for planning brand communication programmes and campaigns may help in developing more effective communication.
4. Pick one public and one private university and compare their corporate brands' main values to BAU. Analyse how these three higher education brands reflect their core values to their owned media (i.e. website, mobile site, mobile application, official social media accounts and so on).
5. Discuss how generation Y would respond to higher education institutions in offline and online communication contexts. Which of their specific characteristics may have an influence on their potential positive and negative responses?

References

Ashfort, B. E. and Mael, F. (1989) "Social identity theory and the organisation." *Academy of Management Review* 14(1), pp. 20–39.

Balmer, J. M. T. (1998) "Corporate identity and the advent of corporate marketing." *Journal of Marketing Management* 14(8), pp. 963–996.

Balmer, J. M. T. (2001) "Corporate identity, corporate branding and corporate marketing: Seeing through the fog." *European Journal of Marketing* 33(3/4), pp. 248–291.

Balmer, J. M. T. (2011) "Corporate marketing myopia and the inexorable rise of a corporate marketing logic: Perspectives from identity-based views of the firm." *European Journal of Marketing* 45(9/10), pp. 1329–1352.

Balmer, J. M. T. and Gray, E. R. (2003) "Corporate brands: What are they? What of them?" *European Journal of Marketing* 37(7/8), pp. 972–997.

Balmer, J. M. T. and Greyser, S. A. (2006) "Corporate marketing: Integrating corporate identity, corporate branding, corporate communications, corporate image and corporate reputation." *European Journal of Marketing* 40(7/8), pp. 730–741.

Balmer, J. M. T. and Liao, M.-N. (2007) "Student corporate brand identification: An exploratory case study." *Corporate Communications: An International Journal* 12(4), pp. 356–375.

Barrett, L. R. (1996) "On students as customers – Some warnings from America." *Higher Education Review* 28(3), pp. 70–71.

Batra, R. and Keller, K. L. (2017) "Integrating marketing communications: New findings, new lessons, and new ideas." *Journal of Marketing*: AMA/MSI Special Issue 80(November), pp. 122–145.

Belch, G. E. and Belch, M. A. (2018) *Advertising and Promotion: An Integrated Marketing Communications Perspective* (11th edition). New York, NY: McGraw-Hill International Edition.

Berger, K. A. and Wallingford, H. P. (1997) "Developing advertising and promotion strategies for higher education." *Journal of Marketing for Higher Education* 7(4), pp. 61–72.

Blythe, J. (2006) *The Essentials of Marketing Communications* (3rd edition). Essex, UK: Pearson Hall.

Busch, R., Seidenspinner, M., and Unger F. (2007) *Marketing Communication Policies*. Heidelberg: Springer.

Caruana, A., Ramaseshan, B., and Ewing, M. T. (1998) "Do universities that are more market orientated perform better?" *International Journal of Public Sector Management* 11(1), pp. 55–70.

Cassidy, R. (2013) "The role of brand orientation in the higher education sector: A student-perceived paradigm." *Asia Pacific Journal of Marketing and Logistics* 25(5), pp. 803–820.

Chapleo, C. (2010) "What defines 'successful' university brands?" *International Journal of Public Sector Management* 23(2), pp. 169–183.

Copley, J. (2007) "Audio and video podcasts of lectures for campus-based students: Production and evaluation of student use." *Innovations in Education and Teaching International* 44(4), pp. 387–399.

Cornelissen, J. (2017) *Corporate Communication: A Guide to Theory and Practice* (5th edition). London: Sage Publications.

Cowles, D. L. and Kiecker, P. (1998) "Reconceptualizing the promotional mix: The challenge of a changing marketing communications environment." *American Marketing Association. Conference Proceedings*; 9, ProQuest Central, pp. 15–25.

Dahlen, M., Lange, F., and Smith, T. (2010) *Marketing Communication: A Brand Narrative Approach*. Sussex, UK: John Wiley & Sons.

Dean, D., Arroyo-Gamez, R. E., Punjaisric, K., and Pich, C. (2016) "Internal brand co-creation: The experiential brand meaning cycle in higher education." *Journal of Business Research* 69(8), pp. 3041–3048.

De Chernatony, L. (2001) "A model for strategically building brands." *Journal of Brand Management* 9(1), pp. 32–44.

De Chernatony, L., Cottam, S., and Segal-Horn, S. (2006) "Communicating services brands' values internally and externally." *Service Industries Journal* 26(8), pp. 819–836.

De Pelsmacker, P., Geuens, M., and Van den Bergh, J. (2013) *Marketing Communications*. London: Pearson.

DiFonzo, N. and Bordia, P. (2007) "Rumor, gossip and urban legends." *Diogenes* 54(1), pp. 19–35.

Dowling, G. R. (1993) "Developing your company image into a corporate asset." *Long Range Planning* 26(2), pp. 101–109.

Downey, G. L. (1986) "Ideology and the clamshell identity: Organizational dilemmas in the anti-nuclear power movement." *Social Problems* 33(5), pp. 357–373.

Duncan, T. and Moriarty, S. E. (1998) "A communication-based marketing model for managing relationships." *Journal of Marketing* 62(2), pp. 1–13.

Dutton, J. E., Dukerich, J. M., and Harquail, C. V. (1994) "Organizational images and member identification." *Administrative Science Quarterly* 39(2), pp. 239–263.

Edmiston-Strasser, D. M. (2009) "An examination of integrated marketing communication in U.S. public institutions of higher education." *Journal of Marketing for Higher Education* 19(2), pp. 142–165.

Eggins, H. (2007) *The Changing Academic Profession: Implications for The Asia Pacific Region*. Hangzhou, China: UNESCO Forum on Higher Education, Research and Knowledge.

Finne, Å. and Strandvik, T. (2012) "Invisible communication: A challenge to established marketing communication." *European Business Review* 24(2), pp. 120–133.

Gelb, B. D. and Rangarajan, D. (2014) "Employee contributions to brand equity." *California Management Review* 56(2), pp. 95–112.

Gioia, D. and Patvardhan, S. (2012) "Identity as process and flow," in M. Schultz, S. Maguire, A. Langley, and H. Tsoukas (eds), *Constructing Identity an and Around Organizations*. Oxford: Oxford University Press, pp. 50–62.

Gioia, D. A., Schultz, M., and Corley, K. G. (2000) "Organisational identity, image and adaptive instability." *Academy of Management Review* 25(1), pp. 63–81.

Godwin-Jones, R. (2005) "Messaging, gaming, peer-to-peer sharing: Language learning strategies & tools for the millennial generation." *Language Learning and Technology* 9(1), pp. 17–22.

Gomes, L. and Murphy, J. (2003) "An exploratory study of marketing international education online." *International Journal of Educational Management*, 17(3), pp. 116–125.

Grace, D. and O'Cass, A. (2005) "Examining the effects of service brand communications on brand evaluation." *Journal of Product & Brand Management* 14(2), pp. 106–116.

Gregory, A. (2007) "Involving stakeholders in developing corporate brands: The communication dimension." *Journal of Marketing Management* 23(1/2), pp. 59–73.

Gromark, J. and Melin, F. (2013) "From market orientation to brand orientation in the public sector." *Journal of Marketing Management* 29(9/10), pp. 1099–1123.

Gronroos, C. (1990) "Relationship approach to marketing in service contexts: The marketing and organizational behavior interface." *Journal of Business Research*, 20(1), pp. 3–11.

Grunig, J. E. (1993) "Image and substance: From symbolic to behavioral relationships." *Public Relations Review* 19(2), pp. 121–139.

Halal, W. E. (2000) "Corporate community: A theory of the firm uniting profitability and responsibility." *Strategy & Leadership* 28(2), pp. 10–16.

Harris, A. L. and Rea, A. (2009) "Web 2.0 and virtual world technologies: A growing impact on IS education." *Journal of Information Systems Education* 20(2), pp. 137–144.

Harris, F. and De Chernatony, L. (2001) "Corporate branding and corporate brand performance." *European Journal of Marketing* 35(3/4), pp. 441–456.

Hatch, M. J. and Schultz, M. (1997) "Relations between organisational culture identity and image." *European Journal of Marketing* 31(3/5), pp. 356–365.

Hatch, M. J. and Schultz, M. (2002) "The dynamics of organizational identity." *Human Relations* 55(8), pp. 989–1018.

Hatch, M. J. and Schultz, M. (2003) "Bringing the corporation into corporate branding." *European Journal of Marketing* 37(7/8), pp. 1041–1064.

Hatch, M. J. and Schultz, M. (2010) "Toward a theory of brand co-creation with implications for brand governance." *Journal of Brand Management* 17(8), pp. 590–604.

Hemsley-Brown, J. and Goonawardana, S. (2007) "Brand harmonization in the international higher education market." *Journal of Business Research* 60(9), pp. 942–948.

Hemsley-Brown, J. and Oplatka, I. (2006) "Universities in a competitive global marketplace: A systematic review of the literature on higher education marketing." *International Journal of Public Sector Management* 19(4), pp. 316–338.

Ind, N. and Bjerke, R. (2007) "The concept of participatory market orientation: An organisation-wide approach to enhancing brand equity." *Journal of Brand Management* 15(2), pp. 135–145.

Ivy, J. (2008) "A new higher education marketing mix: The 7Ps for MBA marketing." *International Journal of Educational Management* 22(4), pp. 288–299.

Karaosmanoglu, E. and Melewar, T C (2006) "Corporate communications, identity and image: A research agenda." *Journal of Brand Management* 14(1–2), pp. 196–206.

Keller, K. L. (2001) "Mastering the marketing communications mix: Micro and macro perspectives on integrated marketing communication programs." *Journal of Marketing Management* 17(7–8), pp. 819–847.

Keller, K. L. (2009) "Building strong brands in a modern marketing communications environment." *Journal of Marketing Communications* 15(2–3), pp. 139–155.

Khanna, M., Jacob, I., and Yadav, N. (2014) "Identifying and analyzing touchpoints for building a higher education brand." *Journal of Marketing for Higher Education* 24(1), pp. 122–143.

Kietzmann, J. H., Hermkens, K., McCarthy, I. P., and Silvestre, B. S. (2011) "Social media? Get serious! Understanding the functional building blocks of social media." *Business Horizons* 54(3), pp. 241–251.

Kinser, K. (2006) "From Main Street to Wall Street: For-profit higher education." *ASHE Higher Education Report* 31(5), pp. 1–155.

Kiriakidou, O. and Millward, L. J. (2000) "Corporate identity: External reality or internal fit." *Corporate Communications: An International Journal* (5)1, pp. 49–58.
Kitchen, P. J. and De Pelsmacker, P. (2004) *Integrated Marketing Communications: A Primer*. Oxford and New York: Routledge Taylor and Francis.
Laroche, M., Habibi, M. R., and Richard, M. O. (2013) "To be or not to be in social media: How brand loyalty is affected by social media?" *International Journal of Information Management* 33(1), pp. 76–82.
Lauer, L. D. (2007) "Advertising can be an effective integrated marketing tool." *Journal of Marketing for Higher Education* 17(1), pp. 13–15.
Lindberg-Repo, K. and Grönroos, C. (1999) "Word-of-mouth referrals in the domain of relationship marketing." *Australasian Marketing Journal* (AMJ), Vol. 7(1), pp. 109–117.
Lii, Y. S. and Lee, M. (2012) "Doing right leads to doing well: When the type of CSR and reputation interact to affect consumer evaluations of the firm." *Journal of Business Ethics* 105(1), pp. 69–81.
Lowrie, A. (2007) "Branding higher education: Equivalence and difference in developing identity." *Journal of Business Research* 60(9), pp. 990–999.
Maringe, F. (2006) "University and course choice: Implications for positioning, recruitment and marketing." *International Journal of Educational Management* 20(6), pp. 466–479.
Meenaghan, T. (1995) "The role of advertising in brand image development." *Journal of Product and Brand Management* 4(4), pp. 23–34.
Melewar, T C (2003) "Determinants of the corporate identity construct: A review of the literature." *Journal of Marketing Communications* 9(4), pp. 195–220.
Melewar, T C, Foroudi, P., Dinnie, K., and Nguyen, B. (2018) "The role of corporate identity management in the higher education sector: An exploratory case study." *Journal of Marketing Communications* Vol. 24(4), pp. 337–359.
Melewar, T C and Karaosmanoglu, E. (2006) "Seven dimensions of corporate identity: A categorisation from the practitioners' perspectives." *European Journal of Marketing* 40(7/8), pp. 846–869.
Merz, M. A., He, Yi, and Vargo, S. L. (2009) "The evolving brand logic: A service-dominant logic perspective." *Journal of the Academy of Marketing Science* 37(3), pp. 328–344.
Moogan, Y. J. (2011) "Can a higher education institution's marketing strategy improve the student-institution match?" *International Journal of Educational Management* 25(6), pp. 570–589.
Muñiz, A. M. and O'Guinn Jr, T. C. (2001) "Brand community." *Journal of Consumer Research* 27(4), pp. 412–432.
Muñiz, A. M. and Schau, Jr, H. J. (2005) "Religiosity in the abandoned Apple Newton brand community." *Journal of Consumer Research* 31(4,) pp. 737–747.
Nevzat, R., Amca, Y., Tanova, C., and Amca, H. (2016) "Role of social media community in strengthening trust and loyalty for a university." *Computers in Human Behavior* 65, pp. 550–559.
Olins, W. (1989) *Corporate Identity: Making Business Strategy Visible through Design*. London: Thames and Hudson.
Peruta, A. and Shields, A. B. (2018) "Marketing your university on social media: A content analysis of facebook post types and formats." *Journal of Marketing for Higher Education* 27(1), pp. 1–17.

Porcu, L., del Barrio-Garcia, S., and Kitchen, P. (2012) "How Integrated Marketing Communications (IMC) works? A theoretical review and an analysis of its main drivers and effects." *Comunicacion Y Sociedad* XXV(1), pp. 313–348.

Pusser, B. (2002) *Higher Education, The Emerging Market and the Public Good.* The Knowledge Economy and the Postsecondary Education: A Workshop Report. Retrieved from www.nap.edu/openbook/0309082927/html/105.html.

Ramos, A. and Cota, S. (2008) *Search Engine Marketing.* New York, NY: McGraw-Hill, Inc.

Royo-Vela, M. and Hünermund, U. (2016) "Effects of inbound marketing communications on HEIs' brand equity: The mediating role of the student's decision-making process. An exploratory research." *Journal of Marketing for Higher Education* 26(2), pp. 143–167.

Rutter, R., Roper, S., and Lettice, F. (2016) "Social media interaction, the university brand and recruitment performance." *Journal of Business Research* 69(8), pp. 3096–3104.

Saichaie, K. and Morphew, C. C. (2014) "What college and university websites reveal about the purposes of higher education." *The Journal of Higher Education* 85(4), pp. 499–530.

Saurombe, M., Barkhuizen, E. N., and Schutte, N. E. (2017) "Management perceptions of a higher educational brand for the attraction of talented academic staff." *SA Journal of Human Resource Management* 15(1), pp. 1–10.

Schüller, D. and Rasticová, M. (2011) "Marketing communications mix of universities-communication with students in an increasing competitive university environment." *Journal of competitiveness* 3(3), pp. 58–71.

Schultz, D. and Kitchen, P. (2004) "Managing the changes in corporate branding and communication: Closing and re-opening the corporate umbrella." *Corporate Reputation Review* 6(4), pp. 347–366.

Schultz, D., Macdonald, E. K., and Baines, P. R. (2012) "Best practice: Integrated marketing communications." *Admap* November, pp. 44–45.

Schultz, D. E. and Schultz, H. F. (2004) *IMC: The Next Generation.* New York: McGraw-Hill.

Sevier, R. A. (1999) *Much Ado about Something: Understanding the Strategic Opportunities Afforded by Integrated Marketing.* Cedar Rapids, IA: Stamats Communications.

Shih, B. Y., Chen, C. Y., and Chen, Z. S. (2013) "An empirical study of an internet marketing strategy for search engine optimization." *Human Factors and Ergonomics in Manufacturing and Service Industries* 23(6), pp. 528–540.

Shimp, T. A. and Andrews, J. C. (2013) *Advertising Promotion and Other Aspects of Integrated Marketing Communications* (9th edition). Mason, USA: South Western Cengage Learning.

Swanson, S. R. and Kelley, S. W. (2001) "Service recovery attributions and word-of-mouth intentions." *European Journal of Marketing* 35(1/2), pp. 194–211.

Thomson, K. and Hecker, L. (2001) "Value-adding communication: Innovation in employee communication and internal marketing." *Journal of Communication Management* 5(1), pp. 48–58.

Turban, D. B. and Greening, D. W. (1997) "Corporate social performance and organizational attractiveness to prospective employees." *Academy of Management Journal* 40(3), pp. 658–672.

Van Riel, C. B. M. (1995) *Principles of Corporate Communication*, Hertfordshire, England: Prentice Hall.
Van Riel, C. B. and Balmer, J. M. T. (1997) "Corporate identity: The concept, its measurement and management." *European Journal of Marketing* 31(5/6), pp. 340–355.
Van Riel, C. B. and Fombrun, C. J. (2007) *Essentials of corporate communication: Implementing practices for effective reputation management.* London: Routledge.
Varey, R. J. and White, J. (2000) "The corporate communication system of managing." *Corporate Communications: An International Journal* 5(1), pp. 5–12.
Vargo, S. L. and Lusch, R. F. (2004) "Evolving to a new dominant logic for marketing." *Journal of Marketing* 68(1), pp. 1–17.
Wæraas, A. and Solbakk, M. N. (2009) "Defining the essence of a university: Lessons from higher education branding." *Higher Education* 57(4), pp. 449–462.
Whisman, R. (2009) "Internal branding: A university's most valuable intangible asset." *Journal of Product & Brand Management* 18(5), pp. 367–370.
Williams Jr, R. L. and Omar, M. (2014) "Brand management to higher education through the use of the Brand Flux Model™ – The case of Arcadia University" *Journal of Marketing for Higher Education* 24(2), pp. 222–242.
Yeshin, T. (1998) *Integrated Marketing Communications.* Oxford, UK: Butterworth-Heinemann.
YOK. (2018). Council of Higher Education in Turkey, www.yok.gov.tr/web/guest/yok-ten-universitelere-kalkinma-cagrisi
Yucel, E. (undated) *Message From the President,* available at https://bauglobal.com/message-from-the-president/ (accessed 4 May 2018).

7 Corporate design
What makes a favourable university logo?

Pantea Foroudi and Bang Nguyen

1 Introduction

Today's environment is more and more visually oriented. The university's logo is a language that communicates to its stakeholders, independent of verbal information (Melewar et al., 2017). The importance of the logo, and particularly the role of corporate and brand logos to create a sustainable competitive advantage, has received the attention of marketing scholars (Foroudi et al., 2014, 2016, 2017; Henderson and Cote, 1998). A well-designed corporate logo will result in a sophisticated corporate image, secure corporate reputation and loyalty, and ultimately increase profits.

Logos are ubiquitous in the marketplace and the average consumer encounters a multitude on any given day (Hagtvedt, 2011). Companies communicate with business, using the elements of their corporate logos to illustrate product differentiation (Henderson and Cote, 1998; Olins, 1989). The main elements that influence a corporate logo are; (1) colour (Bottomley and Doyle, 2006); (2) typeface (Henderson et al., 2004); (3) design and aesthetic appeal (Alessandri, 2001); and (4) corporate name (Leitch and Motion, 1999). So, why is the corporate logo imperative?

The corporate logo is the first and most crucial step in the process of building a company's visual identity (Melewar and Saunders, 1998). Developing a corporate visual identity (CVI) is a process that leads to the revelation of the organisation's corporate identity through the use of visual forms (Van den Bosch et al., 2006). The creation of a corporate visual identity (e.g. logo) is very costly and challenging for the organization (Henderson and Cote, 1998) and managers make every effort to create a favourable corporate logo, which communicates corporate identity in a reliable manner to the market (Van den Bosch et al., 2005).

The corporate logo is the 'heart and soul of a company' (Chajet and Shachtman, 1991, p. 28). The notion of corporate logo is linked to the concept of corporate identity. Researchers (Balmer, 2001; Van den Bosch et al., 2006) assert that the corporate logo is used as a corporate identity's roots, which affect people's judgements and behaviour (Van den Bosch et al., 2006). Corporate identity is defined by Balmer et al. (2007) as: who is the company? (actual identity); who does the company want to be? (desired and ideal identity); how does the company communicate its identity? (communicated identity); how is the company identity conceived by others? (conceived identity); and, how is the company to understand identity as a holistic phenomenon? These five main themes are related to the internal/external nature of a corporation's identity (Balmer et al., 2007). Therefore, there is increasing pressure on organizations to create their corporate logo based on the company's corporate identity and plan their communication strategies carefully. Despite the potentially significant role of the favourable university logo as a university's signature and communication tools, little empirical research has examined how the favourable university logo should be selected and depicted to obtain specific communication and visual objectives.

Chapter 7 considers how corporate design and visual identity influence branding in higher education. The aim is to enable readers to comprehend how universities organize and manage their corporate design and visual identity (in particular the university logo) in different parts of the organization. Furthermore, the chapter presents important aspects of decision making processes, influencing stakeholders' perceptions towards visual identity in higher education branding. Theories on corporate design and visual identity are reviewed and extant research presented. This chapter commences by summarizing the discussion around a London-based university's corporate visual identity programme. Next, the author clarifies research methods. Afterwards, the method is outlined and the findings from the analysis address issues which the university should modify in its visual identity and conceptual model is proposed. Finally, research contributions and limitations are summarized along with suggestions for future research.

Learning objectives

Given the significance of the corporate logo and building upon the evidence discussed, it is useful to investigate the concept further in order to complement existing studies. This research investigates the corporate logo with three objectives, which address the general goals:

- It explores the concept of the university logo and its dimensions.
- It identifies the factors that are most likely to have a significant influence on the favourable university logo (antecedents of the favourable university logo).
- It develops a conceptual framework concerning the relationships between a favourable university logo, its antecedents and its consequences.

2 Review of the literature on logos

A logo is the signature of a company with an essential communication and distinctiveness, which can reflect a company's image. A logo is a specific visual presentation of an organization's name and is sometimes used interchangeably with a symbol, which actually means the sign or shape used for representing a company. The corporate logo is defined in each paradigm through its own lens. For instance, marketing academics focus on the corporate and human personality and assert that the corporate logo is a sign of promises to the customer; it can become a type of shorthand for the personality of the organization and its values. Every company has its own personality, an intellectual and distinctive behaviour that serves to discriminate one firm from another. The corporate logo is at the root of corporate identity as well as being the main element of corporate visual identity (Balmer, 2001). A corporate logo is used to condense the personality of a firm and its values in order for it to be effectively presented to stakeholders. Developing a visually memorable brand is essential to any branding efforts. This chapter focuses on the university brand's visual identity, referring to an assembly of visual cues by which an audience can recognize the company and distinguish it from others.

Marketing and advertising researchers who have studied the visual expressions of the logo (Kenney and Scott, 2003; McQuarrie and Mick, 2003). Henderson and Cote (1998) state that the corporate logo is used as a company's signature (Melewar, 2003). Studies of the marketing perspective concentrate on consumers as primary receivers and argue that the corporate logo is used to lead to favourable company attitudes and directly influence purchase intentions, which can affect a company's financial performance (Bloch, 1995; Henderson et al., 2004). Furthermore, the corporate logo is used as a key economic advantage in lowering customer search costs (Cohen, 1991) and helps transcend global boundaries and language barriers (Kohli et al., 2002). The corporate logo is used to elicit aesthetic responses (Bloch, 1995; Pittard et al., 2007). Marketing literature is very similar to design literature and will be discussed in the next section.

Design literature refers to the corporate logo as a set of elements (colour, typeface, name, and design) that gives prominence to a company's products and services; it enables customers to distinguish and identify a brand or a company (Bennett, 1995; Leitch and Motion, 1999; Mollerup, 1999). They regard the corporate logo as an essential component of stimulus that draws an emotional reaction from consumers (Alessandri, 2001; Berlyne, 1971; Lewicki, 1986). Graphic designers and consultants regard the concept of the corporate logo as the way in which an organization communicates with the public (Balmer, 1998).

Like marketing research, the organizational literature centres on the corporate logo as a clear instrument for expressing organizational characteristics (Foroudi et al., 2017). Corporate visual identity (CVI) 'plays a significant role in the way an organization presents itself to both internal and external stakeholders' (Van den Bosch et al., 2006, p. 871). The organizational authors consider the corporate logo to be more than just a visual presentation of the organization and believe it is crucial for communication with users. The corporate logo is exhibited in the image that a company expresses to its audiences as a product differentiator, to create a favourable corporate image and corporate reputation (LeBlanc and Nguyen, 1996).

In this section, to understand the corporate logo better, the different elements of a corporate logo, such as colour (Baker and Balmer, 1997; Gabrielsen et al., 2000; Tavassoli, 2001), typeface (Henderson et al., 2004), design (Alessandri, 2001) and corporate name (Henderson et al., 2003; Melewar, 2003; Napoles, 1988) are discussed. Building a favourable image through corporate logo design, chiefly needs tools such as fonts, colour, corporate name, and design. Corporate logos are 'almost exclusively thought of as visual phenomena, many include company names or product names which, of course, are pronounceable. Other audible aspects may also be relevant' (Mollerup, 1999, p. 74). These basic elements, translated into a physical effect, help to develop the corporate identity.

Defining the corporate name – corporate name is the expression of corporate uniqueness of the company in the mindset of the stakeholders, and a brand that is distinctive from its competitors. For example, a name as a word or phrase can constitute the distinctive designation of an organization. It may be easy to assume that a corporate logo identifies its company or product by representing its corporate name. Marketing and design researchers (e.g. Henderson et al., 2003; Melewar, 2003; Napoles, 1988; Siegel, 1989) have devoted more attention to the name of the company as a component of the logo. Psychologists, economists and sociologists have given attention to names by researching symbology to develop theories on the power of logos and names to evoke attention and demonstrate desired responses (Koku, 1997). Moreover, scholars and researchers have also shown their interest and focused on the implications of a corporate name or change in name. Foroudi et al. (2014) state that the corporate name is inextricably linked to the company's promised and expected attributes.

Defining colour – colour is a constituent of corporate visual identity, communicates the positioning of an organization, and is a medium of communication information. It induces emotions and moods, expresses personality, influences an individual's perceptions and behaviour, and helps organizations position or differentiates themselves from competitors. A framework of these visual identity elements will be developed. Today, companies realize the value and power of a logo and its colour to classify their products or services and differentiate themselves from other companies or products as well as communicate information about their quality, value and reliability. Colour 'induces moods and emotions, influences consumers' perceptions and behaviour and helps companies position or differentiate from the competition' (Aslam, 2006, p. 15). Lichtle (2007) states the possible interactive effects between colour and an individual's mood before viewing an advertisement. Jenkins (1991, p. 163) states that colour is an expressive tool in terms of visual identity and depends for its effort on two quite distinct considerations: (1) an association with natural phenomena and (2) an association with received cultural references (Baker and Balmer, 1997). Colours can affect and persuade responses based on both instincts and associations and can predict consumer behaviour (Aslam, 2006). Consumer behaviour research states that communication impacts on individuals' behaviours and attitudes (Brown and Reingen, 1987).

Defining design – logo design is becoming more and more important as a means of differentiation to distinguish companies from their competitors. Logo selection is a challenge for an organization (Henderson and Cote, 1998) and a well-designed corporate logo allows for easy recognition and quick association. A logo is vital in terms of what it is able to communicate about the company in the market and to its customers. The corporate logo has the potential to express formal characteristics and these characteristics, described by Henderson and Cote (1998), are dependent upon the firm's objective. Cohen (1991), Peter (1989), Robertson (1989) and Vartorella (1990) believe that a well-designed corporate logo and all desired goals are high on correct recognition, effect, and a familiar, clear meaning. Bloch (1995) stated that corporate logo perception can be an aesthetic response and creates an essential component of stimulus that can draw the attention and emotional reaction of consumers (Berlyne, 1971; Bloch, 1995; Veryzer, 1993).

Defining typeface – typeface is the style, size and arrangement of the letters in a piece of printing, which is a key communication objective that is articulated through the corporate logo and espoused by the managers and may have both a favourable and an unfavourable impact on consumers' attitudes toward the company and raise emotional responses from those consumers. A typeface can contribute to increasing a company's value. Typeface design is a significant visual tool for accomplishing corporate communication objectives (Childers and Jass, 2002; Henderson et al., 2004; McCarthy and Mothersbaugh, 2002; Tantillo et al., 1995) and plays an important role in the way an organization presents itself to both external and internal stakeholders. In the field of corporate logo, a typeface can communicate numerous messages to an audience. A typeface can express feelings that reflect a company's personality and a company's culture. A company's typeface is crucial in helping people to recognize the organization and recall its image. It may even reaffirm trust in the organization and can affect people's judgments and behaviour (Doyle and Bottomley, 2002; Gabrielsen et al., 2000).

The corporate typeface is the core of an organization (Baker and Balmer, 1997; Van den Bosch et al., 2005); to present the physical facet demands sophistication. Rowden (2000) suggests that a typeface is the voice of character and 'the best typography has grace and a certain invisibility' (p. 185). According to aesthetics research, there is a connection between a typeface's characteristics and its influence on consumer responses (Childers and Jass, 2002). Typeface design can rely on an understanding of a particular cultural heritage, which can be lost in other cultures (Doyle and Bottomley, 2002; Gabrielsen et al., 2000). Childers and Jass (2002, p. 2) mentioned corporate typeface as 'the art or skill of designing communication by means of the printed word'.

Research method

In the following section, the chapter presents a study that was conducted to attain insights into issues and discover factors that influence the design of a university's logo, and whether or not a university logo can satisfactorily communicate a company's identity via integrated marketing communication, image and reputation to develop loyalty. This study employs multi-disciplinary primary qualitative data collection (interviews and focus groups).

In-depth interviews and group discussions are very useful in combination (Palmer, 2011; Palmer and Gallagher, 2007; Ritchie et al., 2003) as a valuable resource that brings a new perspective to existing knowledge (Ritchie et al., 2003) and improves the richness of data in hand. The data collected from the interviews and focus groups supplied information and insights to this research and helped to add more data, which was not identified in the literature review. The personal interviews provide information and insights into personal experiences of respondents; interactions between respondents in focus groups highlight social beliefs, practices and perceptions of a social group.

Twelve in-depth interviews were arranged with managing directors and design managers who are involved in the implementation of corporate visual identity. All interviews were conducted face-to-face at their offices. Interview time was approximately 75 minutes. All were recorded and transcribed verbatim. In addition to interviews, seven focus groups were conducted with a total of 39 internal stakeholders (22 women and 17 men) to inspire an adequate level of group discussion and interaction on university logos. The culturally diverse respondents' age ranged from 18 to 45 years, with a mean of 28 years. The data were collected employing undergraduates, postgraduates, PhD researchers, and academics. The interview protocol was developed according to the recommendation from Foroudi et al. (2014, 2016, 2017) to conduct in-depth semi-structured interviews with an emerging qualitative protocol and direct questions were designed to understand the participants' crucial beliefs, opinions, perceptions, and attitudes toward logos.

To examine how the validity and reliability of a study are affected by the qualitative researchers' perceptions and hence to eradicate bias and increase the study's truthfulness, the triangulation method was used in qualitative research. Creswell and Miller (2000) described triangulation as:

'a validity procedure where researchers search for convergence among multiple and different sources of information to form themes or categories in a study' (p. 126). The codes were designed by addressing the research questions, problem areas, and/or key constructs (Foroudi et al., 2017). Then, QSR NVivo software was employed for data administration, data storage, retrieval, interpretation of the entire text and inter-relationships of codes. Afterwards, the qualitative results were examined once the data gathering stage was accomplished. The substantive statements which were directly associated with research questions were revised. In order to ascertain the frequency of responses to satisfy the demands of the methodology, the interviews were transcribed. By identifying a significant word, the comments obtained through the open questions were scanned and linked straightforwardly to the research question in order to deliver a final theory.

Findings and discussion

A literature review indicates that concepts of the university's logo, its antecedents and consequences are not clearly identified. Based on literature and qualitative studies, Figure 7.1 identifies the above gaps and illustrates the conceptual framework that identifies key research constructs. Generating a multiple stakeholders' (managers, employees, and students) level conceptual framework demonstrates: (1) the concept of the university logo and its dimensions; (2) the factors that are most likely to have a significance influence on the favourable university logo (antecedents of the favourable university logo); and (3) development and empirical assessment of a conceptual framework concerning the relationships between a favourable university logo, its antecedents and its consequences.

Components of a university logo

The content analysis has identified four components of the corporate logo (1) name, (2) colour, (3) design/graphics, and (4) typeface. There are countless dimensions of logos that characterize the perceptions of customers regarding a logo. Though the scope of this inquiry is limited, those dimensions are referred to in related literature and by participants in the interviews and focus groups. This research supports the dimensions generated from previous study findings.

Stakeholders' perception towards university name – the corporate name is enormously significant in today's businesses to keep loyal customers, establish a competitive edge and enhance the establishment image. Therefore, many researchers highlight the importance of the corporate name in sustaining a competitive advantage in today's competitive global market (Foroudi et al., 2017). Several studies have been developed about the association between corporate name and logo, which has been researched from different approaches (Childers and Houston, 1984; Koku, 1997; Lutz and Lutz, 1977). Corporate name can be defined as the most pervasive element in corporate and brand communications that identifies a company and increases recognition speed (Foroudi et al., 2014, 2016, 2017). With regard to the functional part of the entire corporate logo, the 'university name' as described by Foroudi et al. (2017), was described in participants' comments as a contributing factor towards the university image. For instance, a focus group participant said

> as soon as I saw the name of the university, I realised that it is located in London however I was quite confused with the name as it means quite non-sense for the name of the university ... I was not sure if I could trust the university as where I can study.

A respondent in follow-up interviews stated:

> the name of the university is the most important key to attract international students. I think our uni's name is not very recognisable and not easy to explain, but it is us, our name has not changed but we changed the colour and logos couple of times. Our name differentiates us to other HEs

> I think we always can see logo and names together and design cannot communicate without a name ... the name reflects the quality and characteristics of the uni.

Stakeholders' perception towards university colour – the findings of the current study show that colour as an element of the corporate logo is important as a reflection of the company's values and characteristics (Baker and Balmer, 1997). Participants made numerous comments on the effective use of the right colour in logo design and its influences on consumers' perceptions and behaviour in the marketplace (Aslam, 2006).

> I think the colour is interesting because culturally it is very bold in certain countries. The red is quite full on. We're not quite brash, but quite strong in our colour palette. It possibly lacks subtlety, but I think we are trying to make quite a bold ambitions statement. So I think it works for us.

The focus group members (representing students) discussed more practical issues, to which experts pay less attention. For example, one focus group member commented that: 'the colour of our uni is bold in some nations, ambitious angle, lucky colour, strong vibrant colours and right colour palette ... it is memorable and very consistent in all over the uni'.

Stakeholders' perception towards university design – design can be defined as a creative process that conveys a message or creates effective communications for companies (Andriopoulos and Gotsi, 2001). Design can serve as an integral part of supporting the corporate logo, even though it may not act as a primary factor (Henderson and Cote, 1998). Effectiveness and usability is extremely important in the logo creation process. Previous research paid attention to design as a means of differentiation to distinguish companies from their competitors (Robertson, 1989; Vartorella, 1990). Similarly, in the current study, a design manager comments on some aspects of the design, for example:

> the design should illustrates something memorable, to create impression, the personality of the company, but it is not easy as we are aiming to approach different culture and nationalities ... most of our students and staff are international with different perception and the design should be a way that makes all happy ... we have tried to design the logo and visual cues of the uni very carefully and I think we were quite successful.

Stakeholders' perception towards university typeface – typeface design can rely on an understanding of a particular cultural heritage, which can be lost in other cultures (Foroudi *et al.*, 2014). Henderson *et al.* (2004) emphasize the value of the typeface expressed through the corporate logo, which is also espoused by managers. This is important because organizations need to create an important strategic impression in the marketplace (Somerick, 2000; Spaeth, 1995; Tantillo *et al.*, 1995). Identifiable typefaces increase the likelihood of achieving greater feasibility and visibility (Melewar and Saunders, 2000) and a positive image in the marketplace. As mentioned by an interviewee, 'I think our typeface is appropriate, really nice typeface, really modern, which actually stood out as something modern'.

Antecedents of the university logo

The literature and qualitative study propose university identity and strategy as two key components of a university logo. Findings from the qualitative study indicate that a company identity should be reflected in companies, which is wedded to customer decisions when choosing what to purchase. Additionally, the textual analysis of interviews reveals a focus on what the company stands for, communication and the distinctiveness of the logo, which influences their perception. Managers state that the corporate logo should communicate a reliable message that needs to be enhanced to communicate the personality of the company. The following comments illustrate managers' assessment of this finding:

> we considered the philosophy of the university in our design ... it shows the heritage of our place, it is clear that who we are, what are

our beliefs ... communicates the individuality of our identity ... our new logo presents our brand, guideline, and personality.

The corporate logo is the official graphical design for a company and the uniqueness of the design requires significant creativity, which must match a firm's strategy: it should be unique and creative in its design. When the strategy is recognized, the corporate visual identity makes the organization memorable and well-known through its corporate logos (Foroudi et al., 2014). In addition, a good design can engage an audience by asking them to visually interrelate with the logo. In order to create a new corporate visual identity and changes in the logo, organizations have to invest large amounts of money. Symbolism has a greater role and has grown from its original purpose of increasing organizational visibility to a position where it is seen as having a role in communicating corporate strategy. A consultant participant commented that:

> like other universities, our brand is quite recognizable. We are pleased with the quality of our students and believe they have deep relationship with our brand. In our worldwide campuses, all recognize us from our name and logo ... we have updated our logo to reflect our new strategy and with the new design, we have stronger positioning in the market and the design can support the vision for the future of the university.

Consequences of the university logo

Based on the literature and qualitative study, the key outcomes of the university logo were acknowledged as integrated marketing communication, university image, reputation/trust creation, engagement, commitment, and loyalty. In addition, attractiveness, familiarity, and recognisability were identified as the key moderators between (1) integrated marketing communication and university image and (2) university logo and university image.

Stakeholders' perception towards university integrated marketing communication – integrated marketing communications are the strategic co-ordination of all messages and media employed by an organization to produce maximum impact amongst relevant target audiences (Foroudi *et al.*, 2017). By integrating the communication strategies, synergies are created among different forms of communication. All forms of communication express an image and seek an integrated approach to articulate company's identity in coherent and harmonized messages through external and internal forms of communication. Gilly and Wolfinbarger (1998) analysed the impact of advertising upon an internal audience and the importance of involving employees in communications; they stressed the need for integrated and consistent communications. Communication effectiveness may relate to previous familiarity of the advertised brand or company (Campbell and Keller, 2003). Participants referred to a logo as the identity of a company, which needs to be fashionable and modern to provide and ensure positive and reliable communications and it should be consistent in all company stationery, promotion, public relations and social media. Universities harmonize both internal and external communications to generate favourable images of the company for target audiences.

Stakeholders' perception of university image – the importance of the impact of the company's logo on positive and desired attributes to evoke a more positive image of an organization has been recognized by previous studies (Foroudi *et al.*, 2014; 2016; 2017). The findings of the qualitative study showed how a fit between the logo and the university image enhanced consumers' perceptions of the university, which in turn led to more positive evaluations of the participants' performance. Those findings were consistent with prior research (Henderson and colleagues, 1998, 2003; Janiszewski and Meyvis, 2001; Pittard *et al.*, 2007). This relationship has been highlighted by respondents and manager participants in the following comments:

> So, I would say it's chiefly how our uni can be seen from the outside. It is critical in two respects. One is in the recruiting [process] of the students, in which we think about the university's global image. Another fundamental is the university research reputation, these are two areas where the university's identity becomes critical. Our image helps us to survive in the competitive market and be profitable ... also we need to consider how and what we communicate to our stakeholders through media.

Stakeholders' perception towards reputation/trust creation – anticipation of the corporate reputation is built up by the corporate image through the corporate logo. The importance of corporate reputation is particularly evident when the customers trust the company and its product. One of the interviewees illustrated the importance of corporate reputation: 'I joined the university as I believed I could trust the place and I could build my future by investing my time studying'. As such, the company's logo impacts on positive and desired attributes and can add value to the reputation of an organization. It has been argued that a well-orchestrated corporate image is deemed to be a major contribution to creating corporate reputation. A participant explained that creating trust among the team, students and staff is important, which can impact on reputation. For example,

> people know that here is quite a good place to place to work compared to other universities in London.... However, we have to find a

way to synergize that individual reputation with the overall goals of the institution, which I don't think we have quite achieved yet.

Another participant mentioned that there are many factors which influence on the reputation of the company but logo and visual cues have key roles, mainly when people see the organization for the first time.

Stakeholders' perception of attractiveness, familiarity, and recognizability – organizations invest large amounts of money in developing and implementing a corporate logo and expect important benefits from it. The use of the corporate logo improves the attractiveness and distinctiveness of corporate images for external and internal audiences. An organization's instruments make stakeholders' association more visible. Distinctiveness lies in the unique position of the company in the minds of stakeholders and can be achieved through strategic alignment and emotionally attractive features, and by drawing attention using favourable messages. Organizations create an attractive corporate visual identity and tack it onto a wide range of products, hoping that it means something similar to employees and consumers. Some reflections on the logo and attractiveness are offered by a focus group participant,

> The university as an individual brand has a high aesthetic attractiveness which attracts us as students and employees ... the visual identity of the uni draws attention to its attractiveness and beauty ... the attractiveness of the brand and logo has impacted our perceptions.

Research on company and product familiarity and qualitative studies have an impactful influence on the relationships between logo and image, also impacting on the relationships between integrated corporate communication and image (Chadwick and Walters, 2009; Melewar and Saunders, 1998). Furthermore, the direction of the interaction of product familiarity with a company depends on the corporate logo (Melewar and Saunders, 1998). Similarly, the current findings from the qualitative study illustrate these relationships.

> The name and logo of the uni have uses in all social media, signs, and websites that can reach the buying public and communicate the worth of the university. Thus, everything is related to the design of our university's logo. I believe the work of the logo goes on even after the university's identity and image has been established ... the name and logo inspire an optimistic personal response which contains a sense of familiarity which benefits the uni and succeeds in contradiction of our competitors.

Recognisability of product and service are extremely important to today's businesses in order to attract maximum attention and situate the

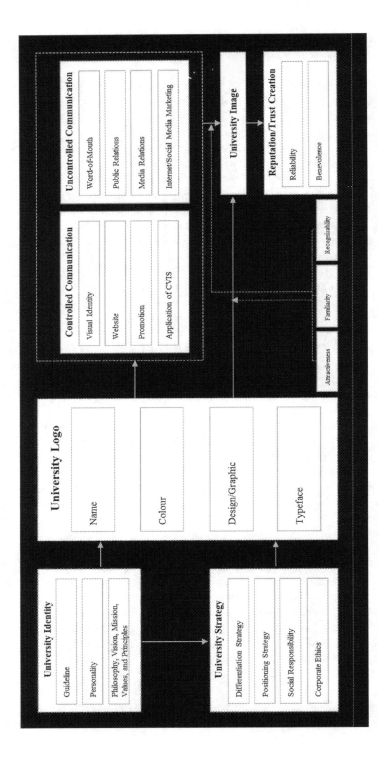

Figure 7.1 Research model.
Source: Developed by the research based on review literature and qualitative study.

company in customers' minds for a long time. Therefore, many marketing scholars emphasize the importance of the relationship between corporate logo and product and service recognisability to sustain a competitive advantage in today's competitive global market (Henderson and Cote, 1998). A high quality corporate logo was reported in participants' comments as a contributing factor leading to a favourable corporate image. Companies employ logos to maintain success in a marketplace. Similarly, the findings from the qualitative study show that 'the name and logo of a brand should be recognisable and second ... illustrates and reflects company's values and identity of the place'.

3 Managerial implications

This research offers managerial contributions for decision-makers and graphic designers who wish to understand the entirety of the relationship between a favourable university logo and the factors in its antecedents (corporate name, typeface, design, and colour) from the internal stakeholders' perspective and its effect on a favourable university image and reputation. Findings from the research in this chapter have vital managerial implications, presenting an inclusive picture of the whole situation in which a favourable university logo can be constructed within a company to achieve a favourable image of the organization in the consumer's mind. In other words, a clear understating of the dimensions of the relevant concepts can assist managers and designers to devise a favourable university logo, which will create strong marketing communication, image and reputation.

By understanding the market needs, as well as the company's strengths and weaknesses, managers will be able to make the right decision in selecting a logo favourable for targeting and responding to market needs. In practice, different managers set out to create a sense of shared vision by reducing dysfunctional conflict and promoting a sense of shared values and communication. Furthermore, managers should be more responsive to the university's corporate logo by taking into account that responsiveness was found to have the greatest influence on the university's outcomes. Importantly, this chapter helps consultants and managers to understand whether the university's logo communicates a reliable message and the personality of the company to the target audience.

As discussed earlier, the corporate logo as a main element of corporate visual identity (Balmer, 2001; Bromley, 2001) evokes an emotional response in the minds of consumers (Henderson and Cote, 1998; Olins, 1978, 1989; Van den Bosch et al., 2005). Thus, it is fruitful for a company's designers, and communication managers to note the importance of the emotional aspect of the corporate logo as a key element of corporate identity rather than simply focusing on what is fashionable and modern.

Admittedly, three variables are investigated in this chapter's research, namely, attractiveness, familiarity and recognisability. These constructs are the key moderators between logo and image, and logo and integrated marketing communication. In this respect, advertising and marketing managers should concentrate on consistency in corporate communications, in order to learn which beliefs, attitudes, impressions and associations held by consumers can be matched to corporate identity. Furthermore, managers should place more emphasis on the corporate logo as the signature of a company and less on the content to be placed in adverts. These three variables (attractiveness, familiarity and recognisability) are likely to play an important role in encouraging positive consumer perception.

4 Conclusion

This chapter discussed a qualitative study that sought to address the research aim (to develop a comprehensive understanding of the university logo, its elements, antecedents and consequences) and the corresponding research questions. A framework model of the implementation and determinants of a corporate logo was developed on the basis of literature reviews and the qualitative study alike.

While the chapter provides some suggestions to extend the current body of knowledge in the literature on the corporate logo and corporate visual identity, this study is exploratory in nature. Replication of the study is needed in order to gain greater generalisability and validity for the identified relationships. In this respect, further study should investigate whether the domain of a favourable corporate logo construct modifies or changes and how the association in the proposed framework would differ with the type of corporate logo being investigated. Furthermore, a future study could explore whether the relationships found in this study are also valid in other countries.

5 Case study – university's new look: cues used by stakeholders in evaluating university logos – a case of Brunel, University London

> Everyday routines and activities in an entity do not simply happen but occur because of tradition or history ... the answer of where does the company come from, can be hidden in company's history and founder.
> (Foroudi, 2015, p. 28)

As there was no documentary material from the library, or from the school on the web etc., this case study has been designed mainly using Dr Mohammad Mahdi Foroudi's (2015) PhD research.

Brunel and higher education: learning from re-branding

Higher education is becoming a global phenomenon, particularly in the main English-speaking countries. The modern university is more like a 'stakeholder university' than a 'republic of scholars'. In the competitive global market, the university needs to market itself in a climate of international competition to attract and attain high quality students and academic staff at a global-level. The competition is no longer limited by national borders. Education has become a global business sector and resembles an industry, which develops challenges and increased stress on corporate image and reputation. Universities recognize students as customers and they have discovered the importance of implementing strategies to maintain and enhance their competitiveness based on a set of unique characteristics.

Brunel University London is one of these universities. Brunel, as a middle-ranked London-based institution, constitutes a key case study for in-depth organizational analysis as it has a leading role in the UK education sector and has a distinctive and modern building. Brunel has a long history of education, back to 1798, through its predecessor colleges, Borough Road College, Maria Grey College, Shoreditch College, and the West London Institute of Higher Education, and also through Acton Technical College, then Brunel College. In 1966, the university, located on the outskirts of Uxbridge, UK, was named after the Victorian engineer, Isambard Kingdom Brunel, one of the most versatile and audacious engineers of the nineteenth century.

In a highly competitive environment, Brunel, like other service providers, has worked to develop and protect its identity and brand by communicating messages consistently. Thus, the multiple internal stakeholders of the university are a group of respondents who have experience in receiving internal messages in their school and are representative of internal stakeholders in providing information about different aspects of the concepts in the study.

In August 2014, the university re-branded and changed its name to 'Brunel University London'. The new corporate identity emphasizes the corporate visual identity and includes modifications in the university logo, typeface, colour and name. A branding and corporate identity researcher conducted research related to visual identity of London-based-universities to understand what the perceptions of international students are concerning global corporate logo favourability and how logos can impact on their perceptions of integrated marketing communication? The researcher believes that a company's logo creates the first impression and is the most important aspect of a company in communicating the identity and personality of the company. The main objective of this case study was to review the perception of internal stakeholders towards the CVI of Brunel University *'after the changes'*. Did policy makers and managers decide to re-brand the university to become visual identity-focused as an appropriate approach to closing the gap between brand values and perception to improve corporate image and reputation?

Corporate visual identity enhances consumers' knowledge about an organization. Researchers (Van den Bosch *et al.*, 2006; Brooks *et al.*, 2005) noted that repositioning, modernizing, managing change, promoting growth, and starting over, all require a new identity. Mergers, acquisitions, restructuring, repositioning, changing marketplaces and takeovers often lead to a new corporate logo. Companies change their corporate logo to become up-to-date and modern (Foroudi et al., 2014). The company's corporate logo impacts on positive and desired attributes and can add value to the reputation of an organization. It has been argued that a well-orchestrated corporate strategy is deemed to be a major contribution to creating corporate reputation. Participants explained:

> I think the University's overall strategy is not clear to staff, not well defined, not enough. It is important to communicate it better, in more details. By communicating with deans and heads of services, is that part of making it clearer for staff in terms of understanding the overall strategy of the university. They are clear about the objectives and journey. But there is an anxiety, so it is crucial for us to do what we need to do, to get some synergy.
>
> (Senior Lecturer)

> The university's corporate branding has a consistent short and long time strategic framework, which I think includes a school's activities and is designed by the top management at the school and I think was aligned based on the school's brand identity. It presents the company's values, both emotional and functional by building the clear connection among strategic vision, organization culture and stakeholder image, consumers, customers, government, and etc. We should consider the difficulties such as aligning internal and external stakeholders, and create credible and authentic identity.
>
> (Professor)

> I think the school changed its strategy and for this reason they need to revise the school's visual identity. Our new name and logo shows as the clues to distinguish the changes in the school. I think all changes appears on our communication to students and staffs. I think our name and logo are the main expression of the Brunel, which people can identify us and differentiate us from others.
>
> (Manager)

The above quotations are consistent with corporate strategy and corporate identity researchers (Balmer, 2001) as well as the organizational behaviour researchers (Albert and Whetten, 1985). They assert that management is responsible for conveying the same message to internal and external audiences. Moreover, a senior lecturer participant stated that:

> I strongly believe that a strategy means nothing unless it is fully communicated all the way through the organization. It should never be

kept to the managers who plan it. It is quite sad when you observe that the top management changes the company's strategy without engaging with team members. I think good strategy should be simple, clear, credible, motivating and it reflects the uniqueness of the organization. I think managers work a lot but I think it ends up looking the same or worse than last year. But the logo or our brands looks different and I think the culture of the organization is still the same as it used to be, but still confusing to us. The school strategy is like a story of how a business is going to grow and expand and how to drive growth. It starts by scanning the environment and taking a view of where the market is headed. People here are not clear what their roles are and if the strategies fail, what is going to happens.

Brand structure is the part of corporate structure that is concerned with the branding of the products, business units and the corporate umbrella and how they appear to an organization's audience. It is closely related to brand strategy, which refers to the way firms mix and match their corporate, house and individual brand names on their products (Gray and Smeltzer, 1985). Several respondents were likely to see the university as a brand. For instance,

> 'people think we are pioneering, our reputation is innovation'. 'We have a great brand values, we are innovative, determined, and mainly to people we are modern.... We are high quality. We are leaders, creative, forward thinking, ambitious, and quite aggressive. We communicate all these points to our students. We are keeping up with the speed of that change'.

Another respondent added

> Our branding was related to the alignment of employee behaviour with our brand values. Internal branding or aligning the behaviour of employees with brand values has impact on competitive markets. UK universities are the most valuable intangible asset for the government. I don't think the school realised the importance of the relationship between internal branding and support from the academic employees.

Another lecture added

> In spite of huge complexity. Brunel has a clear brand, we are a university, and the uni has its own brand, as a business school. It illustrates things such as what we teach, what is the key school research cluster.... But as a characteristic brand, we were struggling and I think it was the way we had to add the London word to the unique name ... I think it was very confused but better now.... We try to sell ourselves;

hopefully the launch of our new brand might solve the confusion. It present ourselves moving forward ... we are very well branded through our traditional name, sign, logo, or design, or some combination of all, which everyone recognises as us and differentiates us from competitors' offerings.

Furthermore, the respondents granted that branding activities are a way to facilitate employees to sustain the brand of the institution. The comment above signified a positive impact of the messages which are communicated via the institution's activities on employee brand support. The Brunel Business School (BBS) slogan, mission, and vision available on the school's web pages are remembered by staff, therefore directing staff behaviour. Moreover, employees can imitate the leader's behaviour. In particular, an academic employee shared her beliefs on the impacts of branding activities on her employee brand support:

If the Brunel University is our brand, business school, being sub brand, shares the same values and characteristics of the Brunel University London as a parent brand. We use the main University logo and present ourselves as central University activities. However, we have individual marketing and communication strategies.... Our web page is to maintain level of consistency in the user experience.... Like individuals, we have own identity, complex identity and brand. Our university identity differentiates us from its competitors. It allows our stakeholders to recognise, understand and clearly describe the organization concerned.... Our values and ambitions of employees play a key role.... Our visual brand manifests itself in many ways, through logo, typeface and colours, stationery, buildings signage, customer information, vehicles, and every aspect of promotional activity.... The education sector in the UK is crowded and competitive. Business schools compete with each other for students and staff, public funding and commercial income, not only in the UK, Europe, all over the world.... The main reason for rebranding the university was to add the London word to the name, to attain success in such a highly competitive arena is via discrimination, by developing a distinguishing brand personality and set of values which appeal to the school's key audiences.

(Lecturer)

The foundation of our brand is our Brunel logo, our website, packaging and promotional materials, all of which should integrate the school logo to communicate our brand.

I think the school's brand strategy is how, what, where, when and to whom top management plan on communicating and delivering on the school's brand messages. Where the school advertises is part of the university' brand strategy, distribution channels are also part of the school's brand strategy. Also what top management communicates visually and verbally is part of the school brand strategy. We tried to communicate consistent strategic branding to people internally, externally, internationally. Based on my knowledge, it leads to a strong school's brand equity.... Rebranding our school was difficult. Defining our brand was a complex journey of business self-discovery; it was very difficult, time-consuming. By changing our logo, we had to think about what are the changes in school or university's mission? What are the benefits and features of the school's products or services? What do the customers think about us? We had to think about the new brand messaging. Every employee should be aware of the brand attributes. If they can't do this, attempts at establishing a brand will fail.

(Focus Group 3)

As you know, the history of corporate branding emerged from the notion of logo, name and trademarks, which make easy brand awareness and recognition, motivating consumers to have particular expectations of the promise of a brand such as a special quality, distinctive experience, or personal identity.

(Operations Administrator)

In addition, the participants provided their opinions about their impressions of corporate identity on identification as follows:

I always have seen our corporate identity as a collection of visual elements such as logo and slogan, which are used in many applications. Also, it is the core of our organization's existence, which can say it is consistent of our long history, beliefs, philosophy, our ethical and cultural values and strategies. I think it helps to position our school in terms of the markets and competitors and to support the image of an organization and influence on our employees' work ... as staff, my identification towards the school is a particular form of my social identification and I sometimes think I belong to Brunel which make me different with higher prestige to my colleagues in different universities.... The identity is a visual that represents the business of the school and it is the sensory elements which help the stakeholders make a human/emotional connection. Our unique interpersonal identity is related to our personalised bonds of attachment which is derived from common identification with a social group.

(Research Student Administration)

well, I like the blue colour of our identity, it is the main expression of our school. As you can see, we all use and distribute the blue BBS pen to our students, it shows our prestige ... I like the quality of heading papers provided in the conferences. I really like the old design of the logo which we rarely use these days. Interestingly, you can't find as such the typeface and logo of the Brunel University in BBS. Our logo is differentiating us from other Business Schools.

(Senior Lecturer)

The ways we communicate to people demonstrate our personality, who we are. We all have different types of personality, and that might influence on person's individual communication style ... sometimes the lack of interpersonal communication ultimately affects the others. The institution is very similar, we communicate through media and different channels to the public. We aim to communicate the same message through our logo, Brunel Business School as a name, what we are famous at, to all our stakeholders, to transmit coherence, credibility and ethic. Communication is linking the organization to the stakeholders ... we tried to build and attain a positive perception in stakeholders' minds.

(Research Student Administration)

The above discussed the context of the research in terms of its history and branding through its visual design. Higher education institutions have demonstrated the key characteristics of organizations in the organization's corporate visual identity. The questions were answered were 'Where do we come from? and 'Where would the university like to go?' What is needed now is a more precise description of the university identity, its desired position and its strategic intent through its logo design and visual identity as part of strategic growth and development.

6 Further investigation

1 To identify more antecedents of a university's logo.
2 To recognize more consequences of a university's logo.
3 Replication and comparison of this study across different countries.
4 Quantitative examination of the developed conceptual framework.
5 What recommendations will you make to managers regarding continuously improving corporate visual design? Be specific in your answer by comparing the university's CVI with other universities to make your points clearer.
6 How might the proposed conceptual model be applied in different industries?

References

Albert, S. and Whetten, D. A. (1985) "Organisational identity." *Research in Organisational Behaviour* 7, pp. 263–295.

Alessandri, S. W. (2001) "Modelling corporate identity: A concept explication and theoretical explanation." *Corporate Communications: An International Journal* 6(4), pp. 173–182.

Andriopoulos, C. and Gotsi, M. (2001) "Living the corporate identity: Case studies from the creative industry." *Corporate Reputation Review* 4(2), pp. 144–154.

Aslam, M. (2006) "Are you selling the right colour? A cross-cultural review of colour as a marketing cue." *Journal of Marketing Communications* 12(1), pp. 15–30.

Baker, M. J. and Balmer, J. M. T. (1997) "Visual identity: Trappings or substance?" *European Journal of Marketing* 31(5), pp. 366–382.

Balmer, J. M. T. (1998) "Corporate identity and the advent of corporate marketing." *Journal of Marketing Management* 14(8), pp. 963–996.

Balmer, J. M. T. (2001) "Corporate identity, corporate branding and corporate marketing seeing through the fog." *European Journal of Marketing* 35(3)/4, pp. 248–291.

Balmer, J. M. T. Fukukawa, K., and Grey, E. (2007) "The nature and management of ethical corporate identity: A commentary on corporate identity, corporate social responsibility and ethics." *Journal of Business Ethics* 76(1), pp. 7–15.

Bennett, P. D. (1995) *Dictionary of Marketing Terms*. Lincolnwood, IL, USA: McGraw-Hill.

Berlyne, D. E. (1971) *Aesthetics and Psychobiology*. New York: Appleton Century Crofts.

Bloch, P. H. (1995) "Seeking the ideal form: Product design and consumer response." *Journal of Marketing* 59(3), pp. 16–29.

Bottomley, P. A. and Doyle, J. R. (2006) "The interactive effects of colours and products on perceptions of brand logo appropriateness." *Marketing Theory* 6(1), pp. 63–83.

Bromley, D. B. (2001) "Relationships between personal and corporate reputation." *European Journal of Marketing* 35(3/4), pp. 316–334.

Brooks, M., Rosson, P., and Gassmann, H. (2005) "Influences on post-M&A corporate visual identity choices." *Corporate Reputation Review*, 8(2), pp. 136–144.

Brown, J. J. and Reingen, P. H. (1987) "Social ties and word-of-mouth referral behaviour." *Journal of Consumer Research* 14(3), pp. 350–362.

Campbell, M. C. and Keller, K. L. (2003) "Brand familiarity and advertising repetition effects." *Journal of Consumer Research* 30(2), pp. 292–304.

Chadwick, S. and Walters, G. (2009) "Sportswear identification, distinctive design and manufacture logos – Issues from the front line." *The Marketing Review* 9(1), pp. 63–78.

Chajet, C. and Shachtman, T. (1991) *Image by Design: From Corporate Vision to Business Reality*. Boston: McGraw-Hill.

Childers, T. L. and Houston, M. J. (1984) "Conditions for a picture-superiority effect on consumer memory." *Journal of Consumer Research* 11(2), pp. 643–654.

Childers, T. L. and Jass, J. (2002) "All dressed up with something to say: Effects of typeface semantic associations on brand perception and consumer memory." *Journal of Consumer Psychology* 12(2), pp. 93–106.

Cohen, D. (1991) "Trademark strategy revisited." *Journal of Marketing* 55(3), pp. 46–59.

Creswell, J. W. and Miller, D. L. (2000) "Determining validity in qualitative inquiry." *Theory into Practice* 39(3), pp. 124–131.

Dacin, P. and Brown, T. (2002) "Corporate identity and corporate associations: A framework for future research." *Corporate Reputation Review* 5(2/3), pp. 254–253.

Doyle, J. R. and Bottomley, P. A. (2002) "Font appropriateness and brand choice." *Journal of Business Research* 57(8), pp. 873–380.

Foroudi, M. M. (2015) "The corporate identity, architecture, and identification triad: theoretical insights" (Doctoral dissertation, Brunel University London).

Foroudi, P., Dinnie, K., Kitchen, P. J., Melewar, T C, and Foroudi, M. M. (2017) "IMC antecedents and the consequences of planned brand identity in higher education." *European Journal of Marketing* 51(3), pp. 528–550.

Foroudi, P., Hafeez, K., and Foroudi, M. M. (2016) "Evaluating the impact of corporate logos towards corporate reputation: A case of Persia and Mexico." *Qualitative Market Research: An International Journal* 20(2), pp. 158–180.

Foroudi, P., Melewar, T C, and Gupta, S. (2014) "Linking corporate logo, corporate image, and reputation: An examination of consumer perceptions in the financial setting." *Journal of Business Research (JBR)* 67(11), pp. 2269–2281.

Gabrielsen, G., Kristensen, T., and Hansen, F. (2000) "Corporate design: A tool for testing." *Corporate Communications: An International Journal* 5(2), pp. 113–118.

Gilly, M. C. and Wolfinbarger, M. (1998) "Advertising's internal audience." *Journal of Marketing* 62(1), pp. 69–88.

Gray, E. R. and Smeltzer, L. R. (1985) "SMR forum: Corporate image – An integral part of strategy." *Sloan Management Review* 26(41), p. 73.

Hagtvedt, H. (2011) "The impact of incomplete typeface logos on perceptions of the firm." *Journal of Marketing* 75 (July), pp. 86–93.

Henderson, P. W. and Cote, J. A. (1998) "Guidelines for selecting or modifying logos." *Journal of Marketing* 62(2), pp. 14–30.

Henderson, P. W., Cote, J. A., Meng, L. S., and Schmitt, B. (2003) "Building strong brands in Asia: Selecting the visual components of image to maximize brand strength." *International Journal of Research in Marketing* 20(4), pp. 297–313.

Henderson, P. W., Giese, J., and Cote, J. A. (2004) "Impression management using typeface design." *Journal of Marketing* 68(4), pp. 60–83.

Janiszewski, C. and Meyvis, T. (2001) "Effects of brand logo complexity, repetition, and spacing on processing fluency and judgement." *Journal of Consumer Research* 28(1), pp. 18–32.

Jenkins, N. (1991) *The Business of Image: Visualising the Corporate Message.* London: Kogan Page.

Kenney, K. and Scott, L. M. (2003) "A review of the visual rhetoric literature Introduction," in L. M. Scott and R. Batra, *Persuasive Imagery: A Consumer Response Perspective.* Mahwah NJ: Lawrence Erlbaum, pp. 17–56.

Kohli, C., Suri, R., and Thakor, M. (2002) "Creating effective logos: Insights from theory and practice." *Business Horizons* 45(3), pp. 58–64.

Koku, P. S. (1997) "Corporate name change signaling in the services industry." *Journal of Services Marketing* 11(6), pp. 392–408.
LeBlanc, G. and Nguyen, N. (1996) "Cues used by customers evaluating corporate image in service firms: An empirical study in financial institutions." *International Journal of Service Industry Management* 7(2), pp. 44–56.
Leitch, S. and Motion, J. (1999) "Multiplicity in corporate identity strategy." *Corporate Communications: An International Journal* 4(4), pp. 193–200.
Lewicki, P. (1986) "Processing information about co variations that cannot be articulated." *Journal of Experimental Psychology: Learning, Memory and Cognition* 21(1), pp. 135–146.
Lichtle, M. C. (2007) "The effect of an advertisement's colour on emotions evoked by an ad and attitude towards the ad: The moderating role of the optimal stimulation level." *International Journal of Advertising* 26(1), pp. 37–62.
Lutz, K. A. and Lutz, R. J. (1977) "Effects of interactive imagery on learning: Application to advertising." *Journal of Applied Psychology* 72(2), pp. 493–498.
McCarthy, M. S. and Mothersbaugh, D. L. (2002) "Effects of typographic factors in advertising-based persuasion: A general model and initial empirical tests." *Psychology and Marketing* 19 (July/August), pp. 663–691.
McQuarrie, E. F. and Mick, D. G. (2003) "Visual and verbal rhetorical figures under directed processing versus incidental exposure to advertising." *Journal of Consumer Research* 29(4), pp. 579–587.
Melewar, T C (2003) "Determinants of the corporate identity construct: A review of literature." *Journal of Marketing Communications* 9(3), pp. 195–220.
Melewar, T C, Foroudi, P., Dinnie, K., and Nguyen, B. (2017) "The role of corporate identity management in the higher education sector: An exploratory case study." *Journal of Marketing Communications* 24(4), pp. 337–359.
Melewar, T C, Foroudi, P., Kitchen, P., Gupta, S., and Foroudi, M. M. (2017) "Integrating identity, strategy and communications for trust, loyalty and commitment." *European Journal of Marketing* 51(3), pp. 572–604.
Melewar, T C and Saunders, J. (1998) "Global corporate visual identity systems: Standardization, control and benefits." *International Marketing Review* 15(4), pp. 291–308.
Melewar, T C and Saunders, J. (2000) "Global corporate visual identity systems: Using an extended marketing mix." *European Journal of Marketing* 34(5), pp. 538–550.
Mollerup, P. (1999) *Marks of Excellence, History and Taxonomy of Trademarks*. London: Phaidon Press.
Napoles, V. (1988) *Corporate Identity Design*. New York: Van Nostrand Reinhold.
Olins, W. (1978) *The Corporate Personality: An Inquiry into The Nature of Corporate Identity*. UK: Kynoch Press.
Olins, W. (1989) *Corporate Entity: Making Business Strategy Visible through Design*, London: Thames and Hudson.
Palmer, A. (2011) "Cooperative marketing associations: an investigation into the causes of effectiveness." *Journal of Strategic Marketing* 10(2), pp. 135–156.
Palmer, A. and Gallagher, D. (2007) "Religiosity, relationships and consumption: A study of church going in Ireland." *Consumptions, Markets and Culture* 10(1), pp. 31–50.
Peter, J. P. (1989) "Designing logos." *Folio* 18 (July), pp. 139–141.

Pittard, N., Ewing, M., and Jevons, C. (2007) "Aesthetic theory and logo design: Examining consumer response to proportion across cultures." *International Marketing Review* 24(4), pp. 457–473.

Ritchie, J., Lewis, J., and Elam, G. (2003) "Designing and selecting samples," in J. Ritchie and J. Lewis, *Qualitative Research Practice, A Guide for Social Science Students and Researchers*. CA: Sage Publications.

Robertson, K. R. (1989) "Strategically desirable brand name characteristics." *Journal of Consumer Marketing* 6 (Fall), pp. 61–71.

Rowden, M. (2000) *The Art of Identity: Creating and Managing a Successful Corporate Identity*. UK: Gower Publishing.

Siegel, L. B. (1989) "Planning for a long-life logo." *Marketing Communications* 14 (March), pp. 44–49.

Smithson, J. (2000) "Using and analysing focus groups: Limitations and possibilities." *International Journal of Social Research Methodology* 3(2), pp. 103–119.

Somerick, N. M. (2000) "Practical strategies for avoiding problems in graphic communication." *Public Relations Quarterly* 45(3), pp. 32–34.

Spaeth, T. (1995) "What does it all mean?" *Across the Board* 32 (February), pp. 53–55.

Tantillo, J., Janet, D., and Richard E. M. (1995) "Quantifying perceived differences in type styles: An exploratory study." *Psychology and Marketing* 12(5), pp. 447–457.

Tavassoli, N. T. (2001) "Colour memory and evaluations for alphabetic and logographic brand names." *Journal of Experimental Psychology: Applied* 7(2), pp. 104–111.

Van den Bosch, A. L. M., De Jong, M. D. T., and Elving, W. J. L. (2005) "How corporate visual identity supports reputation." *Corporate Communications: An International Journal* 10(2), pp. 108–116.

Van den Bosch, A. L. M., Elving, W. J. L., and De Jong, M. D. T. (2006) "The impact of organisational characteristics on corporate visual identity." *European Journal of Marketing* 40(7/8), pp. 870–885.

Vartorella, R. W. (1990) "Doing the bright thing with your company logo." *Advertising Age* 61(26), p. 31.

Veryzer, R. W. (1993) "Aesthetic response and the influence of design principles on product preferences." *Advances in Consumer Research* 20(1), pp. 224–228.

8 Brand image and reputation development in higher education institutions

Adele Berndt and Linda D. Hollebeek

1 Introduction

Higher education institutions (HEIs) are tasked with delivering services that differ from those offered by traditional private-sector organizations. Despite this, HEIs are recognizing the importance of branding, and are increasingly creating and using their brand image and reputation to develop and differentiate their services within an increasingly competitive environment. With a positive brand image affecting student enrolments, sponsorship and reputation, many contemporary HEIs are developing promotional strategies, tactics, and materials (e.g. brochures, websites, social media pages) to optimize their image and communication.

After reading this chapter you should be able to:

- Comment on the importance of a brand image specifically for HEIs.
- Contrast views regarding branding image models in the context of HEIs.
- Comment on the role of brand identity in the development of brand image for HEIs.
- Explain the tools that are used to communicate brand image to various stakeholders.
- Explain the nature and role of reputation for HEIs.

2 Review of the literature in brand image and reputation in HEI

Higher education has seen a number of trends in recent decades, including reduced government involvement and an associated growing focus on generating profit (marketization), thereby instilling a growing need for HEI marketing to successfully compete in an increasingly competitive environment. This in turn has resulted in increasing efforts to create and communicate a favourable brand image to a diverse group of stakeholders (Brodie *et al.*, 2016; Hollebeek, 2015).

The nature of a brand image

A brand image denotes a product/service's identity and how it is viewed by external stakeholders, including customers. Brand image reflects how the brand is viewed by various stakeholders (Argenti, 2000), including (current/prospective) students, employers, and society at large. A brand image, which is created within the customer's mind, communicates functional and emotional brand-related values (Alwi and Kitchen, 2014). For example, for HEIs (prospective) students' brand image will include knowledge of the institution's offering (e.g. courses, activities, facilities), as well their emotional image-related response (Naidoo and Hollebeek, 2016).

Brand image differs from brand identity. That is, while brand identity reflects a brand's *organization-crafted* representation, brand image denotes the brand's perception by the *external market* (Keller, 2001). HEI-based brand identity is developed by virtue of marketing communications (including social media) attempting to convey it to stakeholders.

Complicating the understanding of brand image, there is a lack of agreement on what factors or dimensions make up HEI brand image (Lafuente-Ruiz-de-Sabando, Zorrilla, and Forcada, 2017). Some researchers have identified institutions' *teaching* and *research* activities as important brand image facets, while others have identified such aspects as *location, graduate employability, internationalization* and *media coverage*.

The importance of creating a strong brand image in HEI

Branding and brand image development is crucial for HEIs in an increasingly complex and competitive market (Hemsley-Brown and Goonawardana, 2007). In addition, declining government funding, and global changes in the tertiary education sector play an important role (Balaji, Roy, and Sadeque, 2016).

Due to these pressures, the development of a competitive advantage is important as it can be used as a basis for differentiation. The brand image (which could be associated with the institution's heritage, or research outputs) can raise the HEI's profile, thereby increasing institutional prestige and stakeholder preference. The development of a strong brand image offers numerous advantages to HEIs when interacting with their internal and external stakeholders and serves as a shortcut to reflect the HEI's quality (Jevons, 2006).

Benefits to (prospective) students

An important benefit of a strong brand image lies in the quality and number of prospective students the HEI could attract. Previous research suggests an institution's brand image as a key driver of students' HEI choice (Hemsley-Brown and Oplatka, 2006). A favourable HEI image sends signals about quality and trust (Balaji *et al.*, 2016), which is important when deciding where to study. A brand image enables students to identify their preferred HEIs, and serves as a basis for life-long engagement with the HEI (Stephenson and Yerger, 2014).

In addition, students are increasingly mobile, that is, they are willing to move to attend an HEI of their choice (Hemsley-Brown and Goonawardana, 2007), thus not limiting their market to a specific location. Institutional image also impacts on students' expectations that develop prior, during, and after their studies. That is, having studied at a reputable HEI imparts an expectation of future career success. Further, the ability to attract quality students impacts the HEI's future as they can improve its brand image once they enter the workplace.

Benefits to other internal stakeholders

Employees are critical to service organizations. In HEIs, faculty members and administrators are key customer-facing employees (Wilson, Zeithaml, Bitner, and Gremler, 2012). In their professional capacity faculty also interact with society and business, thereby further contributing to developing institutional brand image. Sample engagements include education, research, and developing employment possibilities for students (Dean *et al.*, 2016). A strong brand image can also lead to broader community-based invitations and networking or contact opportunities.

Not only can a brand image be used to attract students, it can also be deployed to attract quality faculty members (Chapleo, 2010; Hemsley-Brown and Goonawardana, 2007). In some disciplines there is a shortage of faculty, and an HEI's brand image and reputation can influence an academic's employment-related decision-making. The HEI's brand image is also important in faculty retention and productivity management (e.g. research outputs and teaching excellence) (Hemsley-Brown *et al.*, 2016). Educators and researchers would typically prefer to associate with HEIs offering a high quality (vs ambiguous) brand image and will tend to disseminate institution-related word of mouth (Brodie *et al.*, 2011; Hollebeek, 2011). A further effect of a high quality institutional brand image lies in its impact on staff management, including faculty members' allocated research and teaching loads (Jevons, 2006).

Benefits to external stakeholders

There are various external stakeholders who are influenced by institutional brand image. Having completed their tertiary studies, alumni play an important role in communicating the institution's image to others, including their employers. They will also influence others regarding the quality of their education and acquired skills, thereby helping to build the institution's reputation within their employing organizations, as well as in the business sector (Groeger, Moroko, and Hollebeek, 2016).

A high quality brand image not only helps in attracting quality students, but also assists in attracting sponsorships and (financial) support (Hemsley-Brown et al., 2016) from alumni and other donors (Stephenson and Yerger, 2014) in the alumni network or the wider business community. These donations or sponsorships can be used to develop facilities (e.g. buildings) or to support research.

The government is an additional key stakeholder that is responsible for developing the policies and legislation that regulate the awarding of degrees, as well as relevant regulations in the broader business sector. HEIs offering executive education will tend to understand the broader business sector's needs. This will enable them to generate revenue streams through research and teaching targeted at professionals and their employers (e.g. short courses specifically designed to meet focal employers' needs).

An HEI's brand image is not just important at a national level, but also on the international stage, including through the financial resources accruing from international students. Declining government revenue has required HEIs to attract fee-paying students, thereby increasing the importance of a strong international brand image. This is necessary to attract high-quality international students.

Brand image strategies in HEIs

With the increasing attention given to brand image in for-profit organizations, the question emerges as to its relevance for HEIs. Some believe brand image development is not an important activity for HEIs as the values that comprise brand identity/image cannot be easily portrayed to others. For example, how can HEI values such as freedom of speech, independence, and objectivity be reflected in a brand image (Wæraas and Solbakk, 2009)?

As brand image is used to differentiate HEIs (Melewar and Akel, 2005), it raises another issue. That is, if developing a positive brand image is something each HEI is doing, how then, can institutions differentiate themselves from one another (Argenti, 2000; Wæraas and Solbakk, 2009)? Therefore, is it possible to find a unique position, particularly given HEIs' common usage of such terms as 'world-class' and 'leading'?

Despite these challenges associated with institutional brand image development, stakeholders will hold some HEI-related brand image. It therefore becomes important to proactively manage brand image, and communicate focal brand-related activities and benefits to society.

Building a strong HEI brand image

While brand image is an important strategic tool for HEIs, research into HEI-based branding and brand image remains relatively limited

(Hemsley-Brown and Oplatka, 2006; Hemsley-Brown et al., 2016; Jevons, 2006; Wæraas and Solbakk, 2009; Wilson and Elliot, 2016). While some research has been conducted on the role of institutional heritage (Bulotaite, 2003), brand identity (Lowrie, 2007), and the role of online institutional branding (Opoku, Abratt, and Pitt, 2006), important HEI-based brand image-related gaps remain. For example, theorizing about institutional brand image development remains scarce (Lafuente-Ruiz-de-Sabando et al., 2017). In addition, while there is some insight into HEI branding (Hemsley-Brown and Oplatka, 2006), we did not identify any models that consider HEIs' unique environment and stakeholders. Furthermore, while service marketing or for-profit organization-based insight has been applied to institutional branding, these do not always reflect HEIs' unique characteristics and needs (Hemsley-Brown and Oplatka, 2006) nor its complexities (Chapleo, 2008, 2011).

Are HEI-based brand image building strategies the same as in other sectors?

The answer to this question is debated by academics. Yes, say Opoku et al. (2006), as they highlight the brand building-related similarities in HEIs, versus for-profit brands. Consequently, the application of for-profit branding-based insight and strategies is expected to generate valuable outcomes.

However, other academics adopt a different view, based on the following rationale. First, the nature of HEIs and their operating contexts differ from for-profit contexts, rendering traditional brand management strategies and techniques inadequate for HEIs (Chapleo, 2008; Jevons, 2006; Temple, 2006). HEIs are viewed as more complex due to the complex stakeholder network involved in developing an institutional brand image (Alexander, Jaakkola, and Hollebeek, 2017). For example, HEIs comprise various internal stakeholders (e.g. students, employees), as well as external stakeholders (e.g. alumni, graduate employers) (Wilson and Elliot, 2016). The institution's brand image therefore is impacted not only by the organization's brand communications, but also by the actions of its administrators, faculty and students. Further, in HEIs a great deal of the work is also conducted by students (paying customers), with their skills developing over time (Groeger et al., 2016; Hollebeek, Srivastava, and Chen, 2016; Temple, 2006). This means that by the time customers (graduates) leave the organization, their skill and competence levels will have changed (increased).

Second, HEIs are able to develop strong customer/staff emotional bonds and attachment, including through their brand-related heritage (Chapleo, 2008). For example, Oxford and Harvard Universities incorporate years of tradition and history in their brand images. Graduates can develop a lifelong attachment to 'their' institution, which can in turn generate future revenue for the institution (e.g. by children being encouraged to attend the specific institution).

A third argument is linked to HEIs' task and societal expectations of their task. HEIs have traditionally been funded by governments (i.e. taxpayers), which has placed expectations on HEIs in terms of their responsibility for delivery of quality graduates who meet structural needs within the economy and who are able to contribute positively to society (e.g. by not being unemployed for extended periods). Traditional branding models tend to overlook these societal expectations.

Fourth, traditional brand management strategies tend to be inadequate in the HEI market as its environment comprises several unique characteristics. In the case of traditional products and services, organizations sell to any consumer who is willing and able to pay. However, HEIs are able to evaluate and select students who they believe are suitable to take specific courses and not accept others. That is, customers' ability to pay is not the critical selection criterion. Reasons for not offering students a place could be linked to their (sub-standard) academic results, although some HEIs reserve places for particular (e.g. ethnic, gender) minorities, limiting the number of available places for other groups.

In more traditional HEIs, internal resistance to the use of marketing and branding strategies may also exist (Argenti, 2000; Jevons, 2006). This is important because while all parties (including faculty and administrators) are involved in developing the institution's brand image, some actors may not support its implementation.

A final argument asks what brand image development involves for HEIs and questions whether this is necessary. Some view branding as being closer to public relations (PR) or reputation management (Temple, 2006). Shattock (2003) views a university brand from the perspective of reputation and corporate image (Temple, 2006), which begs the question as to whether university brands actually exist. As a result, HEIs cannot really differentiate themselves, as illustrated by Jevons (2006). Universities that are uncertain about what is important for the brand, their students, or other stakeholders, grasp at less-than-differentiating value propositions. An example of this is seen in a US university that used the advertising tag line of 'one of Florida's 11 public universities'.

Despite these differing views, it remains essential for HEIs to develop a clear brand identity and image. However, further theorizing in this area is needed.

Building a brand image

While brand image exists in stakeholders' minds, HEIs need to proactively determine how they will go about developing their desired brand image. Brand image development thus starts within the HEI. The stages comprising this process are shown in Figure 8.1.

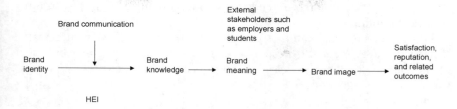

Figure 8.1 Brand image development.
Source: adapted from Kapferer (2012); Berthon, Pitt, and Campbell (2009); Wilson and Elliot (2016).

First steps: brand identity development (see Chapter 2)

To develop a brand image, it is important that the organization has a brand identity it can communicate to its stakeholders (Kapferer, 2012). For example, corporate culture is part of HEI branding (Wæraas and Solbakk, 2009), thereby ensuring that shared employee vision and purpose is of key importance (Wæraas and Solbakk, 2009). HEIs require clearly articulated institutional values and a clear vision (strategic agenda) that needs to reflect their audiences' (e.g. customers') needs and values. Brand identity development would also emphasize the importance of employees 'living the brand' (Wæraas and Solbakk, 2009), while adopting a shared organizational vision derived by interacting with HEI management, colleagues and students.

The importance of brand-related communication for brand identity development

After determining the HEI's desired identity, key brand-related content is communicated to the HEI's various audiences. This process includes the development of promotional material (e.g. advertising, logos, online media). An integrated marketing communication-based program is developed to target the organization's stakeholders. For example, communications aimed at prospective students may focus on such issues as the quality of education and future employability, while those aimed at graduates' future employers would focus on key graduate skills.

University rankings are widely used to communicate HEI quality and reputation, thereby assisting the development of brand image. HEIs tend to regularly communicate their upward movement in relevant rankings. Double (or dual) degrees represent a particular type of HEI alliance that allows students to obtain their qualifications from two HEIs at once (Naidoo and Hollebeek, 2016). A critical success factor for such double degrees is stakeholder support of the individual institution's, and the particular alliance's brand image and their respective fit. In addition, accreditation (e.g. AACSB or EQUIS) can serve to strengthen the HEIs' brand image, which therefore tends to be explicitly included in institution-related communications.

HEI-based communication to its (external) stakeholders is necessary (Melewar and Akel, 2005), which needs to not only be consistent in terms of its content, but also in selecting appropriate communication channels for particular stakeholders.

Brand image development

The literature identifies two key components that contribute to brand image development, including brand-related meaning and knowledge (Alwi and Kitchen, 2014; Balaji *et al.*, 2016). The receiver therefore needs to know (and interpret) the content of HEI-related communication while also understanding the message.

a Developing brand knowledge

Brand knowledge refers to the factual knowledge that a student (or other stakeholder) holds about an HEI, which provides a basis for institutional differentiation (Wilson and Elliot, 2016). Brand knowledge develops through the actor's exposure to brand-related communication messages and channels, which may fulfil differing objectives (Keller, 2003). For example, while organizations search for talented employees, the institution's educational standards are critical to potential students. This means that an HEI needs to communicate different information to various groups, which the parties can use to clearly connect to the brand. From these, functional and emotional HEI-related values will develop. HEIs can develop stakeholders' brand-related knowledge in various areas (e.g. through research reports/publications). HEIs may also communicate the successes of their graduates, or achievements of their faculty in the media (including social media) and on their websites as part of this effort.

b Creating brand meaning

From an actor's brand-related communication and knowledge, HEIs will derive a particular brand meaning (Berthon, Pitt, and Campbell, 2009; Wilson and Elliot, 2016). If there is no shared institution-related meaning between the institution and its audiences (e.g. prospective customers), effective communication has not taken place. This is important as brand image development is based on adequate sender/receiver communication, that is, the development of prospective students' HEI image as *desired* by the organization. A gap between (prospective) students' perceived, and the organization's intended brand meaning may occur. Brand meaning can also differ across institutional stakeholders (e.g. students vs faculty) and may change over time as a result of stakeholders' interactions with the brand. For example, while current students may have been attracted to the HEI based on a particular perceived brand meaning, this continues to develop during and after their studies (Dennis *et al.*, 2016).

High quality brand image outcomes: satisfaction, reputation and related outcomes

Numerous outcomes are associated with the creation of a positive brand image, including consumer (student) satisfaction and loyalty, organizational reputation, etc.

Satisfaction reflects the extent to which the overall service meets (or exceeds) customer expectations (Wilson *et al.*, 2012). A positive brand image influences customer expectations as well as perceptions, thereby affecting satisfaction. Extensive research shows that brand image impacts on students' HEI satisfaction, though a negative relationship between these concepts has also been identified (Lafuente-Ruiz-de-Sabando *et al.*, 2017). Satisfaction in turn contributes to HEI loyalty, and the development of institutional reputation.

Other related outcomes include the development of brand identification among students, as well as faculty. Brand identification refers to actors' attachment or sense of belonging towards the institution (Balaji *et al.*, 2016), thereby impacting actors' self-identity through their association with a particular school. High levels of student commitment are seen in individuals making institution-related contributions beyond their traditional role expectations (Balaji *et al.*, 2016), including by being involved in extracurricular or social activities and societies. These activities in turn exert an effect on alumni support through their relationship with the HEI and affect other variables, such as the HEI's future donations. High brand identification also increases the likelihood of students acting as brand ambassadors (Balaji *et al.*, 2016; Stephenson and Yerger, 2014).

For faculty, institutional identification may be linked to (a) particular institutional centre(s), department(s) or unit(s), as opposed to the broader institution per se. For example, an institution may have several colleges (units) where college identification is stronger than that with the institution at large (Jevons, 2006). The faculty still represent the image of the HEI in their academic activities and reflect its mission and values.

Measuring brand image

While a positive brand image has been reported to generate enhanced consumer brand awareness and sales, HEIs' brand image links to student enrolments only *indirectly* (e.g. given consumers' high involvement decision-making that has long-term consequences e.g. in terms of graduate employability, etc.), thereby complicating the measurement process.

While a favourable brand image will have a range of positive outcomes, there is no consensus on the concept's dimensions, or its suitable measurement (Lafuente-Ruiz-de-Sabando et al., 2017). While HEIs make vast brand-related (including promotional) investments, they tend to lack accountability regarding the efficiency of these investments (Jevons, 2006).

University reputation: issues and management

Reputation, which reflects stakeholders' overall perception of an organization (Argenti, 2000), impacts the extent to which the institution is able to influence stakeholder actions and its environment. While Frost and Cooke (1999) refer to reputation as organizational image, others view the concept as the actors' evaluation of organizational performance. Thus, for some, reputation is a function of corporate communication, while, for others, it is linked to stakeholders' experiences with the organization. Communicating relevant academic achievements and positive outcomes (e.g. accreditations) can thus contribute to the development of institutional reputation. The importance of reputation here lies in its link to brand image (Nguyen and LeBlanc, 2001).

Reputable HEIs are able to charge higher prices for their offerings, and will tend to have a lower employee churn rate (Argenti, 2000). In addition, they are also likely to receive more applications from quality students, and would also be able to select/reject students without their decision significantly affecting the institution's reputation (Dean et al., 2016).

While many scholars believe brand image and reputation to be differing constructs, Frost and Cooke (1999) view these as aspects of 'the same thing'. Therefore, while these may be distinct theoretically, in a practical sense they may exhibit some degree of overlap (Chapleo, 2008).

Reputation drivers

Several *controllable* factors influence institutional reputation (Frost and Cooke, 1999), including:

- Communication, including traditional communicative forms, institutional branding tools (e.g. logo), and new media (e.g. social media-based) communications.
- The HEI's brand identity that reflects how it wishes to be seen (Frost and Cooke, 1999) which is a reflection of its mission and vision.
- Physical evidence in the campus and facilities (e.g. aspects of the service's physical delivery location (servicescape), staff presentation, etc.) (Bitner, 1992).
- Stakeholder (e.g. customer, staff) interactions (e.g. customer service) (Cockburn, 2017) contribute to the development of institutional reputation (Frost and Cooke, 1999). These also contribute to word-of-mouth,

which can significantly influence potential students' institution-related decision-making.
- The institution's position in relevant rankings (Argenti, 2000), which tend to be used in institutional brand communication (particularly for highly ranked institutions). However, the ranking needs to be important to the target audience and reflect a significant aspect for the target market.
- University, faculty and facilities actions (Nguyen and LeBlanc, 2001). Examples of these actions on institutional reputation can be seen in recent discussions regarding the salary levels of chancellors in UK universities that exceed those of leading business executives, or faculty plagiarizing or committing other ethical infractions in their research (e.g. fabricating their data).
- Inter-institutional alliances can also influence reputation (Kalafatis et al., 2016). Examples include double-degrees (Naidoo and Hollebeek, 2016), or overseas campuses that bear the name of the parent institution (e.g. Monash University's Sunway Campus in Malaysia), thereby enabling the transfer of the parent institution's reputational benefits to the other party, for mutual benefit.

Reputation management

Institutional reputation management is a continual communicative process about the organization and its activities. Frost and Cooke (1999) suggest that institutional reputation management begins with the establishment of a clear brand identity, followed by transparent institutional communication to its relevant stakeholder groups. Implementing these values in day-to-day offline (e.g. face-to-face) and online (e.g. social media-based) stakeholder interactions represents an integral part of institutional reputation management. An overview of brand image and reputation's effects on key institutional stakeholders is provided in Table 8.1.

3 Managerial implications

HEI brand identity, image and reputation building represent an important strategic activity with wide-ranging effects on students, faculty and other institutional stakeholders. It is an important contributor to the institutional climate that will impact on students' institution-related perceptions and faculty's job engagement and satisfaction.

The development of a positive academic environment is a key part of this climate. Therefore, the institution's internal stakeholders need to collaborate to deliver a synergistic student (and employer) experience. In addition, the development of students' relevant transferable skills during their degree is of key importance in shaping institutional brand image and reputation. Institutions are thus advised to establish relevant student bodies

Table 8.1 Brand image/reputation's effects on key institutional stakeholders

Internal stakeholders	
Administrators	While the role of deans and administrators is critical in the development of the institutional mission/vision, their specific role in institutional brand image development remains poorly understood.
Faculty	Faculty's importance can be used in the institution's brand-related development (e.g. promotion). Faculty are critical in brand image/reputation formation and maintenance, including through their direct encounters with customers/students.
External stakeholders	
Students and alumni	At various points in time, prospective students will choose a particular institution to study at, thereby taking on the role of student, followed by those of graduate and then alumnus/a. They have a powerful influence on the HEI brand.
Employers and business organisations	Academic research lags behind in uncovering insight into the business sector's perceptions of the institution, students, graduates, etc.
Government and general public/society	As a major educational stakeholder, government decision-making in this area has far-reaching (inter)national ramifications, which remain underexplored to date.

and societies that help students nurture important skills (e.g. debating skills through a debating society).

In light of integrated marketing communications (IMC), the institution's key attributes or benefits need to be communicated in a consistent manner to (prospective) students. Institutional IMC will also need to take into account the unique needs and preferences (in terms of both content and media channels) of relevant stakeholder groups.

4 Conclusion

This chapter has focused on the process of HEI-based brand identity, image and reputation development, which begins with a clearly defined, unique brand identity communicated to relevant stakeholders (e.g. prospective/current students). Once the brand image is created, it needs to be maintained to ensure it remains relevant.

Further development and testing of HEI branding models is required, in particular models that explain how brand identity creates brand image for the institution's various stakeholder groups. To date, HEI-based brand image remains unclear, thereby necessitating the undertaking of further research in this area.

Relatedly, methodological rigour in the domain of brand image/reputation represents another focus area of debate, including in HEIs.

Consequently, more comprehensive measures need to be developed, and also merit further research.

5 Case study

Well-known HEIs, such as Harvard University and Oxford University, have a heritage that helps drive their reputational development. However, building a brand image for a new university can be challenging. Key among these challenges are (a) successful market entry and (b) developing a brand image that differentiates the institution in highly competitive (or saturated) markets.

One HEI that has successfully developed a favourable brand image is Nanyang Technological University in Singapore. Not only does it rank in the top 5 of Young Universities and the top 5 in Asia, but it also appears in rankings that include traditional institutions. Established in 1981, it has rapidly moved up regional, national and international rankings.

Nanyang Technological University offers double-major degrees at the Bachelor level (e.g. a double-major in Accounting and Marketing). Double-majors are also offered across functional areas, such as Engineering and Science. At the Masters level, double-degree programs are offered in conjunction with the University of St. Gallen (Switzerland), ESSEC (France) and Waseda University (Japan). Research and teaching excellence represent an integral part of the institution's strategy. In addition, 31 per cent of students are classified as international students.

Nanyang Technological University uses a range of traditional and new media, including its website and social media (e.g. Facebook, Twitter). Traditional communication forms include press releases, speeches and media reports. News updates are placed on the website, and there are regular postings on Facebook and other social media platforms (Hollebeek, Glynn, and Brodie, 2014). Posts may address student-related activities, or research achievements, etc.

The institution has numerous alumni and many scientists, entrepreneurs and celebrities have Nanyang Technological University as their *alma mater* (e.g. the founders of Foodpanda, the Reebonz group and Sunseap Leasing, Singapore's largest clean energy provider) (Anon, 2016).

6 Further investigation

Based on these analyses, we suggest the following avenues for further research in this area:

- Investigation into the key drivers in students' HEI decision-making.
- Exploring the role of institutional brand identity, image and reputation in students' study decisions.
- Examining the effect of a change of dean (or other leading management team members) on an HEI's brand identity, image and reputation.

- Exploring employers' needs and their associated recruitment-related decision-making for new graduates and more senior positions.
- Assessing how an HEI-related crisis (e.g. through unfavourable media coverage) affects HEIs' brand identity, image and reputation.

References

Alexander, M., Jaakkola, E., and Hollebeek, L. (2017) "Zooming out: Actor engagement beyond the dyadic." *Journal of Service Management* 29(3), pp. 333–351.

Alwi, S. F. S., and Kitchen, P. J. (2014) "Projecting corporate brand image and behavioral response in business schools: Cognitive or affective brand attributes?" *Journal of Business Research* 67(11), pp. 2324–2336.

Anon. (2016) NTU alumni entrepreneurs making it big [Press release]. Retrieved from http://enewsletter.ntu.edu.sg/ntulink/Jun-Aug%202016/Pages/cs5.aspx?AspxAutoDetectCookieSupport=1.

Argenti, P. (2000) "Branding B-schools: Reputation management for MBA programs." *Corporate Reputation Review* 3(2), pp. 171–178.

Balaji, M., Roy, S. K., and Sadeque, S. (2016) "Antecedents and consequences of university brand identification." *Journal of Business Research* 69(8), pp. 3023–3032.

Berthon, P., Pitt, L. F., and Campbell, C. (2009) "Does brand meaning exist in similarity or singularity?" *Journal of Business Research* 62(3), pp. 356–361.

Bitner, M. J. (1992) "Servicescapes: The impact of physical surroundings on customers and employees." *The Journal of Marketing* 56(2), pp. 57–71.

Brodie, R., Fehrer, J., Jaakkola, E., Hollebeek, L., and Conduit, J. (2016) *From customer to actor engagement: exploring a broadened conceptual domain.* Paper presented at the Proceedings of the 2016 EMAC Annual Conference.

Brodie, R., Hollebeek, L., Jurić, B., and Ilić, A. (2011) "Customer engagement: Conceptual domain, fundamental propositions, and implications for research." *Journal of Service Research* 14(3), pp. 252–271.

Bulotaite, N. (2003) "University heritage – an institutional tool for branding and marketing." *Higher Education in Europe, Vol. XXVIII, No. 4, December 2003,* 28(4), pp. 449–454.

Chapleo, C. (2008) "External perceptions of successful university brands." *International Journal of Educational Advancement* 8(3–4), pp. 126–135.

Chapleo, C. (2010) "What defines 'successful' university brands?" *International Journal of public sector management* 23(2), pp. 169–183.

Chapleo, C. (2011) "Exploring rationales for branding a university: Should we be seeking to measure branding in UK universities?" *Journal of Brand Management* 18(6), pp. 411–422.

Cockburn, S. (2017) 4 areas that influence brand reputation. Retrieved from http://growingsocialbiz.com/4-areas-that-influence-brand-reputation/.

Dean, D., Arroyo-Gamez, R. E., Punjaisri, K., and Pich, C. (2016) "Internal brand co-creation: The experiential brand meaning cycle in higher education." *Journal of Business Research* 69(8), pp. 3041–3048.

Dennis, C., Papagiannidis, S., Alamanos, E., and Bourlakis, M. (2016) "The role of brand attachment strength in higher education." *Journal of Business Research* 69(8), pp. 3049–3057.

Frost, A. R., and Cooke, C. (1999) "Brand v reputation: Managing an intangible asset." *Journal of Brand Management* 7(2), pp. 81–87.

Groeger, L., Moroko, L., and Hollebeek, L. (2016) "Capturing value from non-paying consumers' engagement behaviours: field evidence and development of a theoretical model." *Journal of Strategic Marketing* 24(3–4), pp. 190–209.

Hemsley-Brown, J. and Goonawardana, S. (2007) "Brand harmonization in the international higher education market." *Journal of Business Research* 60(9), pp. 942–948.

Hemsley-Brown, J., Melewar, T., Nguyen, B., and Wilson, E. J. (2016) "Exploring brand identity, meaning, image, and reputation (BIMIR) in higher education." *Journal of Business Research* 69(8), pp. 3019–3022.

Hemsley-Brown, J. and Oplatka, I. (2006) "Universities in a competitive global marketplace: A systematic review of the literature on higher education marketing." *International Journal of Public Sector Management* 19(4), pp. 316–338.

Hollebeek, L. (2011) "Exploring customer brand engagement: Definition and themes." *Journal of Strategic Marketing* 19(7), pp. 555–573.

Hollebeek, L. (2015) "Exploring customer engagement: A multi-stakeholder perspective," in R. Brodie, L. Hollebeek, and J. Conduit (eds), *Customer Engagement: Contemporary Issues and Challenges*. Singapore: Routledge, pp. 67–82.

Hollebeek, L., Glynn, M. S., and Brodie, R. J. (2014) "Consumer brand engagement in social media: Conceptualization, scale development and validation." *Journal of Interactive Marketing* 28(2), pp. 149–165.

Hollebeek, L., Srivastava, R. K., and Chen, T. (2016) "SD logic–informed customer engagement: Integrative framework, revised fundamental propositions, and application to CRM." *Journal of the Academy of Marketing Science*, September, pp. 1–25. DOI 10.1007/s11747-016-0494-5.

Jevons, C. (2006) "Universities: A prime example of branding going wrong." *Journal of Product & Brand Management* 15(7), pp. 466–467.

Kalafatis, S. P., Ledden, L., Riley, D., and Singh, J. (2016) "The added value of brand alliances in higher education." *Journal of Business Research* 69(8), pp. 3122–3132.

Kapferer, J.-N. (2012) *The New Strategic Brand Management Advanced Insights and Strategic Thinking* (5th edition). London; Philadelphia: Kogan Page.

Keller, K. L. (2001) Building customer-based brand equity: A blueprint for creating strong brands (01–107). Retrieved from www.mktg.uni-svishtov.bg.

Keller, K. L. (2003) "Brand synthesis: The multidimensionality of brand knowledge." *Journal of Consumer Research* 29(4), pp. 595–600.

Lafuente-Ruiz-de-Sabando, A., Zorrilla, P., and Forcada, J. (2017) "A review of higher education image and reputation literature: Knowledge gaps and a research agenda." *European Research on Management and Business Economics* 24(1), pp. 8–16.

Lowrie, A. (2007) "Branding higher education: Equivalence and difference in developing identity." *Journal of Business Research* 60(9), pp. 990–999.

Melewar, T. and Akel, S. (2005) "The role of corporate identity in the higher education sector: A case study." *Corporate Communications: An International Journal* 10(1), pp. 41–57.

Naidoo, V. and Hollebeek, L. D. (2016) "Higher education brand alliances: Investigating consumers' dual-degree purchase intentions." *Journal of Business Research* 69(8), pp. 3113–3121.

Nguyen, N. and LeBlanc, G. (2001) "Image and reputation of higher education institutions in students' retention decisions." *International Journal of Educational Management* 15(6), pp. 303–311.

Opoku, R., Abratt, R., and Pitt, L. (2006) "Communicating brand personality: Are the websites doing the talking for the top South African Business Schools?" *Journal of Brand Management* 14(1–2), pp. 20–39.

Shattock, M. L. (2003) *Managing Successful Universities*. Maidenhead: SRHE/ Open University Press.

Stephenson, A. L. and Yerger, D. B. (2014) "Does brand identification transform alumni into university advocates?" *International Review on Public and Non-profit Marketing* 11(3), pp. 243–262.

Temple, P. (2006) "Branding higher education: Illusion or reality?" *Perspective* 10(1), pp. 15–19.

Wæraas, A. and Solbakk, M. N. (2009) "Defining the essence of a university: Lessons from higher education branding." *Higher Education* 57(4), p. 449.

Wilson, A., Zeithaml, V. A., Bitner, M. J., and Gremler, D. D. (2012) *Services Marketing: Integrating Customer Focus Across the Firm* (2nd European edition). London: McGraw-Hill.

Wilson, E. J. and Elliot, E. A. (2016) "Brand meaning in higher education: Leaving the shallows via deep metaphors." *Journal of Business Research* 69(8), pp. 3058–3068.

Further reading

Bruno, A. J. (2015) https://blog.trendkite.com/trendkite-blog/brand-image-vs-reputation-what-s-the-difference.

Tanksalvala, S. (n.d.) The importance of understanding your university's reputation. http://stateofinnovation.com/the-importance-of-understanding-your-universitys-reputation-and-rankings.

Torrillo, J. (2014) *Academic Reputation is the Most Important Factor in College Choice*, March 19, www.reputationmanagement.com/blog/academic-reputation-important-factor-college-choice/.

9 Co-creation of value
A customer-integration approach

Tim Hughes and Ian Brooks

1 Introduction

The idea of students as consumers of higher education is problematical in a number of ways. The approach taken in this chapter is to consider higher education as an example of co-creation of value between the student and the university: 'Maybe the education service is one of the best representative examples of the value co-creation approach: if students do not work on their own, they cannot get a result regardless of lecturer performance' (Díaz-Méndez and Gummesson, 2012, p. 578).

The framework for co-creation utilized in this chapter comes from Service-Dominant Logic [S-D Logic] (Vargo and Lusch, 2004). This is an alternative explanation of markets to the established Goods-Dominant Logic. S-D Logic is put forward as a more satisfactory theoretical basis that explains the way markets operate. In particular, S-D Logic is compelling in analysing a complex and interactive service offering such as higher education: 'Higher education, as a service, has some specific characteristics. These include the high level of active involvement demanded of the individuals accessing the service; a prolonged service relationship, and a great variety in the nature of the service offered' (Chalcraft, Hilton, and Hughes, 2015).

After reading this chapter, you should be able to:

- Critique the market-based view of students as customers.
- Distinguish between a Goods-Dominant Logic and Service-Dominant Logic, as an explanation of markets.
- Consider the implications of co-creation of value for higher education.

2 Review of the literature on co-creation of value

The student as customer

The increasing influence of market competition on higher education has been a subject for discussion for some time (Williams, 1995). Critics of the market approach claim that treating students as consumers is detrimental to education outcomes (Molesworth, Nixon, and Scullion, 2009; Arum and Roksa, 2011), leading to a focus on short term gains rather than scholarly development. In particular, treating the student as a customer can lead to one-sided expectations that tutors are responsible for the student's learning rather than the student taking personal responsibility (Ng and Forbes, 2009). However, the extent to which this has actually happened is challenged (Koris *et al.*, 2015) and there is some evidence that most students do not express a customer orientation towards their education (Saunders, 2015).

Presenting higher education as a market is then the subject of debate. A particular problem is that the student as customer view does lead to assumptions on how a market works that are not appropriate for analysing the provision of higher education. The idea that the student is a consumer who expects to receive a degree in return for a fee payment suggests an exchange view of the market stemming from a Goods-Dominant Logic. However, there is an alternative view of the market that may be more appropriate. Vargo and Lusch's (2004) concept of S-D Logic is put forward as a more satisfactory explanation of markets, based on co-creation of value-in-use rather than value-in-exchange.

The next section discusses the ideas around co-creation of value and S-D Logic in preparation for applying these ideas to higher education.

Co-creation of value and S-D Logic

Vargo and Lusch's seminal (2004) paper identified how marketing has shifted its dominant logic away from the exchange of tangible goods (Goods-Dominant Logic) towards the exchange of intangibles, specialized skills, and knowledge and processes (S-D Logic). It is important to understand that Vargo and Lusch are not talking about a move away from goods towards services. They are claiming a new perspective on how the market works. Thus it is an explanation of both goods and services marketing. Value is only created when goods or service are consumed, in contrast to traditional economic theory that emphasizes value in exchange (e.g. value is conceptualized as the payment received for a product or service).

The idea that value is created in use is important. Value-in-use recognizes that customers are co-creators of their own value and they determine what is of value (Lusch and Vargo, 2006; Vargo and Lusch, 2008a). The customer creates value for himself or herself, but while interacting with the customer, the supplier can influence the process of value creation (Grönroos and Ravald, 2011). Starting with this idea, the strategic role of any supplier is therefore to support its customers in creating value (Ballantyne, Williams, and Aitken, 2011).

Co-creation of value should not be confused with service co-production. Value creation is a customer perception and each customer will perceive the value received in their own unique way. In some cases, the customer may also co-produce the service, for example by using self-service at supermarket checkouts. Mixing service co-production with value creation may have contributed to confusion in the earlier literature on S-D Logic (Vargo and Lusch, 2008b). Value is always co-created and sometimes may involve elements of co-production.

A central and prevailing theme of S-D Logic is that value is created by service-for-service exchange (Vargo and Lusch, 2004, 2008b, 2016, 2017). S-D Logic, by emphasizing service provision, highlights the purpose that motivates relationships – 'That is, the purpose of interaction, and thus relationship, is value co-creation through mutual service provision' (Vargo, 2009, p. 378). Higher education can be seen as service, in which skills and knowledge are applied to gain new insights for the benefit of stakeholders. Prime stakeholders in this are students. Lecturers combine their knowledge with that of the students to develop the students' resources in terms of knowledge and skills.

Co-creation of value and higher education

Vargo and Lusch (2016) have recently restated the core ideas of S-D Logic as fundamental axioms, based on ten years of debate. Value co-creation takes place through **actors** taking part in **resource integration** and **service exchange**, enabled and constrained by **institutions and institutional arrangements**, establishing **service eco-systems** of **value creation**. Table 9.1 takes these ideas and adapts them to the higher education context.

In higher education, value is co-created between lecturers and their students, but there are many other actors who contribute. The student experience is shaped by administration and support staff, the involvement of industry, and not least, by interacting with other students.

The actors integrate operant resources (Lusch and Vargo, 2011). Operant resources typically involve knowledge and skills (Vargo and Lusch 2004, 2008a) and it is the integration of the operant resources, from the actors, that creates value (Löbler, 2011; Lusch and Vargo, 2011; Kleineltankamp *et al.*, 2012). When lecturers interact with students, both parties bring in a range of operant resources. A resource integration perspective encourages an examination of the nature of the resource inputs from the actors and a consideration of how these resources may change and develop in the process. An actor can be involved in resource integration at varying levels from very active to passive (Löbler, 2013). For example, a student, in developing as an independent learner over the course of their degree, should become more active in directing their own learning, requiring different resource inputs from their lecturers over time. The concept is also useful in considering types of students. A postgraduate part-time MBA student will bring operant resources from their work experience and will benefit from an approach that integrates this experience with the theoretical knowledge of the lecturer

Table 9.1 Application of core ideas from S-D Logic to higher education

Vargo and Lusch's (2016) core ideas of value co-creation	Application to higher education
Actors	Value co-creation takes place amongst generic actors (Axiom 2). This is more complex than thinking about customer/supplier. In higher education, value is co-created between lecturers, students, administrators, support staff, networks connected to the university and others.
Resource integration	All economic and social actors are resource integrators (Axiom 3). Students come into higher education with a range of existing knowledge and skills. Lecturers integrate their knowledge with that of their students in the course of teaching and learning. Thus, learning can be seen as the development of the students' operant resources over time.
Service exchange	Service is the fundamental basis of exchange (Axiom 1). Value is created by service exchange. Lecturers and other staff provide service, but value is only created when students engage with the service.
Institutions and institutional arrangements	Value co-creation is coordinated through actor-generated institutions and institutional arrangements (Axiom 5). The contexts of the different types of students are highly significant in understanding how they learn and utilize knowledge.
Service eco-systems	Higher education takes place within a service eco-system. A service ecosystem perspective enables managers to view their organization from a broader and more enlightening perspective (Greer, Lush, and Vargo, 2016).
Value creation	Value is always uniquely and phenomenologically determined by the beneficiary (Axiom 4). Academics and students will have a range of different perceptions in relation to the value of the educational experience and its longer term impact on each student's career. Value can be seen in utilisation and, in the case of education, utilisation may not take place until many years after the original provision of service. The challenge in this is that at the point of delivery utilisation potential may not be obvious.

effectively. In addition, the students benefit from interacting with each other and integrating knowledge across different sectors. While a traditional value-in-exchange approach concentrates on the organization's resources, S-D Logic takes account of how value is created by the interaction of all actors in integrating their resources (Dziewanowska, 2017).

In addition to integrating resources, the actors are involved in service exchange. Actors in the higher education institution provide a service to students, but value is only created when students are influenced by the service provided. The level of engagement in the service exchange may vary and this may have significant implications for the value created. Actors in higher education do not create value just by offering the service; it requires student engagement with the service for value to be created. Within S-D Logic, the core service in a university is a learning experience that is co-created and emergent (Ng and Forbes, 2009). Lusch and Wu, (2012, p. 4) put it this way:

> At the very least, a service perspective provides us a means of holistically perceiving students' needs. Therefore, the value of a lecture is not something the instructor produces alone. The value of a lecture, as service, is always co-created with the students.

Institutions and institutional logics are the formal and informal constraints (rules and norms) that shape actors' behaviour in resource integration (Edvardsson *et al.*, 2014). Higher education institutions have their own logics that influence their expectations of students and impact on the way students are treated. Understanding the role that these institutional norms play in shaping behaviour and perceptions is highly relevant. At the same time, it is useful to consider the differing institutional logics that have shaped the previous education of students. For example, international students will have been educated previously in many different contexts. Students may have come from institutions that encourage rote learning and discourage questioning and criticality.

Co-creation takes place within a service eco-system, a relatively self-contained system for co-creating mutual value through service exchange (Vargo and Lusch, 2014). Higher education institutions are part of an eco-system containing schools, colleges, the business community, the public sector, charities etc. The idea of an eco-system reminds us of how universities are linked to the economy and society. Pressures for universities to demonstrate economic and social impact across many advanced economies (Watson *et al.*, 2011; Perkmann *et al.*, 2013) reflect policy-makers' expectations in this respect.

Axiom 4 underlines the need to consider perspectives on value from different points of view. According to S-D Logic terminology, lecturers provide students with a value proposition (Díaz-Méndez and Gummesson, 2012). If the value proposition is sufficiently motivating the actors (the students) commit their operant resources to the value creation process (Ballantyne and Varey, 2006). Therefore, universities present a value proposition, at a high level, to attract students to choose a particular institution in the first place. Determining value at an individual level can be highly complex due to the gap between the provision of the service and the use of the knowledge or skills provided. There is a challenge in determining the usefulness of knowledge provided well ahead of utilization. For

Table 9.2 Key issues

The idea of the student as customer can be problematical in considering higher education

However, many of the problems with this approach can be seen to stem from a transactional, Goods-Dominant view of the market

Service-Dominant logic provides an alternative approach based on co-creation of value in use

In Service-Dominant logic, higher education is the provision of service, involving integration of resources

Institutions coordinate service exchange in service eco systems

Value will be perceived differently by all the actors involved

It is important to recognise the responsibility the student has for co-creating his or her own value

---

example, the full benefits of learning about management or marketing strategy might not be apparent until the student has worked his or her way up to a level in a company where they have to make strategic decisions.

While value can be co-created, it can also be co-destroyed (Plé and Chumpitaz Cáceres, 2010) as a result of non-positive outcomes from actor-to-actor interactions (Prior and Marcos-Cuevas, 2016). At a less extreme level, defective co-creation can occur when the actors under-participate, failing to input resources of sufficient quality or quantity to facilitate value co-creation (Greer, 2015), or when role conflicts occur (Chowdhury, Gruber and Zolkiewski, 2016). It is important to recognize the responsibility the student has for co-creating his or her own value.

3 Managerial implications

What are the implications of taking a co-creative approach to higher education management?

The role of the university

A co-creative approach, based on S-D Logic, challenges universities to take on board how they create value in the wider service eco-system:

> It is essential that higher education recognize that what the university produces on campus, in the classroom, or online and packages to create an output (a college degree) is only the starting point of a longer process that co-creates value.
>
> (Lusch and Wu, 2012, p. 5)

The expectation of universities in relation to their role in society and the economy has been discussed extensively in the literature (Perkmann *et al.*, 2013). Universities are now seen as integral to regional innovation and economic development (Etzkowitz, 2011; Mackenzie and Zhang, 2014) and there are pressures for the higher education sector to be more outward facing and engaged with society and the economy across the world (Watson et al., 2011).

A service ecosystem perspective enables managers to view their organization from a broader and more enlightening perspective (Greer, Lusch, and Vargo, 2016). Engagement and interaction in society and the economy requires universities to be outward facing and open beyond the academic community. This is a challenge for many academics unused to moving between the different communities of academia and practice (Shrivastava and Mitroff, 1984). Universities could provide greater support for academics in engaging with society and the economy. This includes providing training and mentoring for younger academics. PhD programmes could include a greater emphasis on how research is utilized. Academic careers are traditionally built on producing academic journal articles, but incentives to encourage the generation of wider impact from research would be valuable in encouraging wider engagement. The inclusion in the UK Research Evaluation Framework (REF) of Impact Case Studies provides an opportunity to demonstrate effective dissemination and impact of research outside the academic community.

As well as creating an internal environment that is supportive of academic engagement, universities need to be proactive in developing collaborative eco-systems (Rothwell, 1994, Perkmann et al., 2013). Reaching out to actors in communities outside the university is not new; however, there is plenty of room for further development. A starting point is to identify key stakeholder groups in the wider community. Taking business and management as an example, connections with practitioners are frequently used to keep the syllabus up to date with current practice; to provide students with work experience; to bring in external speakers; and to provide graduates with job opportunities. Thus the value of the student experience in applied subjects, such as business and management, can be seen to be enhanced greatly by engagement with the business community.

The student experience

In higher education, value is co-created between a number of different actors including lecturers, students, administrators, support staff, networks connected to the university and others. Student satisfaction is impacted by a range of elements in their overall educational experience. Therefore, a holistic approach needs to be adopted rather than dealing with each dimension in isolation in creating a valued education (Lai et al., 2015). This requires universities to understand the overall experience of students from the student's point of view.

This is not easy because value is always uniquely and phenomenologically determined by the beneficiary (Axiom 4). Hence value will be perceived differently by all the actors involved. While universities cannot cater for every individual student's whim it is possible to relate to the needs of different groups. For example international student cohorts coming from a range of backgrounds will perceive their experience in the light of their educational backgrounds and cultures. The contexts of the different types of students are highly significant in understanding how they learn and utilize knowledge. Effective resource integration requires an understanding that students come into higher education with a range of existing knowledge and skills.

A co-creative approach requires universities to take a user perspective and this can be challenging for a large institution organized around functions and faculties. Supporting individuals through providing personal tutors who engage with individual students throughout their educational experience is one approach, but this does require engagement of the student with the process.

Student engagement

As discussed earlier in the chapter, taking a value-in-exchange approach to considering the student as customer implies that tutors are responsible for student learning, ignoring the role that students have to play as active and responsible learners. In S-D Logic the supplier offers value propositions, but does not create value. The customers, as users, create value for themselves, facilitated by the supplier (Gronroos, 2011). In the higher education context the role of the university is to provide the conditions in which students can create their own value. This requires a new approach recognizing their limited control over students, according to Wardley, Bélanger and Nadeau, (2017, p. 1010):

> One must be cognizant of the fact that the goal of engaging students in the co-creation of value is one that is fundamentally outside of institutional control. Students have decision-making independence which means that they cannot be tightly controlled by administration and this is evident through the strong support for the new definition of autonomy. Consequently, institutions need to develop strategies encouraging, managing, and enhancing student involvement without having ultimate control over the students and their behaviours.

Wardley *et al.* (2017) go on to itemize elements of engagement that institutions should provide to support students in their personal growth. These include: the autonomy given to students in carrying out their work; the degree to which the students feel responsible for their work; the meaningfulness of the tasks and skills required; the feedback provided and organizational support provided.

Interaction is a key concept in co-creation. The supplier seeks opportunities to become a co-creator of value, but this can only be realized when opportunities for interaction with customers exist. Providing opportunities for interaction may start long before the acceptance of a student at a university. The use of social networks replaces the passive view of customers with an active view in which applicants are invited to use their own initiative rather than simply react to predetermined marketing activities (Fagerstrøm and Ghinea, 2013). Social media strategies can allow interactive co-creation from early on (Fujita, Harrigan, and Soutar, 2017).

How far should the role of the student as co-creator extend? There is an argument that students should have a limited role in co-designing their courses because of their lack of experience and knowledge of what they might need to learn for their future. Thus students should be seen as customers or collaborators, but not as co-designers, according to Fleischman, Raciti, and Lawley (2015). However, there may be situations in which students can become co-designers of their educational experience. In the case study, provided at the end of this chapter, we present an example of an innovative degree 'Team Entrepreneurship', provided by a UK university, in which the students can design their own degree experience within a university-supported structure.

4 Conclusion

While S-D Logic has been debated since 2004 there has been only limited research into the implications of S-D Logic in contexts of application. As previously mentioned, higher education provides a particularly interesting context for understanding co-creation because of the proactive nature of the role of students in their education and because of the prolonged nature of the interaction between the student and the educational institution.

The co-creation perspective suggests many areas for further research. It would be of great interest to explore perceptions of value of current students compared with alumni, who have the benefit of viewing the value of their education in the context of how it has helped them in their careers and practice. A wider perspective can be added by looking at perceptions of value amongst employers of the university's students in different subject areas. New technology is increasingly impacting on the student experience and there is much to learn about the role of digital technology and face-to-face interaction in co-creation of the student journey.

Universities across the world have to show the wider impact of their activities on society at large and a co-creation approach could be informative in guiding this. For example, there is much to do in mapping the service eco-systems of a university and understanding how different actors in the eco-systems engage and interact with the university.

5 Case study – the team entrepreneurship course at Bristol Business School

The Team Entrepreneurship course (UWE Bristol, 2017) at the University of the West of England provides an illuminating case study in relation to co-creation of value. The course, with its formal title of BA (Hons) Business (Team Entrepreneurship), enrolled the first cohort of 37 undergraduates in September 2013 (UWE Bristol, 2013). The aim of the course is to produce graduates with degrees plus experience of running their own businesses.

The course structure is ground-breaking – no classrooms, compulsory lectures or exams – the degree course is based on methods pioneered in Finland and also run successfully in Spain and Hungary. The undergraduates join together in teams which run a wide array of business projects. The emphasis of the course is on learning-by-doing, whilst building team enterprises. There are no traditional classroom lectures. There are no exams.

At launch, course leader Carol Jarvis from UWE's Bristol Business School said,

> Running a real business – devising a product or service and selling it to customers – is what drives the students' learning. All students have an equal financial stake in the companies they create and will learn to manage the risks and rewards this entails.

The course is based on the Team Academy programme developed by Johannes Partanen in Finland in 1993 (Tiimiakatemia, 2013; Partanen, 2015). There is now a network of institutions delivering Tiimiakatemia courses in 12 countries (Tiimiakatemia Global, 2016). The programme handbook (Rivers, 2017, p. 4) states the guiding principles for the course:

However, there is a series of written assignments, which enable the Team Entrepreneurs (TEs) to demonstrate their mastery of theory, concepts, and models through reading and application in enterprises. These assignments are grouped into mandatory modules through which academic credit is gained. The modules are organized in three strands throughout the three years, developing individuals, teams, and ventures. Modules have

Table 9.3

'Not students	But team entrepreneurs
Not classrooms	But an open plan office
Not teaching	But learning
Not teachers	But coaches
Not simulations	But real ventures
Not control	But self-organizing'

specified learning objectives and recommended reading but the teams will seek additional learning as they identify their need for it. For example, one final year assignment is based on the TEs providing consultancy-style advice to the first and second year TE teams.

The framework of S-D logic provides a lens to view elements of co-creation on the Team Entrepreneurship course and to make comparisons with more traditional undergraduate business courses.

Key actors

The main actors involved are much the same as on a more traditional course: the students, their tutors, module and programme leaders and visiting practitioners. What is different is the roles played by the actors. The Team Entrepreneurs are expected to be highly proactive in organizing their work and study to meet their individual and group aims. Tutors are coaches with the aim of facilitating TEs in achieving these aims. Module leaders have to provide academic frameworks and assessment that maintain rigour within this more fluid environment. The Programme Leader is responsible for maintaining and developing the unique value proposition. Business leaders and other practitioners are encouraged to be more closely involved with the programme on an ongoing basis than in traditional courses.

Resource integration

TEs come to the course with their own individual knowledge, skills, and capabilities (operant resources), as do all students. However the TEs integrate their resources with each other by working together in teams to create businesses across the whole timeframe of the degree and often beyond this.

TEs integrate their operant resources with those of academic staff, as do traditional students. But the nature of the programme, as a business incubator, encourages integration with less traditional resources, as may be required by the needs of the businesses they are developing. For example, a team of TEs founded a food catering and delivery business, Pelico (Mason-Jones, 2017). They negotiated the use of UWE kitchen facilities (operand resources) and researched food business processes (operant resources from other actors) to launch and run a food service business. The TEs integrated a range of resources and through this learning-by-doing they significantly enhanced their own operant resources.

Service exchange

It follows that the service exchange between the TEs and the university develops to meet the different needs of TEs trying to establish a business and varies from that of typical undergraduate programmes. The university needs to be flexible in understanding its role in providing service to the students.

Most importantly the greatest value is co-created when TEs work with practitioners and academics to apply appropriate theory to the reality experienced in their business start-ups. This exchange is facilitated by the Team Coaches and it requires the university to be closely linked with the business community and to be able to broker and facilitate substantial practitioner support on an ongoing basis.

Institutions and institutional arrangements

Universities, faculties and subject fields have established cultures and ways of working. The Team Entrepreneurship guiding principles (Rivers, 2017) encourage different ways of thinking and working and diverge from university institutional norms.

The Team Academy programme (Tiimiakatemia, 2013; Partanen, 2015) and partner institutions, delivering the programme globally, influence the culture developed within the TE programme and the TE teams and TE-generated businesses start to create new institutional arrangements.

Service eco-systems

The University provides a broad service eco-system with academics and practitioners in a wide range of disciplines. While the access to service in this ecosystem is largely predetermined on more traditional programmes, the TEs can negotiate access to actors and resources within the wider eco-system, as the need arises in their business development. Furthermore, the TE programme can be seen as a service eco-system in itself, working within the wider eco-system of the Tiimiakatemia Global network of similar courses.

Value creation

Evidence of value creation will be most significant in terms of the lifetime impact on the TEs. The UWE Bristol course has only been running for a few years, but the Finnish experience is that, at two years after graduation, 42 per cent of students are entrepreneurs and the businesses they create provide additional value in extending the Tiimiakatemia eco-system. As the UWE Bristol programme started in 2013, it is only possible to use shorter-term proxy measures at this stage. The instruments in use in England are the National Student Survey (NSS) and Destination of Leavers from Higher Education survey (DLHE). For the first graduating TE cohort:

> DLHE and NSS data shows high levels of attainment and satisfaction, with 100% of graduates saying that the programme prepared them

well for starting their own business. Graduates not running their own companies are proving to be highly employable within professional and managerial roles.

(University Alliance, 2017)

In the short time that the UWE Bristol course has been running, there have been other recognitions of the value created. TEs from UWE Bristol have been named Student Director of the Year by the Institute of Directors for both 2016 (Institute of Directors, 2016) and 2017 (Director Magazine, 2017). Future research needs to be done to quantify the value creation of businesses founded as a result of the programme as they develop. There is also a broader value creation in the UK from the contribution of these cohorts of TEs towards economic growth.

Value for the university, seen from an exchange point of view, is the tuition fee income. However, a broader view of value, as perceived within S-D Logic, recognizes that the programme provides pedagogic learning on new ways to engage with students and that the engagement of students in the Bristol community through their businesses contributes to the University's brand and future student recruitment.

In the global context, the TEs and the course contribute value towards the achievement of a number of the United Nations Sustainable Development Goals (SDGs), notably SDG 4 Quality Education target 4.4: 'By 2030, substantially increase the number of youth and adults who have relevant skills, including technical and vocational skills, for employment, decent jobs and entrepreneurship' (United Nations General Assembly, 2015).

Conclusions

The case study provides a particular example of co-creation of value in higher education. The Team Entrepreneurship approach would not be suitable for all business students. Recruitment is strict in terms of selecting students who are suited to this type of learning. Staff selection is based on ability to engage with business and to facilitate the students' learning in the course of developing a business. S-D Logic provides a useful lens to view co-creation in the case and to compare the case with a more traditional approach.

Useful links

Mason-Jones, S. (2017) *A first taste of Pelico – a new Bristol business*. Available from: http://365bristol.com/story/2017/06/08/the-first-taste-of-pelico-a-new-bristol-business/4788/

Tiimiakatemia (2013) *Tiimiakatemia in a nutshell*. Available from: www.tiimiakatemia.fi/en/tiimiakatemia/tiimiakatemia-nutshell/

6 Further investigation

1. What are the implications of thinking about higher education as a service in which value is co-created in use, against thinking about higher education as a service that is consumed by students?
2. What are the services and elements of service provided to students in higher education and where are the best opportunities for universities to improve the value provided to students?
3. How can universities be more effective in engaging all types of students to study?
4. How far should students be involved in co-designing the courses they study?
5. In what ways should co-creation between lecturers and students vary at different levels of study (e.g. levels 1–3 of undergraduate courses and undergraduate/postgraduate levels)?

References

Arum, R. and Roksa, J. (2011) *Academically Adrift: Limited Learning on College Campuses*. Chicago, IL: The University of Chicago Press.

Ballantyne, D. and Varey, R. J. (2006) "Creating value in use through marketing interaction: The exchange logic of relating, communicating and knowing." *Marketing Theory* 6(35), pp. 335–348.

Ballantyne, D., Williams, J., and Aitken, R. (2011) "Introduction to service dominant logic: From proposition to practice." *Industrial Marketing Management* 40(2), pp. 179–180.

Chalcraft, D., Hilton, T., and Hughes, T. (2015) "Customer, collaborator or co-creator? What is the role of the student in a changing higher education servicescape?" *Journal of Marketing in Higher Education* 25(1), pp. 1–4.

Chowdhury, I. N. Gruber, T. B., and Zolkiewski, J. (2016) "Every cloud has a silver lining – Exploring the dark side of value co-creation in B2B service networks." *Industrial Marketing Management* 55, pp. 97–109.

Díaz-Méndez, M. and Gummesson, E. (2012) "Value co-creation and university teaching quality: Consequences for the European Higher Education Area (EHEA)." *Journal of Service Management* 23(4), pp. 571–592, https://doi.org/10.1108/09564231211260422.

Director Magazine. (2017) *Director of the Year – Alex Gatehouse, Co-founder and CEO, Pelico*. Available from: www.director.co.uk/alex-gatehouse-student-director-22953-2/ [accessed 14 February 2018].

Dziewanowska, K. (2017) "Value types in higher education – Students' perspective." *Journal of Higher Education Policy and Management* 39(3), pp. 235–246, DOI:10.1080/1360080X.2017.1299981.

Edvardsson, B., Kleinaltenkamp, M., Tronvoll, B., McHugh, P., and Windahl, C. (2014) "Institutional logics matter when coordinating resource integration." *Marketing Theory* 14(3), pp. 291–309.

Etzkowitz, H. (2011) "Normative change in science and the birth of the Triple Helix." *Social Science Information* 50(3–4), pp. 549–568.

Fagerstrøm, A. and Ghinea, G. (2013) "Co-creation of value in higher education: Using social network marketing in the recruitment of students." *Journal of Higher Education Policy and Management* 35(1), pp. 45–53. DOI: 10.1080/1360080X.2013.748524.

Fleischman, D., Raciti, M., and Lawley, M. (2015) "Degrees of co-creation: An exploratory study of perceptions of international students' role in community engagement experiences." *Journal of Marketing for Higher Education* 25(1), pp. 85–103. DOI:10.1080/08841241.2014.986254.

Fujita, M., Harrigan, P., and Soutar, G. (2017) "A netnography of a university's social media brand community: Exploring collaborative co-creation tactics." *Journal of Global Scholars of Marketing Science* 27(2), pp. 148–164. DOI: 10.1080/21639159.2017.1283798.

Greer, C. R., Lusch, R. F., and Vargo, S. L. (2016) "A service perspective: Key managerial insights from service-dominant (S-D) logic." *Organizational Dynamics* 45, pp. 28–38.

Greer, D. (2015) "Defective co-creation." *European Journal of Marketing* 49(1/2), pp. 238–261. http://dx.doi.org/10.1108/EJM-07-2012-0411.

Grönroos, C. (2011) "A service perspective on business relationships." *Industrial Marketing Management* 40(2), pp. 240–247.

Grönroos, C. and Ravald, A. (2011) "Service as business logic: Implications for value creation and marketing." *Journal of Service Management* 22(1), pp. 5–22.

Institute of Directors. (2016) *IoD announces Director of the Year Awards 2016 winners*. Available from: www.iod.com/news/news/articles/IoD-announces-Director-of-the-Year-Awards-2016-winners [accessed 26 February 2018].

Kleineltankamp, K., Brodie, R., Frow, P., Hughes, T., Peters, L., and Woratschek, H. (2012) "Resource Integration." *Marketing Theory* 12(2), pp. 201–205.

Koris, R., Örtenblad, A., Kerem, K., and Ojala, T. (2015) "Student-customer orientation at a higher education institution: The perspective of undergraduate business students." *Journal of Marketing for Higher Education* 25(1), pp. 29–44. DOI:10.1080/08841241.2014.972486.

Lai, M. M., Lau, S. H., Mohamad Yusof, N. A., and Chew, K. W. (2015) "Assessing antecedents and consequences of student satisfaction in higher education: Evidence from Malaysia." *Journal of Marketing for Higher Education* 25(1), pp. 45–69. DOI:10.1080/08841241.2015.1042097.

Löbler, H. (2011) "Position and potential of service-dominant logic – Evaluated in an 'ism' frame for further development." *Marketing Theory* 11(1), pp. 51–73.

Löbler, H. (2013) "Service-dominant networks." *Journal of Service Management*, 24(4), pp. 420–434. http://dx.doi.org/10.1108/JOSM-01-2013-0019.

Lusch, R. F. and Vargo, S. L. (2006) "Service-dominant logic: Reactions, reflections and refinements." *Marketing Theory* 6(3), pp. 281–288.

Lusch, R. F. and Vargo, S. L. (2011) "Viewpoint service-dominant logic: A necessary step." *European Journal of Marketing* 45(7/8), pp. 1298–1309.

Lusch, R. and Wu, C. (2012) "A service science perspective on higher education. Center for American Progress." August 1–12. Downloaded on 15/01/18 from www.Americanprogress.org/issues/education/reports/2012/08/13/11972/a-service-science-perspective-on-higher-education/.

Mackenzie, N. G. and Zhang, Q. (2014) "A regional perspective on the entrepreneurial university: Practices and policies," in A. Fayolle, and D. T. Redford (eds), *Handbook on the Entrepreneurial University*. Cheltenham: Edward Elgar, pp. 188–206.

Mason-Jones, S. (2017) A first taste of Pelico – a new Bristol business. Available from: http://365bristol.com/story/2017/06/08/the-first-taste-of-pelico-a-new-bristol-business/4788/ [accessed 26 February 2018].

Molesworth, M. Nixon, E. and Scullion, R. (2009) "Having, being and higher education: The marketisation of the university and the transformation of the student into consumer." *Teaching in Higher Education* 14(3), pp. 277–287. doi:10.1080/13562510902898841.

Ng, I. C. L and Forbes, J. (2009) "Education as service: The understanding of university experience through the service logic." *Journal of Marketing for Higher Education* 19(1), pp. 38–64.

Partanen, J. (2015) *Glimpses of Individual Learning: What Team Coaches Need to Know about Individual Learning and the Practices of Tiimiakatemia. Vol. I.* Finland: Partus.

Perkmann, M., Tartari, V., McKelvey, M., Autio, E., Broström, A., D'Este, P., Fini, R., Geuna, A., Grimaldi, R., Hughes, A., Krabel, S., Kitson, M., Llerena, P., Lissoni, F., Salter, A., and Sobrero, M. (2013) "Academic engagement and commercialisation: A review of the literature on university–industry relations." *Research Policy* 42, pp. 423–442.

Plé, L. and Chumpitaz Cáceres, R. (2010) "Not always co-creation: Introducing interactional co-destruction of value in service-dominant logic." *Journal of Services Marketing* 24(6), pp. 430–437.

Prior, D. D. and Marcos-Cuevas, J. (2016) "Value co-destruction in interfirm relationships: The impact of actor engagement styles." *Marketing Theory* 16(4), pp. 533–552.

Rivers, A. (2017) *Programme Handbook BA(Hons) Business (Team Entrepreneurship) 2017–18.* Bristol: University of the West of England.

Rothwell, R. (1994) "Towards the fifth-generation innovation process." *International Marketing Review* 11(1), pp. 7–31.

Saunders, D. B. (2015) "They do not buy it: Exploring the extent to which entering first-year students view themselves as customers." *Journal of Marketing for Higher Education* 25(1), pp. 5–28. DOI: 10.1080/08841241.2014.969798.

Shrivastava, P. and Mitroff, I. I. (1984) "Enhancing organizational research utilization: The role of decision makers' assumptions." *Academy of Management Review* 9(1), pp. 18–26.

Tiimiakatemia. (2013) Tiimiakatemia in a nutshell. Available from: www.tiimiakatemia.fi/en/tiimiakatemia/tiimiakatemia-nutshell/ [accessed 27 February 2017].

Tiimiakatemia Global. (2016) Tiimiakatemia Global. Available from: www.tiimiakatemia.com/en/ [accessed 14 February 2017].

United Nations General Assembly. (2015) *Transforming our World: The 2030 Agenda for Sustainable Development.* [online]. pp. 1–35. Available from: www.un.org/ga/search/view_doc.asp?symbol=A/RES/70/1&Lang=E.

University Alliance. (2017) *UWE Bristol: Team Entrepreneurship.* Available from: www.unialliance.ac.uk/2017/08/02/uwe-bristol-team-entrepreneurship/ [accessed 26 February 2018].

UWE Bristol. (2013) Learning by doing; UWE Bristol runs new course for budding entrepreneurs. Available from: http://info.uwe.ac.uk/news/uwenews/news.aspx?id=2693 [accessed 14 February 2018].

UWE Bristol. (2017) *BA(Hons) Business (Team Entrepreneurship).* Available from: https://courses.uwe.ac.uk/N191/business-team-entrepreneurship [accessed 14 February 2018].

Vargo, S. L. (2009) "Toward a transcending conceptualization of relationship: A service – dominant logic perspective." *Journal of Business & Industrial Marketing* 24(5/6), pp. 373–379.

Vargo, S. L. and Lusch, R. F. (2004) "Evolving to a new dominant logic for marketing." *Journal of Marketing* 68(1), pp. 1–17.

Vargo, S. L. and Lusch, R. F. (2008a) "Why 'service'." *Journal of the Academy of Marketing Science* 36, pp. 25–38.

Vargo, S. L. and Lusch, R. F. (2008b) "Service-dominant logic: Continuing the evolution." *Journal of the Academy of Marketing Science* 36, pp. 1–10.

Vargo, S. L. and Lusch, R. F. (2014) "Inversions of service-dominant logic." *Marketing Theory* 14(3), pp. 239–248.

Vargo, S. L. and Lusch R. F. (2016) "Institutions and axioms: An extension and update of service-dominant logic." *Journal of the Academy of Marketing Science* 44(1), pp. 5–23.

Vargo, S. L. and Lusch, R. F. (2017) "Service-dominant logic 2025." *International Journal of Research in Marketing* 34(1), pp. 46–67.

Wardley, L. J. Bélanger, C. H. and Nadeau, J. (2017) "A co-creation shift in learning management: Work design for institutional commitment and personal growth." *Higher Education* 74, pp. 997–1013. DOI 10.1007/s10734-016-0090-0.

Watson, D., Hollister, R., Stroud, S.E., and Babcock, E. (2011) *The Engaged University: International Perspectives on Civic Engagement*. Oxford: Routledge.

Williams, G. (1995) "The 'marketization' of higher education: Reforms and potential reforms in higher education finance," in W. D. Dill and B. Sporn (eds), *Emerging Patterns of Social Demand and University Reform: Through a Glass Darkly*. Oxford: Pergamon Press, pp. 170–193.

Part III
Measurement

10 Measuring higher education brand performance and brand impact

Chris Chapleo and Louise Simpson

1 Introduction

As universities strive for improvement across many areas and are faced with much tougher market competition, it is vital for managers to be able to measure brand performance and use the metrics to enable them to continuously improve over time. However, in higher education brand metrics are a relatively new concept and brand itself is still not a word that sits comfortably with some academics (with reputation being much more palatable). Rankings have also become for many the 'go to' metric for brand and institutional performance. Moreover, it is still not agreed in the literature how brand performance and brand impact can be measured in this sector, although practitioners are seemingly striving to address this gap and calls to evaluate the effectiveness of branding are increasing.

This chapter focuses on the management challenges of measuring brand performance, examines the increasing number of metrics and asks whether we have a comprehensive measure? The chapter will explore the core concept of brand equity, and evaluate actionable metrics, including: market share, price premium, loyalty, league tables and rankings as measures of performance. The authors will review the benefits and challenges of using strategic brand measurement and metrics and include practitioner perspectives.

The aim is to enable readers to comprehend how universities organize and manage their brand evaluation strategies. Theories on brand performance and brand impact are reviewed and extant research presented.

After reading this chapter, you should be able to:

- Understand how brand equity relates to HE.
- Evaluate key measures of brand effectiveness in the HE sector.
- Identify core challenges in evaluating HE brands.
- Understand examples of theory and practice in relation to the above.

2 Review of the literature on branding performance in higher education (HE)

Brands are paradoxical – seemingly a simple concept, but on closer inspection inherently psychologically complex and also commonly misunderstood, even by senior personnel in some sectors. The classic brand definition is arguably that of the American Marketing Association (1960) where 'a brand is a distinguishing name and/or symbol intended to identify the goods or services of either one seller or a group of sellers, and to differentiate those goods or services from those of competitors'. This definition, however, has a strong product focus and although many definitions are derived from this, more holistic contemporary definitions argue that the real value of a brand is in the synthesis of functional and emotional meaning with unique associations. This is perhaps best encapsulated as a cluster of functional and emotional values, which promises a particular experience (de Chernatony, 2002).

So perhaps we are closer to some understanding of what is meant by a brand, but by no means is it a consistent and absolute concept. Therefore the challenge of how we evaluate, or even measure brand performance is also open to debate (Aaker, 1996, 2009; de Chernatony and Segal Horn, 2003; Kapferer, 2012). Brand performance is inherently complex; as there is no simple standard for what a brand is, the measures of performance are of course open to interpretation. How we measure concepts such as brand performance also relates to who we are (Van Reil, Stroeker, and Maathuis, 1998).

This ambiguity, however, does not detract from the importance of measuring brand performance. There is a growing academic and practitioner requirement for this with significant and increasing amounts being spent on branding campaigns in higher education (www.insidehighered.com, 2016; www.jamesgmartin.center, 2016; www.hanoverresearch.com, 2014; www.timeshighereducation.com, 2014), whilst an ongoing debate on the marketization of HE and the associated value of branding is evident in academic literature (Hemsley-Brown and Goonawardana, 2007; Gibbs, 2001; Jevons, 2006) and indeed it has been claimed that 'vast sums are spent without clear purpose' (Jevons, 2006, p. 467).

Measurement and valuation of brands has long been a necessity in commercial organizations and, whilst this is arguably still not an exact science, metrics and methods applied commercially offer a logical starting point. However the particular qualities of HE, if not unique, necessitate close consideration in any simplistic application of commercial brand evaluation. Modern universities are often large, complex, quasi-commercial organizations with a particular employee culture (often linked to the deeply rooted concept of academic freedom), sometimes conflicting commercial imperatives and a high degree of governmental influence. They are offering a service which, unlike a hotel or an airline, tends to be a very expensive (in time and/or money) and one-off purchase. By choosing a university, the buyer (or student) becomes de facto part of that brand.

All of these qualities make simplistic application of commercial notions of brand success challenging to say the least. However, there are clear indicators of what may be considered aspects of strong brand performance and the challenge is therefore to consider and evaluate these and hopefully synthesize them into a clearer understanding of what brand performance in HE constitutes.

Brand equity

When, as is the focus of this chapter, measuring and evaluating brand effectiveness is considered, brand equity is arguably the key concept within management theory and practice (Srinivasan, Park, and Change, 2005). It can be argued that strong brand equity is the aim and desired outcome of other areas of branding activity and as such is representative of brand effectiveness. However, this of course depends on exactly how one defines and understands brand equity. Although conceptualization of brand equity is not straightforward, a simple definition is 'the added value with which a given brand endows a product' (Farquar, 1989, p. 24) and this 'added value' translates to a price premium (Aaker, 1996). It therefore logically follows that the aim of most organizations' branding is to increase brand equity but closer examination reveals that this is over simplistic: higher education can, in some circumstances, charge a price premium, but often is more interested in charging an entry premium – the quality of the students adds transactional value to the organization. Thus higher education is not a pure market and the actual concept of brand equity itself is subjective and variable. So, to what extent is brand equity helpful in evaluating higher education brand performance?

Perhaps the most widely cited (and comprehensive) conceptualization of brand equity is that of Keller (Vukasovic, 2015) in his consumer based brand equity (Keller, 2001), but before wider understanding of brand equity is explored, it is appropriate to look at more specific measures such as financial values.

Financial Measurement. The value of many brands is huge, with seven brands valued at over $40 billion in 2014 (Aaker, 2014) and this drives the need to measure brand equity. Despite this, there have been limited consistent quantifiable measures of brand equity (Herremans and Ryans, 1995) although brand consultancies have increasingly sophisticated metrics. Academic work has also looked at measuring reputation, which overlaps brand equity, but is not the same (as examined later) (Fombrun, Gardberg, and Sever, 2000). Part of the inherent challenge in measuring brand equity is that it is defined by stakeholders' subjective and often intangible assessment (Zeithaml, Lemon, and Rust, 2001), but a number of approaches have received wider recognition, as detailed below.

The three core valuation methods employed commercially are Cost-Based Brand Valuation, Market-Based Brand Valuation, and Income Approach Brand Valuation. None of these are simple closed formulae, but rather each is a *process*.

Interbrand, one of the foremost global branding agencies, utilizes a method that involves measuring the financial performance of a company and weighting the differential role of brands in creating extra profits, evaluated as a percentage of the company's market value. This approach considers the brand as an asset that can be accounted for as part of a balance sheet and is the first brand valuation method to receive International Organization for Standardization (ISO) certification ('procedures and methods of measuring the value of a brand'; ISO 10668) in September 2010.

Another key brand agency, Millward Brown use their 'BrandZ' valuation method (www.millwardbrown.com, 2017) and argue that many brand valuation methodologies are similar in their use of 'financial research and sophisticated mathematical formulas to calculate current and future earnings that can be attributed directly to a brand rather than to the corporation'. They believe that their methodology differs in assessing stakeholders and talk about the three BrandZ™ components of brand equity (Meaning, Difference, and Salience) that predispose consumers to choose a brand and pay a premium for it.

Having, in outline, discussed approaches to evaluating brand performance of three foremost branding agencies, we can conclude that 'most' commercial measures take heavy account of financial specifics. This is of course easier to calculate for a wholly commercial organization, where profit, price and turnover all act as highly visible signs of brand strength.

Because brand is most easily measured in fiscal terms, it is not surprising whom agencies seek to serve in their brand valuation methodologies: the financial community (e.g. analysts, shareholders, and investors) and brand owners (e.g. one agency talks of needing to understand the causal links between brand strength, sales, and profits). It is apparent that brand loyalty, market share and price premium are three elements of brand equity that are incorporated to some degree in the majority of commercially utilized brand equity measures. The degree of 'fit' in terms of utilizing these to evaluate university brand performance therefore needs consideration.

Market Share. Given this chapter's authors and core focus, the UK market is used as an example to a large degree. Higher education is not currently a pure market where competitors can expand to absolute potential (although restrictions on the market are being incrementally loosened) and therefore Market Share as a measure of brand performance is only applicable to some extent (where, for example, higher quality AAB students are recruited).

Price Premium is again partly applicable. At postgraduate level and for international students, universities are free to set fees and in some markets this is also the case across the spectrum of courses. However, in many markets, such as the UK, the maximum that institutions can charge for undergraduate courses is limited and this again is therefore not a wholly derestricted market where associations of price premium can be meaningfully investigated.

Loyalty. This again is a partly applicable measure, but with inherent challenges. Brand loyalty is seen as an important brand equity asset (Vukasovic, 2015) but is of greatest relevance where repeat purchase is key. In HE there is some applicability, such as the choice to stay on in an institution for further PG or PhD study, or to endorse the university to others, or to give money to the institution (alumni philanthropy) but 'repeat purchase' in the classic fast moving consumer goods (FMCG) sense does not occur; in fact it may be argued that the main 'work' of the brand is in influencing before and at the point of the initial choice of where to study. This of course focuses on students as the core audience and the loyalty of staff and alumni may be somewhat more measurable.

It seems, therefore, that whilst commercially derived, brand-equity-based performance measures have some applicability, none provides the whole answer as to how we evaluate HE brand performance.

Brand equity is evidently not one distinct concept and it does appear that systematic investigation into this is lacking, but it can broadly be divided into a customer perspective or a company perspective (Huang and Sarigoellue, 2014). However, a certain amount of academic work has been undertaken to apply the idea of brand equity in a meaningful way in the HE context. Many of these studies are somewhat wider in conceptualization and have less explicit financial focus than their commercial equivalents. Vukasovic (2015) argues that Consumer-Based Brand Equity (hereafter referred to as CBBE) (Keller, 2001, 2003) does apply to HE and that it is a construct based around a combination of brand awareness and brand image. Pinar et al. (2014) also utilize CBBE but they draw on wider antecedents and consider it in terms of variables that include brand awareness, perceived quality, brand loyalty, brand trust, personality and brand associations.

It has been suggested that Keller and Lehmann's (2003) Brand Value Chain that integrates three different types of brand equity measure (customer mind set, brand performance and shareholder value) is among the most comprehensive (Huang and Sarigoellue, 2014). It is of course possible to evaluate the value of the endowment of an HEI, which is fairly well correlated with ranking and arguably a proxy for shareholder value. Ultimately, however, there is no direct measure of shareholder value in HE, which therefore makes full applicability difficult.

The role of rankings

Any discussion of brand performance in higher education would be incomplete without consideration of the significant role of league tables, an external measure of perceived quality that, whilst not unique, has become highly influential in this particular sector.

Rankings (or league tables) have been used to evaluate commercial reputation since the 1980s, but HE has been somewhat slower to join this trend. However league tables have now become established as a measure of the perceived quality of universities. The UK has a number of league tables, either driven by the media (The Times Good University Guide and The Guardian Guide), or by the government (the National Student Survey). The US has the US News and World Report that draws from national rankings and global league tables have developed in the last few years, driven by global competition in HE.

This growing role of league tables seems to reflect a need among consumers for what they perceive as objective indicators, driven partly by a cynicism towards perceived manipulative marketing messages and the lack of public performance measures.

The distinction between league tables and reputation needs to be recognized, however: university rankings are not measures of reputation (although they may include it as a construct) but are quantitative scales chosen by the compiler to capture the aggregate quality of universities.

In terms of the implications for measuring brand performance, the inherent challenge of measuring brand means that there is a tendency to deconstruct the concept and attempt to measure the constructs that comprise our context specific interpretation of brand. Rankings are one such key construct that may be argued to be a component of the brand, or viewed as a proxy. Indeed, it has been suggested that many universities adopt brand management primarily to improve their ranking in the HE market (Bunzel, 2007).

It cannot be denied, however, that league table rankings and brand are closely intertwined. Rankings may have a halo effect, whereby rising up a league table becomes a metaphor for the positive attributes of the brand more widely. As such, rankings influence brand hierarchies (Karabel, 2005) and need consideration when measuring brand performance.

Reputation

When considering brand performance in HE a debate that quickly becomes apparent is that of whether *reputation* and *brand* overlap or are actually the same? It may be argued that an educational brand can be equated to academic reputation but closer consideration suggests that this is limiting (Vukasovic, 2015). They are evidently used as synonyms by many and universities prefer to talk of their reputation rather than their brand, implying a weaker management than would be present in an executive company. Reputation means what the public think of a company. Brand tends to mean how the company has decided it should be considered by the public.

Literature argues that an organization can purposefully define and communicate *brand*, but that *reputation* is more difficult to purposefully manage as it comprises impressions of an organization's behaviour (Argenti and Druckenmiller, 2004) and draws strongly from historical actions and assessment (Fombrun and van Riel, 1997). The concept of corporate identity (Melewar and Jenkins, 2002) also needs to be understood as conceptually distinct from brand. Corporate identity is the brand of the parent company and below that there could be a variety of brands used to promote different strands of the company. A university could deploy different brands in the same way for different markets and audiences. There seems to be little doubt, however, that there is a degree of overlap between the terms when commonly used in a university context and it is evident that *reputation* is a more palatable term for many internal stakeholders (particularly academics) to discuss and also enables them to distance themselves from the need to manage a brand!

In practical terms, therefore, branding in universities may often be about enhancing reputation and it is argued that the better brands gain in quality of student and raise the overall academic standing of a university (Bunzel, 2007).

Conceptually, reputation has been suggested as linked to corporate credibility, which in turn is one of the core elements of successful brands (Keller and Aaker, 1998). The relationship between reputation and brand therefore depends on perspective; is reputation an outcome of brand performance or a key construct in assessing brand performance?

In summary (as with brand equity), there are many ways to evaluate reputation. A good reputation may be one outcome of brand performance but, crucially for measuring brand performance, it is also a key dimension in consumer-based models of brand equity (Pinar et al., 2014).

Summary of literature

In summary, it is evident from the literature that brand equity is not one single value, but rather a combination of several major constructs depending on the measurer and the intended end user of the information. The variety of measurement approaches to it is not helpful in operationalizing brand equity to assess brand performance however.

So, it seems fair to conclude that brand equity can be understood as a measure of brand performance but of course brand equity is not wholly defined as a concept. Two broad types of brand equity concept can be identified and these resonate with HE to differing extents: financially based measures of brand performance only capture part of HE's broad mission, whereas consumer based measures (Huang and Sarigoellue, 2014) resonate more strongly.

Pinar et al. (2014) draw on fairly wide consumer-based antecedents and offer brand awareness, perceived quality, brand loyalty, brand trust, personality and brand associations as a set of brand equity dimensions to measure. These, it may be argued, can be measured in HE (for example, perceived quality can be assessed by measuring league tables, career outcomes, entry tariffs, collaborations, and investments, with similar measures of each of the dimensions). The issue is of course that these data are difficult and expensive to collect and therefore in pragmatic terms may not be very widely utilized. However, Pinar *et al.*'s (2014) model does seem to offer a framework from which we can begin to analyse brand performance in its broadest sense.

Key contributions of the relevant literature

Table 10.1

Pinar, M., Trapp, P., Girard, T., and Boyt, T. (2014) "University brand equity: an empirical investigation of its dimensions." *International Journal of Educational Management* 28(6), pp. 616–634.	This paper uses brand equity as a foundation and offers a scale for brand equity measurement, developed through a wide literature review. Findings suggest that some brand equity elements are more important and the paper builds on theory by identifying core and supporting value creating factors that comprise a university brand.
Huang, R. and Sarigoellue, E. (2014) "Assessment of brand equity measures." *International Journal of Market Research* 56(6), pp. 783–806.	Combines survey and market data and assesses two types of brand equity measure. Results suggest that product-market performance measures are better than customer mind set measures for tracking brand equity. This study is a full test of Keller and Lehmann's 2003 brand value chain model on real market data.
Bunzel, D. L. (2007) "Universities sell their brands." *Journal of Product & Brand Management* 16(2), pp. 152–153.	This paper discusses the extent to which brands have an effect on reputation and ranking. It examines branding programmes at universities to look for positive impact on rankings but concludes that there is no significant evidence of deliberate branding activity affecting ranking.
Vukasovic, T. (2015) "Managing consumer-based brand equity in higher education." *Managing Global Transitions* 13(1), pp. 75–90.	This examines brand equity theory and its applicability to international HE. A conceptual model based on Keller's customer based brand equity model is proposed and tested (in a Slovenian Faculty). Findings suggest that image related determinants (service, symbolic and financial) are major dimensions of brand equity.

Table 10.1 Continued

Chapleo, C. (2011) "Exploring rationales for branding a university: Should we be seeking to measure branding in UK universities?" *Journal of Brand Management* 18(6), pp. 411–422.	This paper looks at how and why branding in HE should be evaluated. It uses exploratory research interviews with HE markets professionals. Findings are that there is no consistent view of the objectives of branding and whilst some qualitative and quantitative measures are suggested, more consistency would be of value.
De Chernatony, L. and Segal-Horn, S. (2003) "The criteria for successful services brands." *European Journal of Marketing* 37(7/8), pp. 1095–1118.	This paper offers a model of service branding based on literature, but verified by interviews with 28 consultants. The findings offer qualitative criteria for success and highlight the importance of shared values in a service organisation.
Keller, K. L. (2001) Building customer-based brand equity: A blueprint for creating strong brands, MSI (available at www.msi.org/reports/building-customer-based-brand-equity-a-blueprint-for-creating-strong-brands/?login=required, accessed 30.12.18).	Keller's Customer Based Brand Equity model, first proposed in 1993 and built upon in this paper, is arguably the most widely accepted conceptualisation of brand equity. The model proposes four key steps that allow organisations to build effective brands.
Srinivasan, V., Park, C. S., and Chang, D. R. (2005) "An approach to the measurement, analysis, and prediction of brand equity and its sources." *Management Science* 51(9), pp. 1433–1448.	This paper proposes a new approach for measuring and predicting a brand's equity in product based markets. The approach incorporates three sources of brand equity and evaluates how much each contributes. This provides capability to analyse the impact of marketing strategies on brand equity and the method is applied to the mobile phone market in Korea. Findings suggest that it has good face validity and convergent validity.
Keller, K. L. and Lehmann, D. R. (2003) „How do brands create value?" *Marketing Management* 12(3), pp. 26–26.	This paper proposes a brand equity measurement system called the 'brand value chain' as an integrated approach to understanding the value created by brands. It is essentially a conceptual model rather than the result of empirical testing.

3 Managerial implications and a practitioner perspective: avoiding the dark art of branding

Universities definitely view 'brand' as if it were Tolkien's eponymous ring, forged in Mordor to control Middle Earth. Academics realize it might give the university power and influence, but it is a suspect force, designed to destroy faculty liberty, placing power in the hands of the marketers (those pesky orcs) and senior management (aka the Dark Lord Sauron). This paradox was very evident when I was a communications director at Cambridge University where there was a strong reluctance to talk about and manage brand, even though he University *was* a huge global brand.

Experts tend to define reputation as what the public thinks of an organization whilst brand is what the organization presents as its main product and identity. It's rather like the subtle difference between character (what people say about you – i.e. reputation) and identity (what you say about yourself – i.e. your personal brand). Reputation is the restaurant review and brand is the chef's speciality dish. As reputation is the major test of whether the brand works, both tend to be used interchangeably, which makes for complexity!

To avoid the dastardly b word, universities have always been very content to talk about reputation, putting the emphasis on audience evaluation, rather than considered identity – which would imply management choices have been made! A positive reputation results in rises in student numbers, grades, research income, alumni giving etc. It helps recruit the best faculty and win research funding. What is there not to like? Universities have always valued priority stakeholders, agreed corporate shields and colours, and created ceremonies and buildings that amplify their personalities and pedagogy. In a marketing world, all of this would be called branding. But in the university world, it tends to be called reputation management, or nothing at all! '*It's just how we run the university*'.

Brand impact in higher education

So, it's important to recognize that the absence of branding as a term doesn't mean it isn't happening as a concept or as a managed process in higher education. There are many studies of brand impact in higher education, albeit under the term reputation. McKnight and Paugh (1999) show that top students are more drawn to the university name whereas less qualified applicants take more note of slogans. Dick and Basu (1994), showed that university reputation deepens loyalty, which leads to greater support, affinity and giving. A reputable university does not need 'selling' to parents of loan guarantors as employers look at where students have gone, as much as, or possibly more than, their subject or grades (Roberts and Thompson, 2007). Sung and Yang (2008) found students considered the external prestige of their institution (again a brand avoidance term) to be four times more important than their own experience of that institution. The more recent higher education brand book published by CASE, The Challenge of Being Distinctive, again avoids the b word, but urges universities to be real, relevant and rare (Baker and Myers, 2017) in order to 'build a powerful brand'.

The rise of reputation management in response to rankings

Reputation has however become much more centre stage for universities because world rankings and other KPIs like student satisfaction, graduate employment, teaching scores and student-staff ratios are all so publicly accessible. Thus the public can compare one university with another – whether they are parents, students, academics thinking of changing jobs, or a research council choosing which university to invest in. Rankings have become a de facto expression or proxy for reputation and brand. The research we have done through the World 100 Reputation Network has shown that the power of a university's brand as exemplified through ranking drives the academic job market, PhD student choice, and international rankings themselves (Simpson *et al.*, 2014–2017). When we have asked academics how they evaluate the reputation or brand power of global universities, they nearly always talk of rankings straight away. The reputation surveys of Quacquarelli Symonds (QS) and Times Higher Education (THE) are the main indicators on which their world rankings are compiled.

Market and media forces

Rankings are not the only reason that reputation is an important professional job in the UK, with communications and marketing directors in some universities earning more than professors. The high price of a university education and the diminution of the graduate premium (i.e. the difference between what you would earn as a graduate compared to someone who goes straight into work aged 18) has also meant that the public are looking for evidence of value for money from universities. There's also the immediacy of news today, with a bad news story travelling very fast and putting a dent in a university's reputation – and a good news story of a cancer treatment being all over the world instantly. So, universities know that the more they manage their reputations, the more they are likely to reap the benefits. If their names are amplified, if they work hard to be visible, and global, and avoid crises, they are most likely to be well thought of and be higher ranked – so brand is a virtuous circle, not a malevolent ring.

How does one measure brand or reputation in higher education?

Cynics would say, you just have to look at which universities are the hardest to get into, and there you have your brand indicator. Others say the biggest brands are the oldest ones because they are the richest – hence Oxford, Cambridge and Harvard rise to the top in their own countries and across the world. Yet this historical index is changing as Asian governments invest heavily in their own institutions to make them into super brands.

The term brand equity is not really ever used in higher education, except by academics writing about brand! There is no stock market on which to list universities' 'value' to shareholders that might also denote the brand or reputation. Clearly there are many financial measures for universities – such as the value of their endowment, the amount institutions bring in in terms of research funding, the price of a degree, or the amount they raise for philanthropy. But there is no valuation of the brand or reputation per se in higher education, as discussed in one of the authors' MPhil research (Simpson, 2011).

Academics who have looked into this area (such as Pinar *et al.*, 2014), normally test audience valuations of different educational assets, including reputation. Yet researchers have disagreed for years over whether reputation or brand should be seen as an asset in its own right, or as the aggregation of all assets. Studies of 'brand equity' also tend to be limited because they normally only research equity with students (only one of a university's critical audiences when it comes to reputation). They tend to research only small sample populations, and each study sets about the research in a different way, using different terms (for example, students might be asked to order a long list of assets, including 'reputation', 'faculty', and 'place' whilst another study might assess 'brand', 'academic studies', and 'student experience'). Perceptions of values can also be skewed by the regulatory and macroeconomic environment, so perceptions of the value of scholarships or price will be different in Germany (where university places are free) to the US (where an international degree will be expensive). Audience is another variable – if academics are asked about reputation, they will give a very different answer to students and alumni will come up with their own priorities!

The rankings may be a proxy of brand power but they still only measure academic and business views within their reputational survey elements. So how do you tell where your brand strengths lie as a university, or where your reputation stands with wider audiences? There are established professional ways to measure a university's reputation or brand power, including qualitative phone interviews, mass surveys, media monitoring and measuring, and public performance measures (rankings, NSI scores etc.). Through one of the author's consultancy, The Knowledge Partnership, we deploy these methods for client universities to test their reputations and the ideal is a mix of qualitative interviews and quantitative data, as well as analysis of what a university is saying about itself in marketing and communications.

We are also trying to innovate in this field of measuring a university's brand. We have devised a university brand tracker (with 11 leading UK universities) using simple questions which are put to much wider audiences than those interrogated in ranking surveys. We use the adapted net promoter question, 'on a scale of 1 to 10, how likely are you to recommend this university?' along with more bespoke questions for each audience. The trick has been to make the surveys incredibly short to get high response numbers. We ask people to name (unprompted) the top universities in the UK and the world. This allows us to cut the data by audience – parent/business/student – etc., and look at it over time, as the questions are repeated each year. The final data is arranged in colourful bar charts and other visual formats for instant analysis online. The clients – usually the marketing director or market research manager – share the tracker with their teams and sometimes leadership to give a strong sense of brand performance in relation to their close competitors.

4 Conclusion

Brand understanding and evaluation are increasingly necessary and topical in modern HE. Whilst the particular qualities and culture of the sector do not make this a straightforward proposition, marketing practice is now well versed in this and theory is fast developing and exploring some interesting challenges. The field will hopefully benefit from ongoing insights that enable us to manage HE brands (and reputations) in mutually advantageous ways.

5 Case study: Newcastle University – creating a stronger brand position

We also help individual universities measure their reputation and strengthen their brand. The following case study explains one such process with Newcastle University.

Newcastle University is a traditional high quality northern university, with industrial heritage and a strong medical school. With a new VC and an appetite for a stronger international reputation amongst the wider leadership team, we were commissioned to help them research their reputation and define their brand position.

We used our reputation tool, ADMIRE, based on academic branding work (Aaker, Davies and Chun, Fombrun, Keller etc.), combined with market research and our own practitioner knowledge of the higher education environment.

Step one is to understand what the university brand is – or, in academic speak, what is its reputation. We implemented our fast Triple Test, a survey just for senior leaders and communicators, which elicits what they think the key messages are. The brevity of the tool (only three answers for each question) means that they can't 'waffle on' and not come to a view (some academics have been known to provide a short thesis when we explore what the university brand is, arguing both for and against each view they submit!). This gave us an insightful picture of a very friendly university that thought its brand personality should be more dynamic and international.

Workshops with senior managers and staff helped us understand what Newcastle's assets were, and whether or not there was a consistent brand. Interestingly, staff saw the brand position as anchored around the concept of the civic university. Some loved this, but others felt 'civic' was rather outdated for a global enterprise and wanted something more ambitious. We also analysed data, media performance and the university's website to understand how they presented themselves.

Interviews with stakeholders then provided a 360 degree view of the university. Stakeholders also confirmed that 'civic' as a brand position was worthy but dull. People said Newcastle was lacking profile outside the North East: 'They need to be positioned as international, not regional!' was a common cry.

This public view was confirmed through survey data. Market research with prospective postgraduate students showed that students were choosing Newcastle because of its research reputation, but others turned it down because it was not so well known around the world. The university also has the problem of a namesake in Australia, creating brand confusion amongst some international audiences. Whilst Newcastle University (UK) is much older and more highly ranked, the University of Newcastle (Australia) is punching above its weight and has the better website. Forty per cent of prospective students felt there was a risk of brand confusion.

We also discovered that the features that Newcastle excelled in (community engagement, and campus location) were not of high priority to academics and employers, who were more interested in international reputation, international engagement and ability to attract top quality students. There was also little awareness of what made Newcastle's teaching distinctive. Its strapline 'Excellence with a purpose' was felt to point towards further rather than higher education.

The final stage of the brand process involved testing new themes and messages with critical audiences – international employers, international academics, staff, students, and prospective students. Five research themes aimed at creating a sharper identity were tested to see if they were acceptable, and manifested real strengths. There is no point creating a brand that is not true! All came through well, apart from Social Justice, which was seen as relevant but confusing as a concept. Straplines were explored, with staff throwing out most of them or disagreeing over favourites.

The final conclusions were that Newcastle was a good university, but not top tier. It was hiding some of its best assets (like being a member of the prestigious Russell Group and being a leader in the field of medicine) and it was too focused on the vibrant city rather than the intellectual assets that it deserved to shout about.

We presented our data sets and findings to the senior management committee chaired by the VC, Chris Day. Our final recommendations – taking into account everyone's views – were to position the brand around being a quality international university rather than a friendly civic university. We suggested they drop the strapline, as few high quality universities use straplines. We recommended they use their international logo to highlight their UK and overseas campuses to avoid confusion with Australia. We suggested that their internet descriptor – the first piece of text anyone sees when looking for Newcastle – be changed, from an emphasis on the splendours of the city, to their quality and their Russell Group imprimatur.

We suggested three clear values, rather than the long list they had previously used – excellence, creativity and impact – which seemed to capture the broad strengths of the university, whilst embodying the former 'excellence with a purpose' in a bolder way.

The recommendations were all accepted and even the Vice-Chancellor seemed happy to back away from a strapline he rather liked! The academics and directors of corporate affairs and marketing now have the job of making it all zing with creativity and marketing flair. They know the challenge is to occupy the international quality university brand without losing the warm city personality beneath. But hopefully, the reputational data and wide brand views we drew together give them the evidence for change.

6 Further investigation

1 Explore what you understand as the differences between brand and reputation in terms of conceptualization and management.
2 Explore the cultural challenges that are, if not unique, evident in HE and how these can best be addressed through internal and external communications.
3 Consider the increasing marketization of HE; what are the philosophical arguments for and against this?
4 It may be argued that higher education has a particularly diverse stakeholder environment. The challenge of what this means for brand management, in particular brand evaluation, needs investigation.

References

Aaker, D. A. (1996) "Measuring brand equity across products and markets." *California Management Review* 38(3), pp. 102–120.
Aaker, D. A. (2009) *Managing Brand Equity*. New York, USA: Simon and Schuster.
Aaker, D. (2014) *Aaker on Branding: 20 Principles that Drive Success*. New York, USA: Morgan James Publishing.
American Marketing Association. (1960) *Marketing Definitions; A Glossary of Marketing Terms*. Chicago, IL: AMA.
Argenti, P. A. and Druckenmiller, B. (2004) "Reputation and the corporate brand." *Corporate Reputation Review* 6(4), pp. 368–374.
Baker, S. and Myers, A. (2017) *The Challenge of Being Distinctive*. Washington DC: CASE.

Bunzel, D. L. (2007) "Universities sell their brands." *Journal of Product & Brand Management* 16(2), pp. 152–153.

Chapleo, C. (2011) "Exploring rationales for branding a university: Should we be seeking to measure branding in UK universities?" *Journal of Brand Management* 18(6), pp. 411–422.

De Chernatony, L. (2002) "Would a brand smell any sweeter by a corporate name?" *Corporate Reputation Review* 5(2–1), pp. 114–132.

De Chernatony, L. and Segal-Horn, S. (2003) "The criteria for successful services brands." *European Journal of Marketing* 37(7/8), pp. 1095–1118.

Dick, A. S. and Basu, K. (1994) "Customer loyalty: Toward an integrated conceptual framework." *Journal of the Academy of Marketing Science* 22, pp. 99–113.

Farquhar, P. H. (1989) "Managing brand equity." *Marketing Research* 1(3), pp. 24–33.

Fombrun, C. J., Gardberg, N. A., and Sever, J. M. (2000) "The Reputation Quotient SM: A multi-stakeholder measure of corporate reputation." *Journal of Brand Management* 7(4), pp. 241–255.

Fombrun, C. J. and Van Riel, C. B. (1997) "The reputational landscape." *Corporate Reputation Review* 1(2), pp. 5–13.

Gibbs, P. (2001) "Higher education as a market: A problem or solution?" *Studies in Higher Education* 26(1), pp. 85–94.

Hanover Research. (2014) www.hanoverresearch.com/media/Trends-in-Higher-Education-Marketing-Recruitment-and-Technology-2.pdf (accessed 20 November 2017).

Hemsley-Brown, J. and Goonawardana, S. (2007) "Brand harmonization in the international higher education market." *Journal of Business Research* 60(9), pp. 942–948.

Herremans, I. M. and Ryans, J. K. (1995). "The case for better measurement and reporting of marketing performance." *Business Horizons* 38(5), pp. 51–60.

Huang, R. and Sarigoellue, E. (2014) "Assessment of brand equity measures." *International Journal of Market Research* 56(6), pp. 783–806.

Inside Higher Education. (2016) www.insidehighered.com/views/2016/04/18/too-much-being-spent-higher-education-marketing-assault-essay (accessed 20 November 2017).

James G. Martin Centre. (2016) www.jamesgmartin.center/2016/08/universities-spend-big-money-public-relations (accessed 20 November 2017).

Jevons, C. (2006) "Universities: A prime example of branding going wrong." *Journal of Product & Brand Management* 15(7), pp. 466–467.

Kapferer, J. N. (2012) *The New Strategic Brand Management: Advanced Insights and Strategic Thinking*. London, UK: Kogan Page publishers.

Karabel, J. (2005) *The Chosen. The Hidden History of Admission and Exclusion at Harvard, Yale and Princeton*. Boston: Houghton Mifflin.

Keller, K. L. (2001) *Building Customer-based Brand Equity: A Blueprint for Creating Strong Brands*. Cambridge, MA: Marketing Science Institute.

Keller, K. L. (2003) "Brand synthesis: The multidimensionality of brand knowledge." *Journal of Consumer Research* 29(4), pp. 595–600.

Keller, K. L. and Aaker, D. A. (1998) "The impact of corporate marketing on a company's brand extensions." *Corporate Reputation Review* 1(4), pp. 356–378.

Keller, K. L. and Lehmann, D. R. (2003) "How do brands create value?" *Marketing Management* 12(3), pp. 26–26.

Keller, K. L. and Lehmann, D. R. (2006) "Brands and branding: Research findings and future priorities." *Marketing Science* 25(6), pp. 740–759.

McKnight, O. T. and Paugh, R. (1999) *Advertising Slogans and University Marketing: an Exploratory Study of Brand-fit and Cognition in Higher Education*. Marketing Management Association Proceedings January 1999. Available from: http://works.bepress.com/oscar_mcknight/2/ (accessed 15 March 2018).

Melewar, T C and Jenkins, E. (2002) "Defining the corporate identity construct." *Corporate Reputation Review* 5(1), pp. 76–90.

Millward Brown. (2015) www.millwardbrown.com/brandz/top-indian-brands/2015/brand-valuation-methodology (accessed 21 November 2017).

Pinar, M., Trapp, P., Girard, T., and E. Boyt, T. (2014) "University brand equity: An empirical investigation of its dimensions." *International Journal of Educational Management* 28(6), pp. 616–634.

Roberts, D. and Thompson, L. (2007) *Reputation Management for Universities, Working Paper. Series 2. Managing Reputation in Higher Education. University League Tables and Their Impact on Student Recruitment*. Leeds: The Knowledge Partnership. Available from: www.theknowledgepartnership.com/docsandpdf/leaguetablefinalreport.pdf (accessed 15 March 2018).

Simpson, L. (2011) The management and impact of international rankings on reputation in higher education. University of Manchester MPhil. Available at: www.escholar.manchester.ac.uk/api/datastream?publicationPid=uk-ac-man-scw:132370&datastreamId=FULL-TEXT.PDF (accessed 15 March 2018).

Simpson, L. (2017) *The Ranking Influencers: How Academics and Employers Determine the Best Universities*. Summary available at: http://theworld100.com/wp-content/uploads/2017/10/The-Ranking-Influencers-Report-1-Executive-Summary-1.pdf (accessed 15 March 2018).

Srinivasan, V., Park, C. S., and Chang, D. R. (2005) "An approach to the measurement, analysis, and prediction of brand equity and its sources." *Management Science* 51(9), pp. 1433–1448.

Sung, M. and Yang, S. (2008) "Toward the model of university image: The influence of brand personality, external prestige, and reputation." *Journal of Public Relations Research* 20(4), pp. 357–376.

Times Higher Education Supplement. (2014) www.timeshighereducation.com/news/marketing-spend-up-but-applications-fail-to-follow-suit/2012107.article. (accessed 20 November 2017).

Van Riel, C. B., Stroeker, N. E., and Maathuis, O. J. M. (1998) "Measuring corporate images." *Corporate Reputation Review* 1(4), pp. 313–326.

Vukasovic, T. (2015) "Managing consumer-based brand equity in higher education." *Managing Global Transitions* 13(1), pp. 75–90.

Zeithaml, V. A., Lemon, K. N. and Rust, R. T. (2001) *Driving Customer Equity: How Customer Lifetime Value is Reshaping Corporate Strategy*. New York, USA: Simon and Schuster.

11 Building a trustworthy university brand

An inside-out approach

Sanjit Kumar Roy, Saalem Sadeque, and Sathyaprakash Balaji Makam

1 Introduction

In today's competitive environment, higher education institutions (hereafter HEIs) are struggling to develop a competitive edge in the marketplace. Extant literature suggests that branding can offer HEIs an opportunity to help stakeholders differentiate them from competitors, build reputation, and attract prospective students (Chapleo, 2015). Strong brands can determine the success of HEIs as these act as surrogates for the quality and credibility of services offered to the students. This reduces students' perceived risk and increases their trust in the HEI (Khanna, Jacob, and Yadav, 2014).

HEIs are investing heavily in promotional activities with a view to increasing their brand awareness and equity and attracting potential students. Higher brand equity indicates better performance, lower risk, positive image, and lower search costs which allow prospective students to choose one university over others (Mourad, Ennew, and Kortam, 2011). The value of a stronger brand varies depending on the unique characteristics of the universities. For example, the Ivy League universities derive brand equity from the reputation and prestige of the universities (Rauschnabel *et al.*, 2016). For other universities, the brand value can depend on trust of the HEI, value for money, familiarity, location, and infrastructure (Dennis *et al.*, 2016). HEIs with greater brand equity can benefit from high student loyalty, which can translate to higher retention rates of existing students and higher probability of alumni involvement. Consequently, branding has become part of the lexicon of HEI and many universities have embraced branding strategy by investing significant amount of resources in branding endeavours.

However, there exist mixed results as HEIs have failed to successfully adopt brand management strategies and apply the highly complex branding process and activities in the higher education setting. Many HEIs are focusing on 'quick-fix' solutions such as redesigning the logo or crest, crafting a catchy tagline, or running an expensive advertising campaign that fizzles out quickly, providing transient benefits. Moreover, there is a growing body of research that questions the suitability and effectiveness of such outside-in branding approaches in an HEI context as they might actually threaten the institutional integrity and institutional commitment of the university (Chapleo and Reader, 2014).

To address the above issue, this chapter develops a study that proposes an 'inside-out' approach for HEI branding, since students play a particularly crucial role as they represent the HEI to the public and it is through their experience an institution's brand is developed (Cassidy and Wymer, 2015). Branding efforts that engage students in the form of student citizenship behaviours can contribute to building a strong and trustworthy higher education brand. Moreover, students' interaction with staff and others shape the HEI brand values and service quality (Melewar and Akel, 2005). This inside-out approach requires excellent brand communication to connect students to the HEI brand values and perceptions (Goi, Goi, and Wong, 2014). As student behaviours are largely dependent on the psychological relationship they maintain with the HEI, brand communication can evoke university identification among students by contributing to their knowledge and belief in the higher education brand (Scharf and Correia, 2015). Moreover, students who identify strongly with the HEI are likely to feel more committed to the HEI brand and engage in citizenship behaviours that contribute to an HEI's branding effort. Thus, HEIs can turn students into 'university ambassadors' by focusing on an inside-out approach to branding. However, empirical research on how HEIs can engage students in citizenship behaviours that contribute towards developing a trustworthy higher education brand is relatively scarce and the current study addresses this research gap.

The study conducted in this chapter aims to propose and examine an inside-out approach to building a trustworthy HEI brand from the students' perspective. As trust determines the relationship strength students have with the HEI (Kharouf, Sekhon, and Roy, 2015), this study proposes that building a trustworthy university brand is crucial in developing a strong university brand. This study extends research in higher education literature in two ways. First, it offers an inside-out branding approach for turning students into university ambassadors that contributes to developing a strong higher education brand. Second, this study shows how brand communication can evoke identification and commitment and motivate students to engage in brand-building citizenship behaviours, which can ultimately engender university trust. The findings of the study have major implications in light of the evidence (Busteed, 2013) that only a small percentage of students are actively engaged with their HEIs.

The rest of the chapter is organized as follows. First, a review of literature on the constructs used in the research model is provided along with the proposed hypotheses. Next, the research methods used are explained, followed by data analysis and results. The chapter concludes with discussion of managerial implications along with limitations and further investigation.

After reading this chapter, you should be able to:

1   Understand the critical role of communication in building an HEI brand.
2   Understand how to build a trustworthy HEI brand from the students' perspective.
3   Understand the critical role played by HEI brand identity in building trust in HEIs.
4   Critically examine the role of student citizenship behaviours in the case of HEI brands.
5   Understand the critical role of branding strategy for HEIs.

2 Review of the literature on higher education branding

Figure 11.1 presents the research framework for the chapter's study. We propose that university brand communication influences students' identification and commitment with the university, which in turn affects their citizenship behaviours towards the university. Further, we propose that university trust is determined by the citizenship behaviours performed by the students.

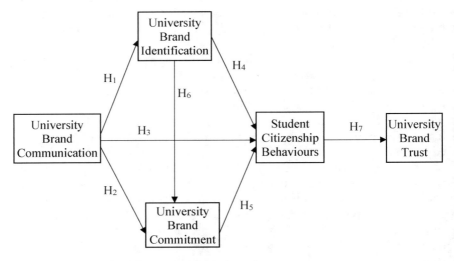

Figure 11.1 Conceptual framework of the study.

University brand communication and university identification

University brand communication involves the communication between university and students that serves the purpose of identifying, expressing and sharing the meaning of the university with students. Prior studies contend that brand communication plays a key role in developing organization identity among stakeholders. For example, Bhattacharya and Sen (2003) suggest that consumers acquire knowledge about an organization's identity from messages delivered through company-sponsored communication channels. Similarly, Postmes, Tanis, and de Wit (2001) argue that communication that flows from organizational hierarchy can aid in the self-definition of the organization and subsequently employees' self-definition within it. Kuenzel and Vaux Halliday (2008) reported that corporate communication is positively related to brand identification. In addition, other studies have reported that internal communication can lead to greater organizational identification through communication climate (i.e. trustworthiness of communication and receptivity of employee communication) and through perceptions of internal marketing orientation (Ferdous and Polonsky, 2014).

According to Social Identity Theory (SIT; Abrams and Hogg, 1998), an individual's identity is more congruent with that of the organization when organizational identity matches the individual's own identity. This is likely to make individuals feel more committed toward the organization. In the HEI context, students are more likely to identify themselves with the university when they are more familiar with the university's identity-revealing communications, such as the mission statement, values represented by the university, and the benefits of studying at the university. This is more likely to occur when the values communicated by the university match the values of individual students. Therefore, we propose that:

> H_1: *University brand communication is positively related to university identification.*

University brand communications and university brand commitment

Prior studies suggest that university brand communication can increase commitment towards the organization. For example, Vallaster and de Chernatony (2005) argued that internal brand communication is related to creating commitment among employees. Brand communication that flows from the top-level organizational hierarchy predicts employee commitment best compared to informal forms of communication such as communication between workers or colleagues (Postmes *et al.*, 2001). Baumgarth and

Schmidt (2010) note that brand communications allow consumers to have clear and consistent brand information and knowledge. It is argued that brand communications can create brand imagery and arouse feelings and thoughts within consumers which, in turn, can reduce uncertainty, increase purchase intention, and enhance perceived quality through effective brand communications. University brand communications transmit its mission, vision, and values and enable students to identify with the university (Mourad, Ennew, and Kortam 2011). Further, effective and successful brand communication by the university can lead to higher commitment towards the university as students are more likely to be familiar with the university's brand position and values. Therefore, we propose that:

> H_2: *University brand communication is positively related to university brand commitment.*

University brand communication and student citizenship behaviour

Successful brand communication is essential to develop strong brand relationships with students. Prior studies show internal brand communication to employees can positively influence citizenship behaviour through job satisfaction and organizational identification (Ferdous and Polonsky, 2014) and organization commitment (Yu et al., 2018). In the context of HEI, internal brand communication could help internalize the university's brand values among the students who are more likely to engage in positive word-of-mouth about the university, show more willingness to donate to the university, buy merchandise with university logos (Stephenson and Yerger, 2014), and suggest improvement to the university. These behaviours are collectively termed student citizenship behaviour. Therefore,

> H_3: *University brand communication is positively related to student citizenship behaviour.*

University identification and student citizenship behaviour

Organizational behaviour and marketing literature suggest that organizational or brand identification is positively related to customer citizenship behaviour (CCB) (Stokburger-Sauer, Ratneshwar, and Sen, 2012). CCB is defined as 'voluntary and discretionary behaviours that are not required for the successful production and/or delivery of the service but that, in the aggregate, help the service organization overall' (Groth, 2005, p. 11). It is argued that students who identify with a university are likely to perceive it as part of their selves and this motivates them to engage in university supportive behaviours. Balaji, Roy, and Sadeque (2016) show that university identification is positively related to supportive behaviours such as advocacy intentions, affiliation, participation activities and feedback. Based on social exchange theory (SET) (Emerson, 1976), it is hypothesized that students who identify strongly with the university will engage in student citizenship behaviours. Thus,

> H_4: *University identification is positively related to student citizenship behaviour*

University brand commitment and student citizenship behaviour

Brand commitment is defined as 'the extent of psychological attachment of employees to the brand, which influences their willingness to exert extra effort towards reaching brand goals, in other words, to exert brand citizenship behaviour' (Burmann and Zeplin, 2005, p. 284). Bettencourt (1997) argued that commitment is an attitude toward the organization that should lead to customer citizenship behaviour. According to SET (Emerson, 1976), individuals who feel committed toward an organization are more likely to be interested in the well-being of the organization and are more likely to engage in citizenship behaviours. Prior studies have reported positive relationships between commitment and citizenship behaviour (Yi and Gong, 2008). In the context of HEI, students who feel committed toward their university would be willing to take actions for the well-being of the university. Accordingly, it is hypothesized that students who show greater university brand commitment are more likely to engage in student citizenship behaviours such as making positive recommendations, providing suggestions for improvement, showing affiliation intentions, and participating in future activities by the university.

> H_5: *University brand commitment is positively related to student citizenship behaviour.*

University identification and university brand commitment

Prior studies support the relationship between brand identification and brand commitment (Punjaisri, Evanschitzky, and Wilson, 2009). Brand identification is the cognitive element of self-definition and commitment is the evaluative aspect which influences the relationship. Students who strongly identify with the values of a faculty within a university are also most likely to show a greater degree of commitment toward that faculty. In the HEI context, identifying with the values and position of the university will help complete self-identities of the students who will, in turn, show more commitment toward the university in order to maintain the relationship between themselves and the university (Elbedweihy and Jayawardhena, 2014).

> H₆: *University identification is positively related to university brand commitment.*

Student citizenship behaviour to university trust

Ghosh, Whipple, and Bryan (2001) define trust as the degree to which a student is willing to rely on or have faith and confidence in HEIs to take appropriate steps that benefit him or her, for example, achieving the student's learning and career objectives. In accordance with SET (Emerson, 1976), students are likely to reciprocate by engaging in voluntary behaviours when they feel that they have received exceptional service. Vivek, Beatty, and Morgan (2012) note that customer engagement is a combination of behavioural response with an emotional context. These authors note that higher customer engagement can lead to increased trust. Individuals who engage in company supportive behaviours are likely to be highly engaged and involved with the company. Dennis *et al.* (2016) report that the brand image of an HEI is positively related to brand trust. In the context of HEI, brand communication by the university influences brand image projected to the students. We contend that the relationship between university brand communication and trust works through university brand commitment, university identification and student citizenship behaviours.

> H₇: *Student citizenship behaviour is positively related to university trust.*

Method – sample, instrument, and data collection

A self-administered survey was used to collect responses from students enrolled in a business degree program at one private university in Malaysia. These students were from different specializations such as marketing, finance, accounting, human resource management, banking, and international business. Participation in the survey was voluntary and it was administered during class. The survey was anonymous and a student representative was asked to distribute and collect questionnaires to ensure that students did not feel compelled to participate in the survey. A total of 365 valid and usable responses were obtained for the study.

The measurement items and scales for the study were adapted from previous literature. The survey questionnaire was created using a standard instrument development procedure that first involved extensive review of literature on higher education and brand management. The measurement items collected from the literature review were then reviewed by three subject matter experts from the participating university in order to confirm their face validity and content validity, and to comment on clarity and completeness. All measurement items were measured on a 7-point Likert scale ranging from 1 (*strongly disagree*) to 7 (*strongly agree*).

University brand communication was measured with the scales provided by Baumgarth and Schmidt (2010) and Matanda and Ndubisi (2013). University brand commitment was measured using scales adapted from Rothwell, Herbert, and Rothwell (2008). University identification was measured with a scale adapted from Jones and Kim (2011). The scales to measure university trust were adapted from Sampaio *et al.* (2012). Student citizenship behaviours included voluntary and helpful behaviours such as advocacy intentions, suggestions for improvement, university affiliation, and participation in future activities, measured with scales adapted from Zeithaml, Berry, and Parasuraman (1996), Bove *et al.* (2009) Johnson and Rapp (2010) and Stephenson and Yerger (2014). Scales are shown in Table 11.1.

Of the 365 responses collected for the study 53 per cent were from males and 47 per cent were from females. Sixty-six per cent of the respondents were in the age group 21–26 years and 43 per cent of the respondents were in the first year of the degree program. Seventy-six per cent of the respondents were Malaysian nationals.

Data analysis

Partial least squares structural equation modelling (PLS-SEM) with Smart-PLS 3.0 was used in this study, taking into account the sample size and exploratory nature of the study (Hair *et al.*, 2012). The model consists of five latent variables of which one was an exogenous variable (university brand communication) and four were endogenous variables (university brand commitment, university identification, student citizenship behaviours, and university trust). Student citizenship behaviour was conceptualized as a Type I reflective second-order construct consisting of reflective first-order constructs of advocacy intentions, suggestions for improvements, university affiliation, and participation in future events. The model evaluations in the study were assessed using the effect size, significance levels, and *t*-values of the structural paths, and R-square values of the endogenous variables (Chin, 1998). Bootstrap resampling and a blindfold approach were used to test the reliability and validity of the proposed research model.

Table 11.1 Measurement model results

Constructs and items	λ	t	A	ρ	AVE
University brand communication (UBC)			0.81	0.87	0.57
I am familiar with the university communication (e.g. magazines, newsletters, brochures, emails, etc.)	0.73	21.44			
I am made aware of the overall policies and events of my university	0.81	29.60			
Communications (newsletters, magazines, website, social media, etc.) are adequate within this university	0.64	14.92			
I am familiar with the university brand style guide	0.74	18.33			
I am regularly notified of important changes in the university	0.83	43.00			
University commitment (UC)			0.84	0.89	0.67
I talk up this university to my friends as a great university to be at	0.81	37.18			
I am proud to tell others that I am at this university	0.84	40.93			
I really care about this university and its future	0.79	32.27			
For me this is the best of all universities to be a member of	0.84	52.37			
University identification (UI)			0.78	0.81	0.70
This university reflects who I am	0.86	49.24			
I find it easy to identify with the university	0.85	42.79			
This university has a great deal of personal meaning for me	0.80	30.36			
Student citizenship behaviour (SCB)			0.88	0.92	0.74
Advocacy intentions					
I will recommend this university to others	0.71*	13.82			
I will recommend this university to those who ask or seek my advice	0.91	83.07			
I will recommend it to others on the university social media (e.g. Facebook)	0.88	58.28			
I will recommend it to others on my social media (e.g. Facebook)	0.88	65.35			
I will post positive comments about the university on my social media (e.g. Facebook)	0.78	30.05			

	λ	t	α/ρ/AVE
Suggestions for improvement (SI)	0.72*	14.79	
I would make suggestions to the university as to how it can be improved	0.81	23.63	0.86 0.90 0.70
I would let the university know of ways that could make it better serve my needs	0.86	28.90	
I would share my opinions with the university if I felt they might be of benefit	0.85	34.65	
I would contribute ideas to the university that could help it improve service	0.81	26.18	
University affiliation (UA)	0.81*	35.36	
I would often wear clothes (apparel) with the university logo or name	0.86	46.88	0.87 0.92 0.80
I would display a sticker (e.g. car or self) with the university logo or name	0.91	74.41	
I would often display merchandize (e.g. umbrella) with the university name or logo	0.90	74.29	
Participation in university activities (PA)	0.75*	29.04	
I would attend future events being sponsored by the university	0.94	108.0	0.86 0.93 0.81
I would attend future functions held by the university	0.92	85.49	
University trust (UT)			
Very undependable/very dependable	0.89	40.79	0.88 0.92 0.73
Very incompetent/very competent	0.92	50.23	
Of very low integrity/of very high integrity	0.91	40.61	
Very unresponsive/very responsive	0.70	9.19	

Notes

λ – Standardized loading; *t* – *t*-value; α – Cronbach's alpha; ρ – Composite reliability; AVE – Average variance extracted; * – Second-order factor loadings and *t*-values.

Results – measurement reliability and validation

The construct reliability, convergent validity, discriminant validity, and nomological validity test were applied to all constructs. The psychometric properties of all latent constructs are presented in Table 11.1. As seen in Table 11.1, the standardized loadings (λ) of each reflective measurement item on its corresponding latent construct were greater than the threshold levels of 0.50 and were all significant at $p < 0.01$ and therefore convergent validity was achieved (Hair, Ringle, and Sarstedt, 2011). The Cronbach's alpha values (α) and composite reliability (ρ) for all latent constructs were above 0.70, supporting adequate reliability of the multi-item scales. All average variance extracted (AVE) was greater than the 0.50 threshold level, supporting convergent validity of the latent constructs (Hair et al., 2011).

As seen in Table 11.2, the discriminant validity was supported as the AVE for each construct was greater than the squared correlation with other constructs (Fornell and Larcker, 1981). The nomological validity was assessed using the measure of explained variance. The R^2 values of university brand commitment, university identification, and student citizenship behaviours were 0.36, 0.33, and 0.45 respectively, which were large effect sizes (~26%; Cohen, 1992). This indicates that the model has good predictive power. The goodness-of-fit (GOF), which was calculated as the geometric mean of average R^2 (0.30) and average communality (0.59), was 0.42 and suggested satisfactory fit to the model (Tenenhaus et al., 2005).

Student citizenship behaviour conceptualized as a higher-order construct in the study was empirically supported as the indicator weights for each first-level construct i.e. advocacy intentions ($\beta = 0.71$, $t = 13.82$, $p < 0.01$), suggestions for improvement ($\beta = 0.72$, $t = 14.79$, $p < 0.01$), university affiliation ($\beta = 0.81$, $t = 35.36$, $p < 0.01$), and participation in future activities ($\beta = 0.75$, $t = 29.04$, $p < 0.01$) were significant. The reliability and AVE of the first-order constructs exceeded the threshold levels of 0.7 and 0.5 respectively. Additionally, R^2 of each first-order construct exceeded 0.5 and the dimensional correlations were less than the second-order factor loadings. This supports the higher-order conceptualization of student citizenship behaviours.

The test of potential common method bias was carried out using the Harman's one-factor test (Podsakoff et al., 2003). This test was conducted through entering all the measurement items in an exploratory factor analysis using IBM SPSS 21.0. The sample would have a common method bias problem if a single construct explained more than 50 per cent of the extracted variance (Podsakoff et al., 2003). The results show that the first factor explained 31.1 per cent of variance for the sample and therefore suggest that common method variance might not be a problem in this study.

Table 11.2 Descriptive statistics and discriminant validity

	1	2	3	4	5	6	7	8
1 University brand communication	(0.57)	0.18	0.33	0.16	0.10	0.12	0.25	0.06
2 University commitment	0.43	(0.67)	0.34	0.48	0.04	0.18	0.07	0.05
3 University identification	0.58	0.58	(0.70)	0.35	0.07	0.14	0.11	0.04
4 Advocacy intentions	0.40	0.69	0.59	(0.73)	0.04	0.15	0.11	0.06
5 Suggestions for improvement	0.31	0.21	0.26	0.21	(0.74)	0.15	0.18	0.02
6 University affiliation	0.35	0.43	0.37	0.39	0.39	(0.70)	0.35	0.00
7 Participation in university activities	0.50	0.27	0.31	0.33	0.43	0.59	(0.80)	0.03
8 University trust	0.25	0.23	0.21	0.24	0.14	0.07	0.18	(0.81)
Mean	4.90	4.64	4.26	4.43	5.01	4.42	4.62	4.46
Standard deviation	0.94	1.17	0.92	1.23	0.97	1.25	1.27	1.32

Notes
Diagonal values represent average variance extracted. Lower half of the diagonal represents the correlations between the constructs and upper half of the diagonal represents square of the correlations between the constructs.

Structural model and hypotheses testing

A blindfold approach was carried out to evaluate the predictive validity of the structural model. The means of the cross-validated (CV) communality (H^2) and redundancy (F^2) indicated that the quality of structural model is well above the recommended standard of 0.30 (Tenenhaus et al., 2005). In fact, the average CV-communality (H^2) was 0.59 and average CV-redundancy (F^2) was 0.31. The average variance accounted (AVA) for the model was 0.65, which was greater than the cut-off value of 0.10 (Falk and Miller, 1992). These results suggest that the model exhibits adequate explanatory power.

Table 11.3 presents the estimated path coefficients and t-values of the hypothesized paths. A bootstrapping resampling method using 5000 resamples was used to estimate the t-values. The results confirmed the research hypotheses. Particularly in support of H_1, H_2, and H_3, university brand communication was found to have a positive impact on university identification ($\beta=0.58$, $t=13.9$, $p<0.01$), university brand commitment ($\beta=0.15$, $t=2.84$, $p<0.01$), and student citizenship behaviours ($\beta=0.25$, $t=4.77$, $p<0.01$). H_4 was supported as university identification positively impacted student citizenship behaviour ($\beta=0.19$, $t=2.81$, $p<0.01$). Similarly, H_5 received support as university brand commitment was found to have a positive impact on student citizenship behaviour ($\beta=0.36$, $t=4.97$, $p<0.01$). University identification was found to have a positive impact on university brand commitment ($\beta=0.50$, $t=9.66$, $p<0.01$), supporting H_6. Finally, H_7 was supported as student citizenship behaviour had a positive impact on university trust ($\beta=0.22$, $t=4.19$, $p<0.01$).

Table 11.3 Structural model results

	Structural paths	β	t-values
H_1	University brand communication → University identification	0.58	13.9*
H_2	University brand communication → University brand commitment	0.15	2.84*
H_3	University brand communication → Student citizenship behaviour	0.25	4.77*
H_4	University identification → Student citizenship behaviour	0.19	2.81*
H_5	University brand commitment → Student citizenship behaviour	0.36	4.97*
H_6	University identification → University brand commitment	0.50	9.66*
H_7	Student citizenship behaviour → University trust	0.22	4.19*

Notes
β – standardized loadings; t–t-value; *$p<0.01$.

Mediation analysis

A post-hoc mediation analysis tested the mediation role of university brand commitment and university identification in the relationship between university brand communication and student citizenship behaviour, using the Preacher and Hayes (2008) procedure. The latent variables scores obtained using SmartPLS were analysed using the SPSS routine developed by Preacher and Hayes (2008) for generating the 95 percentile confidence intervals. The results show that the confidence intervals contained no zeros, thus supporting the mediating role of university brand identification (indirect effect = 0.11, LCI = 0.05, UCI = 0.17) and commitment (indirect effect = 0.05, LCI = 0.01, UCI = 0.10). These findings suggest a mediation role of university brand identification and university commitment. Similarly, student citizenship behaviour was found to mediate the relationship between university brand commitment, university identification, and university trust.

Discussion – theoretical implications

The study findings contribute to the higher education literature in three ways. First, despite growing interest in citizenship behaviours (Balaji, 2014) few studies have explored the student citizenship behaviours in the higher education context. In particular, little empirical research has addressed how universities can turn students into university brand ambassadors and motivate them to engage in supportive behaviours that promote the university's branding efforts. As citizenship behaviours are crucial and have a significant influence on how the university brand is seen by prospective students, current students, and other stakeholders, the present study considers students' citizenship behaviours in developing the university brand. This study extends the research conducted by Stephenson and Yerger (2014) which noted that the students' interpretation of university brand determines their supportive behaviours. In the case of this research, it is shown that university brand communication promotes university brand through student citizenship behaviours such as word-of-mouth, suggestions for improvement, affiliation, and participation in future activities.

Second, the study finds empirical support for the role of brand communication in promoting students' citizenship behaviours. In particular, university brand communication was found to positively influence the student citizenship behaviours both directly and indirectly through university identification and university brand commitment. The study findings concur with past brand management work (Punjaisri and Wilson, 2011) that university branding efforts enhance student citizenship behaviours. Further, this study also offers important insights into how brand communication can foster student citizenship behaviours. By showing that university identification and university brand commitment mediates the effects of university brand communication; this study provides a better understanding of how branding efforts can turn students into university ambassadors. It is argued that successful brand communication strategies provide students with a sense of belonging and encourage their commitment towards the university. This motivates students to engage in student citizenship behaviours and reinforce their relationship with the university. These findings confirm that an internal orientation can improve the success of the university brand.

Finally, an important finding of this study is that student citizenship behaviours positively influence students' trust in the university. As brand trust has been considered as a key variable in determining the nature of consumer-brand relationship and brand strength (Kharouf, Sekhon, and Roy, 2015), this study empirically demonstrates that students exerting citizenship behaviours promote the university brand through the effects of trust. Moreover, this study extends previous studies that have proposed but not empirically examined the effects of branding efforts on student citizenship behaviours and the student-university relationship.

3 Managerial implications

The findings of this chapter's study have important implications for HEIs and managers in developing a strong university brand. HEIs can employ internal branding efforts as a brand management strategy for engaging students in student citizenship behaviours and thereby strengthen the university brand. As brand communication is a requisite for internal branding efforts, the university can persuade students to turn into brand ambassadors and support the university's brand by engaging in and internal brand communication strategy. Also, the university managers can stimulate the students' identification with the university through brand communication efforts that enhance the students' fit, knowledge, and belief in the university brand. On the other hand, the university managers can deploy brand communication programs to enhance students' attitude towards the university as well as enhance their commitment towards the university.

As university identification and university brand commitment act as a partial mediator in the relationship between university brand communication and student citizenship behaviours, higher education managers should pay attention to students' attitude towards the university brand as influenced by university brand communication. The mediating effects suggest that when university brand communication effectively influences the students' identification and commitment for the university, student citizenship behaviours can be more effectively impacted through brand communication programs. Thus, higher education managers can use brand communication programs to directly shape students' identification with the university and engage them in university supportive behaviours that support the university's brand.

Importantly, the university can use various communication channels such as newsletters, magazines, website, emails, blog, social media, and others to clearly communicate with the students, inform them about university policies and policy changes, update them about university events, and apprise them of what the university stands for and promises to students. For example, the University of Northampton developed a highly engaging brand campaign named 'raising the bar' to improve internal awareness and deliver the core brand message and values to its students and other stakeholders. This research supports such branding efforts as they help students better understand university goals, characteristics, and personality. Such efforts motivate students to identify with the university and engage in supportive behaviours. However, successful implementation of internal branding efforts can be challenging as students might consider university branding and brand issues as irrelevant. Thus, university managers should carefully evaluate and consider students' potential responses before implementing such branding endeavours. One of the ways by which universities can address this is through leadership programs such as those for student ambassadors and civic engagement. When students engage with the university through such branding programs they build personal relationship and reciprocate by engaging in greater levels of student citizenship behaviours. Moreover, students who highly identify with the university feel committed and turn into genuine university ambassadors.

4 Conclusion

Although citizenship behaviours have been acknowledged to play an important role in developing brand equity, the higher education literature has given limited attention on the role of student citizenship behaviours in the HEI context. Previous literature on higher education has largely focused on brand reputation and brand image in attracting and retaining students (Merchant et al., 2015). Recently, however, it has been realized that branding efforts focused on students are crucial in developing a trustworthy university brand (Idris and Whitfield, 2014). This has become even more critical given the challenges faced by higher education institutions in building and maintaining a strong brand. In response to the above gaps in the higher education literature, the study presented in this chapter has addressed the following related questions: what is the role of branding efforts for student citizenship behaviour management? And what can higher education institutes do to build a trustworthy university brand? To address these research questions, the study proposed an inside-out approach for developing the university brand. Particularly, this chapter proposes that university brand communication can promote students' identification and commitment towards the university. This promotes student citizenship behaviours, thereby strengthening the university brand. The empirical findings of the study provide evidence for these relationships between university brand communication, university brand commitment, university identification, student citizenship behaviours, and university trust.

5 Case study

One of the well-known universities in Australia decided to rebrand itself after almost four decades. It launched a new logo and new brand slogan. The logo was redesigned for the stakeholders of the digital era to create warmth and friendliness in the market. The ultimate agenda was to build sustainable competitive advantage in the global higher education market. The university needs to be more active and visibly trustworthy in the present times where the information asymmetry between the university and its stakeholders is slowly disappearing.

The strategy behind the rebranding exercise was to connect and engage with present and future students and other stakeholders on both the national and global stages. The new brand slogan was used to market the HEI brand and communicate with current students, potential students and other stakeholders in the higher education market.

The market research agency entrusted to rebrand the university utilized the new brand campaign launched in print media, on campus, and through television and social media channels.

The new ad campaign was designed to connect and engage with students at every touch point, both physical and digital. The brand communication strategy was designed to engender commitment and create an image in the minds of stakeholders. The ad features inspiring stories of students and researchers who have been successful and appeal to potential students.

The university needs to portray the extensive set of cultural values which it has built over the last few decades so as to reinforce its image and build trust in the minds of HEI stakeholders (e.g. students). Change is risky in any sector, especially in the HE sector. For this university the challenge is far greater because the unified identity of the brand needs to be preserved and at the same time the new brand image needs to be communicated to students. The new logo was just one element of the visual identity of the brand which also included a new colour and other visual elements to reinforce the newness of the brand. The new visual identity was pretested before the final launch. Brands and their identities are built over a period of time, utilizing visual as well as other elements of brand identity. An integrated campaign was used to communicate and connect with the students so as to engender trust in the university brand.

Based on the brief case study, please discuss the following questions:

- Why did the university opt for the rebranding exercise after four decades?
- What were the key elements of the identity of an HEI's brand identity?

- How can HEIs use brand communication elements and the elements of brand identity to build a trustworthy brand?
- What is the role of student citizenship behaviours and student commitment in engendering trust in HEI brands?

6 Further investigation

While the study described in this chapter offers important theoretical and practical implications for turning students into university ambassadors through brand communication or internal branding efforts, it also has some limitations that offer opportunities for future research. First, the study was carried out at one private university in Malaysia. Thus, further research is required to establish the generalizability of the study findings across other universities and countries. Second, as this study relied on cross-section data, future research can complement it with additional longitudinal studies and experimental data to provide more decisive evidence of causality among the study variables. Finally, this study considered only university brand communication in encouraging students to engage in student citizenship behaviours. As brand leadership and HR-related brand activities are identified in the literature as other key branding efforts (Burmann and Zeplin, 2005), future studies can examine their role in developing the university brand.

References

Abrams, D. and Hogg, M. A. (1998) "Prospects for research in group processes and intergroup relations." *Group Processes & Intergroup Relations* 1(1), pp. 7–20.

Balaji, M. S. (2014) "Managing customer citizenship behavior: A relationship perspective." *Journal of Strategic Marketing* 22(3), pp. 222–239.

Balaji, M. S., Roy, S. K., and Sadeque, S. (2016) "Antecedents and consequences of university brand identification." *Journal of Business Research* 69(8), pp. 3023–3032.

Baumgarth, C. and Schmidt, M. (2010) "How strong is the business-to-business brand in the workforce? An empirically-tested model of 'internal brand equity' in a business-to-business setting." *Industrial Marketing Management* 39(8), pp. 1250–1260.

Bettencourt, L. A. (1997) "Customer voluntary performance: Customers as partners in service delivery." *Journal of Retailing* 73(3), pp. 383–406.

Bhattacharya, C. B. and Sen, S. (2003) "Consumer-company identification: A framework for understanding consumers' relationships with companies." *Journal of Marketing* 67(2), pp. 76–88.

Bove, L. L., Pervan, S. J., Beatty, S. E., and Shiu, E. (2009) "Service worker role in encouraging customer organizational citizenship behaviors." *Journal of Business Research* 62(7), pp. 698–705.

Burmann, C. and Zeplin, S. (2005) "Building brand commitment: A behavioral approach to internal brand management." *Journal of Brand Management* 12(4), pp. 279–300.

Busteed, B. (2013) The school cliff: Student engagement drops with each school year. *Gallup*, accessed from http://news.gallup.com/opinion/gallup/170525/school-cliff-student-engagement-drops-school-year.aspx. (accessed 19 January 2018).

Cassidy, R. and Wymer, W. (2015) "The impact of brand strength on satisfaction, loyalty and WOM: An empirical examination in the higher education sector." *Journal of Brand Management* 22(2), pp. 117–135.

Chapleo, C. (2015) "Brands in higher education: Challenges and potential strategies." *International Studies of Management & Organization* 45(2), pp. 150–163.

Chapleo, C. and Reader, P. (2014) "Higher education brands and data," in M. E. Menon, D. G. Terkla, and P. Gibbs (eds), *Using Data to Improve Higher Education*. Rotterdam: Sense Publishers, pp. 81–91.

Chin, W. W. (1998) "Commentary: Issues and opinion on structural equation modeling." *MIS Quarterly*, 22(1), pp. vii–xvi.

Cohen, J. (1992) "A power primer." *Psychological bulletin* 112(1), p. 155.

Dennis, C., Papagiannidis, S., Alamanos, E., and Bourlakis, M. (2016) "The role of brand attachment strength in higher education." *Journal of Business Research* 69(8), pp. 3049–3057.

Elbedweihy, A. M. and Jayawardhena, C. (2014) "Consumer-brand identification: A social identity based review and research directions." *The Marketing Review* 14(2), pp. 205–228.

Emerson, R. M. (1976) "Social exchange theory." *Annual Review of Sociology* 2(1), pp. 335–362.

Falk, R. F. and Miller, N. B. (1992) *A Primer of Soft Modeling*. OH, USA: University of Akron Press.

Ferdous, A. S. and Polonsky, M. (2014) "The impact of frontline employees' perceptions of internal marketing on employee outcomes." *Journal of Strategic Marketing* 22(4), pp. 300–315.

Fornell, C. and Larcker, D. F. (1981) "Evaluating structural equation models with unobservable variables and measurement error." *Journal of Marketing Research* 18(1), pp. 39–50.

Ghosh, A. K., Whipple, T. W., and Bryan, G. A. (2001) "Student trust and its antecedents in higher education." *The Journal of Higher Education* 72(3), pp. 322–340.

Goi, M. T., Goi, C. L., and Wong, D. (2014) "Constructing a brand identity scale for higher education institutions." *Journal of Marketing for Higher Education* 24(1), pp. 59–74.

Groth, M. (2005) "Customers as good soldiers: Examining citizenship behaviors in internet service deliveries." *Journal of Management* 31(1), pp. 7–27.

Hair, J. F., Ringle, C. M., and Sarstedt, M. (2011) "PLS-SEM: Indeed a silver bullet." *Journal of Marketing Theory and Practice* 19(2), pp. 139–152.

Hair, J. F., Sarstedt, M., Ringle, C. M., and Mena, J. A. (2012) "An assessment of the use of partial least squares structural equation modeling in marketing research." *Journal of the Academy of Marketing Science* 40(3), pp. 414–433.

Idris, M. Z. and Whitfield, T. A. (2014) "Swayed by the logo and name: Does university branding work?" *Journal of Marketing for Higher Education* 24(1), pp. 41–58.

Johnson, J. W. and Rapp, A. (2010) "A more comprehensive understanding and measure of customer helping behavior." *Journal of Business Research* 63(8), pp. 787–792.

Jones, R. and Kim, Y. K. (2011) "Single-brand retailers: Building brand loyalty in the off-line environment." *Journal of Retailing and Consumer Services* 18(4), pp. 333–340.

Khanna, M., Jacob, I., and Yadav, N. (2014) "Identifying and analyzing touchpoints for building a higher education brand." *Journal of Marketing for Higher Education* 24(1), pp. 122–143.

Kharouf, H., Sekhon, H., and Roy, S. K. (2015) "The components of trustworthiness for higher education: A transnational perspective." *Studies in Higher Education* 40(7), pp. 1239–1255.

Kuenzel, S. and Vaux Halliday, S. (2008) "Investigating antecedents and consequences of brand identification." *Journal of Product & Brand Management* 17(5), pp. 293–304.

Matanda, M. J. and Ndubisi, N. O. (2013) "Internal marketing, internal branding, and organisational outcomes: The moderating role of perceived goal congruence." *Journal of Marketing Management* 29(9–10), pp. 1030–1055.

Melewar, T C and Akel, S. (2005) "The role of corporate identity in the higher education sector: A case study." *Corporate Communications: An International Journal* 10(1), pp. 41–57.

Merchant, A., Rose, G. M., Moody, G., and Mathews, L. (2015) "Effect of university heritage and reputation on attitudes of prospective students." *International Journal of Nonprofit and Voluntary Sector Marketing* 20(1), pp. 25–37.

Mourad, M., Ennew, C., and Kortam, W. (2011) "Brand equity in higher education." *Marketing Intelligence & Planning* 29(4), pp. 403–420.

Podsakoff, P. M., MacKenzie, S. B., Lee, J. Y., and Podsakoff, N. P. (2003) "Common method biases in behavioral research: A critical review of the literature and recommended remedies." *Journal of Applied Psychology* 88(5), p. 879.

Postmes, T., Tanis, M., and De Wit, B. (2001) "Communication and commitment in organizations: A social identity approach." *Group Processes & Intergroup Relations* 4(3), pp. 227–246.

Preacher, K. J. and Hayes, A. F. (2008) "Asymptotic and resampling strategies for assessing and comparing indirect effects in multiple mediator models." *Behavior Research Methods* 40(3), pp. 879–891.

Punjaisri, K., Evanschitzky, H., and Wilson, A. (2009) "Internal branding: An enabler of employees' brand-supporting behaviours." *Journal of Service Management* 20(2), pp. 209–226.

Punjaisri, K. and Wilson, A. (2011) "Internal branding process: key mechanisms, outcomes and moderating factors." *European Journal of Marketing* 45(9/10), pp. 1521–1537.

Rauschnabel, P. A., Krey, N., Babin, B. J., and Ivens, B. S. (2016) "Brand management in higher education: The university brand personality scale." *Journal of Business Research* 69(8), pp. 3077–3086.

Rothwell, A., Herbert, I., and Rothwell, F. (2008) "Self-perceived employability: Construction and initial validation of a scale for university students." *Journal of Vocational Behavior* 73(1), pp. 1–12.

Sampaio, C. H., Perin, M. G., Simões, C., and Kleinowski, H. (2012) "Students' trust, value and loyalty: Evidence from higher education in Brazil." *Journal of Marketing for Higher Education* 22(1), pp. 83–100.

Scharf, E. R. and Correia, R. B. (2015) "Identification with a higher education institution through communication of the brand," in *The Sustainable Global Marketplace*. Ruston, LA: Springer, Cham, pp. 478–481.

Stephenson, A. L. and B. Yerger, D. (2014) "Optimizing engagement: Brand identification and alumni donation behaviors." *International Journal of Educational Management* 28(6), pp. 765–778.

Stokburger-Sauer, N., Ratneshwar, S., and Sen, S. (2012) "Drivers of consumer–brand identification." *International Journal of Research in Marketing* 29(4), pp. 406–418.

Tenenhaus, M., Vinzi, V. E., Chatelin, Y. M., and Lauro, C. (2005) "PLS path modeling." *Computational Statistics & Data Analysis* 48(1), pp. 159–205.

Vallaster, C. and de Chernatony, L. (2005) "Internationalisation of services brands: The role of leadership during the internal brand building process." *Journal of Marketing Management* 21(1–2), pp. 181–203.

Vivek, S. D., Beatty, S. E., and Morgan, R. M. (2012) "Customer engagement: Exploring customer relationships beyond purchase." *Journal of Marketing Theory and Practice* 20(2), pp. 122–146.

Yi, Y. and Gong, T. (2008) "The effects of customer justice perception and affect on customer citizenship behavior and customer dysfunctional behavior." *Industrial Marketing Management* 37(7), pp. 767–783.

Yu, Q., Asaad, Y., Yen, D. A., and Gupta, S. (2018) "IMO and internal branding outcomes: An employee perspective in UK HE." *Studies in Higher Education* 43(1), pp. 37–56.

Zeithaml, V. A., Berry, L. L., and Parasuraman, A. (1996) "The behavioral consequences of service quality." *The Journal of Marketing* 60(2), pp. 31–46.

12 Scale development in higher education

University corporate brand image, student satisfaction, and student behavioural intention

Sharifah Faridah Syed Alwi and Norbani Che-Ha

1 Introduction

It has long been debated within academic circles that, in order to triumph in the highly competitive environment today, universities require a systematic approach to understanding and designing their branding strategies (Syed Alwi and Kitchen, 2014; Chapleo, 2010; Balmer and Liao, 2007; Bennett and Ali-Choudhury, 2009; Curtis, Abratt, and Minor, 2009; Davies and Chun, 2008; Hemsley-Brown and Goonawardana, 2007; Melewar and Akel, 2005). Chapleo (2010) explains that the education sector should be treated as a 'corporation brand' rather than 'service/product brand', because product brand strategy cannot influence/impact ranking positions. Rather, the corporate brand image and reputation are more influential (Chapleo, 2010). Similarly, Gioia and Corley (2002) raised the question: 'What is the university beyond ranking and how can a university sustain itself?' This is a consideration that needs to be explored beyond ranking position since the ranking measures are still disputed.

The higher education sector, and business schools in particular, is generally growing (Antunes and Thomas, 2007). By having a reputable image, a business school will benefit in many ways including not only ranking position, but also increased enrolment of excellent students, attracting funding opportunities, top employer recruitment, and alumni donations (Davies and Chun, 2008). However, to date, limited empirical research has focused on the corporate brand image within the business school context, its antecedent, and behavioural outcome (e.g. Davies and Chun, 2008; Hemsley-Brown and Oplatka, 2006; Melewar and Akel, 2005). Nevertheless, the importance of this sector is gaining prominence with increased publication on the subject matter (e.g. Syed Alwi and Kitchen, 2014) and a special section in a journal dedicated to this sector (see Hemsley-Brown *et al.*, 2016). Hence, the study conducted in this chapter attempts to add to the wider literature by demonstrating how universities can develop and design their own corporate brand image via what the study termed 'university corporate brand image'.

The chapter's research questions are as follows:

1 What are the university corporate brand images in the case of business schools?
2 Are these university brand images presented by multi-dimensional constructs?
3 Do university corporate brand images have a direct effect on students' satisfaction and students' behavioural intentions?
4 Does student satisfaction necessarily explain relevant recommendation/ behavioural intention?

At the end of this chapter, readers should be able to:

- Understand what is meant by corporate brand image, especially in the context of university/institution/business school.
- Appreciate ways in which corporate brand image within the university context could be measured: functional, emotional and symbolic.
- Understand how to position and differentiate using corporate brand within a business school context: prestigious, chic and competence.
- Explain what factors prompt students to recommend a business school.

The chapter is divided as follows. First, we discuss the importance of positioning a business school using corporate brand image. We then define the corporate brand image and discuss the possible scales that could be used to measure business schools. We later explain our methodology and data analysis. The final section discusses our findings and concludes the study by highlighting the strategic positioning of a university corporate brand.

2 Review of the literature in higher education and branding

Corporate brand as a strategic educational positioning for business schools

The importance of positioning a business school's corporate brand has been well-acknowledged (Argenti, 2000; Melewar and Akel, 2005; Balmer and Liao, 2007; Hemsley-Brown and Goonawardana, 2007; Davies and Chun, 2008; Curtis et al., 2009; Bennet and Choudhry, 2009; Chapleo, 2010; Hemsley-Brown et al., 2016). Substantial budget is also allocated for branding activities in many higher education institutions (HEIs) (Chapleo, 2007). Yet, managing corporate brand strategies is seemingly difficult because many organizations lack proper understanding of how to manage their corporate brand strategies (Curtis et al., 2009). To date, very few scholars have attempted to provide empirical research on managing corporate branding within HEIs (Davies and Chun, 2008). This is perhaps because education branding research is less developed (Chapleo, 2010). Hemsley-Brown and Oplatka (2006) pointed out that research on higher education branding is still at an early stage with much still needed from both an exploratory and a strategic perspective. In particular, Curtis et al. (2009) focused on corporate brand management in a USA HEI: Embry-Riddle Aeronautical University, also known as ERAU; Melewar and Akel (2005) explored the corporate identity of Warwick University in the UK; Davies and Chun (2008) examined how to build corporate brand identity for Manchester Business School, UK; Bennett and Choudhury (2009) investigated the educational services and brand covenant of HEIs (former polytechnics) in East London, UK; and Hemsley-Brown and Goonawardana (2007) explored how to harmonize a brand within a corporate brand, (focusing on brand architecture) in one of the HEIs in the USA, while Syed Alwi and Kitchen (2014) did so in a Malaysian business school. With the few empirical exceptions above, most of the previous studies on corporate branding and corporate identity of business schools remain at conceptual or theoretical levels (Curtis et al., 2009).

Generally, corporate marketing has several marketing tactics, including corporate identity and image (Balmer and Gray, 2003); the end product of a corporate brand is usually corporate image (Curtis et al., 2009). As observed by many scholars, university corporate brand image does not rely on its product branding strategy, rather it is more about 'associations, emotions, images and faces' (or corporate brand image) (Chapleo, 2010, p. 173; Davies and Chun, 2008). Scholars also note that the role of university branding is to build, manage, and develop these impressions (Chapleo, 2010). Nevertheless, we are beginning to see the emergence of diverse empirical research (e.g. Syed Alwi and Kitchen, 2014; Hemsley-Brown et al., 2016), which indicate the need to extend the topic beyond product (program) brand strategy which is the current study's objective.

What is university corporate brand image and how can it be measured?

A corporation or business school can position its corporate brand through the development of a reputable image across multiple fields (Balmer and Liao, 2007). Positioning business schools based on corporate brand image (represented by values) is perceived to be relevant when marketing a service or HEI/business school (Bennett and Choudhury, 2009; Hatch and Schultz, 2009) because organizations are able to differentiate themselves and build their institutional values (Blanton, 2007). Building corporate brand image and reputation by understanding the values or personality behind the brand is necessary because values and personality are closely related to the constituent components of corporate marketing mix and help explain the covenant aspect of the brand (what is promised and expected) (Balmer and Gray, 2003). For example, some prestigious universities explain how students could form an identification with them, which in turn could prompt further referrals to their colleagues or whoever seeks their advice when pursuing their studies. Blanton (2007) explains that people tend to support institutions that are well-recognized. This will then lead to a clearer strategic brand positioning and provide the basis for branding strategy in business schools (Davies and Chun, 2008; Belanger, Mount, and Wilson, 2002). Corporate brand image can be positioned in several ways: functional, emotional and symbolic. This has resulted in a number of ways of measuring the construct in the past as it differs depending on which sector/industry or context is being researched, which is the subject of the following paragraphs.

First, attributes used to measure brand image in some way are also adopted in the understanding of store brand image, corporate brand image, company reputation, customer satisfaction and service quality in many different industries. Three types of methodological approach were found in earlier related literature concerning brand image evaluation. On the one hand, past studies have evaluated brand image on the basis of a more rational or functional approach, for example service quality, price, product performance. These measures are commonly used in the context of retail store and brand image studies.

On the other hand, some more emotional or symbolic brand attributes are employed to measure corporate brand image and reputation. For example, adapted scales are usually derived from human personality traits (e.g. friendly, innovative, honest, chic) or symbolic features (e.g. symbol, heritage element, brand name or logo that are associated with the corporation or university (Burghausen and Balmer, 2014)). The measures are commonly found in corporate branding and reputation studies (see Davies and Chun, 2008; Rojas-Mendez, Podlech, and Olave, 2004; Davies et al., 2004). By using metaphorical expression, specifically the personification approach (i.e. by viewing the company as a person), these studies have examined corporate brand images or brand personalities in various settings (e.g. retailing industry, services, higher education, and automobile manufacture).

The third perspective is where scales and measures were combined (rational, emotional and/or symbolic) were all used to measure corporate brand image and reputation of a corporation or institution (see for example, Syed Alwi and Kitchen, 2014). This is because separating these measures/constructs will have some effect on corporate brands (Anisimova, 2007). Additionally, Brown (1998, p. 217) defined corporate association as 'cognition, affect evaluations (that consumers attach to specific cognitions or affects) summary evaluations and patterns of associations (e.g. schemata, scripts) with respect to a particular company'. This may be due to the fact that an image of a company refers to not only 'what we hear and see from the company's messages (impression formed from other people's opinion or media advertising), but experience of its product (the direct contact the consumer has with the product)', (Ind, 1997, p. 5). Consistent with this notion, Patterson (1999, p. 419) defines brand image as 'consumer perceptions of brand attributes and associations from which those consumers derive symbolic value'. This suggests that brand image attributes (regardless of whether they encompass product or service related attributes) might be relevant when consumers evaluate the brand image of a retail store, or a business school, which is the context of the present study.

In the higher education context, an institution's image consists of two components: functional (which is related to tangibles such as product or service offered) and emotional (which is the psychological dimension that is manifested by feelings and attitudes towards an institution) (Nguyen and LeBlanc, 2001). Despite the importance of functional elements, it is the emotional elements that help in universities' brand differentiation and positioning, which in the long-term will impact/improve their ranking position (Chapleo, 2010).

Despite the importance of product brand strategy within the university environment, an appreciation of the emotional side of a university's corporate brand offers guidance not only when delivering the university's message to relevant audiences, but also in helping the university to decide on what message or image to convey, and which user imagery or endorser should be chosen to represent the university brand in advertising campaigns. It may also help the company to establish or define or re-establish/re-define its brand positioning based on the corporate brand image perceived by its stakeholders. By incorporating the metaphor of personality traits (which is more influenced by the emotional or affective elements as explained earlier) to measure universities' corporate brand image, this study hopes to add to existing knowledge, not only regarding the feasibility of this methodological approach, but also on the applicability of these emotional elements for the present context of the study, particularly where knowledge is very limited.

The current study thus regards business schools as a type of emotional component. Explicitly, the study defines corporate brand image as the sum of values that represent an organization (Ind, 1997) and these values or perceptions held by stakeholders are based on their accumulated experiences with an organization (Davies *et al.*, 2003; Goldsmith, Lafferty, and Newell, 2000). Thus, corporate brand image is about the consumer's emotional response to a brand that leads to the personification of brand attributes, and this is then used to differentiate between alternative offerings (Patterson, 1999). Similarly, Chapleo (2010) and Bulotaite (2003) suggest that when someone mentions the name of a university it will immediately evoke the emotional association and images.

In particular, the current study adopts corporate brand image scales from Davies et al., (2003, 2004) namely the 'Corporate Character Scale'. The Corporate Character Scale identifies seven dimensions (agreeableness; enterprise; competence; chic; ruthlessness, informality, and machismo, consisting of 49 items – see Table 12.1) in order to measure the business school corporate brand image as the construct is regarded as more emotional and affective in nature (Davies et al., 2004).

Satisfaction and behavioural intention: the measures

In this study, respondents or students were asked to indicate their level of satisfaction with the university in their second semester and later, since the study is more concerned with assessment over time. Students were screened on the basis of their previous experiences with the business schools to ensure a truer representation of satisfaction. It is suggested that when respondents have more time to assess the corporate or institutional brand, a more accurate reflection of their satisfaction levels emerges (Roper, 2004). Two different studies have been used to help determine the multi-item satisfaction measures in this study. Four items have been adopted from Davies and Chun (2002) and another two items from Oliver (1997). The recommendation/behavioural intention construct was operationalized as: (1) the students recommending the school to others; and (2) the repurchase or pursue intention concerning the school in future. Explicitly, the items were adopted from Zeithaml, Berry, and Parasuraman, (1996) to represent the behavioural intention. All items were measured using a five-point Likert scale; see Table 12.1 for the detail measures used for the study.

Therefore, achievement of corporate brand equity (e.g. the corporate brand image) of a business school lies with image and reputation, not satisfaction with the school (happy and proud with the school) or behavioural intention (recommending the school to others). Thus, focusing on the corporate brand of business schools may hopefully help to establish not only differentiation and preference at organizational, individual product or service levels (Chapleo, 2010; Curtis et al., 2009), but also positive behavioural responses such as overall image of the school, satisfaction and loyalty. The diagram below (Figure 12.1) illustrates the study's research proposition.

Data collection and respondents' backgrounds

Relevant surveys were distributed to four business schools and a state-owned university in Malaysia. Although the US still dominates the top rankings for business schools in advanced countries and has the largest market share, followed by Europe (particularly the UK) and third, Australia, business schools are also growing in developing economies such as

Table 12.1 Items/dimensions of corporate brand image, satisfaction and behavioural intention

Constructs/sources	Dimensions	Item measures
University Corporate Brand	Agreeableness	Friendly, Pleasant, Open, Straightforward Concerned, Reassuring, Supportive, Agreeable Honest, Sincere, Socially-responsible, Trustworthy
Image (Davies *et al.*, 2003, 2004)	Competence	Reliable, Secure, Hardworking Ambitious, Achievement-oriented, Leading Technical, Corporate
	Enterprise	Cool, Trendy, Young Imaginative, Up-to-date, Exciting, Innovative Extrovert, Daring
	Chic	Charming, Stylish, Elegant Prestigious, Exclusive, Refined Snobby, Elitist
	Ruthlessness	Arrogant, Aggressive, Selfish Inward-looking, Authoritarian, Controlling
	Machismo	Masculine, Tough, Rugged
	Informality	Casual, Simple, Easy-going
Satisfaction Oliver (1997) Davies and Chun (2002)		Happy studying at the business school Pleased to be associated with the school School has a distinct brand personality School has a unique identity Affinity with the school
Behavioural Intention Zeithaml *et al.* (1996)		Recommend to friends and family Encourage others First choice when considering pursuing studies Say positive things about the University

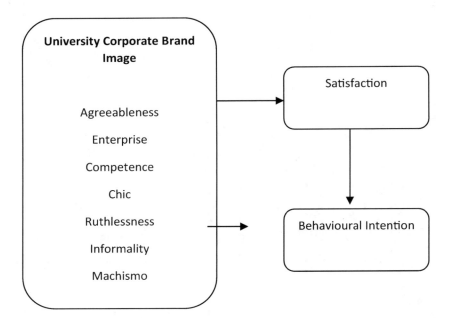

Figure 12.1 The study's research proposition.

in the Middle East and Asia (China, Hong Kong and Malaysia (Hawawini, 2005, p. 770). In particular, Malaysia offers a welcoming environment for higher education in general, with a large potential target market, which makes it a highly attractive academic destination. This creates a competitive atmosphere among these business schools in attracting top students. With regard to data collection, the study received permission from the Malaysian Ministry of Higher Education (MOHE) and the deans of business schools to administer the survey to MBA students in-class in the four business schools. Students were briefed and the questionnaires distributed during their break time or shortly after classes. In total, the usable questionnaires collected were 553 and in order to explore the study's research question, structural equation modelling was performed.

The study data consists of 261 male and 292 female respondents. The respondents represented the wider population of Malaysia with an ethnic composition as follows: 48 per cent Malay, 30.1 per cent Chinese, 11.3 per cent Indian, and 10.6 per cent others, (Population, & Housing Census, Malaysia, 2017). The respondents were mainly MBA students between 25–34 years of age. Most of the students (80%) were in their first or second year of their MBA program, which reflected the program structure (i.e. the program duration is approximately two years including two semesters of research dissertation within the Malaysian context).

Data analysis and discussion

All constructs and items were validated by a rigorous technique – structural equation modelling. Since the underlying factor structure of the corporate character scale had been specified a priori, confirmatory factor analysis (CFA) appeared to be more appropriate than exploratory factor analysis (EFA) (Byrne, 2001). The study performed first and second order (latent) methods as proposed (Byrne, 2001; Hair et al., 1998; Garver and Menzter, 1999). The second order model 'would allow a stronger statement by the researcher as to the dimensionality of the construct' (Hair et al., 1998, p. 626). Second, to meet the objective of construct validation of the corporate brand image scale, Garver and Mentzer (1999) explain that both first and second order are necessary to ensure the underlying theoretical structure is tested for unidimensionality and reliability. Finally, testing the corporate brand image in the first and second order models would help to determine which dimensions represent the university corporate brand image. The analysis then proceeds to 'Step Two Approach' known as the Structural Full or Equation Model (the SEM). The full model in general deals with testing one's theoretical model (Anderson and Gerbing, 1988). The analysis was conducted using the latest version of the AMOS 20 statistical package by the default method – maximum likelihood (ML).

First order model

The initial result showed a poor fit and needed to be re-specified. For example, the result of ($\chi^2_{(1106)} = 3841$, $p < 0.001$); $\chi^2/df = 3.5$; GFI = 0.731; TLI = 0.657; CFI = 0.678; RMSEA = 0.094 suggests that there were misfits in the model. Items that are cross-loaded in more than one dimension were relaxed one at a time as proposed by Long (1983) and insignificant parameters were excluded from the study. In addition, relaxing parameters, removal or addition of items (or parameters) from one dimension to another dimension, which is highly cross-loaded, was also a part of1 this study. However, any removal, exclusion or addition of parameters need to be performed based on theoretical, statistical and practical considerations (Bagozzi and Heatherton, 1994). The final result indicated that five dimensions (Agreeableness, Enterprise, Competence, Chic and Machismo) represent university corporate brand images. Goodness-of-fit statistics show that the online model [$\chi^2_{(289)} = 630.79$; $p < 0.001$; $\chi^2/df - 2.1$; GFI–0.905; CFI–0.922; TLI–0.915; RMSEA 0.006] fits the data well. Convergent validity were all supported in this study with all parameter estimates (i.e. the item's standardized loadings >0.5, (Kline, 1998) and all items were statistically significant at $p < 0.001$ (Anderson and Gerbing, 1988) as shown in Figure 12.2. In terms of variance explained by each dimension, online corporate brand image explains 72 per cent, 79 per cent, 89 per cent, 97 per cent and 99 per cent of the variance associated with the

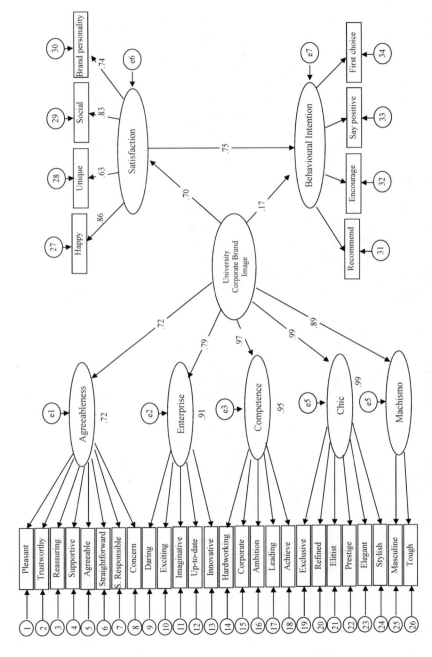

Figure 12.2 University corporate brand image, satisfaction and behavioural intention.

dimensions Agreeableness, Machismo, Enterprise, Competence and Chic respectively and this represented the university corporate brand image.

Satisfaction and behavioural items were analysed separately in the measurement model phase. Specifically, they were analysed in a first order measurement and were then combined with the second order model in a full structural model (as exhibited in Figure 12.2). The result of the full model: [$\chi^2_{(316)} = 1072$, $p < 0.001$; $\chi^2/df = 2$; GFI = 0.905; CFI = 0.918; TLI = 0.911; RMSEA = 0.064] fits the data very well. In order to explore research questions 3 and 4 on the direct effect, customer satisfaction and behavioural intention were included in the full structural model. The results show, in particular, that both directions have significant positive effects on the university corporate brand image as proposed. These results thus show that first, while empirical research on university corporate brand image has been limited, as addressed earlier, five dimensions determine it: Agreeableness, Machismo, Enterprise, Competence and Chic, with Competence and Chic representing the dominant dimensions. Second, in addition to customer satisfaction, consumers' behavioural intention/recommendation is also explained by university corporate brand image; and finally, a happy (satisfied) student will positively recommend the university to her/his colleagues and consider further study options. Hence, these results answer all four research questions addressed at the beginning of the chapter.

3 Managerial implications

Several managerial implications arise from the chapter. First, the study emphasizes looking at the important dimensions to be addressed by educators/school administrators, business school deans and marketing departments of universities. The current chapter stresses that both *Chic* (e.g. Prestigious, Exclusivity, Refined, Elitist, elegant and Stylish) and *Competence* (Hard Working, Corporate, Leading, Achievement-Oriented) represent the business school/university corporate brand image and it is important that they are equally highlighted in the corporate brand positioning strategy of business schools. Since university corporate brand image is seen as a more emotional or affective construct (Davies *et al.*, 2004), the study uses human personality traits to measure the construct. Therefore, this could help the business school to understand its corporate brand image better and perhaps more effectively, as through personality traits, these factors (Chic and Competence) may be considered not only at a strategic level but at a tactical level. For example, they may be considered when designing university marketing communication campaigns – in website design/social media – with a view to having a more corporate look and addressing mission/vision or a slogan which connects to *Leading* and communicates any *Prestigious element* arising from their heritage (if applicable). Also, these elements explain the high impact on students' satisfaction and potential positive recommendation of the business schools/institutions in the future. Therefore, the study's practical contribution and its managerial implications can be seen in the context of defining strategy, positioning and the tactical approach of business schools in a higher education context.

4 Conclusion

As discussed, there are several ways in which corporate brand image could be measured regardless of contexts (e.g. university, institution, banking, automobile industry, or retailing). The basis upon which these measures are conceptualized and operationalized are commonly: functional, emotional and symbolic elements. The current study adopted an emotional type of measures, using human personality traits, because the setting investigated (i.e. business schools) is seen as more suited to 'abstract level and emotional basis/images' (Chapleo, 2010; Davies and Chun, 2008). The study found that the most two important values/emotional dimensions of how business schools could be differentiated and positioned are based on *Chic* and *Competence*. These emotional values also impact student happiness (satisfaction) and future behavioural intention (i.e. to positively recommend the business school to others).

The current chapter investigated four business schools in Malaysia. Further research could look into other business schools to explore if these values/dimensions (e.g. Chic and Competence) apply in other business school settings across the globe with broader samples which include a myriad of stakeholders (e.g. industries, employees and school administrators). This could be potentially explored since this activity will provide a broader or holistic picture of the university corporate brand image, which may help to identify a more effective or clearer corporate brand positioning. Also, since business schools or universities could be positioned and differentiated in several ways as discussed (e.g. functional, emotional and symbolic), combining and exploring them in a single/cross sectional manner would be interesting since we focus only on one aspect (the emotional concept of corporate brand image) in this study. A comparative assessment could be done in a cross-cultural study, to understand which element features in which business school and in which geographic region/location, since brand could be perceived differently in different settings (Aaker, 1997).

5 Case study: to brand or not to brand – a case of a graduate business school

Ranked as no. 1 in the country and among the top 20 in the region, Arian University (AU), established in the early 1900s, is well known for its academic achievements. AU offers more than 57 education programmes across disciplines, and business education is one of them. Business education has been offered since the mid-1960s.

In 1997, the pressing need to meet the growing demand for postgraduate business education led to the setting up of Arian Graduate School of Business (AGSB). Since then, AGSB has offered three postgraduate programmes, the Masters in Business Administration (MBA), Masters in Management (MM), and Doctor of Philosophy (PhD).

Twenty years since its inception, many at AGSB feel that their activities and achievements are overshadowed by AU in general. Many outsiders fail to differentiate between AGSB and its parent university, AU. They tend to remember AU the most. Remembering AU potentially means AGSB is lost among the many faculties and centres at AU. Some at AGSB feel that it is high time for the school to have its own identity. This is important because it has to stand out from many other business schools that are available nowadays. Some however, feel that the AU brand name is important. It is the brand that everyone knows and associates with.

AGSB itself is not short of its academic accomplishments. It is the only business school in the country with Triple Crown accreditations from international accreditation bodies, hence it has a leading and prestigious image. One accreditation is for the highest standard met in postgraduate business education. AGSB has also been placed in the 'top business school' category by an international body for its Masters programmes. It is the only business school in that category in the country. All of these international accolades are recognition of top quality programmes offered by AGSB. These programmes are supported and taught by international academics trained by top universities across the world.

The recognition of its academic excellence attracts many students from many countries, which gives it the highest composition of international students in the country. Moreover, as a result of its reputation, many professional accounting and finance bodies are affiliated with the institution. The hallmark of success was achieved when AGSB was sponsored to build an iconic and state-of-the-art building by a private donor, in order to house all of its activities and provide efficient teaching and learning environments for its academics and students.

6 Further investigation

1 What could be the potential brand positioning for AGSB? List all possible answers.
2 How does AU differentiate itself among its competitors within the country?
3 On what basis is this differentiation founded?
4 If AGSB decides to rebrand itself, suggest the best possible way to carry out its research.

References

Aaker, J. L. (1997) "Dimensions of brand personality." *Journal of Marketing Research* 34(3), pp. 347–356.

Anderson, J. C. and Gerbing, D. W. (1988) "Structural equation modelling in practice: A review and recommended two-step approach." *Psychological Bulletin* 103(3), pp. 411–423.

Anisimova, T. A. (2007) "The effects of corporate brand attributes on attitudinal and behavioural consumer loyalty." *Journal of Consumer Marketing* 24(7), pp. 395–405.

Antunes, D. and Thomas, H. (2007) "The competitive (dis)advantages of European business schools." *Long Range Planning* 40(3), pp. 382–404.

Argenti, P. (2000) "Branding b-schools: Reputation management for MBA programs." *Corporate Reputation Review* 3(2), pp. 171–178.

Bagozzi, R. P. and Heatherton, T. F. (1994) "A general approach to representing multifaceted personality constructs: Application to state self-esteem." *Structural Equation Modelling* 1(1), pp. 35–67.

Balmer, J. M. T. and Gray, E. R. (2003) "Corporate brands: What are they? What of them?" *European Journal of Marketing* 37(7/8), pp. 972–997.

Balmer, J. M. T. and Liao, M.-N. (2007) "Student corporate brand identification: An exploratory case study." *Corporate Communications: An International Journal* 12(4), pp. 356–375.

Belanger, C., Mount, J., and Wilson, M. (2002) "Institutional image and retention." *Tertiary Education and Management* 8(3), pp. 217–230.

Bennett, R. and Ali-Choudhury, R. (2009) "Prospective students' perceptions of university brands: An empirical study." *Journal of Marketing for Higher Education* 19(1), pp. 85–107.

Blanton, J. (2007) "Engagement as a brand position in the higher education marketplace." *International Journal of Educational Advancement* 7(2), pp. 143–154.

Brown, T. J. (1998) "Corporate associations in marketing: Antecedents and consequences." *Corporate Reputation Review* 1(3), pp. 215–233.

Bulotaite, N. (2003) "University heritage – An institutional tool for branding and marketing." *Higher Education in Europe* 28(4), pp. 449–454.

Burghausen, M. and Balmer, J. M. (2014) "Corporate heritage identity management and the multi-modal implementation of a corporate heritage identity." *Journal of Business Research* 67(11), pp. 2311–2323.

Byrne, M. B. (2001) *Structural Equation Modelling with AMOS: Basic Concepts, Applications and Programming.* NJ, USA: Lawrence Erlbaum Associates.

Chapleo, C. (2007) "Barriers to brand building in UK universities?" *International Journal of Nonprofit and Voluntary Sector Marketing* 12(1), pp. 23–32.

Chapleo, C. (2010) "What defines 'successful' university brands?" *International Journal of Public Sector Management* 23(2), pp. 169–183.

Curtis, T., Abratt, R., and Minor, W. (2009) "Corporate brand management in higher education: The case of ERAU." *Journal of Product & Brand Management* 18(6), pp. 404–413.

Davies, G. and Chun, R. (2002) "Gaps between the internal and external perceptions of the corporate brand." *Corporate Reputation Review* 5(2/3), pp. 144–158.

Davies, G. and Chun, R. (2008) "Projecting corporate character in the branding of business school," in T C Melewar (ed.), *Facets of Corporate Identity, Communication and Reputation*. UK: Routledge, pp. 163–177.

Davies, G., Chun. R., Da Silva, R., and Roper, S. (2003) *Corporate Reputation and Competitiveness*. UK: Routledge.

Davies, G., Chun, R., Da Silva, R., and Roper, S. (2004) "Corporate character scale to assess employee and customer views of organisation reputation." *Corporate Reputation Review* 7(2), pp. 125–146.

Garver, M. S. and Mentzer, J. T. (1999) "Logistics research methods: Employing structural equation modelling to test for construct validity." *Journal of Business Logistics* 20(1), pp. 33–57.

Gioia, D. A. and Corley, K. G. (2002) "Being good versus looking good: Business school rankings and the circean transformation from substance to image." *Academy of Management Learning and Education* 1(1), pp. 107–120.

Goldsmith, R. E., Lafferty, B. A., and Newell, S. J. (2000) "The influence of corporate credibility on consumer attitudes and purchase intent." *Corporate Reputation Review* 3(4), pp. 304–318.

Hair, F. J., Anderson, E. R., Tatham, L. R., and Black, C. W. (1998) *Multivariate Data Analysis*. NJ: Prentice-Hall Inc.

Hatch, M. J. and Schultz, M. (2009) "Of bricks and brands: From corporate to enterprise branding." *Organizational Dynamics* 38(2), pp. 117–130.

Hawawini, G. (2005) "The future of business schools." *Journal of Management Development* 24(9), pp. 770–782.

Hemsley-Brown, J. and Goonawardana, S. (2007) "Brand harmonization in the international higher education market." *Journal of Business Research* 60(9), pp. 942–948.

Hemsley-Brown, J., Melewar, T C, Nguyen, B., and Wilson, E. J. (2016) "Exploring brand identity, meaning, image, and reputation (BIMIR) in higher education: A special section." *Journal of Business Research* 69(8), pp. 3019–3022.

Hemsley-Brown, J. and Oplatka, I. (2006) "Universities in a competitive global marketplace: A systematic review of the literature on higher education marketing." *International Journal of Public Sector Management* 19(4), pp. 316–338.

Ind, N. (1997) *The Corporate Brand*. UK: Macmillan Press Ltd.

Keller, K. L. (2003) "Brand synthesis: The multidimensionality of brand Knowledge." *Journal of Consumer Research* 29(4), pp. 595–600.

Kline, R. (1998) *Principles and Practice of Structural Equation Modelling*. New York: The Guildford Press.

Long, S. J. (1983) *Confirmatory Factor Analysis: A Preface to Lisrel*. CA: Sage.

Melewar, T C and Akel, S. (2005) "The role of corporate identity in the higher education sector: A case study." *Corporate Communications: An International Journal* 10(1), pp. 41–57.

Nguyen, N. and LeBlanc, G. (2001) "Image and reputation of higher education institutions in students' retention decisions." *The International Journal of Educational Management* 15(6), pp. 303–311.

Oliver, R. L. (1997) *Satisfaction: A Behavioural Perspective on the Consumer*. MA: McGraw-Hill.

Patterson, M. (1999) "Re-appraising the concept of brand image." *Journal of Brand Management* 6(6), pp. 409–426.

Population & Housing Census, Malaysia. (2017) www.dosm.gov.my/v1/?English/pressdemo.htm (accessed 15 March 2018).

Rojas-Mendez, I. J., Podlech, E. I., and Olave, S. E. (2004) "The Ford Brand Personality in Chile." *Corporate Reputation Review* 7(3), pp. 232–251.

Roper, S. (2004) *Corporate Branding: A Reputational Perspective in Business-to-Business Markets*, Unpublished Doctoral Thesis, Manchester Business School, University of Manchester.

Syed Alwi, S. F. and Kitchen, P. J. (2014) "Projecting corporate brand image and behavioural response in business schools: Cognitive or affective brand attributes?" *Journal of Business Research* 67(11), pp. 2324–2336.

Zeithaml, V. A., Berry, L. L., and Parasuraman, A. (1996) "The behavioral consequences of Service quality." *Journal of Marketing* 60(2), pp. 31–46.

13 Evaluating branding scales in higher education

Lesley Ledden, Stavros P. Kalafatis, and Ilia Protopapa

1 Introduction

Only a cursory glance through extant literature in higher education (HE) marketing is necessary to confirm the view that increased competition and marketization has led to a transformation of marketing thought and practice in the HE sector. Despite resistance and criticism, marketing concepts derived from mainstream consumer and industrial marketing literature are now widely adopted and implemented in the HE context. Branding is one such concept that has garnered widespread attention, both as a management strategy to enable HE institutions (HEIs) to develop and manage their identity and image and as the basis for understanding how stakeholders perceive and evaluate HEIs. Brand image, brand personality and brand reputation represent just a few of the employed measures. The focus of this chapter is on evaluating the relevance and empirical robustness of such measures in the HE context, with the aim to guide HE researchers and managers when making decisions related to the operationalization of branding scales.

The scope of the chapter is as follows. First, we acknowledge the contribution of interpretivist approaches in uncovering deep and nuanced insight through brand narratives derived from qualitative data. However, such studies do not apply enumerated measurement scales and thus fall outside the scope of this chapter. Specifically, the present chapter aligns with positivist ontology and concentrates on studies that employ a quantitative approach in the measurement of branding concepts in studies of HEIs. It comments on the applicability of such scales to the HE context and evaluates the robustness of branding scales in terms of relevance (i.e. conceptual fit) and psychometric performance (i.e. reliability and validity; all scales under review are multi-item). Excluded from the chapter is commentary on the theoretical robustness of the conceptual models in which the branding scales are used or examination of the functional interrelationships between model constructs. Lastly, since HE brand scale development is covered in Chapter 12, the present chapter does not include related debate. However, it is inevitable that there will be some overlap in the content of the two chapters.

Methodology

Academic journal papers published in peer reviewed journals on the subject of branding in HE constitute the unit of analysis. The data collection commenced by using keyword searches for the terms 'brands', 'branding', 'higher education', 'HE', and 'university/ies'. Using our university's library database as the sample frame, our search yielded a total of 82 papers. Each paper was read to establish its suitability for inclusion in the sample for analysis, i.e. to confirm that branding constructs were employed and, if so, whether these were measured quantitatively. The resultant 25 papers, when reviewed, enabled the identification of a further 17 eligible papers, resulting in a total sample size of 42 papers for the analysis that informs the discussions in this chapter.

Learning objectives

After reading this chapter you should be able to:

1. Understand the importance of content validity in specifying the conceptual domain of a scale.
2. Appreciate the factors that should be taken into account in order to avoid errors when borrowing scales.
3. Understand the requirements for credibility and the need to demonstrate rigour when specifying sources of borrowed scales.
4. Appreciate the accepted conventions for testing the psychometric properties of a scale.
5. Critically evaluate the use of scales to measure branding concepts as applied in HE research and evaluate their adherence to good practice.

2 Review of the literature in the use of multi-item scales in HE branding

Overview of papers reviewed

Using the Chartered Association of Business Schools (CABS) Academic Journal Guide 2018 we classified the 42 papers under review. Table 13.1 shows that the majority are published in either unranked journals (29%) or those ranked first (49%). Although the evidence indicates that the majority (83%) of the reviewed papers are published in lower ranked journals we are cognisant of the discussions and objections regarding the construction and use of the CABS list and acknowledge that quality is often found in lower ranked journals. Therefore, we examine each publication on its merits rather than being 'influenced' by the ranking of the journal. In terms of journals, the *International Journal of Educational Management* (CABS rank 1; five papers), *Journal of Marketing for Higher Education* (CABS rank 1; 11

Table 13.1 Number of papers and quality of source publication

Year	Journal quality according to CABS					Total
	Not ranked	1	2	3	4 or 4*	
2001		1				1
2002	1					1
2003		1				1
2004						0
2005						0
2006	1	1				2
2007		1				1
2008	1	2				3
2009		1	1			2
2010		1				1
2011	3					3
2012	1					1
2013		2				2
2014	2	6*		1		9
2015	2	1	1			4
2016	2			6**		8
2017		2				2
2018		1				1
Total	13	20	2	7	0	42
Cumulative %	29%	78%	83%	100%		

Notes
* 3 from special issue in the *Journal of Marketing for Higher Education*;
** all 6 from special section in the *Journal of Business Research*.

papers) and the *Journal of Business Research* (CABS rank 3; seven papers) contributed the greatest concentration of publications with scales related to branding of higher education. There are two observations: (a) given that the time span is 17 years, the number of papers under review is quite small; and (b) this paucity would have been greater if not for the two special issues.

Turning to Table 13.2, this indicates the brand concepts that are investigated therein, their frequency of appearance, and the authors employing the constructs. A total of 35 brand concepts were identified, 17 of which featured in single papers while others occurred more frequently across the corpus; in particular, brand reputation featured in 12 papers, brand image in ten, brand personality and brand loyalty in nine, and brand identification in eight. Brand prestige appears in five papers with brand equity and brand trust appearing in four.

Our examination of the 42 papers reveals that the majority of the scales used, 67 per cent, are adopted from non-HE specific marketing literature (55% consumer, 12% b2b), with the 18 per cent of papers in organizational studies the second highest contributor. HE specific publications account for 9 per cent while the remaining 6 per cent come from psychology or non-profit

Table 13.2 Branding constructs used in HE research

Construct	No. of papers	Authors
Brand alliance attitudes	2	Naidoo and Hollebeek (2016); Wilkins et al. (2017)
Brand association	2	Pinar et al. (2014); Chen (2017)
Brand attachment	1	Dennis et al. (2016)
Brand attitude	1	Erdoğmuş and Ergun (2016)
Brand attributes	1	Syed Alwi and Kitchen (2014)
Brand awareness	2	Brewer and Zhao (2010); Pinar et al. (2014)
Brand commitment	2	Dennis et al. (2016); Nguyen et al. (2016)
Brand competence	1	Jillapalli and Jillapalli (2014)
Brand consciousness	1	Naidoo and Hollebeek (2016)
Brand credibility	1	Wilkins et al. (2017)
Brand emotions	1	Pinar et al. (2014)
Brand engagement	1	Šramová (2015)
Brand environment	1	Pinar et al. (2014)
Brand equity	4	Teh and Salleh (2011); Jillapalli and Jillapalli (2014); Pinar et al. (2014); Dennis et al. (2016)
Brand familiarity	1	Naidoo and Hollebeek (2016)
Brand fit	1	Naidoo and Hollebeek (2016)
Brand identification	8	Polyoma (2011); Porter et al. (2011), Stephenson and Yerger (2014a, 2014b, 2016), Palmer et al. (2016); Hefferan et al. (2018); Wilkins et al. (2017)
Brand identity	3	Bosch et al. (2006a, 2006b); *Goi et al. (2014); Dennis et al. (2016
Brand image	10	Nguyen and LeBlanc (2001); Palacio et al. (2002); *Arpan et al. (2003); Bosch et al. (2006); Clemes et al. (2008); Brown and Massaro (2009); Sultan and Wong (2012); Syed Alwi and Kitchen (2014); Dennis et al. (2016); Nguyen et al. (2016)
Brand interpretation	2	Stephenson and Yerger (2014a, 2014b)
Brand knowledge	1	Balaji et al. (2016)
Brand loyalty	9	Nguyen and LeBlanc (2001); Brown and Mazzarol (2009); Syed Alwi and Kitchen (2014); *Pinar et al. (2014); Casidy (2014a); Casidy and Wymer (2015); Erdoğmuş and Ergun (2016); Palmer et al. (2016); Hefferan et al. (2018)
Brand meaning	2	Teh and Salleh (2011); Dennis et al. (2016)
Brand orientation	2	Casidy (2014a, 2014b)
Brand perceptions	1	Bennett and Ali-Choudhury (2009)

Table 13.2 Continued

Construct	No. of papers	Authors
Brand performance	1	Nguyen et al. (2016)
Brand personality	9	Bosch et al. (2006); Sung and Yang (2008); Opoku et al. (2008); Polyoma (2011); Watkins and Gonzenbach (2013); Syed Alwi and Kitchen (2014); Thongthip and Polyorat (2015); Balaji et al. (2016); *Rauschnabel et al. (2016)
Brand prestige	5	Sung and Yang (2008); Porter et al. (2011), Stephenson and Yerger (2014a, 2014b); Balaji et al. (2016)
Brand quality	3	*Pinar et al. (2014); Jillapalli and Jillapalli (2014); Dennis et al. (2016)
Brand relationship	1	Bosch et al. (2006a, 2006b)
Brand relevance	1	Bosch et al. (2006a, 2006b)
Brand reputation	12	Nguyen and LeBlanc (2001); *Alessandri et al. (2006); Bosch et al. (2006a, 2006b); Sung and Yang (2008); Brewer and Zhao (2010); *Parahoo et al. (2013); Jillapalli and Jillapalli (2014); *Pinar et al. (2014); Elsharnouby (2015); Dennis et al. (2016); Nguyen et al. (2016); Hefferan et al. (2018)
Brand strength	3	Judson et al. (2008); Casidy and Wymer (2015); Khanna et al. (2014)
Brand support	1	Palmer et al. (2016)
Brand trust	4	*Pinar et al. (2014); Naidoo and Hollebeek (2016); Wilkins et al. (2017); Hefferan et al. (2018)

Note
* These papers contain some degree of scale development.

sources. Our conclusion is that a notable majority of scales employed in HE branding research are 'borrowed' from other disciplines or domains.

Although the practice of borrowing scales is extensively applied in marketing research, such practice is often problematic because some scales; (a) fail to perform adequately in terms of psychometric properties; and/or (b) require considerable purification before reaching accepted benchmarks. Furthermore, Kalafatis, Sarpong and Sharif (2005) found that the use of alternative scales measuring the same construct results in differential functional relationships, depending on the coverage of the underlying domain. Gilmore and McMullan (2009, p. 646) in their review of service quality scales conclude that

> The constant theme emerging from contemporary writers in this area is the importance of understanding what is to be measured, including a

detailed conceptual framework of the construct and its constituent parts.... Rather than using 'off the peg', widely used methodologies with some or little adaptation to the particular situation, more thought needs to be given to the service specific research objectives and the unique needs of a service context.

Engelland, Alsford and Taylor (2001, p. 152) – a 'must read' for anyone planning to borrow scales from any business or management field – endorse this view, stating:

occasionally research using these scales has reported anomalies in their psychometric performance, resulting in cautions to 'borrow with care.' While paradigms for new scale development are well known and accepted in the marketing literature, the necessary precautions required in using borrowed scales are not well understood.

Our evaluation of the scales reported on in Table 13.2 reveals four main recurring themes that exemplify the above-mentioned concerns relating to borrowing scales and our associated discussion aims to assist the reader in understanding (and thus avoiding) the resultant problems that can occur. We specify these themes as Secret Sources, Muddy Modification, Dubious Derivation, and Confounded Construal, each of which is explained and illustrated with examples. The final part of this section examines issues relating to Testing the Psychometric Properties. Before moving on, we should clarify that it is not our intention to invalidate or question the research from which the examples are drawn – rather, we use published material simply for illustrative purposes to enable the learning outcomes to be achieved.

Secret sources

Specification of the source(s) from which a scale is borrowed and/or detailed explanation of the methodology undertaken in identifying the scale items are both necessary conditions through which to ensure scientific clarity and establish credibility of the scale. The lack of provision of theoretical definition and relevant information raises questions about whether the resulting scale truly reflects the underlying construct. In other words, scales (or modifications of established scales) must demonstrate content validity (remember that face validity is not on its own sufficient) which, in the absence of formal tests, is assessed by reference to theoretically-guided (i.e. from literature) generation of scale items and expert judgement of the appropriateness of the items.

To exemplify, we turn to Nguyen and LeBlanc (2001, p. 306) who state their intention to use direct measures in the absence of consensus on valid scales for two of the model constructs. The scale items are presented in the paper's Appendix. However, at the same time (a) there is no mention and critique of the scales that are not valid and (b) if we accept (a), the authors had the opportunity to embark on a scale development exercise rather than introducing scale items whose source and relevance cannot be substantiated. In another example Chen (2017, p. 977) presents a scale for brand association (with student trust and student commitment similarly reported) that is 'adapted from the literature review ... and previous research'. However, the specific source of the scale remains undisclosed. Though the reporting of acceptable Cronbach's α to confirm reliability is helpful in terms of assessing the scale's psychometric properties, it does not mitigate the omission of the scale's source.

Muddy modification

Irrespective of the domain of the source, borrowing scales invariably necessitates some form of modification, adaptation or contextualization. The former implies adding or removing scale items while the latter refers to changes in wording according to the research context (for cross-national research see Douglas and Nijssen, 2003). For guidelines on good practice we refer the reader to Engelland et al. (2001), Finn and Kayande (2004) and Hardesty and Bearden (2004).

Our example refers to Teh and Salleh (2011, p. 220) where we read:

> To better differentiate it from 'brand identity' and 'brand experience', brand meaning is operationalised as a multi-dimensional construct (Martinez and de Chernatony, 2004) comprising three dimensions (Keller, 2001) ... namely (a) brand 'strength' – meaning how strong is the HEI's brand (nine items adapted from Palacio et al., 2002), (b) brand 'favourability' – describing how important or valuable is the HEI's brand (three items adapted from Palacio et al., 2002 and Lampo, 2001), and (c) brand 'uniqueness' – capturing how distinctive is the HEI's brand (five items adapted from Martinez & de Chernatony, 2004; Keller, 2001 and Palacio et al., 2002).

Although the authors should be commended for stating the meaning of the construct domains and specification of the sources used, closer inspection raises questions, namely: (a) we could not find measures of brand strength or favourability in Palacio et al. (2002); (b) Lampo (2001) refers to an unpublished PhD thesis, while our search identified a 2004 paper by Berry and Lampo (Branding labour-intensive services, *Business Strategy Review*, 15(1):18–25) that does not provide scale items; and (c) the papers by Martinez and de Chernatony (2004), Palacio et al. (2002) and Keller (2001) do not provide scale items. The lack of explanation regarding the way in which the source scales were adapted and the omission of the full list (as compared to partially-worded examples on page 221) of the scale items makes it difficult to judge the suitability of the measures. Reporting Cronbach's alpha during a pre-test and pilot test is helpful. However, since it provides only a partial evaluation, complete confidence in the scale is tenuous. Formal testing of the psychometric properties of the scales during the main study would have strengthened the study's robustness.

Dubious derivation

Credibility is a fundamental prerequisite for research running through all aspects of its execution, including the sources it draws upon. The criteria of credibility include (a) reputation, (b) ability to see, and (c) expertise (Brigham Young University, 2018). In the context of scale derivation, reputation relates to the reliability of a source; ability to see refers to whether the source can be accessed; and expertise associates to evidence of the source's specialized knowledge. Our two examples fail to meet one or more of these criteria when it comes to evaluating the credibility of a borrowed scale's source.

In the first, Bosch *et al.* (2006a) conceptualize brand identity as a higher order construct that they operationalize based on Coop (2004), which we can see from the paper's references is an unpublished PhD thesis. Also cited in the paper is a two-page summary of the thesis by Coop that appears in a practitioner magazine one year later, however the scale items are not included. In the second example, Brown and Mazzarol (2009, p. 86) say 'items used to develop the IMAGE dimension were drawn from an unpublished research study', which is cited as a Masters' level dissertation. We carried out a literature search to determine whether the scale was subsequently published in a verifiable source; unfortunately, our efforts did not return any results. From both examples we conclude that the lack of peer review scrutiny by the academic community of scales that are borrowed from unpublished (and thus unverifiable) sources can dent the credibility of the research.

Confounded construal

Accepting the need for modification of borrowed scales, clarity of purpose and conceptual coherency should underpin the adopted process. Confusing logic, unsubstantiated decisions and radical alterations comprise the integrity of the original scale and result in 'unsafe' operationalizations. In our illustrative example we turn to Judson *et al.* (2008), where brand strength is 'gauged using scales derived from the work of Michaels, Cron, Dubinsky, and Joachimisthaler (1988) and Aurand, Gorchels, and Bishop (2004)'. Examination of the supporting references finds that Michaels *et al.* (1988) study is in the b2b domain (published some 19 years earlier) and does not contain the focal construct of brand strength and neither does the paper include a list of scale items (readers are invited to contact the

Aurand *et al.* (2004, p. 165)	Judson *et al.* (2008, p. 62)
Human resources involvement in internal branding	Perceived university brand private university participants
Statement	Statement
The (brand) values are reinforced through internal communications	The university is at present, or has been, involved in promoting its brand image over the past two years
Training is provided to help employees use these values	The university clearly stands for something distinctive
The skill set necessary to deliver these values is considered in staffing decisions	The university communicates a clear message concerning its brand image to administrators
Annual performance reviews include metrics on delivering the values	Administrator has the same perceptions of the university's brand image as prospective students
Departmental plans include employees' roles in living the brand values	

Figure 13.1 Scale for internal branding in Aurand *et al.* (2004) and implementation of brand strength in Judson *et al.* (2008).

authors). In Aurand *et al.* (2004) the context of the study is human resources staff's involvement in internal branding. Figure 13.1 presents the scale items of the latter publication alongside those in Judson *et al.* (2008), where it can be seen that there is a lack of specific mapping of the original scale (on the left of the figure) to its later, borrowed version (on the right).

Testing the psychometric properties

Psychometric properties refer to the validity and reliability of a scale. As part of scale development DeVellis (2017) and Netemeyer *et al.* (2003) present and evaluate the various procedures and formal tests designed to assess reliability and validity according to classical test theory, exemplified in Churchill (1979), and therefore apply only to reflective multi-item scales. Briefly, reliability refers to the consistency of the scale and 'is concerned with that portion of measurement that is due to permanent effects that persist from sample to sample' (Netemeyer *et al.*, 2003, p. 10). There are various formal tests of reliability where we expect to see information about the scale items (i.e. size and significance of their loadings with the intended construct) and indices of internal consistency (Cronbach's alpha) and composite reliability (CR). Validity 'refers to how well a measure actually measures the construct it is intended to measure' (Netemeyer, Bearden, and Sharma, 2003, p. 11). Convergent and discriminant are the two validity tests that we expect researchers to report. Although the often-quoted multitrait-multimethod matrix (MTMM) can test for both types of validity, its application is rare; instead, the expectation is that papers should include information about average variance extracted (AVE) and the Fornell and Larker criterion. Scale item cross loadings, exploratory factor analysis (EFA) and, in the case of PLS, the heterotrait-monotrait ratio (HTMT) can be used. Application of confirmatory factor analysis (CFA) under covariance (e.g. LISREL, AMOS etc.) or examination of the outer model under variance (e.g. SmartPLS) structural equation modelling should be reported.

Table 13.3 shows the number of papers under analysis in this chapter and the reported validity and reliability tests, leading to two main observations: (a) a considerable number of studies carry out a full 'set' of tests (41%); and (b) this is especially evident in recent publications (73% of publications since 2015). Therefore, there is evidence of increasing technical competence in terms of formal tests of the adopted scales. Nonetheless, this conclusion must be tempered by the following comment in Finn and Kayande's (2004, p. 49) investigation on issues of scale modification:

> Similarly, the common practice of scale refinement based on an item's impact when scaling respondents ... often results in changes to the scale that are counter-productive when the application area requires the scaling of other objects of measurement (here retailers and retailers by dimensions). This is an important finding of our cross-validation research.

3 Managerial implications

The main purpose of multi-item scales is to obtain a valid and reliable metric for the construct(s) of interest. Although developing, testing and using such scales is, predominantly, the domain of researchers, the results

Table 13.3 Number of papers and tests of psychometric properties

Type of test	Number of papers	Year of publication
No information	2	2010, 2015
Content analysis	1	2008
Cronbach's alpha only	9	2001, 2006, 2008, 2011, 2011, 2011, 2014, 2014, 2015
Factor/Principle Component Analysis and Cronbach's alpha	9	2002, 2003, 2007, 2009, 2009, 2013, 2013, 2016, 2016
Factor/Principle Component Analysis, CFA a and Cronbach's alpha	2	2014, 2014
CFA only	1	2008
CFA, Cronbach's alpha and AVE	1	2006
CFA, Cronbach's alpha, CR, AVE and Fornell and Larcker criterion	17	2012, 2014, 2014, 2014, 2014, 2014, 2015, 2015, 2016, 2016, 2016, 2016, 2016, 2016, 2017, 2017, 2018

have direct relevance to practice in two substantive ways, (a) scales are used in developing theory that (should) inform practice and (b) as Rauschnabel *et al.* (2016, p. 3084) quite correctly state, a scale provides 'managers with an assessment tool for measuring their institution's as well as competitors' [*insert name of relevant branding construct*]'. It is self-evident that the above points are predicated on the integrity of the adopted scales; consequently, questions of 'trust' and related implications for managerial usefulness are pertinent.

In this chapter we identify five main issues that marketing managers in the HE domain must consider when 'accepting' results of research using multi-item scales and employing scales in operational activities such as development of promotional material. We identify lack of rigorous and theoretically supported modifications as having a major impact in the integrity of the adopted scales and warn against compromises. In other words, scales which fail to meet any of the identified issues are problematic and therefore findings should be considered only as indicative or at best partial. In addition, as the following comment from Babin *et al.* (2016, p. 3137) indicates, preoccupation with technical excellence is not sufficient: 'even rigorous CFA examinations, which remain critically important, do not mean very much when the items lack face validity'. In addition, in Section 5, we show the 'dangers' of transferring scales to HE even when such scales are widely applied in other fields or domains and found to be valid and reliable.

Despite the above warnings, we appreciate that our position could be considered as a purist's view and recognize the limitations of developing HE specific scales for all constructs and incorporating such scales in developing theory. In addition, we acknowledge that much of the reported research adheres to good practices of scientific enquiry and therefore has both academic and managerial merit. We therefore suggest that, during the developmental period, managers should (a) examine the source of the borrowed scale to ensure its credibility and the quality of the publication in which the scale is reported, (b) scrutinize the logic behind the adoption of a non-HE specific scale and examine the debate leading to or guiding scale modifications, with emphasis on theoretical grounding and logical alignment to HE, (c) starting with consideration of the problem at hand, specify the information needed and then map against the published scales, and (d) complement textual evaluation with qualitative methods such as observations, input from experts and in-depth interviews with the intended target market (see Gilmore and McMullan, 2009).

4 Conclusion

The aim of this chapter is to review evidence related to the use of multi-item scales in the study of branding in the HE domain. Overall, we find limited employment of such scales in the specific domain. Our search returned 42 papers and if we exclude the papers in special issues (see Table 13.1) the number drops to 33. Excepting operationalizations of some scales in Bennett and Ali-Choudhury (2009) and Brown and Mazzarol (2009), the reviewed scales are reflective.

Although we find scales developed specifically for HE (see Arpan, Raney, and Zivnuska, 2003; Alessandri, Yang, and Kinsey, 2006; Parahoo, Harvey, and Tamim, 2013; Goi, Goi, and Wong, 2014; Pinar et al., 2014; Rauschnabel et al., 2016) the majority of the multi-item scales employed are borrowed. Our analysis indicates that adaptations or modifications designed to contextualize the borrowed scales are infrequently fully explained and neither do they follow good practice. In addition, on evidence from HE specific scales, we find limited transferability to HE of even widely employed and highly reputable borrowed multi-item scales. Our conclusion leads to the need for the development of new scales or rigorous contextualization of borrowed scales. The most worrying corollary of our findings is the degree of confidence we can attribute to reported functional relationships of constructs operationalized through non-HE specific scales. We therefore suggest that there is urgent need for an in-depth examination of the stability of the reported functional relationships of constructs operationalized using scales borrowed from other fields and/or disciplines. In Section 5 we provide an example of how such an investigation can be carried out.

5 Case study: comparing HE-specific to 'general' scales

Elsewhere in this chapter we comment and question, on both conceptual and operational grounds, the use of borrowed multi-item scales developed and/or published in non-HE contexts. To examine whether our concerns about transferability of general scales to HE are justifiable, we need an appropriate methodology. We are aware of formal tests for scale invariance but not of how to assess whether or not two scales are equivalent in terms of adequately measuring the same construct (not to be confused with the KMO sampling adequacy test in EFA). As Rossiter (2008, p. 380) clearly articulates, significant correlations between alternative scales of the same construct or of such scales with antecedents and outcomes of the construct 'says nothing about which is the more valid'.

We could consider ourselves as subject experts and/or use a panel of experts in the assessment process. Although such an approach is commended by Engelland et al. (2001) it does not overcome the lack of a benchmark that guides views and opinions. Accepting the subjective nature of our logic we suggest that a recently published HE specific scale that adheres to good practices of scale development and is published in a highly reputable journal can act as a benchmark against which to examine alternative operationalizations. Having reviewed the evidence we consider that the UBPS scale of brand personality developed by Rauschnabel et al. (2016) and published in the *Journal of Business Research* (CABS 3) meets our criteria for a benchmark – the base scale. Further, according to Table 13.2, brand personality is one of the more often researched constructs and its operationalizations in a number of studies are based on Aaker's (1997) highly regarded and extensively applied conceptualization (Google Scholar reports 8,424 citations). Before moving on, as previously mentioned in Section 2, we should again clarify that it is not our intention to invalidate or question the research that is critiqued here; we use published material for illustrative purposes only.

In Table 13.4 in the first column we present the structure and operationalization (i.e. scale items) of the UBPS (base scale). To provide context and a point of comparison the second column contains Aaker's (1997) brand personality scale followed by operationalizations in seven HE specific studies.

Let's examine the dimensionality of the brand personality construct. Given consensus about the anthropomorphic and thus the inherently complex nature of brand personality, the unidimensional treatment by some authors is problematic. The inclusion of traits and self-concept (both multi-faceted constructs) in Balaji et al. (2016) indicates a lack of conceptual alignment with the adopted operationalization: 'University personality refers to the extent to which students consider the personality traits.... University brand personality is based on the idea that people select products and/or brands that correspond to their self-concept' (p. 3024). Similarly, mention of 'the personification metaphor' in Sung and Yang (2008) implies the need for a measure commensurate to the indicated complexity of the construct. In Bosch et al. (2006b), the following implies confusion between scale items and dimensions: 'Brand personality can also be viewed as the set of human characteristics associated with a brand and can be measured along five dimensions, namely sincerity, level of excitement, competence, sophistication, and ruggedness (Coop 2004: 114)' (pp. 12–13). We therefore conclude that the unidimensional operationalizations of brand personality in the above papers do not accord with the corresponding descriptions or conceptual definitions. While evidence of meeting psychometric benchmarks demonstrates understanding of good practice in terms of the general process of testing the measurement model, it does not overcome our stated concerns.

Focusing on the multi-dimensional scales, the UBPS identifies six dimensions while the studies that adopt Aaker (1997) conceptualize brand personality using five dimensions. Before we compare the base scale to those in the other HE publications there are six important observations regarding the adoption of Aaker's scale.

1   There is confusion as to what constitutes a dimension and what is a facet (or sub-dimension). The identified HE publications omit to account for the higher order structure of Aaker's scale, for example 'down-to-earth' is a facet (dimension) in Aaker while it is a scale item in Watkins and Gonzenbach (2013).

Table 13.4 Operationalisations of brand personality in HE, with the inclusion of Aaker as a point of reference (1997)

Rauschnabel et al. (2016) UBPS (base scale)	Aaker (1997)	Opoku et al. (2008)	Watkins and Gonzenbach (2013)	Polyorat (2011)	Thongthip and Polyorat (2015)	Balaji et al. (2016)	Bosch et al. (2006)	Sung and Yang (2008)
Sincerity (humane, helpful, friendly, trustworthy, fair)	Sincerity Down to earth (down-to-earth, family-orientated, small town) Honesty (honest, sincere, real) Wholesomeness (wholesome, original) Cheerfulness (cheerful, friendly, sentimental)	Sincerity (domestic, honest, genuine, cheerful)	Sincerity (down-to-earth, family oriented, small-town, cheerful, and sentimental)	Sincerity Excitement Competence Sophistication Ruggedness No scale items presented for any of the above dimensions	Sincerity Excitement Competence Sophistication Ruggedness No scale items presented for any of the above dimensions	• Friendly • Stable • Practical • Warmth	The XXX brand: • reflects sophistication • is resilient (strong) • is superior to competition • has a strong personality	• Friendly • Stable • Practical • Warmth
Lively (athletic, dynamic, lively, creative)	Excitement Daring (daring, trendy, exciting) Spirited (spirited, cool, young) Imagination (imaginative, unique) Contemporary (up-to-date, independent, contemporary)	Excitement (daring, spirited, imaginative, up to date)	Excitement (trendy, excited, cool, young, spirited, imaginative, unique, and up-to-date)					

Conscientiousness (organized, competent, structured, effective)	Competence Reliability (reliable, hard working, secure) Intelligence (intelligent, technical, corporate) Success (successful, leader, confident)	Competence (reliable, responsible, dependable, efficient)	Competence (hardworking, intelligent, technical, and leader)
Prestige (accepted, leading, reputable, successful, considerable)	Sophistication Class (upper class, good-looking, glamorous) Charm (charming, feminine, smooth)	Sophistication (glamorous, presentation, charming, romantic)	Sophistication (glamorous and feminine)
Appeal (attractive, productive, special)	Ruggedness Masculinity (outdoorsy, masculine, western) Toughness (tough, rugged)	Ruggedness (tough, strong, outdoorsy, rugged)	
Cosmopolitan (networked, international, cosmopolitan,) Psychometric properties			

continued

Table 13.4 Continued

	Rauschnabel et al. (2016) UBPS (base scale)	Aaker (1997)	Opoku et al. (2008)	Watkins and Gonzenbach (2013)	Polyorat (2011)	Thongthip and Polyorat (2015)	Balaji et al. (2016)	Bosch et al. (2006)	Sung and Yang (2008)
	EFA, CFA, Cronbach's α; CR, AVE, Fornell and Larcker discriminant validity		Content analysis thus not applicable	EFA, Cronbach's α	Cronbach's α	No information	PLS loadings; Cronbach's α; CR; AVE; Fornell and Larcker discriminant validity		CFA; Cronbach's α
Source(s)			Aaker (1997); marketing; wide variety of consumer brands including service				Sung and Yang (2008); PR, HE	Coop (2004); marketing, unclear	Chatman and Jen (1994); organisational studies; services Davies et al. (2004); organisational studies; retail, airlines; banks Sung and Tinkham (2005); marketing; food/beverage; media, personal care; automotive; luxury; technology; alcohol; retail; leisure goods

Evaluating branding scales 249

2   We observe variation in the number of scale items: four in Opoku, Hultman, and Saheli-Sangari (2008) and five in Watkins and Gonzenbach (2013), while in Watkins and Gonzenbach (2013) there is item redundancy where 21 items of Aaker's scale are omitted (p. 26).
3   In Opoku et al. (2008) we find the items 'domestic' and 'genuine' that are not in Aaker's original sincerity dimension.
4   Polyorat (2011) and Thongthip and Polyorat (2015) mention the original Aaker scale but do not present any of the scale items in their studies
5   With the exception of Opoku et al. (2008), there is insufficient information about the scales' psychometric properties.
6   We appreciate that scales can be complex and collecting data may involve considerable methodological challenges. However, compromising the integrity of a measure invalidates tests of its functional relationships with other constructs which in turn leads to questionable development of theory and suspect managerial guidelines. To illustrate the point and re-emphasize earlier concerns about content validity, the Watkins and Gonzenbach (2013) operationalization contains three items from the down-to-earth (down-to-earth, family oriented and small-town) and two from the cheerfulness (cheerful, and sentimental) facet. Consequently, we may question whether the author's comment that 'Dartmouth's athletic logo was identified with the sincerity brand dimension' (p. 2) is accurate or should be reworded to: 'Dartmouth's athletic logo was identified with down-to-earth and cheerfulness facets of sincerity'.

We move on to discuss the substantive issue of scale equivalence between the base scale and Aaker's scale by examining three questions, (1) lack of sub-dimensions (or facets) in the UBPS, (2) whether or not there are similar or common dimensions, and (3) in the case of similar dimensions, whether they share comparable operationalizations or scale items. Each is discussed in turn.

We suggest that contextual framing of the two scales answers the first question. Aaker's scale is derived from a study across a wide range of consumer domains (products and services) and therefore represents a generic model that reflects inter-product/service category nuances while the UBPS is context specific and consequently has a narrower remit.

In the second question (are there are common dimensions?), commentary in Rauschnabel et al. (2016, pp. 3083–3084) indicates both convergence and divergence. In terms of convergence we find reference to Aaker in three of the six dimensions of the UBPS, 'Sincerity ... shares similarities with the sincerity dimension of the Aaker brand personality scale', 'the lively dimension of UBPS is somewhat similar to the excitement dimension of general brand personality (Aaker, 1997; Bosnjak et al., 2007)' and 'In Aaker's (1997) scale, the competence factor shows similarity with the conscientiousness factor discovered here'. On the other hand, the lack of any similar comparative commentary for the prestige, appeal and cosmopolitan dimensions of the UBPS indicates divergence.

To address the third question (do the common operationalizations share scale items?) we focus on the convergent dimensions. Examining the various operationalizations of 'sincerity', 'friendly' is the single shared scale item and use of synonyms does not add to this list. Rauschnabel *et al.* (2016, p. 3083) explain 'The differences expressed by items such as fairness and helpfulness might arise from the strong interaction between students and universities. In contrast, Aaker's sincerity items focus less on personal interactions'. Lack of similar scale items reflects differential emphasis, with the UBPS emphasizing athletic and creative aspects while dynamism and energy are prominent in Aaker's scale. Finally, scale items such as 'organized' and 'structured' in the UBPS relate to educational and administrative experiences that are mainly internal while competence in Aaker is manifested by externally directed scale items.

Our analysis leads us to suggest that, in addition to incomplete operationalizations in HE studies, the Aaker model has limited applicability or transferability to HE. The 'sophistication' and 'ruggedness' dimensions do not map to the UBPS while omission of 'prestige', 'appeal' and 'cosmopolitan' narrow its content validity. Furthermore, even when we find commonalities, these are at a high level of abstraction, resulting in differential operationalizations. At this point we like to make sure that, (a) our conclusions are comparative in nature and therefore we do not suggest that the UBPS is not an answer to Rossiter's (2017) calls for an optimal standard measure (OSM) and (b) we do not claim that our conclusions have generalisability beyond the information in our analysis.

6 Further investigation

The below are suggested discussion/assessment questions for students.

1   Brand reputation is one of the most often examined constructs in HE research. With the case study in this chapter as a guide, critically evaluate the adopted scales. Assume that you are involved with research that includes reputation of an educational institution as one of its constructs. Using your analysis, suggest an appropriate operationalization.
2   As Palmer, Koenig-Lewis, and Asaad (2016, p. 3035) state 'Brand loyalty and support are important concepts in higher education'. Your task is to critically examine the operationalizations of brand loyalty applied to HE research and comment on whether the adopted operationalizations affect the functional relationships of brand loyalty with its antecedents.

3   Examine the manner in which Balaji, Roy, and Sadeque (2016) operationalize brand knowledge. Compare the adopted operationalization with the source and consider the activities undertaken to ensure the face and content validity (pp. 3037–3038). From the perspective of a reviewer of the paper, provide comments to the authors including remedial actions and suggestions for improvement.
4   In their paper Nguyen *et al.* (2016, p. 3107) state

> Commitment is an enduring desire to maintain a long-term relationship with higher education.... Such commitment reflects the students' motivation to continue the relationship with the university, for instance by continuing their postgraduate studies at the same institution

and they treat commitment as a unidimensional construct. Reading the extract, a question arises whether commitment is unidimensional. Accepting HE as a form of service, review recent articles that examine the role of commitment in services and comment on the dimensionality of commitment in HE.

5   One of the constructs in Bennett and Ali-Choudhury (2009) is cognitive responses. On page 106 the authors present the sources of their operationalization. Your task is to review the sources and comment on the adopted scale.

References (we do not include references for the source scales)

Aaker, J. L. (1997) "Dimensions of brand personality." *Journal of Marketing Research* 34(3), pp. 347–356.

Alessandri, S., Yang, S. U., and Kinsey, D. (2006) "An integrative approach to university visual identity and reputation." *Corporate Reputation Review* 9(4), pp. 258–270.

Arpan, L., Raney, A., and Zivnuska, S. (2003) "A cognitive approach to understanding university image." *Corporate Communications: An International Journal* 8(2), pp. 97–113.

Aurand, T. W., Gorchels, L., and Bishop, T. R. (2004) "Human resource management's role in internal branding: an opportunity for cross-functional brand message synergy." *Journal of Product and Brand Management* 14(3), pp. 163–169.

Babin, B. J., Griffin, M., and Hair, J. F. Jr (2016) "Heresies and sacred cows in scholarly marketing publications." *Journal of Business Research* 69(8), pp. 3133–3138.

Balaji, M., Roy, S., and Sadeque, S. (2016) "Antecedents and consequences of university brand identification." *Journal of Business Research* 69(8), pp. 3023–3032.

Bennett, R. and Ali-Choudhury, R. (2009) "Prospective students' perceptions of university brands: An empirical study." *Journal of Marketing for Higher Education* 19(1), pp. 85–107.

Berry, L. and Lampo, S. (2004) "Branding labour-intensive services." *Business Strategy Review* 15(1), pp. 18–25.

Bosch, J., Venter, E., Han, Y., and Boshoff, C. (2006a) "The impact of brand identity on the perceived brand image of a merged higher education institution: Part one." *Management Dynamics* 15(2), pp. 10–30.

Bosch, J., Venter, E., Han, Y., and Boshoff, C. (2006b) "The impact of brand identity on the perceived brand image of a merged higher education institution: Part two." *Management Dynamics* 15(3), pp. 36–47.

Brewer, A. and Zhao, J. (2010) "The impact of a pathway college on reputation and brand awareness for its affiliated university in Sydney." *International Journal of Educational Management* 24(1), pp. 34–47.

Brigham Young University Website (2018) *Step-by-Step Guide & Research Rescue: Evaluating Credibility*; http://guides.lib.byu.edu/c.php?g=216340&p=1428399 (accessed 31 March 2018).

Brown, R. and Mazzarol, M. (2009) "The importance of institutional image to student satisfaction and loyalty within higher education." *Higher Education* 58(1), pp. 81–95.

CABS. (2018) *Chartered Association of Business Schools Academic Journal Guide 2018*, available at: https://charteredabs.org/academic-journal-guide-2018/, (accessed 29 January 2018).

Chen, Y. C. (2017) "The relationships between brand association, trust, commitment, and satisfaction of higher education institutions." *International Journal of Educational Management* 31(7), pp. 973–985.

Churchill, G. A. Jr (1979) "A paradigm for developing better measures of marketing constructs." *Journal of Marketing Research* 16(1), pp. 64–73.

Clemes, M., Gan, C., and Kao, T. (2008) "University student satisfaction: An empirical analysis." *Journal of Marketing for Higher Education* 17(2), pp. 292–325.

Coop, W. F. (2004) *Brand Identity as a Driver of Brand Commitment*. Unpublished doctoral thesis, Cape Technikon, Cape Town.

Dennis, C., Papagiannidis, S., Alamanos, E., and Bourlakis, M. (2016) "The role of brand attachment strength in higher education." *Journal of Business Research* 69(8), pp. 3049–3057.

DeVellis, R. F. (2017) *Scale Development: Theory and Applications* (4th edition), 26 Applied Social Research Methods Series. London: Sage Publications Inc.

Douglas, S. P. and Nijssen, E. J. (2003) "On the use of 'borrowed' scales in cross-national research: A cautionary note." *International Marketing Review* 20(6), pp. 621–642.

Engelland, B. T., Alsford, B. L., and Taylor, R. D. (2001) "Caution and precaution on the use of 'borrowed' scales in marketing research," in T. A. Slater (ed.) *Marketing Advances in Pedagogy, Process and Philosophy*. New Orleans: Society of Marketing Advances, pp. 152–153.

Elsharnouby, T. H. (2015) "Student co-creation behavior in higher education: The role of satisfaction with the university experience." *Journal of Marketing for Higher Education* 25(2), pp. 238–262.

Finn, A. and Kayande, U. (2004) "Scale modification: Alternative approaches and their consequences." *Journal of Retailing* 80, pp. 37–52.

Gilmore, A. and McMullan, R. (2009) "Scales in services marketing research: A critique and way forward." *European Journal of Marketing* 43(5/6), pp. 640–651.

Goi, M. T., Goi, C. L., and Wong, D. (2014) "Constructing a brand identity scale for higher education institutions." *Journal of Marketing for Higher Education* 24(1), pp. 59–74.

Hardesty, D. M. and Bearden, W. O. (2004) "The use of expert judges in scale development. Implications for improving face validity of measures of unobservable constructs." *Journal of Business Research* 57(2), pp. 98–107.

Judson, K., Aurand, T., Gorchels, L., and Gordon, G. (2008) "Building a university brand from within: University adminstrators' perspectives of internal branding." *Services Marketing Quarterly* 30(1), pp. 54–68.

Kalafatis, S. P, Sarpong, S. Jr, and Sharif, K. J. (2005) "An examination of the stability of operationalisations of multi-item marketing scales." *International Journal of Market Research* 47(3), pp. 255–266.

Michaels, R. E., Cron, W. L., Dubinsky, A. J., and Joachimsthaler, E. A. (1988) "Influence of formalization on the organizational commitment and work alienation of salespeople and industrial buyers." *Journal of Marketing Research* 25(4), pp. 376–383.

Naidoo, V. and Hollebeek, L. D. (2016) "Higher education brand alliances: Investigating consumers' dual-degree purchase intentions." *Journal of Business Research* 69(8), pp. 3113–3121.

Netemeyer, R. G., Bearden, W. O., and Sharma, S. (2003) *Scaling Procedures*. London: Sage Publications Inc.

Nguyen, B., Yu, X., Melewar, T C, and Hemsley-Brown, J. (2016) "Brand ambidexterity and commitment in higher education: An exploratory study." *Journal of Business Research* 69(8), pp. 3105–3112.

Nguyen, N. and LeBlanc, G. (2001) "Image and reputation of higher education institutions in students' retention decisions." *International Journal of Educational Management* 15(6), pp. 303–311.

Opoku, R. A., Hultman, M., and Saheli-Sangari, E. (2008) "Positioning in market space: The evaluation of Swedish universities' online brand personalities." *Journal of Marketing for Higher Education* 18(1), pp. 124–144.

Palacio, A. B., Díaz Meneses, G., and Pérez Pérez, P. (2002) "The configuration of the university image and its relationship with the satisfaction of students." *Journal of Educational Administration* 40(5), pp. 486–505.

Palmer, A., Koenig-Lewis, N., and Asaad, Y. (2016) "Brand identification in higher education: A conditional process analysis." *Journal of Business Research* 69(8), pp. 3033–3040.

Parahoo, S. K., Harvey, H. L., and Tamim, R. M. (2013) "Factors influencing student satisfaction in universities in the Gulf Region: Does gender of students matter?" *Journal of Marketing for Higher Education* 23(2), pp. 135–154.

Pinar, M., Trapp, P., Girard, T., and Boyt, T. E. (2014) "University brand equity: An empirical investigation of its dimensions." *International Journal of Educational Management* 28(6), pp. 616–634.

Polyorat, K. (2011) "The influence of brand personality dimensions on brand identification and word -of-mouth: The case study of a university rand in Thailand." *Asian Journal of Business Research* 1(1), pp. 1–18.

Porter, T., Hartman, K., and Johnson, J. S. (2011) "Books and balls: Antecedents and outcomes of college identifications." *Research in Higher Education Journal* 13, pp. 1–14.

Rauschnabel, P. A., Krey, N., Babin, B. J., and Ivens, B. S. (2016) "Brand management in higher education: The University Brand Personality Scale." *Journal of Business Research* 69(8), pp. 3077–3086.

Rossiter, J. R. (2008) "Content validity of measures of abstract constructs in management and organizational research." *British Journal of Management* 19, pp. 380–388.

Rossiter, J. R. (2017) "Optimal standard measures for marketing." *Journal of Marketing Management* 33(5/6), pp. 313–326.

Šramová, B. (2015) "Brand engagement for university students in depending on the structure of values." *Procedia – Social and Behavioral Sciences* 174, pp. 2519–2523.

Stephenson, A. L. and Yerger, D. B. (2014a) "Optimizing engagement: Brand identification and alumni donation behaviors." *International Journal of Educational Management* 28(6), pp. 765–778.

Stephenson, A. L. and Yerger, D. B. (2014b) "Does brand identification transform alumni into university advocates?" *International Review on Public and Nonprofit Marketing* 11(3), pp. 243–262.

Stephenson, A. L. and Yerger, D. B. (2016) "How pretrial expectations and anticipated obstacles impact university brand identification." *Journal of Promotion Management* 22(6), pp. 853–873.

Sultan, P. and Yin Wong, H. (2012) "Service quality in a higher education context: An integrated model." *Asia Pacific Journal of Marketing and Logistics* 24(5), pp. 755–784.

Sung, M. and Yang, S. U. (2008) "Toward the model of university image: The influence of brand personality, external prestige, and reputation." *Journal of Public Relations Research* 20(4), pp. 357–376.

Syed Alwi, S. F. and Kitchen, P. J. (2014) "Projecting corporate brand image and behavioral response in business schools: Cognitive or affective brand attributes?" *Journal of Business Research* 67(11), pp. 2324–2336.

Teh, G. M. and Salleh, A. H. M. (2011) "Impact of brand meaning on brand equity of higher educational institutions in Malaysia." *World Journal of Management* 3(2), pp. 218–228.

Thongthip, W. and Polyorat, K. (2015) "The influence of brand personality dimensions on perceived service quality and perceived service value." *The Business & Management Review* 6(4), pp. 22–27.

Watkins, B. and Gonzenbach, W. (2013) "Assessing university brand personality through logos: An analysis of the use of academics and athletics in university branding." *Journal of Marketing for Higher Education* 23(1), pp. 15–33.

Wilkins, S., Butt, M. M., and Heffernan, T. (2017) "International brand alliances and co-branding: Antecedents of cognitive dissonance and student satisfaction with co-branded higher education programs." *Journal of Marketing for Higher Education* https://doi.org/10.1080/08841241.2017.1393785.

14 Conclusion to *Strategic Brand Management in Higher Education*

Bang Nguyen, T C Melewar, and Jane Hemsley-Brown

There is a distinct gap for a book of this type, reflecting the maturity of branding deployment and the growing awareness of effects in higher education. The quality of chapter contributions in this book is high and insightful, which is unsurprising given the qualifications and track record of selected chapter authors. The editors also have the skills and experiences necessary to assist contributors where necessary and the result is a book with a balance of theoretical, methodological and empirical studies that are expected to appeal to an international audience. Apart from the traditional marketing courses, the text will be useful in courses such as: Brand Management, Brand Strategy, International Business, International Marketing, Marketing Management, Consumer Behaviour and so on. These courses are very widely taught globally. All undergraduate students in business or management have the option to take services marketing or consumer marketing options and many do. Marketing Management is a required course for MBA programmes worldwide and for many MSc programmes in business. The book has worldwide appeal for those interested in branding in the higher education sector.

'Strategic Brand Management in Higher Education' is an edited book, which serves as a supplementary text for advanced undergraduates and postgraduates and a key resource for academics working in higher education marketing, public sector marketing management, and broader subject areas of corporate branding and marketing management. It is not a textbook aimed at core undergraduate courses, neither is it a research monograph. We envisioned the edited book to be an authoritative reference work of branding in higher education, as it's the first of its kind, and we believe that we have achieved this objective. As a result, 'Strategic Brand Management in Higher Education' provides Master's students, final year undergraduate students and doctoral students in business and marketing with a comprehensive treatment of the nature of higher education branding. The book is also of significant interest to academics who are using brand management solutions to deploy branding successfully. It explores current research and practices in different areas and from different perspectives. The text serves as an invaluable resource for marketing and branding academics requiring more than anecdotal evidence of different branding applications. Readers will find it interesting to compare and contrast different situations covering important aspects related to strategy, planning and measurement. The book includes an interesting mix of theory, research findings and practices that engenders confidence in academics, practitioners and students of both marketing and brand management alike.

In the concluding chapter, we highlight critical elements and managerial lessons for branding in higher education, followed by a presentation of important branding lessons: areas which we believe will have great implications for the higher education branding literature.

1 Managerial implications arising from the book

Our book treated the nature of strategic brand management in the higher education context comprehensively. By drawing from varying perspectives, it explored research and practices in very different institutions. This section will briefly go through each of the chapters in terms of key implications for management and practice.

In the first part of the book, guidelines about strategic perspectives in higher education branding were recommended. Chapter 2 proposed a framework that aims to encourage HEI brand managers to focus on three key questions: what is their core business mix; who are their stakeholders; and how can they draw on their ecosystem to co-create their brand identity? The key managerial implication for many HEIs therefore is that education is one business focus and students are one, albeit important, stakeholder within their ecosystem. HEIs therefore need move their focus from the students at the centre of the ecosystem to consider other stakeholders and the ecosystem as a whole when considering brand identity. This wider perspective highlights that brand identity is not linear, brands are intricately intertwined (Bergvall, 2006, p. 174) and co-creation takes place on a number of different levels with a wide range of direct and indirect actors. HEIs need to take a wider, holistic approach to brand identity.

Chapter 3 proposes that the development of a strong corporate brand and its implementation call for higher education leaders to address and integrate innovative features into their brand definition and management. Of particular interest are leadership, corporate branding consistency and co-creation, and internal brand living. The leadership vision for the HEI constitutes a core aspect in brand building. Brand leaders are strategists who set the tone for behaviour and the strategic direction of the organization. The connection between the higher education institution culture and the CB is articulated in the connection of the institution's mission/vision and values, as initially defined by the institution's leadership (also reflected in the organizational culture). In particular, the presentation of an institution's mission and values becomes a feature of expression of the corporate brand (Simões, Singh, and Perin, 2015). The perception of brand meaning that stakeholders hold, tends to be aligned with the mission of the university (Wilson and Eliot, 2016). There is a dilution in the organization's borders where consumers and other stakeholders become co-creators of value (da Silveira, Lages, and Simões 2013). Such intertwinedness of roles between consumers (and other stakeholders) and the higher education brand lead to the strengthening of the relevance of a strong connection between organizational and culture and branding. The organizational culture ought to set the tone and platforms for brand co-creation.

Chapter 4 recommends that a university could enhance brand support behaviour from the academic staff by communicating to them institutional brand values via transformational leaders and internal branding activities. In practice, it could be a useful guide for the management team of educational institutions as well as those in other industries, above all, service industries, to encourage brand support effectively. Moreover, this chapter suggests that the brand support behaviour of employees can be directly affected by transformational leaders, immediate leaders in particular. Thus, apart from operating internal branding activities, ensuring the existence of transformational leaders within the organization is another way for management to encourage the building of brand support.

Chapter 5 suggests that in order to cope with increased competition, it is likely that colleges and universities will become more differentiated and have more distinct strategic missions in terms of the type of students and stakeholders they wish to attract, programs they want to offer, and the role of research and scholarship in their academic life. It is important to highlight that enhancing a higher education institution's prestige and market share will pass through the stages of adopting market orientation, putting customers first, being responsive to potential students' needs and considering who the competitors are from the students' perspective. Successful university brands should keep saying as loudly as possible why the academic institution is different (instead of just offering more of the same), to ensure a shared brand meaning and foster internal commitment to the brand, facilitating internal culture change, on top of enhancing institutional reputation externally.

Chapter 6 highlights the role of corporate communications in HEIs' brand communication to stakeholders. The following are suggested for HEIs: first, HEIs should have a managerial approach that provides an environment that is open to interaction and value exchange that nurtures the organizational culture among its members. Commonly shared values help academic and administrative staff to identify with their university and hence help them to be motivated to produce better research to contribute to society at large. Second, marketing communications should be geared to creating awareness, association, and salience in higher education as a means of building trust, eliciting emotions, inspiring action, instilling loyalty, and connecting with prospective students, alumni, and other stakeholders through personal and non-personal connections. Third, and especially, the most suitable and relevant content generation for various social media platforms such as Facebook, Instagram, YouTube, and LinkedIn plays a pivotal role in dealing with the potential harm of uncontrolled communication to the brand positioning of HEIs. A well-managed approach to the use of owned media can help reduce the risk of the creation of negative images and reputations by engaging a broader array of audiences and in that way they can disseminate favourable information about themselves. Last, a budget should be drawn up and the effectiveness of programmes should be assessed on the basis of prospective return on investments.

Chapter 7 offers managerial contributions for decision-makers and graphic designers who wish to understand the entirety of the relationship between a favourable university logo and the factors in its antecedents (corporate name, typeface, design, and colour) from the internal stakeholders' perspective and its effect on a favourable university image and reputation. In other words, a clear understanding of the dimensions of the relevant concepts can assist managers and designers to devise a favourable university logo, which will create a strong marketing communication, image and reputation. Three variables are investigated in this chapter's research, namely, attractiveness, familiarity and recognisability. These constructs are the key moderators between logo and image and logo and integrated marketing communication. In this respect, advertising and marketing managers should concentrate on consistency in corporate communications, in order to learn which beliefs, attitudes, impressions, and associations held by consumers can be matched to corporate identity.

Chapter 8 suggests that brand identity, image and reputation are important contributors to the institutional climate that will impact on students' institution-related perceptions and faculty's job engagement and satisfaction. The development of a positive academic environment is a key part of this climate. Therefore, the institution's internal stakeholders need to collaborate to deliver a synergistic student (and employer) experience. In addition, the development of students' relevant transferable skills during their degree is of key importance in shaping institutional brand image and reputation. Institutions are thus advised to establish relevant student bodies and societies that help students nurture important skills (e.g. debating skills through a debating society). Further, in light of integrated marketing communications (IMC), the institution's key attributes or benefits need to be communicated in a consistent manner to (prospective) students. Institutional IMC will also need to take into account the unique needs and preferences (in terms of both content and media channels) of relevant stakeholder groups.

Chapter 9 proposes that a co-creative approach, based on S-D Logic, challenges universities to take on board how they create value in the wider service eco-system. For example, a service ecosystem perspective enables managers to view their organization from a broader and more enlightening perspective (Greer, Lusch, and Vargo, 2016). Engagement and interaction in society and the economy requires universities to be outward facing and open beyond the academic community. Universities could provide greater support for academics in engaging with society and the economy. This includes providing training and mentoring for younger academics. Further, a starting point is to identify key stakeholder groups in the wider community. Taking business and management, as an example, connections with practitioners are frequently used to keep the syllabus up to date with current practice; to provide students with work experience; to bring in external speakers; and to provide graduates with job opportunities. Thus the value of the student experience in applied subjects, such as business and management, can be seen to be enhanced greatly by engagement with the business community.

Chapter 10 comments that rankings may be a proxy of brand power but they still only measure academic and business views within their reputational survey elements. So how do universities tell where their brand strengths lie, or where their reputation stands with wider audiences? There are established professional ways to measure a university's reputation or brand power, including qualitative phone interviews, mass surveys, media monitoring and measuring, and public performance measures (rankings, NSI scores etc.). Through the authors' consultancy, The Knowledge Partnership, they deploy these methods for client universities to test their reputations and the ideal is a mix of qualitative interviews and quantitative data, as well as analysis of what a university is saying about itself in marketing and communications.

Chapter 11 shows that HEIs can employ internal branding efforts as a brand management strategy for engaging students in student citizenship behaviours and thereby strengthen the university brand. As brand communication is a requisite for internal branding efforts, the university can persuade students to turn into brand ambassadors and support the university's brand by engaging in internal brand communication strategy. Also, the university managers can stimulate the students' identification with the university through brand communication efforts that enhance the students' fit, knowledge, and belief in the university brand. On the other hand, the university managers can deploy brand communication programs to enhance students' attitude towards the university as well as enhance their commitment towards the university.

Chapter 12 emphasizes looking at the important dimensions to be addressed by educators/school administrators, business school deans, and marketing departments of universities. It stresses that both *Chic* (e.g. Prestigious, Exclusivity, Refined, Elitist, Elegant and Stylish) and *Competence* (Hard Working, Corporate, Leading, Achievement-Oriented) all represent the business school/university corporate brand image and they are equally importantly highlighted in the corporate brand positioning strategy of business schools. In addition, the chapter could help a business school to understand its corporate brand image better and perhaps more effectively, as if it were a set of personality traits. These factors (Chic and Competence) may be considered not only at strategic level but at tactical level. For example, they may be considered when designing university marketing communication campaigns – in website design/social media – to have a more corporate image look, addressing mission/vision or slogan.

In chapter 13, we recognize the limitations of developing HE specific scales for all constructs and incorporating such scales in developing theory. Yet, it is acknowledged that much of the reported research adheres to good practices of scientific enquiry and therefore has both academic and managerial merit. Therefore, it is suggested that, during the developmental period, managers should; (a) examine the source of the borrowed scale to ensure its credibility and the quality of the publication in which the scale is reported; (b) scrutinize the logic behind the adoption of a non-HE specific scale and examine the debate leading to or guiding scale modifications, with emphasis on theoretical grounding and logical alignment to HE; (c) starting with consideration of the problem at hand, specify the information needed and then map against the published scales; and finally (d) complement textual evaluation with qualitative methods such as observations, input from experts and in-depth interviews with the intended target market.

2 Important branding lessons

The following section presents more managerial implications that are more case and context specific, including MBA programs and online programs. Finally, some guidelines are made about how to build a brand in higher education (Nguyen, Hemsley-Brown, and Melewar, 2016).

Branding business schools and MBA programs

From the business schools' perspective, the MBA is often a 'flagship' program with the highest external visibility, and which defines the success of the nature, scope, and success of the institution itself (Heslop and Nadeau, 2010). To successfully market an MBA program, Heslop and Nadeau (2010) suggest that the business school must understand what target students want to experience during their studies and want to achieve as the result of attaining their degree. Having this knowledge enables them to effectively position and brand their institution and MBA, ensuring that they attract the best students and faculty.

The MBA program comes in various forms: full daytime MBAs of two years in length, high-intensity one-year programs, executive MBAs (EMBAs) designed for working managers in current jobs, and MBAs with specializations in international business, technology management and various professional fields. As business schools seek to expand their nonlocal markets, they are launching online or videoconference MBAs and opening national and international satellite campuses. In major cities, prospective students will have many choices from more than one local university, offering one or more MBA programs, as well as programs delivered by business schools in nearby cities, through online or distance education, and other international institutions. With increasing competition, diversity of products and prices, and market maturity, Nicholls et al. (1995) note that institutions practicing effective marketing will be more likely to prosper. Segev, Raveh, and Farjoun (1999) argue that focusing on their curriculum offering, MBA programs have multiple ways to successfully compete and differentiate themselves. Goldgehn and Kane (1997) also recommend the need to consider positioning in order to increase the value of the MBA. Thus, differentiating and positioning through brand development is considerably more important and a cornerstone of such effective marketing (Heslop and Nadeau, 2010).

Researchers suggest that students' expectations affect how the MBA is perceived and, hence, its brand image. Some of these expectations include; (1) program inputs: student experiences in terms of what goes into the program, including the quality of their fellow students and faculty; (2) program processes outcomes: the actual student experiences in taking the program; and (3) program completion outcomes: what students will experience as the result of program completion. Some of these outcome expectations occur in the early stages of the program, some outcomes involve experiences as the result of program elements completion (developing new skills and abilities in strategic thinking, team management, building contacts), and some occur in the long-term (obtaining a job after graduation and having a fulfilling career). Heslop and Nadeau (2010) note that these experience expectations (for each of the three elements – inputs, processes, and outcomes) of applicants to an MBA program comprise the MBA's brand image. Thus, in order to develop an effective brand or to understand brand positioning, the views of target customers concerning expected benefits or outcomes must be determined and positively affected.

However, opponents of customer-centric approaches to education suggest that adaptation of the education product to customer demands may simply erode quality (Argenti, 2000; Pfeffer and Fong, 2004). Yet, for MBAs, Taylor and Reed (1995) note that marketing of higher education does not mean taking a totally student-centric perspective, but rather – as in other marketing settings – that the needs of various stakeholders must be balanced. Dailey et al., (2006) adds that, for the MBA program, identifying the needs of different student groups will help shape unique marketing strategies. In addition, Driscoll and Wicks (1998) note that focusing on differentiation of offerings, namely, concentrations and specialization, executive and co-op programs, and online delivery options, MBA programs can further enhance their branding and program quality. Such segmentation attempts may suit the students' demographics better, including their maturity, work experience, and learning needs (Heslop and Nadeau, 2010).

Nicholls et al. (1995) note that it is somewhat ironic that MBA degree programs' marketing efforts are so rudimentary and do not make use of the marketing principles and internal marketing resources that they have and teach. They identify that MBA programs have multiple customers, both direct and indirect, and marketing needs to address multiple points in the value chain: those who influence the decision maker/client of the program, the client (the MBA applicant/student), those who are the client's clients (those to whom the client wishes to market themselves), and future employers and current employers who often sponsor students and may pay the costs, particularly for EMBA programs (Heslop and Nadeau, 2010; Nicholls et al., 1995).

People who are in the process of choosing an MBA program often get their information from the MBA program rating magazines (Dahlin-Brown, 2005). While there are many questions about the value of the magazine ratings, Brennan, Brodnick, and Pinckley (2007) found that the ratings process poorly represented publicly available data about the institutions. They reveal that the variables used in the ratings reflect a narrow set of underlying factors. While these rating services may be questionable in their value to the students, the magazines continue to publish them regularly due to their popularity, indicating that the information is significant enough to be profitable to the producer. In spite of that, the business schools themselves feel they have value to students and often use these reports in their promotion to students (Heslop and Nadeau, 2010).

Rapert et al. (2004) contend that students are uniquely qualified to assess the quality of their educational experience. They found that quality assessments directly affected student program satisfaction and highlighted that the hallmarks of quality programs include the following seven in-class (process and outcome-based) themes: (1) intellectual growth, (2) overall professionalism, including communication and etiquette skills, (3) specialized training and instruction in one or more functional areas, (4) generalized/integrated instruction, (5) teamwork and group dynamics, (6) devoted and knowledgeable faculty with good teaching skills and real-world experience, (7) classmate and faculty intimacy and the following four outside-classroom (process-based) themes: (1) integration with business community, (2) career preparation services, (3) availability of financial assistance, (4) program clarity with clear goals and open lines of communication between students, faculty, and staff. These themes can usefully be adapted and incorporated into any differentiated promotional program.

Online programs

The growing interest in Internet branding is also evident in higher education, inasmuch as Simmons (2007) refers to it as 'i-branding' and argues that new Internet branding strategies might assist universities in creating distinctiveness while engaging with customers. Rowley (2004) suggests the need to build 'online brand experience' and lists a number of activities including 'resources', 'ease of access', and 'relevance' as contributing elements to this experience (Chapleo, Durán, and Díaz, 2011). In parallel to this development, the popularity of online programs has increased. Grenzky and Maitland (2001) note that increased access to online courses for people in rural areas, working professionals, and single parents, who are unable to attend classes on campus, has proven to be the most positive aspect of distance education. Many non-traditional students are now able to access classes offered online that are comparable to those offered through residential programs (Adams and Eveland, 2007). Indeed, many for-profit online institutions are gaining market share by offering programs similar to those offered through traditional universities in residential settings (Golden, 2006). In the delivery of content, student satisfaction rates tend to match or exceed those for 'traditional' instruction (MacFarland, 1999; Sikora, 2003). While online degrees are now more commonplace, scholars note that the reputation of the granting institution makes a difference to whether the degree is perceived as acceptable (Adams and DeFleur, 2006).

In spite of the presence of high quality online programs in higher education, the rapid growth of online education has raised questions concerning the credibility, quality, and role of these programs in the marketplace (Adams and Eveland, 2007; Wilner and Lee, 2002). Online, for-profit institutions have made national news because of fines for aggressive enrolment techniques, investigations regarding misappropriation of federal grant money, and institutional claims related to transferability of credits (Blumenstyk, 2004). Unfortunately, such unfavourable news about missteps in the distance education industry may have resulted in a loss of credibility for the degrees conferred by properly accredited, online, for-profit institutions and traditional-residential universities that offer online programs (Adams and Eveland, 2007). Nevertheless, the online programs are here to stay and are often considered the higher education model of the future. Increased efforts are made to improve the image of online programs, some of which have included branding identities, standardization, or promoting the varied media methods used to deliver content (Adams and Eveland, 2007).

However, traditional-residential universities have the resources to build competitive advantages over online programs. For example, compared to the online programs, these traditional-residential institutions can offer a wider range of student support services and blended learning, or courses that are attended partly online and partly in a classroom setting (Adams and Eveland, 2007). Traditional institutions and their residential programs also have the distinct advantage of smaller classes, face-to-face contact with instructors, name recognition, and solid reputation to maintain and build their enrolment (Carnevale and Olsen, 2003). Both online accredited and online non-accredited institutions appear to be reaching out to potential students by offering promises of career and personal success (Adams and Eveland, 2007).

How to build a university brand

In building a university brand, managing public perception is at the centre of marketing efforts. According to several studies, brand reputation is the most important determinant of a university's performance. For example, prospective students' risk perception is considered a strong deterrent in their decision-making in general and these risks are particularly alleviated in online degrees. Marketers are advised to use risk relievers such as brand reputation to make programs more attractive. Brand reputation is thus important, as it relieves both financial risk and psychological risk, easing the choice of program and university. Well-known traditional-residential higher education universities with an established brand reputation thus have stronger competitive advantage to promote their programs and should exploit this advantage in their marketing strategies (Adams and Eveland, 2007), both online and offline.

Promotional materials, such as letters, brochures, posters, and booklets should be widely distributed to recruit freshmen, as these traditional marketing tactics play an important role in influencing prospective students' decision-making process (Armstrong and Lumsden, 1999). Websites and social media sites, like Facebook, have the potential to influence college choice by serving as an alternative to published information (Ramasubramanian, Gyure and Mursi, 2002), although for some they may be the most important source due to their interactivity. While web pages may be ideal for communicating 'big idea' concepts and themes to connect a name to an institution (Singer, 1997), social media are effective in their ability to interact, that is, post videos and links, answer queries, and develop a brand community. Both approaches help viewers develop an image of the organization and its products or services (Adams and Eveland, 2007). For the branding of university services, targeted and customized advertisement may further aid in developed an integrated marketing campaign across multiple channels, both online and offline.

Universities cannot be content with simply projecting their brand in terms of teaching and research, as was seemingly the case in the past. Chapleo *et al.* (2011) demonstrate that universities must project the main functional factors to their customers, including both the traditional values of teaching, research or management, and new functional factors such as innovation and international projection. These are key factors for university brands to promote. Chapleo *et al.* (2011) further suggest that universities consider emotional values as essential if they want to stand out. They identified two emotional factors, namely universities' environments and social responsibility. These variables suggest that stakeholders are not only concerned with the functional aspects such as teaching, research and management, but also pay attention to emotional values. Specifically, emotional factors can be a good basis for competitive advantage through the online brand, but as suggested by Chapleo et al. (2011), if a long term credible brand is to be maintained, brand positioning should ultimately be largely consistent with the reality of the brand experience of students attending the institution.

For universities, understanding students' decision-making processes is key. For example, school status and reputation remain important factors affecting students' program selection. For the MBA program, ratings persist as a facilitator of choice, choice justification, and overall, an important measure of the program (Dahlin-Brown, 2005). Therefore, for those universities and MBA programs that do not receive high ratings from business magazines, or other rankings, or which have related reputation weaknesses, Heslop and Nadeau (2010) suggest they seek to enhance their applicant appeal by focusing on outcomes. This could, for instance, be done by using promotional elements, stressing that employers are impressed with their graduates, since this outcome influences students' decision-making. For example, Heslop and Nadeau (2010) suggest that program brochures and ads could feature testimonials from employers who hired graduates and were impressed by their knowledge and capabilities. This is important to ensure credibility in the marketplace, especially if that does not come from rating magazines (Heslop and Nadeau, 2010). Over time, their reputation is enhanced, which in turn, assists in the students' decision making.

However, while branding focused on external communication via advertising and sales promotional efforts is important, Judson, Gorchels, and Aurand (2006) suggest that internal marketing and branding is just as important. Recently, greater emphasis has been given to the delivery of the brand promise to employees. Schiffenbauer (2001) emphasizes that the brand message will lose its credibility if it is not supported by integrated employee behaviour. Schultz and Schultz (2000) maintain that the external brand promise must be properly aligned with actual performance within the organization and that employees are the important internal promise deliverers (Judson et al., 2006). Thus, messages conveyed to the employees of an organization are just as important as those sent to customers. When internal branding efforts are implemented, employees are more likely to understand the brand, take ownership in the brand, and provide evidence of the brand in their organizational responsibilities (Judson et al., 2006).

Conclusion

In the concluding chapter, we have reviewed the managerial implications of branding in the higher education sector. We drew together the previous sections of the book and suggested how to create a successful brand in the higher education sector.

On the whole, our book has covered branding, both at student and university levels, across a range of diverse and contemporary topics. The wealth of insight across the chapters and case studies is useful and relevant for students and academics. The book illustrates that strategy, planning and measurement greatly influence brand development in higher education. Brand management is a complex issue that requires more research, as it is still considered an emerging concept. With this book, we therefore call for more research on branding in higher education, notably as branding is context specific and the unique characteristics of the higher education sector make it necessary to conduct sector-specific further study.

Overall, we hope our suggestions and propositions have inspired branding researchers to engage in these fascinating areas of enquiry in future to further develop frameworks and theories in higher education. Thank you for your interest in our book.

References

Adams, J. and DeFleur, M. H. (2006) "The acceptability of online degrees as a credential for obtaining professional employment." *Communication Education* 55(1), pp. 32–45.

Adams, J. and Eveland, V. (2007) "Marketing online degree programs: How do traditional-residential programs compete?" *Journal of Marketing for Higher Education* 17(1), pp. 67–90.

Argenti, P. (2000) "Branding B-schools: Reputation management for MBA programs." *Corporate Reputation Review* 3(2), pp. 171–178.

Armstrong, J. and Lumsden, D. (1999) "Impact of universities' promotional materials on college choice." *Journal of Marketing for Higher Education* 9(2), p. 84.

Bergvall, S. (2006) "Brand ecosystems," in J. E. Schroeder, M. Salzer-Mörling, and S. Askegaard (eds), *Brand Culture*. Abingdon, Oxon: Taylor & Francis, pp. 1–11.

Blumenstyk, G. (2004) "U. of Phoenix uses pressure in recruiting, report says: Institution disputes charges that it pumps up enrolment through illegal tactics." *The Chronicle of Higher Education* 51(7), A1. http://chronicle.com/weekly/v51/i07/07a00101.htm.

Brennan, J., Brodnick, R., and Pinckley, D. (2007) "De-mystifying the U.S. news rankings: How to understand what matters, what doesn't and what you can actually do about it." *Journal of Marketing for Higher Education* 17(2), pp. 169–188.

Carnevale, D. and Olsen, F. (2003) "How to succeed in distance education." *The Chronicle of Higher Education* 49(40), A31. http://chronicle. com/weekly/v49/i44/44a02501.htm.

Chapleo, C., Durán, M. V. C., and Díaz, A. C. (2011) "Do UK universities communicate their brands effectively through their websites?" *Journal of Marketing for Higher Education* 21(1), pp. 25–46.

Dahlin-Brown, N. (2005) "The perceptual impact of U.S. News & World Report rankings on eight public MBA programs." *Journal of Marketing for Higher Education* 15(2), pp. 155–179.

Dailey, L., Anderson, M., Ingenito, C., Duffy, D., Krimm, P., and Thomson, S. (2006) "Understanding MBA consumer needs and the development of marketing strategy." *Journal of Marketing for Higher Education* 16(1), pp. 143–158.

da Silveira, C., Lages, C., and Simões, C. (2013) "Reconceptualizing brand identity in a dynamic environment." *Journal of Business Research* 66(1), pp. 28–36.

Driscoll, C. and Wicks, D. (1998) "The customer-driven approach in business education: A possible danger?" *Journal of Education for Business* 73(1), pp. 58–61.

Golden, D. (2006) "Online university enrolment soars." *Baltimoresun.com*. Originally published in *The Wall Street Journal*. www.baltimoresun.com/news/education/bal-online0515,0,2692708.story?coll=bal-business-headlines (accessed 29 May 2006).

Goldgehn, L. A. and Kane, K. R. (1997) "Repositioning the MBA: Issues and implications." *Journal of Marketing for Higher Education* 8(1), pp. 15–25.

Greer, C. R., Lusch, R. F., and Vargo, S. L. (2016) "A service perspective: Key managerial insights from service-dominant (S-D) logic." *Organizational Dynamics* 45, pp. 28–38.

Grenzky, J. and Maitland, C. (2001) "Focus on distance education." *Update* 7(2), Washington, DC: National Education Association, Office of Higher Education, 20036.

Heslop, L. A. and Nadeau, J. (2010) "Branding MBA programs: The use of target market desired outcomes for effective brand positioning." *Journal of Marketing for Higher Education* 20(1), pp. 85–117.

Judson, K. M., Gorchels, L., and Aurand, T. W. (2006) "Building a university brand from within: A comparison of coaches' perspectives of internal branding." *Journal of Marketing for Higher Education* 16(1), pp. 97–114.

MacFarland, T. (1999) Fall term 1999 Nova Southeastern University students respond to a broad-based satisfaction survey: A comparison of campus-based students and distance education students. A report published by Nova Southeastern University Research and Planning, Report 01–03, February. ED453 732.

Nguyen, B., Hemsley-Brown, J., and Melewar, T C (2016) "Branding in higher education," in J. Singh, F. D. Riley, and C. Blankson (eds), *The Routledge Companion to Brand Management*. London, UK: Routledge.

Nicholls, J., Harris, J., Morgan, E., Clarke, K. and Sims, D. (1995) "Marketing higher education: The MBA experience." *International Journal of Educational Management* 9(2), pp. 31–38.

Pfeffer, J. and Fong, C. T. (2004) "The business school 'business': Some lessons from the U.S. experience." *Stanford Research Paper Series*. Research paper no. 1855.

Ramasubramanian, S., Gyure, J., and Mursi, N. (2002) "Impact of internet images: Impression-information effects of university web site images." *Journal of Marketing for Higher Education* 12(2), p. 52.

Rapert, M. I., Villiquette, A., Smith, S., and Garretson, J. A. (2004) "The meaning of quality: Expectations of students in pursuit of an MBA." *Journal of Education for Business* 80(1), pp. 17–24.

Rowley, J. (2004) "Online branding." *Online Information Review* 28(2), pp. 131–138.

Schiffenbauer, A. (2001) "Study all of a brand's constituencies." *Marketing News* 35(11), p. 17.

Schultz, D. E. and Schultz, H. (2000) "How to build a billion dollar business-to-business brand." *Marketing Management* 9(2), pp. 22–28.

Segev, E., Raveh, A. and Farjoun, M. (1999) "Conceptual maps of the leading MBA programs in the United States: Core courses, concentration areas." *Strategic Management Journal* 20(6), pp. 549–565.

Sikora, A. (2003) A profile of participation in distance education: 1999–2000. Post-secondary education descriptive analysis reports. National Center for Education Statistics. NCES 2003–017, MPR Associates: Berkeley, CA. 23.

Simmons, G. J. (2007) "I-branding: Developing the Internet as a branding tool." *Marketing Intelligence and Planning* 25(6), pp. 544–562.

Simões, C., Singh, J., and Perin, M. (2015) "Corporate brand expressions in business-to-business companies' websites: Evidence from Brazil and India." *Industrial Marketing Management* 51, pp. 59–68.

Singer, C. (1997) "Say it with tag lines." *ABA Banking Journal* 89(4), p. 80.

Taylor, R. E. and Reed, R. R. (1995) "Situational marketing: Application for higher education institutions." *Journal of Marketing for Higher Education* 6(1), pp. 23–36.

Wilner, A. and Lee, J. (October 2002) *The Promise and the Reality of Distance Education. Update.* Washington, DC: National Education Association, Office of Higher Education.

Wilson, E. and Elliot, E. (2016) "Brand meaning in higher education: Leaving the shallows via deep metaphors." *Journal of Business Research* 69(8), pp. 3058–3068.

Index

Page numbers in **bold** denote tables, those in *italics* denote figures.

3Es for higher education framework 75; in action 82; enhance prestige and market share 75–76; entrepreneurial mind-set 77–78; expanding links and value co-creation 78–79
'4Ps' of the marketing mix 97

Aaker's scale 245, 249–250
academic freedom, concept of 180
advertising: Bahceşehir University (Turkey) 109; commercial content of 98; by higher education institutions 99; for image creation 98; sponsored search advertising 98; traditional forms of 98; university brand in 221
aesthetic designations 4
American Marketing Association 180
Arian Graduate School of Business (AGSB) 229
Arian University (AU) 228–229
average variance accounted (AVA) 208
average variance extracted (AVE) 206, 241

Bahceşehir University (Turkey) 105–111; accounts on social media 108; advertising 109; Bahceşehir-Ugur Education Foundation 105; BAU Istanbul in numbers and honours 107; as best education brand 105; best in 500 big service exporters in education 105; CEO as a spokesperson 108; controlled communication tools 108–110; co-op (cooperative education program) 109; corporate behaviour 108; corporate communications management 108; establishment of 105, **106**; mission of 107; overall view of corporate communication in 110–111; publicity via open days and fairs 110; social media accounts for different departments 110; Society Academy 109; stakeholder engagement 109; vision of 107; visual identity 109; website of 109–110
BAU Global Network *see* Bahceşehir University (Turkey)
BiSoluk Café 108
brand associations 45, 183, 186, 239
brand attributes, personification of 76, 137, 220–221
brand awareness 97, 137, 151, 183, 185, 196
brand bio-ecology 30
brand-building citizenship 197
brand-centred training and development 61–67
brand communication 6–8; *see also* university brand communication
brand communities, development of 103
brand core values 3
brand covenant 3, 219
brand, definitions of 3–4
brand ecosystem 30–31
brand equity 2, 190; BrandZ™ components of 182; of business school 222; concept of 181; consumer-based 183, 185; elements of 182; financial measurement 181–182; in higher education 4; loyalty 183; market share 182; price premium 182–183

Index

brand experience 83, 239, 263, 265
brand 'favourability' 239
brand identity 3, 5, 11, 25, 45, 46, 200, 239, 258; brand ecosystem 30–31; business ecosystems 29–30; 'buy-in' of 84; co-creation of 25, 26–27, 32; defined 26; higher education ecosystems 31–32, 153; managerial implications of 33; review of literature on 26–32; stakeholder theory of 26, 28–29
brand image and reputation 183; advantages of developing 144; benefits to external stakeholders 145–146; benefits to other internal stakeholders 145; benefits to (prospective) students 144–145; case study 155; definition of 221; development of 13, *149*, 150–151; difference with brand identity 144; drivers of 152–153; effects on key institutional stakeholders **154**; for higher education institutions 143–153; importance of brand-related communication for 149–150; importance of creating a strong 144; management of 153; managerial implications of 153–154; measurement of 151–152; nature of 144; organization-crafted representation 144; outcomes of 151; positioning of university brands 5–6; process of building 148; quality of 146; steps in development of 149; strategies for building 146, 147–148; university reputation, issues and management of 152; *see also* university corporate brand image
branding campaigns, in higher education 180
branding constructs, used in HE research **236–237**
branding in higher education: concepts of 2–10; instrument for improving university competitiveness and reputation 5; role of 10
branding scales, in higher education 233–234; Aaker's scale 245; case study 244–250; comparing HE-specific to 'general' scales 244–250; confounded construal 240–241; dubious derivation 240; for internal branding *241*; issues of modification of 242; managerial implications of 242–243; methodology for evaluation of 234; muddy modification 239–240; multi-item scales, review of 234–242; need for modification of 240; overview of papers reviewed 234–238; papers and tests of psychometric properties **242**; practice of 237; secret sources for evaluating 238–239; service quality scales 237; for testing the psychometric properties 241–242; themes for evaluation of 238
brand knowledge, development of 150
brand leadership 50; case study 67–70; characteristics of 60; creating brand support in a university 61; decision making processes 58; development of 58; for higher education institutions (HEIs) 50, 256; influencing employees via internal branding 59–61; on internal branding 61–65; internal communication and training 69–70; managerial implications of 65–66; review of the literature in 59–65; training courses 66; transformational 59–61; in university 59–61
brand loyalty 52, 123, 182, 183, 185, 235, 250
brand management 2, 10, 51, 84; branding business schools 260–265; MBA programs 260–265; nature of 256–260
brand meaning, creation of 150–151
brand name 135, 220, 229
brand performance: brand equity 181–183; brand impact in higher education 188; case study 191–193; implications for measuring 184; management challenges of measuring 179; managerial implications of 187–191; market and media forces 189; reputation and 184–185; review of literature on 180–186; rise of reputation management 189; role of rankings in 183–184
brand personality: concept of 6–8; determination of 7; operationalisations of **246–248**; of university 8
brand power, of global universities 189
brand prestige 235
brand reputation 76, 78, 188, 211, 233, 235, 250, 264

brand strategy, characteristics of 2
brand strength 182, 190, 210, 239–240, 259; implementation of 241
brand success, notion of 181
brand support, in university 11, 58–59, 61, 63–68, 70, 136, 257
brand 'uniqueness' 239
brand valuation: cost-based 182; income approach 182; market-based 182
brand value co-creation 51; concept of 25, 32; process of 26–27; stakeholder-based negotiations 27
Brunel, University London: brand structure of 135; corporate identity 133; corporate structure of 135; higher education 132–138; impacts of branding activities 136; learning from re-branding 132–138; logo of 134
business ecosystems: concept of 29–30; groups of 29; marketing frameworks of 29; Moore's model of 34
business education, moral standards of 69
business schools 217; branding of 2; case study 228–229; corporate brand equity of 222; corporate brand for educational positioning of 218–219; corporate brand image of 222; MBA programs 260–265; mottos and taglines 81; satisfaction and behavioural intention 222
'buy-in' of brand identity 84

Challenge of Being Distinctive, The 188
Chartered Association of Business Schools (CABS) Academic Journal Guide 2018 234
co-creation of value 13; case study 168–171; customer perception of 160–161; Goods-Dominant Logic for 160; and higher education 161–164; institutions and institutional arrangements for 161; by integration of operant resources 161; key issues in 164; managerial implications of 164–167; by resource integration 161; review of the literature on 159–164; role of the university in 164–165; service co-production and 160; Service-Dominant logic (S-D Logic) for 160–164; service eco-systems of 161; by service

exchange 161; student as customer 159–160; student engagement in 166–167; student experience in 165–166
college brand, nature and strength of 32
competition, in higher education 74, 3Es framework for 75–79; case study 84–86; how to successfully compete 79–81; managerial implications of 81–83; review of the literature in 75–81
composite reliability (CR) 206, 241
confirmatory factor analysis (CFA) 225, 241
Consumer-Based Brand Equity (CBBE) 183
consumer-brand relationships 7, 210
consumer marketing 255
consumers' behavioural intention 227
consumers' online search activities 98
Co-op Office partner organizations 109
Cornell University (USA) **49–50**
corporate association 5; definition of 220
corporate brand communication 91; case study 105–111; for communicating organizational values 93; components of 93; controllable areas of 92; and corporate branding in higher education 92–94; digital marketing communications 104; management/organizational communication 94–96; managerial implications of 102–104; marketing communications 96–99; review of the literature on 92–102; role of managerial leadership in 94; strategy for HEIs 104; uncontrolled 99–102; word-of-mouth (WOM) 101
corporate branding (CB) 8; expressing organizational culture in 44–46; in higher education institutions 11, 41; inter-non-member relationships 100; intra-brand community-member 100; notion of 45; practices of 5; principles of 51; as strategic educational positioning for business schools 218–219; value propositions of 99
corporate brand interactions: external-external 100; internal-external 100; internal-internal 100
Corporate Character Scale 222, 225
corporate design 12, 95, 119; university's logo 118

272 Index

corporate identity 96, 99, 132; concept of 185; corporate logo and 118; defined 118–119; main themes of 119; management of 44; notions of 44, 118; sense of belonging 93
corporate marketing 103–105, 111, 219–220
corporate name: definition of 121, 125; stakeholders' perception towards 124–125
corporate reputation, importance of 121, 128, 134
corporate social responsibility (CSR) 96
corporate typeface 122–123
corporate visual identity (CVI) 118, 120–121, 133
corporation brand 217
Cronbach's alpha values 206
cross-validated (CV) communality 208, 242
customer brand preferences 7
customer citizenship behaviour (CCB) 200–201
customer-oriented marketing system 1
customer relationship management 78
customer satisfaction 220, 227
customer's service network 27

database management 98
decision-making process, in higher education 264–265
Destination of Leavers from Higher Education survey (DLHE) 170
digital consumers 103
Digital Manager Europe 86
digital marketing communications 104
direct marketing 97–98
direct response ads 98
direct selling 98

ecosystem blindness 30–31
educational identity 7
education, customer-centric approaches to 261
ESCP Europe Business School 84–86
exploratory factor analysis (EFA) 206, 225, 241

Facebook 69, 99, 101, 103, 110, 155, 258, 264
fast moving consumer goods (FMCG) 183
for-profit institutions 263

goodness-of-fit (GOF) 206, 225
Goods-Dominant Logic 159, 160
governmental funding authorities 8
government scholarships 91

Harman's one-factor test 206
Harvard University (USA) 46, 77, 147, 155
heterotrait-monotrait ratio (HTMT) 241
higher education (HE) 1; application of core ideas from S-D Logic to *162*; brand equity in 4; brand impact in 188; brand metrics 179; competition aspect of 12; components of *80*; corporate branding in 92–94; framework of 31–32; integrated marketing, concept of 97; internal branding in 58–59; limitations of developing 260; role of branding in 10; service ecosystem 26; students as consumers of 159–160; UK HE sector 34–35
higher education branding 219; case study 212–213; conceptual framework of *198*; managerial implications of 210–211; review of the literature on 198–210; university brand communication 199–210; university identification for 199–210
higher education institutions (HEIs) 1, 10, 41, 102, 143, 218; application of these new advertising methods by 99; brand communication programs 12; brand identity 153; brand image and reputation in 143–153; branding of 25; brand managers 33; brand positioning for 12, 103; business ecosystem of 25; competitive edge in the marketplace 196; corporate brand (CB) in 11, 41; corporate communication strategy for 104; framework of 31–32; leadership vision for 50, 256; mission and vision of 104; organizational culture in *see* organizational culture, in HEIs; prestige and market share 84–85; purpose of leadership in 59; stakeholders of 28
human capital 58
human resource development loan funds 67

idealization influence, characteristic of 60, 68

image creation, advertising for 98
individual consideration, characteristic of 60, 69
information requirements, for a university 7
inspiration motivation, characteristic of 68
institutional reputation management 153
institution's prestige and quality, public perceptions of 8
integrated marketing 264; concept of 97
integrated marketing communications (IMC) 97, 149, 154, 258; stakeholders' perception towards 127–128
intellectual stimulation, characteristic of 60, 69
interactive marketing, elements of 98
Interbrand (global branding agency) 182
internal branding 61–65; brand-centred training and development 61–64; communication activities 64–65; in higher education (HE) 58–59; marketing control, theory of 63; organizational goals 63; process control activities 63; scale for 241; task of 61; in universities 61, 62
International Organization for Standardization (ISO) certification 182
Internet branding (i-branding) 262; strategies of 263
Ivy League universities 196

Jarvis, Carol 168
Jaworski, B.J. 60, 63
job opportunities 165, 259
job security 10
Journal of Marketing for Higher Education 2

key performance indicators (KPIs) 63, 70, 189
Knowledge Partnership, The 190, 259

leadership *see* brand leadership
league tables 5–6, 179, 183–184, 186
Likert scale 203, 222
logo, corporate: antecedents of 126–127; for building company's visual identity 118; case study 132–138; colour of 121–122; components of 124–125; defined 120; design of 122; elements that influence 118; for expressing organizational characteristics 120; findings of analysis of 124; for identifying corporate name 121; importance of 118; key economic advantage of 120; learning objectives of 119; managerial implications of 131–132; notion of 118; research method for analysis of 123–124; research model 130; review of the literature on 120–131; role of 118; significance of 119; stakeholders' perception towards 124–125; *see also* university logo

Maastricht University (Netherlands) 47
management communication 93–95; and branding in higher education 94–96
marketing communication 93; and branding in higher education 96–99; to generate brand and product preferences 96–97; options for 98; for promoting products/services 97
marketing management 255
marketing mix, '4Ps' of 97
marketing, of higher education 261
marketization of the university, idea of 42, 52
market share 4, 15, 75–77, 82, 179, 182, 257, 263
mass communications 64, 69, 101
maximum likelihood (ML) method 225
MBA programs: brand image 261; branding business schools and 260–265; decision criteria for selecting 9–10; evaluation of 9; executive MBAs (EMBAs) 260, 262; factors influencing choice of 10; as 'flagship' program 260; Internet branding 262; magazine ratings, value of 262; motivations for pursuing 10; online programs 262; value chain 262
measurement of branding, in higher education 2, 11, 233
media advertising 221
Millward Brown (brand agency) 182; 'BrandZ' valuation method 182
multitrait-multimethod matrix (MTMM) 241

National Student Survey (NSS) 170, 184
National Union of Students (NUS), UK 35
Newcastle University (UK) 191–193
non-profit organizations 96, 104

online brand experience 263
online programs, in higher education: emergence of 2; for-profit institutions 263; growth of 263; traditional-residential universities 263
on-the-job experience 109
organizational communication 93, 99; and branding in higher education 94–96
organizational culture, in HEIs: artifacts of 43; common values and beliefs in 11, 41; and corporate brand 41, 44–46; dimensions of 43–44; espoused beliefs and values 43; levels of 43; literature on 42–46; managerial implications of 46–51; mission statement and core values 45–46; shaping of 43–44
organizational identity 7, 44, 94, 199
Oxford University 155

Partanen, Johannes 168
partial least squares structural equation modelling (PLS-SEM) 203
planning process, of higher education branding 2
price premium 179, 181, 182–183
private-sector organizations 143
product brand, notion of 45
product brand strategy, importance of 221
promotional mix activities 98
public relations (PR) 8, 101, 128, 148

Quacquarelli Symonds (QS) 189
quality: quality assurance training 70; of universities 184

rankings, of universities 183–184; indicators of 189; rise of reputation management in response to 189
relationship-building activities 93
reputation management 148, 189–191; concept of 184–185; in response to rankings 189; stakeholders' perception towards 128–129
research-focused programs 9

reverse mentoring 109

San Diego State University 105
scale development, in higher education 217–218; managerial implications of 227–228; review of the literature in 218–227; for strategic educational positioning for business schools 218–219
Service-Dominant logic (S-D Logic) 13, 26, 30, 100, 159, 164, 167, 169, 171, 258; application of core ideas from 162; co-creation of value and 27, 160–164; concept of 160–161; foundational propositions (FP 6) of 26–27; themes of 161
service quality 68, 197, 220, 237
services marketing 160, 255
Sevier, R.A. 97
social exchange theory (SET) 201
Social Identity Theory (SIT) 199
social justice 192
social media 15, 54, 86, 98–99, 101–103, 108, 128–129, 150, 153, 155, 167, 211–212, 227, 260, 264; accounts for different departments 110
social network interactions 98
Social Responsibility Club 108
Sorbonne University (France) 48
staff-stakeholder interactions 104
stakeholder identification 27; importance of 26, 28
stakeholder management, issue of 11, 28–29
student citizenship behaviours 14, 197; data analysis of 203; descriptive statistics and discriminant validity 207; Harman's one-factor test 206; measurement model results of 204–205; measurement reliability and validation 206; mediation analysis of 209; self-administered survey on 202–203; structural model and hypotheses testing of 208; structural model results of 208; theoretical implications of 209–210; type I reflective second-order construct 203; university brand commitment and 201; university brand communication and 200; university identification 200–201; to university trust 202; voluntary and helpful behaviours 203

student loan funds 67
student perceptions, on choice of university brands 2, 9–10
student recruitment, affect of university's image on 8
students, as consumers of higher education 159–160
symbolic branding 4

Team Entrepreneurs (TEs) 167–171
Team Entrepreneurship course (Bristol Business School) 168–171; institutions and institutional arrangements 170; key actors of 169; module leaders of 169; resource integration 169; S-D logic 169; service eco-systems 170; service exchange 169–170; structure of 168; value creation 170–171
telemarketing 98
Tiimiakatemia Global network 170
Times Higher Education (THE) 77, 189
traditional-residential universities 263
transcendental self-development 42, 46
transformational leadership 59–60; brand support behaviour 61; Burns' theory of 60; characteristics of 60; definitions of 60–61; management training 66
Triple Test survey 191
trust creation, stakeholders' perception towards 128–129
Twitter 99, 101, 110, 155

UK Research Evaluation Framework (REF) of Impact Case Studies 165
uncontrolled communication 12, 92–93, 99–102, 104, 111, 258
United Nations Sustainable Development Goals (SDGs) 171
university brand commitment: and student citizenship behaviour 201; university brand communications and 199–200; university identification and 201–202
university brand communication: commitment towards the organization 199–200; influence on student citizenship behaviour 200; measurement of 203; and university identification 199–210
university branding: brand image and positioning of 5–6; building of 264–265; defined 1; development of 10, 46; objectives of 4, 8; planning process of 2; student perceptions and choice of 9–10
university brand personality 46, 245
university colour: concept of 121–122; stakeholders' perception towards 125
university corporate brand image 218; in advertising campaigns 221; attributes used to measure 220; case study 228–229; data analysis and discussion 225; emotional association and images 221; first order model for analysis of 225–226; items/dimensions of 223; managerial implications of 227–228; measurement of 219–222; recommendation/behavioural intention construct 222; satisfaction and behavioural intention of 222, 223, 226; Structural Full or Equation Model (SEM) for analysis of 225; study's research proposition of 224
university design 122; stakeholders' perception towards 125–126
university education 101, 189
university identification 201, 208; influence on student citizenship behaviour 200–201; and university brand commitment 201–202; university brand communication and 199–210
university image, stakeholders' perception of 128
university league tables 6
university logo 118, 200; antecedents of 126–127; components of 12; consequences of 127; key components of 126; stakeholders' perception of attractiveness, familiarity, and recognizability 129–131; stakeholders' perception of university image 128; stakeholders' perception towards reputation/trust creation 128–129; stakeholders' perception towards university integrated marketing communication 127–128
university mission/vision and values 47–50
University of Coimbra (Portugal) 52–54
University of Minho (Portugal) 48–49
University of Northampton (UK) 211
University of Warwick (UK) 47
university reputation, issues and management of 76, 152, 188

276 Index

university services, branding of 264
university typeface 122–123;
  stakeholders' perception towards 126
university websites 99

value chain 262
values of education 42; co-creation of
  see co-creation of value

word-of-mouth (WOM) messaging 5,
  14, 101, 152, 209
World 100 Reputation Network 189

YouTube 86, 101, 103, 258
Yucel, Enver 107–108

Zhejiang University (China) **50**

Printed in the United States
By Bookmasters